A GUIDE TO THE
MEDIEVAL CASTLES
OF ENGLAND

A GUIDE TO THE MEDIEVAL CASTLES OF ENGLAND

Malcolm Hislop

AN IMPRINT OF PEN & SWORD BOOKS LTD
YORKSHIRE – PHILADELPHIA

First published in Great Britain in 2024 by
PEN & SWORD HISTORY
an imprint of Pen & Sword Books Ltd
Yorkshire – Philadelphia

Copyright © Malcolm Hislop, 2024

ISBN 978-1-39900-110-6

The right of Malcolm Hislop to be identified as the author of this work has been asserted by him in accordance with the Copyright, Designs and Patents Act 1988.

A CIP catalogue record for this book is available from the British Library.

All rights reserved. No part of this book may be reproduced or transmitted in any form or by any means, electronic or mechanical including photocopying, recording or by any information storage and retrieval system, without permission from the Publisher in writing.

Typeset by Concept, Huddersfield, West Yorkshire, HD4 5JL.
Printed and bound in England by CPI Group (UK) Ltd, Croydon, CR0 4YY.

Pen & Sword Books Ltd incorporates the imprints of Aviation, Atlas, Family History, Fiction, Maritime, Military, Discovery, Politics, History, Archaeology, Select, Wharncliffe Local History, Wharncliffe True Crime, Military Classics, Wharncliffe Transport, Leo Cooper, The Praetorian Press, Remember When, White Owl, Seaforth Publishing and Frontline Books.

For a complete list of Pen & Sword titles please contact
PEN & SWORD BOOKS LTD
47 Church Street, Barnsley, South Yorkshire, S70 2AS, England
E-mail: enquiries@pen-and-sword.co.uk
Website: www.pen-and-sword.co.uk
or
PEN & SWORD BOOKS
1950 Lawrence Rd, Havertown, PA 19083, USA
E-mail: uspen-and-sword@casematepublishers.com
Website: www.penandswordbooks.com

CONTENTS

List of Plates vi
Introduction vii
Glossary xv
Gazetteer 1
Castles by County 255
Bibliography 259
Index of People 275

LIST OF PLATES

- I. Beeston: Inner gatehouse from the SW.
- II. Bodiam from the NW.
- III. Brough: Gatehouse and great tower from the SE.
- IV. Carlisle: Outer gatehouse of 1378–83 by John Lewyn.
- V. Conisbrough: Keep from the W.
- VI. Dunstanburgh: Lilburn Tower from the S.
- VII. Goodrich from the SE.
- VIII. London: Western entrance with the Middle Tower in the foreground and the Byward Tower in the background.
- IX. Ludlow: Main residential block with central great hall recessed between the Solar Block (left) and Great Chamber Block (right).
- X. Norwich: Keep from the SW.
- XI. Old Wardour: The gateway flanked by doorways to adjacent rooms, from within the inner courtyard (*c.*1391).
- XII. Rockingham: The gatehouse from the E.
- XIII. Sheriff Hutton from the E.
- XIV. Warkworth: Great tower from the S.

INTRODUCTION TO THE CASTLES OF ENGLAND

For we admirers of the English landscape and its monuments, the sight of a castle, perched on an eminence, or surrounded by water, or rising majestically above the treetops, is an encounter that lifts the spirits, stimulates the imagination, and allows us to escape, if but for a moment, from the humdrum round of existence. After that first emotional response we want to know more, and the better informed we are, the more gratifying the experience of exploring the physical remains of these sometimes confusing relics. Unless they were short lived, most castles contain multiple phases of historic fabric, one imposed upon another, thereby generating three-dimensional palimpsests that must be unravelled if we are to extract the greatest satisfaction from our investigations.

The purpose of this book is to provide an introduction to the most significant medieval castles in England, and, for those who wish to pursue further an interest in particular sites, to indicate, in the references given at the end of the individual entries, where further information can be found. No book of this type can be comprehensive if it is to be publishable for the general market. A selection has to be made, but the sites listed here include the most informative examples, and represent the broad sweep of development that took place over 450 years. The castles have been chosen for architectural and archaeological significance, or their accessibility, or indeed both. To meet the accessibility test the building must either open to the public (even though the annual window of opportunity might be small) or can be read about in books, journals or other media. It should therefore be noted that although not all the selected buildings can be freely visited, most can be studied from afar.

Nearly 400 sites are to be found within the following pages including representatives from all the historic counties, but geographical distribution varies greatly, the greatest concentrations being along the land borders with Scotland and Wales, notably in Northumberland (41 sites), Shropshire (28 sites) and Herefordshire (21 sites). Other significant 'castle counties' are Kent (20 sites), which, with its proximity to continental Europe, might also be considered a border county, and, as might be expected, Yorkshire (37 sites), the largest of the shires. There is also considerable variation in the degree of survival, but there is something to see at most sites encompassed within this book. The exceptions are a few demolished castles, for even though the buildings themselves may have disappeared, in some cases they have influenced the later townscape, and a good deal of satisfaction may be gained from walking around the former extent and imagining how things might have been.

As this is a book about England's *medieval* castles, it takes no account of later monuments even though they might bear the appellation castle. For the purpose of this book 'medieval' broadly equates to the years 1050–1500. Many buildings of this date also incorporate earlier and/or later material, but, in order to maintain the intended focus on the Middle Ages, such elements are treated summarily in the descriptions, even though they may have considerable archaeological or architectural significance for the study of other periods. In imposing the chronological parameters given above, the artillery forts of the C16, which are often considered to be part and parcel of a book such as this, have been excluded. Although provision for guns appears in a number of castles from the later C14, artillery fortification, which has a long history of its own, extending far beyond the medieval period, really deserves a separate publication.

The event that turned England into a land of castles was the Norman Conquest of 1066. Whilst it is true that some castles had been established before that date, notably by Normans in the service of the penultimate Anglo-Saxon king, Edward the Confessor, and also that there is some archaeological evidence for the fortification of Anglo-Saxon noble dwellings, the Conquest and the consolidation of Norman power was accompanied by systematic castle building for strategic purposes: overawing the main centres of population, controlling the principal routes of communication, and holding down the profitable territory of the kingdom.

The majority of these Norman castles were of earth and timber, although invariably the timber has vanished and only the earthworks remain. Of the two main types, the motte and bailey is the most recognizable as a Norman castle: a conspicuous mound, usually forming a truncated cone, sometimes man-made, sometimes natural, though normally modified to some degree, accompanied by one or sometimes more court-yards (baileys), the whole complex defined by banks and/or ditches. Multiple baileys may be the result of subsequent enlargement, but the primary bailey (i.e., that closest to the motte) is often kidney-shaped or crescentic in plan, hugging the mound closely and wrapping itself round a large part of its circumference.

The other major category is the ringwork, so called from its penannular plan: a courtyard defined by a bank and ditch, sometimes with an additional courtyard (or bailey) adjacent. Some of these Norman castles seem to be laid out with scrupulous attention to geometry, suggesting the involvement of a professional and the existence of an ideal; others are less regular, though, in all cases, topography undoubtedly played its part in determining the final form. Regarding classification, excavation has shown that there can be a degree of ambiguity. Some mottes have turned out to be ringworks (e.g. Castle Acre), while some ringworks seem to have been converted to mottes (e.g. Pontesbury); mottes were sometimes added to ringworks. Things are not always as they seem!

The timber element of the defences usually comprised a palisade along the top of the banks and the motte. There is also some archaeological evidence that timber sub-structures and super-structures might be used in maintaining the structural stability of the banks. In addition to a palisade the motte top might also support a tower to be used in observation and defence. Where the motte top was extensive, it might accommodate numerous buildings including the great hall (e.g. Tamworth), but usually the principal domestic buildings would have been in the bailey.

Of course, not all early castles fall neatly into one of these two categories. Where prehistoric, Roman or Anglo-Saxon fortifications already existed they might be reused. Normally these existing fortifications were on a much larger scale than the castles they contained, which therefore occupied only a portion of the site in the

Introduction

form of an inner enclosure, sometimes hard up against two sides of the earlier defences, or, where circumstances allowed (as in the case of an abandoned site like Old Sarum, rather than an occupied fortified settlement), as a freestanding fortification within the old enceinte.

Although most early castles had timber superstructures, a small number were in stone from the outset including the C11 sites of Exeter, Rochester, Richmond and Peveril. The curtain walls of all four sites incorporate a distinctive form of rubble walling known in this country as herringbone masonry, but which seems to be a less formal derivative of the Roman *opus spicatum*. Flat stones are laid at an angle of approximately 45 degrees, stability being ensured by alternating the direction of pitch from course to course to give a zigzag pattern. Herringbone masonry is generally indicative of an early date.

Initially, none of these four castles was provided with a great tower, or keep, though three of them acquired one in the C12, a period in which great towers proliferated. The fashion had begun in the C11, the most notable and ambitious examples being within the royal castles of London and Colchester. Indeed, the former (known as the White Tower) was such a dominating factor of the wider fortress, that the entire complex of fortifications and residential accommodation is still known as the Tower of London, rather than London Castle. Both the White Tower and its counterpart at Colchester were begun in the 1070s by William I (reigned 1066–87). It was left to his son, William (Rufus) II (reigned 1087–1100), to complete the White Tower, and shortly before he died, he may have instigated the construction of two more great towers, at Norwich and Canterbury. On William's untimely death he was succeeded by his brother, Henry I (reigned 1100–35), under whom Norwich and Canterbury were completed, and further royal keeps constructed at Bamburgh, Bridgnorth, Carlisle, Corfe, Portchester and Rochester. These conspicuous buildings not only provided secure and princely accommodation, but also served as symbols of royal authority.

This succession of royal great towers was interrupted by Henry's death and a disputed succession between his nephew, Stephen of Blois, and his daughter, Matilda (Dowager Holy Roman Empress, and wife of the Count of Anjou). Stephen became king (reigned 1135–54), but civil war ensued bringing with it a weakening of central authority and a breakdown of security. Understandably it was also a major castle-building period. During this turbulent period (often known as the Anarchy) many castles were thrown up that had not been sanctioned by the King, and to which the adjective 'adulterine' is given. Stephen himself caused many castles to be constructed in connection with his frequent siege activities of castles and towns, but these, like the adulterine castles, were mostly of earth and timber rather than more lasting materials. The torch had passed to the nobility: great towers were built both by Aubrey de Vere, Earl of Oxford, and William d'Albini, Earl of Sussex, probably to celebrate their elevation to the peerage. Oxford's work at Castle Hedingham, and Sussex's at Castle Rising and Old Buckenham, are all three highly significant buildings that compensate for the disruption to royal patronage. Up to this point all great towers in England had rectilinear plans, a precedent followed at Castle Hedingham and Castle Rising, but the Earl of Sussex's tower of *c.*1140 at Old Buckenham departed from tradition by being given a cylindrical form, so acting as a prototype for the numerous towers of this style that were to follow.

Stephen died in 1154, and the accession of Matilda's son as Henry II (reigned 1154–89) was occasioned by an immediate and widespread destruction of adulterine castles as the King began to restore royal authority. A second wave of destruction took place much later in Henry's reign, after the Assize of Northampton of 1176, which affected the castles held against Henry during the rebellion of his sons in 1173–4. Such edicts are useful contributions to castle history but cannot always be taken at face value; it is evident that sometimes royal orders to demolish were not carried out, or that they were effected less zealously in some cases than in others. In contrast to these acts of destruction, Henry's reign witnessed significant royal castle building: a new castle was built at Orford, Newcastle was rebuilt, and a major reconstruction of Dover embarked upon. All three enterprises included the construction of a new great tower, further examples being raised by Henry at Scarborough, Bowes and Peveril; Henry also ordered the Bishop of Durham to rebuild the keep of Norham on the border with Scotland.

Most of these royal great towers were rectangular, but, following New Buckenham, the plan of Henry's Orford keep was based on a circle. Broadly contemporary with Orford is Conisbrough where Henry's half-brother, Hamelin Plantagenet, Earl of Surrey, also raised a circle-based keep. On the whole, round keeps are rare in England, though instances appeared at Barnard Castle and Chartley in the early C13, and at Longton in Herefordshire close to the Welsh border. Indeed, it was in Wales and the Marches that the cylindrical keep gained a degree of popularity unmatched in England, both in *Marchia Wallia* and in *Pura Wallia*, because they happened to be in vogue at a time when castle building was booming in Wales as a result of conflict and consolidation of territory.

In addition to the keeps, castle building under Henry II incorporated improvements to the treatment of the enceinte, which had hitherto been somewhat uninspired and haphazard in its planning. At both Dover and Orford the curtain wall was studded with a systematic arrangement of rectangular wall towers equipped with regular dispositions of arrow loops; an altogether more scientific approach to defence. The same approach is to be seen in the defences of Framlingham Castle, one of the strongholds demolished by order of the King but rebuilt by Roger Bigod, Earl of Norfolk, soon after Henry's death on similar lines to the inner curtain of Dover, with rectangular wall towers and methodically disposed arrow loops, although here, in contrast to Dover, there was no great tower, a circumstance somewhat at odds with the royal trend for such monuments, which had been widely emulated. However, keepless castles had a long pedigree, extending back to the early Norman ringworks, and just as ringworks co-existed with mottes and baileys, so was the courtyard castle an alternative to the courtyard and keep.

The reconstruction of Dover continued under Henry's son, John (reigned 1199–1216), but instead of the rectangular towers favoured by Henry at Dover and Orford and emulated at Framlingham, this later work is characterized by D-shaped wall towers with rounded fronts and flat backs. They are some of the earliest in England, of a type that was to become highly popular during the C13, and which, in concert with cylindrical towers, would temporarily largely supplant the rectangular wall tower. The advantages of such shapes for the military tactician is that the curving surface provided for a less restricted field of fire by reducing blind spots, and also, its greater deflective properties may have provided some protection against missiles. Similar defensive arrangements were instigated by John at Corfe Castle and Scarborough.

Introduction

The last years of John's reign (1215–16) were blighted by the First Barons' War, a major rebellion supported by the French Dauphin, Prince Louis, who invaded in 1216. A number of rebel castles were destroyed on the orders of the King, and the key royal castles of Dover and Windsor each withstood a siege, though both were damaged. Their defences were reorganised by Henry III (reigned 1216–72) in the early years of his kingship. In addition to his major works at Dover and Winchester, Henry made numerous alterations and additions to the royal castles: at the Tower of London the curtain wall was rebuilt, York Castle was completely rebuilt in stone, and there were major additions at Newcastle, Nottingham, Shrewsbury and Winchester. Henry III's work is characterized by round and D-shaped towers, but also more unusual plans and inventive constructions, amongst which may be counted the beaked towers at Dover, almost unique in England, the quatrefoil keep at York and the interesting two-stage gatehouses at Dover (Constable Gate) and Newcastle (Black Gate). Henry was an aesthete, and his castle building exudes good taste and architectural deliberation, as well as the latest developments in military theory.

A notable baronial castle builder in the early years of Henry's reign was the powerful Earl of Chester, Ranulph de Blundeville, who built new courtyard castles at Beeston and Bolingbroke and rebuilt a motte and bailey in stone at Chartley, where he caused a round keep to be raised on top of the motte. Towards the end of the reign another new courtyard castle of special note was built at Barnwell by the otherwise obscure Berenger le Moyne. To him and his anonymous architect we should be grateful for bequeathing to us a small masterpiece: a quadrangular castle reflecting something of the character of the royal works of the C13, albeit on a smaller scale.

Twin D-shaped towers flank the gatehouse at Barnwell; this general form of central entrance and two flanking drum towers first appeared in King John's Dover gateway, which was the rudimentary basis of a significant development in C13 castle architecture best embodied in England at Tonbridge, built by Gilbert de Clare, Earl of Gloucester, between 1262 and 1295. Tonbridge is the epitome of the 'gatehouse keep', a defended gateway with a major accommodation block attached, giving it something of the quality of a great tower. The Earl of Gloucester built a number of gatehouses on this model in Wales, notably Caerphilly, and the principle was taken up by Edward I's masons in north Wales at Aberystwyth, Harlech and Beaumaris.

Royal spending on castle building during the last quarter of the C13 was indeed concentrated in north Wales as Edward I consolidated his conquest of Gwynedd. Edward's castle-building programme in Wales was initiated in 1277, but one of his major works had begun a little earlier *c.*1275 at the Tower of London and was, for a number of years, carried forward contemporaneously with the Welsh castles. At the Tower, Edward enlarged the castle by building an encompassing outer curtain wall, so creating concentric lines of defence, a system that was employed at several of the royal Welsh castles.

Wales does not fall within the scope of this book, but Edward's very substantial works there, which pulled in building craftsmen from all over his realm, were to inspire the castle builders of late C13 and early C14 England. Caernarfon, the crowning glory of the Welsh project, was particularly influential. As much palace as fortress, its formidable defences were tempered by its aesthetic qualities and its residential attributes. Its massive scale and air of fantasy, together with unusual aspects, such as polygonal towers, decorative stone banding and a proliferation of shouldered arches, grabbed the attention and led to widespread emulation. Moreover, construction took place over an extended period (1283–1330), a circumstance that kept the castle in the public and professional consciousness.[1] In England, the influence of north Wales, especially Caernarfon, has been noted at Acton Burnell, Alnwick, Berwick, Bothal, Brougham, Dunstanburgh, Eccleshall, Haverfordwest, Knaresborough, Lichfield (cathedral close), Maxstoke, Newark, Stokesay, Warwick and Windsor.

Following the subjugation of Wales, Edward I turned his attention to Scotland and attempted to establish his authority over the northern kingdom. The unintended consequence of his invasion of 1296, and the wars that ensued, was a breakdown of security along the Anglo-Scottish border, the northern counties of England becoming particularly vulnerable after the Scottish victory at Bannockburn in 1314. Raiding and intermittent warfare was endemic, the situation lasting until the Union of the Crowns in 1603 when James VI of Scotland also became James I of England. During these centuries of uncertainty, those with the means fortified their homes against raids and invasion, and as a result the border counties have a particularly dense concentration of late medieval fortifications.

Most of these are fortified manor houses are now most obviously represented by the residential tower: the largely self-contained and sometimes freestanding tower house, or the attached solar tower, essentially a chamber block in tower form attached to a hall. Some C13 hall houses were converted into towers.[2] Any outer defences have usually (but not always) disappeared, and the tower is sometimes the only component of a medieval fortress to have survived. Apart from the manor houses, attention was also paid to some of the larger castles by members of the northern nobility who were active in Scotland. The Percys, for example, rebuilt Alnwick between c.1310 and c.1350, and Robert Clifford rebuilt Skipton from c.1310. Later in the century new Northumbrian castles emerged at Ford (1338), Etal (1341), Bothal (1343) and Chillingham (1344).

During the latter half of the C14, even in the turbulent north of England, the emphasis amongst castle builders was on the residential amenities rather than the defences, a preoccupation that is exemplified by Edward III's redevelopment of the domestic accommodation at Windsor between 1350 and 1377, a project that, like Edward I's Welsh construction programme, was supported by the impressment of building workers from large parts of the kingdom, thereby providing opportunity for the dissemination of ideas. The main import of the Windsor project was to highlight the possibilities for large-scale domestic planning within a restricted area.

The sophistication of the scheme for the Windsor royal apartments was emulated in the castle-building boom of Richard II's reign (1377–99), which, despite being engendered in part by the threat of French hostilities in the south, and by the fear of Scottish incursions in the north, was nevertheless more notable for advances in domestic planning than in defence, and for an interest in aesthetics rather than functionality. In the south of England, gun ports appear spasmodically, but aren't always functional, and although corbelled machicolations are not uncommon (e.g., Bodiam, Scotney, Cooling), they give the impression of being as much for show as for defence. The purpose of several eye-catching gateways is likewise ambiguous (e.g. Bodiam, Donnington, Saltwood). Several late C14 castles are concerned with symmetry. Edward III's entirely new castle (1361–75) at Queenborough on the Isle of Sheppey,

---

1. For the influence of Edward I's Welsh castles see Hislop 2020, Chapter 11.
2. On the fortification of the northern border see Dixon 1979, 1992, 1993.

Introduction

for example, was circular with concentric fortifications and domestic apartments lining the inner courtyard. A similar concept, perhaps inspired by Queenborough, is to be found at Old Wardour, though here the plan is hexagonal rather than circular. Bodiam, Farleigh Hungerford and Shirburn are quadrangular.

Of the new baronial castles in the north of England, those built by Sir Richard Scrope at what is now Castle Bolton, by Sir Ralph Lumley at Great Lumley, by Sir Thomas Percy at Wressle, and Sir John Neville at Sheriff Hutton, were, like Bodiam, quadrangular, Lumley and Wressle vying with their southern counterparts for symmetry. The Nevilles also rebuilt castles at Brancepeth and Raby, both in County Durham, and Thomas Percy's elder brother, Henry, Earl of Northumberland, raised a remarkable great tower on top of the Norman motte at Warkworth. Significant works were also carried out at the royal border castles of Carlisle, Roxburgh and Berwick. Yet, here in the north, where there was perhaps more reason to be concerned about security, it is the domestic arrangements that stand out. Nevertheless, it is true to say that the fortifications these late C14 strongholds were provided with were quite sufficient to withstand raiding parties who lacked the means to settle in for a protracted siege and did not carry with them the engines of war. This period saw the culmination of a distinctive form of northern English castle architecture based on the rectangular tower, a component which, from around 1320, had started to eclipse the round-fronted wall towers that had been popular in the C13, and which continued to be the standard in the south. Many of these late C14 castle-building activities in the north are attributable to the Durham master mason John Lewyn, and a recurring theme is the integration of the domestic accommodation with the defences to create compact and internally complex plans.

Apart from the residential tower culture of the border manor houses, the north made few major contributions to castle architecture in the C15. The Midlands, on the other hand, contain several important works of this century. The C14 had seen some significant castle building in the Midlands, notably in Warwickshire: the Earl of Huntingdon's new-build quadrangular castle at Maxstoke, the Earl of Warwick's reconstruction of Warwick, and the Duke of Lancaster's remodelling of the inner courtyard at Kenilworth. All three make use of polygonal towers, a characteristic shared by the great tower raised by the Earl of Stafford on the top of Stafford castle motte. The earliest of the C15 Midlands castles, the royal castle of Tutbury, is also in Staffordshire. In origin an early motte and bailey, it was rebuilt in stone between 1400 and c.1460, mostly during the reign of Henry VI (i.e., from 1421), the work including two great residential wall towers built to a rectangular plan. From 1439 Henry VI's treasurer, Thomas Lord Cromwell, built a new fortified manor house on an old castle site at South Wingfield (Derbyshire). Here too, one of the main features was a great tower of rectangular form projecting from the enceinte.

Slightly earlier, in 1434, Cromwell had begun rebuilding the castle of Tattershall (Lincolnshire) and another great tower, but one of the principal interests of the castle is that it was constructed in brick. Contemporaneously, new brick castles were also being built by Sir John Fastolf at Caister (Norfolk) and by Sir Roger Fiennes at Herstmonceux (Sussex), their round and polygonal towers contrasting with the rectangular model found in the Midlands. For the last of the great castle works in brick we must return to the Midlands where William Lord Hastings began work on a new quadrangular castle at Kirby Muxloe (Leicestershire) in 1480, though his execution three years later meant that it would never be completed.

Lord Hastings' conversion of the old manor house at Ashby de la Zouche (also Leicestershire) into a castle is more likely to have reached fruition. Ashby also has a great tower (the Hastings Tower) on the line of the curtain, perhaps the most architecturally satisfying of all the C15 examples so far mentioned, despite half of the building having been lost. Even so, the castle works of Hastings' nemesis, Richard III, have fared less well. A polygonal great tower at Nottingham (Richard's Tower) attributable to Richard and/or his brother Edward IV, his predecessor on the English throne, has been reduced to its foundations, while the even more ambitious tower that straddled the curtain at Warwick has lost its upper storeys and half its width, and survives only as a single-storey gateway. Attractive though this remnant might be, it is a nevertheless pathetic reminder of the vulnerability of monumental legacies and a fitting symbol of the fate that has overtaken so many of England's castles. We must enjoy them while we may.

GLOSSARY

Abacus (pl. **Abaci**): Horizontal pad(s) between a **Capital** and an arch.
Adulterine castle: A term usually applied to unlicensed castles raised during the civil war, or 'Anarchy' of Stephen's reign.
Alure: The circulatory path around the top of a wall behind the parapet, used as a fighting platform. Also known as a wall walk.
Arcade: A row of arches supported on piers or columns.
Arris: A sharp edge where two surfaces meet at an angle.
Ambulatory: An aisle to the east of the sanctuary linking the side aisles of a church.
Arch-braced collar: A **Collar** supported from each end by arching braces extending from the **Soffits** of the rafters to the soffit of the collar.
Ashlar: An accurately-cut block of fine-grained stone, or a collection of such.
Aumbry: A cupboard incorporated into a stone wall.
Ballflower: A foliate decoration resembling an opening bud, usually associated with the period *c*.1300–30.
Barbican: A fortification positioned in front of a gateway, in the form either of a small courtyard or a passageway.
Barrel-vault: A continuous arched vault extending between two parallel walls.
Batter: An external splay at the base of a wall.
Bartizan: A small overhanging turret at the top of a wall, especially at an angle.
Beakhead: C12 decorative sculpture, typically surrounding an opening, consisting of a series of grotesque heads whose beaks wrap over, or bite, a roll moulding.
Berm: A flat area between two lines of defence, e.g. between a ditch and a curtain wall.
Billet: A decorative linear moulding typical of the Norman **Romanesque**, of short cylindrical or square lengths.
Box machicolation: A rectangular turret corbelled out from the wall of a castle, typically at parapet level, with machicolation slot(s) in the base.
Brattice: see **Hoard**.
Broach: A half-pyramidal construction used in reconciling a right-angled substructure with a cylindrical or conical superstructure.
Burh: Anglo-Saxon fortified town.
Buttery: A service room for the storage of beer and other liquors.
Buttress: A localized thickening of, or projection from, the wall of a building to strengthen or shore up, or to counter lateral thrust from, a roof or vault.
Camber: A slight rise in the centre of a beam.
Camera: A private chamber.
Capital: Carved feature crowning and usually overhanging a column, often decorated with mouldings or sculpture.
Caput: The chief place of a landholding, often a castle.

Castle guard: Obligation to perform garrison duty at a lord's castle as part of the terms of feudal tenure.
Chamber: A more private room than a hall, used as a living room and/or bedroom. See also, **Great chamber**.
Chamber block: A structural division containing at least one chamber, and other rooms, either attached to or detached from a hall.
Chamfer: Narrow face, typically at an angle of 45 degrees, at the junction of two right-angled faces, resulting from the removal of the **Arris**.
Chase: Recess within a wall surface to accommodate a timber.
Clearstorey: The uppermost storey of the central vessel (usually the nave) of a church, or, in a more general sense, an additional, upper, tier of windows in a high ceilinged room.
Close stool: A commode, or portable lavatory.
Collar: A horizontal timber, or beam, extending between a pair of rafters.
Colonette: A diminutive column usually flanking an opening.
Coping: The horizontal masonry covering of a wall.
Corbel table: A decorative row of corbels, usually at the head of a wall, supporting a mini **Arcade**.
Counterscarp: Outer slope of a ditch facing towards the castle.
Cranked: Bent.
Crocket: A stylized curling leaf moulding popular amongst Gothic architects.
Crossing: In a church, the area between the nave (W), choir or chancel (E) and transepts (N and S), directly beneath a central tower.
Crown plate: Horizontal axial roof timber extending the full length of the building, carried by **Crown posts**: To support the **Collars**. Also known as a collar purlin.
Crown post: Vertical roof timber extending from a **Tie beam** to a **Crown plate**, which in turn supports the **Collars**.
Cruck: One of a pair of timbers forming the main components of a type of timber cross-frame. Crucks rise from a point well down the side walls of a building as far as, or close to, the apex of the roof; they carry the **Purlins** and **Ridge piece**.
Curtilage: Land surrounding a dwelling and the buildings and structures within it.
Curvilinear tracery: Tracery making full use of the **Ogee** to create a pattern of continuous curves.
Cushion capital: Capital in the form of a basin with the sides reduced to flat surfaces so that the base is round and the top square.
Cusp: The point created at the intersection of two arcs.
Decorated: A style of English architecture typical of the period $c.1280–1350$.
Demi-figure: Sculptural representation of the upper half of a human figure.
Diaphragm arch: An arch carrying a wall, dividing the interior of a building.
Dogtooth: A linear decoration comprising a series of pyramidal mouldings undercut to give the appearance of being four-leaved. In England it is characteristic of the C13.
Doric: One of the classical orders revived during the Renaissance, and occurring in England from the C16.
Double-pile roof: Two parallel roof spans covering the same building.
Dripstone: See **Hood mould**.
Drum tower: Rounded projecting wall or gatehouse tower.

Glossary

Embrasure: The hollow space behind a window in a thick wall, or the open part of a crenellated parapet.
Enceinte: Continuous ring of fortifications surrounding a castle or town.
Enclosure castle: Keepless castle.
Entablature: Horizontal upper part of a classical order consisting of architrave, frieze and cornice.
Fillet: Narrow rectangular band projecting and extending along the length of a column, shaft or **Roll moulding**.
Fishtail: Fishtail-like splay terminating the arm of a narrow opening.
Fleuron: Sculptural decoration in the form of a stylized flower.
Flush work: The use of flint in combination with another (contrasting) stone to produce a chequer-board pattern.
Forebuilding: Projection from the castle keep containing and protecting the entrance.
Formwork: Temporary timber support for vault webbing designed to the intended shape of the vault.
Gablet: A miniature gable.
Geometric: A division of English Gothic architecture, broadly 1240–1310, named after a style of window tracery made up of geometrical figures.
Great chamber: The principal chamber of the lord's private apartments.
Great hall: Principal room of a medieval great house, used as a communal dining room.
Groin vault: **Vault** formed by the intersection of two **Barrel vaults** at right-angles to one another; the point of juncture produces an **Arris** known as a groin.
Gunport: Opening in a wall designed for firing guns through.
Header: In a brick wall, a brick laid with its end outward, in contrast to a stretcher, which is laid with its side outwards.
Hipped roof: A pitched roof at the end of a building as an alternative to a gable.
Hoard: An overhanging wooden gallery erected on the wall head from which the defence of a castle might be conducted. Hoard is the usual modern term for this type of structure, although **Brattice** may have been a more widely used description in the Middle Ages.
Holloway: An old track in the form of a linear depression within the surrounding landscape.
Hood mould: A moulded band projecting from the wall face above a door or window and following its outline, the hood mould was designed to deflect rainwater from the opening and to ornament the wall surface. Also known as a **Dripstone**.
Impost string: Horizontal block, often moulded, carrying the **Springer** of an arch.
Intersecting tracery: See **Y-tracery**.
Joggling: A means of jointing fine masonry in which there is a break or rebate in the line of the joint to prevent slipping or sliding. Typically used in forming a lintel out of several stones, or **Voussoirs**.
Keel moulding: A rounded moulding coming to a point, in section suggestive of a ship's keel.
Keystone: Voussoir at the apex of an arch.
King post: Vertical roof timber extending from the **Tie beam** to the **Ridge piece**.
Lancet: A narrow pointed window characteristic of the early Gothic style.
Laver: An integral wash basin with a drain.

Lierne vault: A later medieval vault making use of liernes, or minor ribs, connecting one rib with another, rather than emanating from a springing point. The employment of liernes allowed highly decorative configurations of ribs.
Machicolation: Projecting stone gallery at the head of a wall, with slots in the base through which projectiles could be dropped.
Mantlet: A low wall surrounding or placed in front of another building, often a great tower or gatehouse.
Mask: Crude (or minimalist) sculptural representation of a face.
Merlons: The raised parts of a crenellated parapet.
Murder hole: An aperture in a vault, usually over a gateway, either for directing missiles through or as conduits for water to dowse fires.
Narthex: A vestibule, or porch, at the W end of a church, normally extending from N–S across the axis of the building.
Offset: A ledge formed by a narrowing of the upper part of a wall. Used as housings for floor timbers internally.
Ogee: Double curved profile comprising concave and convex parts to form an S shape. A staple of **Curvilinear tracery**.
Oillet: A circular termination to an arrow loop.
Openwork: Perforated stone or woodwork.
Outwork: A fortification outside, but perhaps attached to, the castle enceinte.
Pantry: A service room for the storage of bread.
Peel: Fortification in the form of a palisade; also an enclosure fortified by a palisade.
Pentice: A roofed walkway.
Perpendicular: The last phase of English Gothic architecture dating from *c.*1330 to *c.*1530, characterized by tracery of rectilinear forms.
Pilaster buttress: A flat buttress of small projection, characteristic of **Romanesque** architecture.
Piscina: A sink with drain for washing the Communion vessels, situated at the E end of a church within a mural niche.
Portcullis: Heavy grilled gate operated on a vertical plane between grooves in the flanking stonework.
Postern: A subsidiary gateway, either in a different location to the main gateway or adjacent to it in the form of a pedestrian entrance that can be utilized independently.
Principal rafter: Enlarged rafter at the bay divisions of a roof, designed to carry side **Purlins**.
Purbeck marble: A crystalline form of limestone from Dorset, capable of being given a glossy polish, and therefore desirable as an architectural embellishment.
Purlin: Longitudinal member in a roof structure giving intermediate support to the rafters.
Putlog: A horizontal scaffolding pole placed across the line of a wall, and accommodated in putlog holes, allowing scaffolding to be supported on both sides of the structure.
Pyramid stops: A decorative termination to a **Chamfer** in the form of a half pyramid, or **Broach**. Also known as a broach stop.
Quoin: A corner stone, usually of **Ashlar**.
Rear arch: Arch above a window embrasure.

Glossary

Relieving arch: An arch over an opening to divert the load of the upper wall to either side and so relieve the strain on the lintel.
Respond: Demi-column or corbel set into a wall to carry one end of an arch belonging to an arcade or rib vault.
Revetment: Wall or palisade that buttresses and retains a body of earth like a bank or a motte.
Rib vault: Vault constructed on a framework of arches (ribs), the spaces between the ribs being infilled with stone webbing.
Ridge piece: Horizontal timber extending along the apex (ridge) of a roof to which the upper ends of the rafters are attached.
Ringwork: Name given to the earthwork remains of a timber enclosure castle.
Roll moulding: Moulding usually of three-quarter round section.
Romanesque: An architectural style characterized by round arches, which encompasses both the Anglo-Saxon and Norman periods, i.e. *c.* 600–1200.
Roof truss: The principal transverse timber roof frames.
Rustication: Treatment of ashlar masonry in which the joints are sunk to suggest robustness.
Sally port: A type of **Postern**, supposedly for the purpose of making a sally against a besieger.
Saltire: An heraldic term, essentially two bands forming a St Andrew's cross.
Scarp: Inner slope of a ditch facing away from the castle, or, more generally a steep slope, natural or man-made.
Sedile (pl. **Sedilia**): Seat(s) for clergy recessed into the walls of a church chancel.
Septaria: A conglomerate, found in East Anglia and used there as a building stone.
Shell keep: Stone wall encircling the top of a motte.
Shouldered lintel: Lintel carried on a pair of concave corbels, also known as a Carnarvon/Caernarvon/Caernarfon arch.
Slighting: Deliberate destruction of fortifications to render them indefensible.
Soffit: Underside of a horizontal timber or stone.
Solar: Private residential room on an upper storey within a medieval house, sometimes within a tower (hence, solar tower).
Spandrel: The (roughly triangular) space between an arch and its rectangular frame.
Spine wall: Internal wall extending down the longitudinal centre of a building.
Springer: The bottom **Voussoir** of an arch.
Spurred base: A special form of tower plinth, stemming from a foundation of (usually) square plan which supports a rounded or polygonal tower. The 'spurs' are formed when the plinth is carried up on an incline at the angles.
Squinch: Arch built diagonally across the right-angle formed by two adjoining walls to support an upper structure.
Squint: A narrow window, or opening, angled towards a specific spot within a building, which can thus be viewed from the room.
Stellar vault: Lierne vault in the form of a star.
Stiff leaf: A Gothic sculptural decoration in the form of stylized foliage, typical of the C13.
String/string course: A continuous horizontal moulding on the exterior face of a building, sometimes used to indicate a floor level, but largely decorative in intent.
Supermullion: Vertical glazing bar above the main window lights.
Tau cross: Cross in the form of the letter T.

Tie beam: The principal transverse timber member connecting two walls, on which a roof truss is built.

Tracery: Decorative pattern of stone or timber glazing bars in a Gothic window, typically glazed.

Trumpet capital: A late Romanesque form of capital decorated with stylized elongated scalloping, the components of which resemble trumpets.

Tympanum: The infill stone between a lintel and its relieving arch over a window or doorway, sometimes a recipient of sculptured decoration.

Vault: Stone ceiling, or, a timber construction imitating such.

Vesica: An oval with pointed ends.

Voussoir: One of a series of wedge-shaped stones used in the construction of an arch.

Wall plate: Horizontal timber extending along the top of an outside wall on which the feet of the rafters rest.

Wave moulding: A moulding profile forming a continuous curve convex in the centre and concave on each side, characteristic of the period $c.1290–1350$.

Webbing: The infilled compartments of a rib vault.

Wind brace: A timber roof brace extending from the principal rafters to the **Purlins**.

Y-tracery: A simple form of tracery in which the glazing bars of two lancet lights form a Y-shape. A more elaborate derivative found in larger windows is known as **Intersecting tracery**. Mainly of the period $c.1290–1310$.

Ashby de la Zouche: The Hastings Tower from the north.

GAZETTEER

In the gazetteer below, the sites are arranged alphabetically in a single list, rather than by county or region, thereby favouring searches for particular sites rather than geographical areas. For those who do wish to search geographically, a map of the historic counties is included and a list of castles arranged by county. The gazetteer entries indicate whether or not a site is open to the public, but arrangements vary markedly, so always check opening dates and times before embarking on a trip. In most cases there a few suggestions for further reading; these represent some of the more useful items for those wishing to obtain a greater understanding of individual sites. More comprehensive bibliographies can be found in John Kenyon's *Castles, Town Defences and Artillery Fortifications in the United Kingdom and Ireland: A Bibliography 1945–2006* (Donington: Shaun Tyas). For earlier and later material see the late Philip Davies's *Gatehouse* website (www.gatehouse-gazetteer), which is now maintained by the Castle Studies Group; the bibliographies for individual sites extend to 2017, when Philip Davies died. The annual bibliographies of the Castle Studies Group from 2003 onwards are available on the group's website (www.castlestudies group.org.uk), though the lists 2003–6 are included in Kenyon's book.

Abbreviations used
D = Demolished; EH = English Heritage; NT = National Trust; RCHME = Royal Commission on the Historical Monuments of England.

* * *

ABINGER: Surrey (Private). A motte, situated next to Abinger manor house, famously excavated by Brian Hope-Taylor in 1947–9. In Domesday the manor of Abinger was held by William FitzAnsculf, and, from *c.*1100, by the Paynels of Dudley (qv). The castle was probably built by the tenant, Robert of Abinger, who was in possession from *c.*1090; the second phase is probably the work of his son, William. Excavation of the motte top revealed a series of postholes indicating timber superstructures of two phases dating from *c.*1100 and *c.*1150 respectively, though only in the later phase was the evidence substantial enough to allow a coherent reconstruction. The Phase 2 buildings included a timber palisade around the edge of the motte with a wall walk and a SW gateway; there was also a substantial rectangular building, probably a tower, occupying a central position. Digging in the moat revealed a causeway approximating to the position of the gateway, which would have provided the base for a timber bridge. Hope-Taylor 1950.

ACTON BURNELL: Shropshire (Open – EH). The C13 building known as Acton Burnell Castle was the main residential block of a manorial complex of which the only other aspects to survive above ground level are the two gable ends of a large stone barn some 90m (300ft) to the NE. Built for Robert Burnell (d. 1292), Bishop of Bath and Wells and Chancellor of England, under a licence to crenellate of 1284. Burnell,

Acton Burnell: West front.

who had been born at Acton, also built the adjacent church of St Mary, which is slightly earlier than the castle. Royal craftsmen, notably Walter of Hereford, the master mason of Vale Royal Abbey, Cheshire (1277–90), may have been involved in its design and construction. Despite the appellation of 'castle', there are few visible signs of defence, but the crenellated parapet was functional, there was formerly a moat, and there may have been other outer defences. The house is rectangular with four-storey square turrets at each corner, and a larger turret in the centre of the W front containing a private chamber at the upper level. This central turret was balanced at the E end by a service block, beyond which would have been a kitchen. The main entrance was at first-floor level into the NE turret via an external stair (no longer extant) and thence into the hall, a square room divided longitudinally by a stone arcade (supporting a double-pile roof). Beyond this, to the W, was private accommodation on two storeys served by latrines within the turrets. West 1981.

ADDERLEY (Ethelred's Castle), Shropshire (Private). A motte approximately 7m high (23ft) adapted from a natural mound. A bailey probably lay to the E, a site now occupied by buildings. This castle was probably the caput of the manor of Eldredelei (later Adderley). The lord of Adderley in Domesday was Nigel the Physician, who held it under the Earl of Shrewsbury. In the early C12, after Henry I confiscated the English properties of the Third Earl, Robert de Bellême, Adderley was granted to Alan de Dunstanville. On the death of Walter, the last Dunstanville lord, in 1270, the manor passed to his daughter and heir, Petronilla, whose husband John de la Mare was holding it in 1294. The date of the castle is uncertain, but in the last quarter of the C13 Walter de Dunstanville made a park at Adderley, which was probably associated with the castle. A quantity of pottery recovered from the motte was dated to the later C13. Barker 1957–60; Duckers 2006, 17–18.

ALBERBURY, Shropshire (Visible from the adjacent churchyard). Irregularly polygonal stone-built courtyard castle, the main feature of which is a two-storey rectangular great tower. There was a smaller wall tower at the NW angle of the enclosure, but its form is uncertain. Located at the SW angle and forming part of the enceinte, the keep does not seem to have had any internal divisions in stone. The basement was probably given over to storage, and the first floor occupied by a hall. Alberbury Castle probably formed the caput of the manor of Alberbury; its construction is usually attributed to Fulk FitzWarren III and dated to the early C13. Salter 2001; Duckers 2006, 18–20.

ALDFORD, (Blobb Hill) Cheshire (Visible from the churchyard). Motte and bailey close to a crossing of the river Dee. The first mention of the castle dates from the early C13 (before 1229), but it had probably been in existence by the mid C12, possibly as early as the C11. Both motte and bailey are delineated by a dry ditch and outer bank; there was also an inner bank around at least part of the bailey. The motte was subsequently modified by the addition of a shell-keep in stone, no longer visible; geophysical survey has suggested that it may have contained further stone buildings. Swallow 2012.

ALDINGHAM, (Moat Hill) Lancashire (Visible from the road and seashore). Ringwork/motte situated on the edge of a cliff overlooking Morecambe Bay held by Michael le Fleming in 1127. The castle began life in the C12 as a ringwork; this earthwork was converted to a motte in the C13. The motte has been damaged through sea erosion of the cliff. Elsworth and Mace 2015.

ALLINGTON, Kent (Private). Motte and bailey next to the river Medway, the principal interest of which is a late C13 courtyard castle raised within the bailey. The date of the first castle is unknown, but, in 1174, Allington was one of the adulterine castles destroyed on the orders of Henry II, suggesting that the site had been fortified or refortified during Stephen's reign. The builder, therefore, may have been William of Allington (d. *c*.1183) who held the manor during this period. William's daughter and heiress, Avelina, married Osbert de Longchamp; the couple were probably responsible for a partial reconstruction of William of Allington's castle. In 1279, Allington was sold to Sir Stephen Penchester, Warden of the Cinque Ports and Constable of Dover Castle (qv), and in 1281 he and his wife, Margaret, obtained a licence to crenellate their house of Allington; it was under this authority that they built a compact courtyard castle within the NW corner of the existing bailey. In 1492 Allington was bought by Sir Henry Wyatt (d. 1537), who made considerable alterations to the Penchester residence, including large-scale refenestration and the division of the courtyard by the construction of an E–W service range with a long gallery above. The Wyatts' tenure came to an end in 1554 when it was confiscated by the Crown. Subsequently, the castle passed through a number of hands and was allowed to fall into disrepair. By 1905, when it was purchased by Sir Martin Conway, it was little more than a ruin. Conway restored Allington and much of its present appearance is owed to him and/or his architects W.B. Caröe and Philip Tilden.

The first castle consisted of a motte with a D-shaped bailey to the N. A stretch of walling on the S side of the bailey, constructed of herringbone masonry, may be the earliest stonework; it was incorporated into the subsequent rebuilding of the bailey curtain. The Penchester castle has a sub-rectangular plan, its curtain being augmented by several D-shaped towers and turrets of various sizes, somewhat irregularly disposed. The largest of these is Solomon's Tower, which projects from the

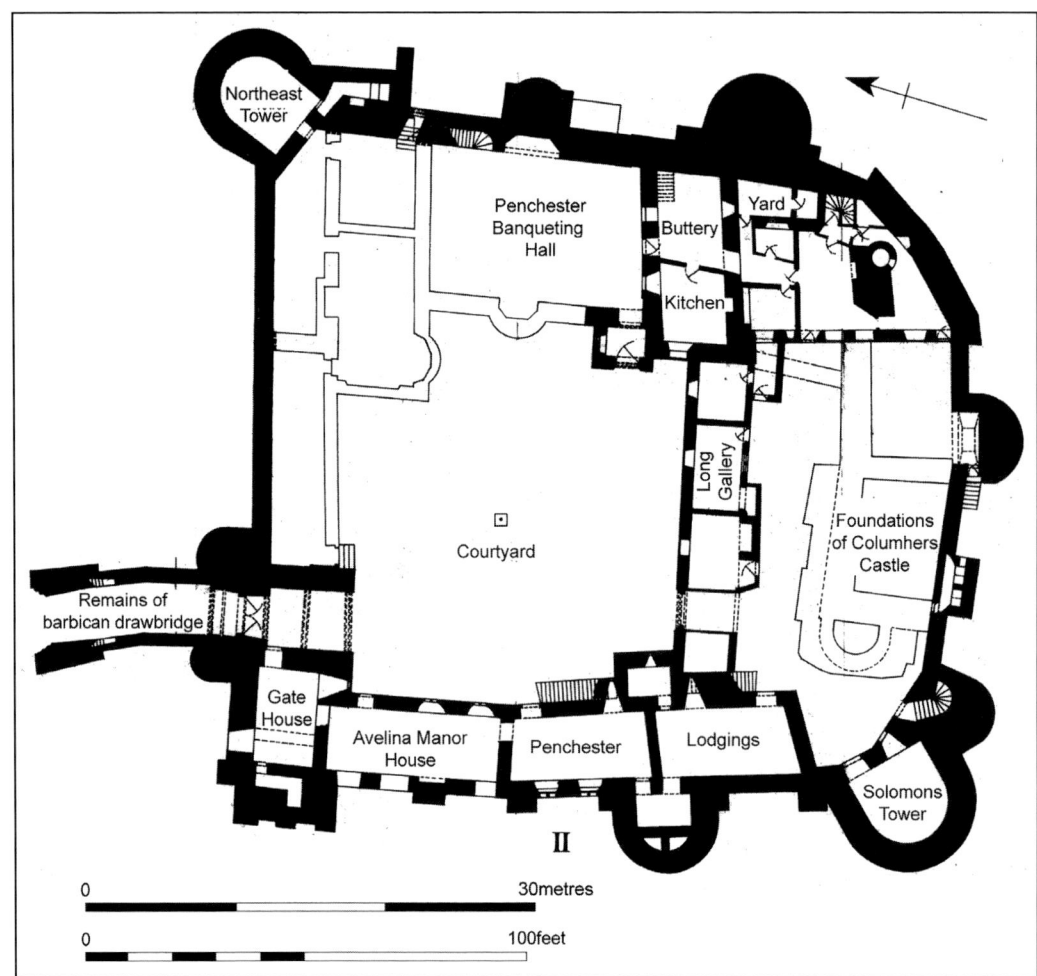

Allington: Ground plan. From Conway 1909.

SW angle; it has an attached staircase turret. Preceding the entrance are the remains of a barbican which contained a drawbridge across the moat. The gateway itself is flanked by a two D-shaped towers of unequal size; this asymmetry recalls some other C13 castle gateways, e.g., Goodrich (qv). The parapet with its C14-style arched machicolations is a Conway-period fabrication. Ranged along the W side of the courtyard are the late C13 Penchester Lodgings, containing some very early brickwork. Conway 1909.

ALNWICK, Northumberland (Open). The seat of the Percy family for the last 700 years, Alnwick is a large stone castle strategically sited on the Great North Road, overlooking a crossing of the river Aln. Dating from *c*.1100, it was substantially redeveloped in the C14 and remodelled in the C18 and C19. First mentioned in 1136, when it was held by Ivo de Vescy, in whose family it remained until 1297 when his descendent, William de Vescy, died without legitimate issue. In the absence of an heir Alnwick was granted to Anthony Bek, Bishop of Durham, who, in 1309, sold it to the Yorkshire nobleman Henry de Percy (d. 1314). Soon after this acquisition Percy began to rebuild the castle, a task that was completed by his son, also Henry (d. 1352).

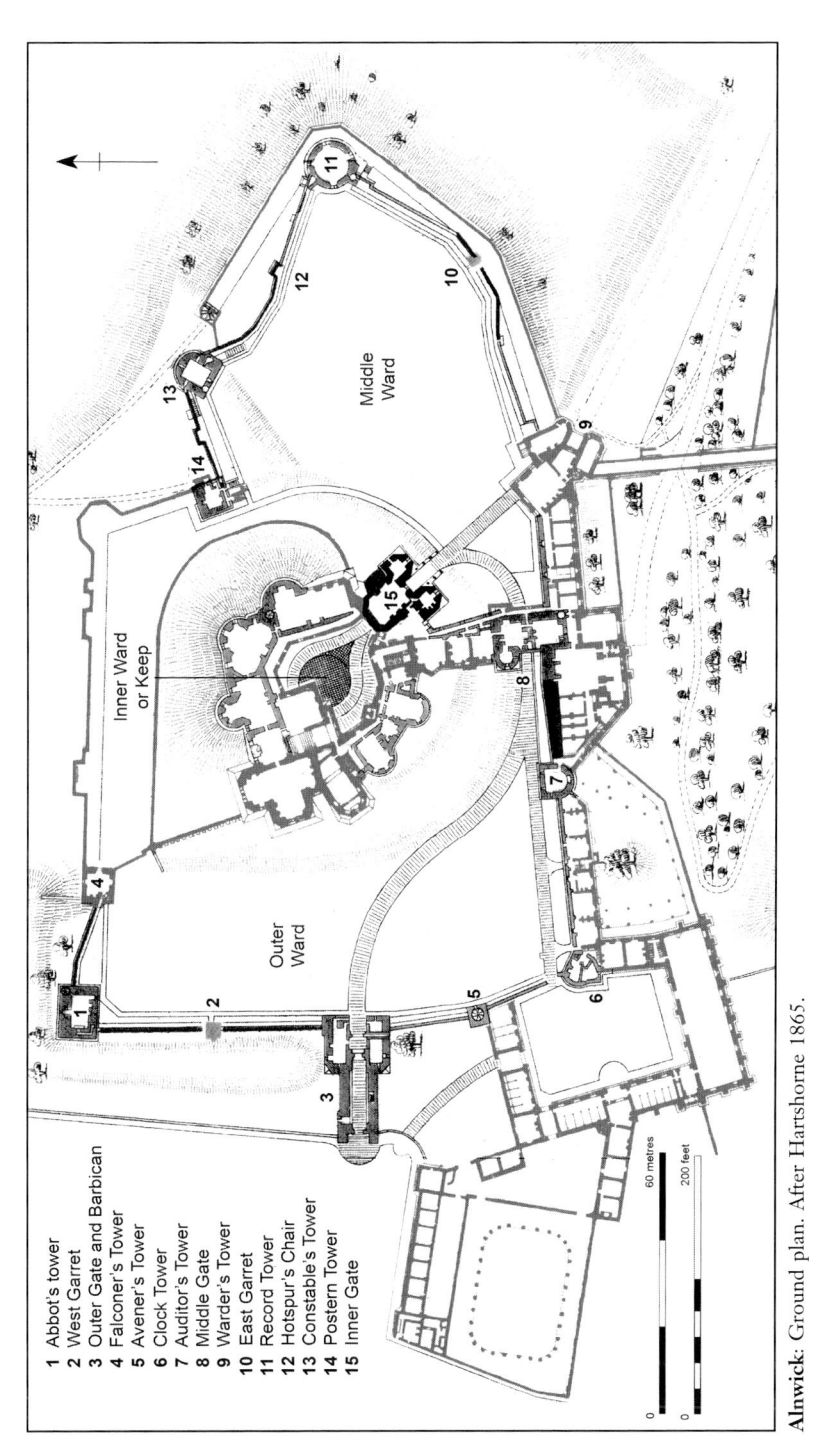

Alnwick: Ground plan. After Hartshorne 1865.

1 Abbot's tower
2 West Garret
3 Outer Gate and Barbican
4 Falconer's Tower
5 Avener's Tower
6 Clock Tower
7 Auditor's Tower
8 Middle Gate
9 Warder's Tower
10 East Garret
11 Record Tower
12 Hotspur's Chair
13 Constable's Tower
14 Postern Tower
15 Inner Gate

By the C18 Alnwick Castle had fallen into ruin, and a programme of refurbishment was carried out in the 1750s and 1760s. However, the results were largely swept away in the 1850s when a major restoration was undertaken by Anthony Salvin. Although a large part of the castle's current character is owed to Salvin, substantial elements of the early fabric survive, and the building remains a significant medieval monument.

The castle was laid out on a modest eminence at the NW edge of the town. To the N, the land falls away for some 500ft (152m) to the river Aln, while its tributary, the Bow Burn (now culverted), formed a natural moat to the S and E. At some stage a moat was dug across the W front. Of the current internal divisions, the outer and middle wards represent the C12 W and E baileys respectively; both retain stretches of early masonry characterized by small, squared blocks, suggesting that the castle may have been built in stone from the start. There is less certainty about the development of the inner ward, or keep, but it is probable that this also formed one of the divisions of the C12 castle (see below), though whether this took the form of a motte or an enclosure has not been verified. A fourth enclosure to the N of the inner ward, bounded by the Gun Terrace, is a creation of the C18 and C19.

Although the later medieval work, which was built with large ashlar blocks, is generally attributed to the Percys, the exact chronology is uncertain, and the one item that can be closely dated is the outer portal of the inner gate (see below) and, by extension (owing to stylistic affinities), the outer gate, both of which must be the work of Henry Percy the younger. Both these buildings have semi-octagonal flanking towers and spurred bases. The plans of the other medieval towers fall into two categories; rectangular or round fronted; the former was becoming fashionable in the N of England from *c*.1315, while the latter started to fall out of favour at around the same time. It is unusual to see them together as part of a single scheme. In this respect it is interesting to note that the round towers are confined to the inner ward and the S and E curtains, from the Clock Tower at the SW angle to the Constable's Tower at the NE angle, suggesting, perhaps, that these areas were the first to be redeveloped. The rectangular towers are concentrated around the N and W curtains.

Of the entrance (W) front only half is now readily apparent, the main features punctuating the curtain being (from the L) the NW corner tower (Abbot's Tower), mid-wall turret (West Garret), and outer gate. The gate, which was situated in the centre of the W elevation, is fronted by a barbican (one of the best preserved in England), which extends across the moat. A semi-circular arched entrance (a recurrent feature of the C14 work) is flanked by square turrets, the heads corbelled out at the sides. Above the entrance a C15 panel contains the Percy emblem of a lion rampant. Figure sculptures surmounting the battlements are mostly replacements for, or emulations of, original features. Formerly, the barbican contained a drawbridge, but the moat has been infilled and the passage paved. The double-battlemented alure was manned from the gatehouse.

Turning L (N) on entering the outer ward are the backs of the West Garret and Abbot's Tower; lastly comes the Falconer's Tower of 1856. Formerly, the curtain extended from the Abbot's Tower to the inner ward and was interspersed by two rectangular turrets. To the S of the outer gate are another mid-wall turret (Avener's Tower) and the three-quarter round SW corner tower (Clock Tower), and, first along the S curtain, the Auditor's Tower. All three were features of the medieval castle, but all have been rebuilt.

Access to the middle ward was via the middle gate, situated at the S end of the dividing wall between the two wards. This gate is contained within a rectangular three-storey structure, with a single (round-fronted) flanking tower, which, like the towers of the inner and outer gates, sits on a spurred base. The upper storeys contained a substantial lodging. Inside the inner ward, moving anti-clockwise around the curtain, the main features are: the Warder's Tower of 1860, Record Tower at the E angle, then, along the NE curtain, a (rebuilt) mid-wall turret (Hotspur's Seat) on the site of a medieval tower, Constable's Tower and Postern Tower. The three-storey Constable's Tower has a well-preserved internal face; At second-floor level a two-light window with mid-height transom and monolithic traceried head, restored, but following the original pattern. Externally, cruciform arrow loops and a twin shoulder-arched and transomed window. From the square Constable's Tower, a length of curtain joined up with the inner ward.

The inner ward, or keep, is usually attributed to Henry Percy the elder; it has been substantially altered, notably through the reconstruction of the NE angle and the remodelling of the interior. As built in the C14 it was studded with a series of seven round-fronted towers, its N front forming part of the outer defences; only five of these towers remain. Like the outer gatehouse, the monumental entrance at the SW angle features twin flanking towers with semi-octagonal fronts, a display of heraldic shields and battlement-topping figure sculptures. The heraldry dates this front to the 1340s, but, beyond the towers, at each end of gate passage, is a C12 gate arch ornamented with chevron mouldings. These are remnants of an earlier gateway which was incorporated into the C14 scheme. That it gave access to a shell-keep surrounded by a ditch, as at Windsor (qv), is probable; an alternative theory that it formed the main entrance to the C12 castle seems less likely. On entering the inner ward, to the R (E) is a C14 well head with three segmental-pointed arches. Otherwise, apart from the gate arch, the medieval character of the courtyard has been lost to Salvin's remodelling. In the C14 the courtyard was larger, but was still lined with residential apartments, partly within the towers, over vaulted undercrofts. The main focus of the accommodation was the first-floor hall on the E side, which communicated with a kitchen block to the N and with a more private suite over the gateway to the S. Goodall 2013a.

ALTON, Staffordshire (Private). A cliff-top stone castle of C12 origin, containing a C19 neo-Gothic mansion. First mentioned in 1176, Alton Castle was probably built by Bertran de Verdun, Sheriff of Leicester and Warwick (1170–84), who died in 1192 while taking part in the Third Crusade. In 1264 it was captured by the Earl of Derby, a supporter of Simon de Montfort, and apparently destroyed. Described as ruinous in 1316, in the following year, whilst being held by the King, it was captured by followers of Thomas, Earl of Lancaster. In 1331 Alton came to the Furnivall family through marriage, when the male line of the Verduns became extinct, and in 1406 it came into the possession of John Talbot, later First Earl of Shrewsbury. In 1847 the castle was reoccupied when a house was built within the enclosure, to the design of A.W.N. Pugin for the Earl of Shrewsbury.

Alton Castle is built on a hill overlooking the Churnet valley to the N, on which side the site is protected by a precipitous cliff. To the S is a great rock-cut ditch, which isolates a small spur of irregular shape. There is every reason to suppose that the castle was built of stone from the outset, and that this material was obtained from the great ditch. Much of the S curtain wall dates from the C12, including a rectangular, open-backed tower with barrel-vaulted ground storey. Both curtain and tower were later heightened, the upper storey of the tower having chamfered angles and a cruciform arrow loop, with basal fishtail splay. This modification may date from the early C13, when a D-shaped wall tower and a gatehouse with twin D-shaped flanking towers were added further to the W. The gatehouse had a sally port beneath the gate passage, which communicated with one of the towers. Cantor 1966.

ALMONDBURY (Castle Hill), Yorkshire West Riding (Open). Castle of three wards within a prehistoric hillfort. First mentioned in a charter of King Stephen (dated 1142–54) confirming Henry de Lacy's possession. The Lacy estates were inherited by Thomas, Earl of Lancaster, following the death of his father-in-law, Henry de Lacy, Earl of Lincoln, in 1311. The castle was excavated between 1939 and 1972.

Orientated NE–SW the extent of de Lacy's castle was co-terminus with the summit of the hillfort and utilized, or reworked, the hillfort defences to create a tripartite division of (from SW–NE) inner, middle and outer wards. The inner ward was isolated by a great ditch 90ft wide and 30ft behind which was a wall-topped bank. It contained a stone keep (its position marked by the Victoria Jubilee Tower) and two wells. The archaeological work suggests that during the later C13 the outer ward was given over to agriculture and that sometime in the early C14 the buildings of the inner ward were demolished, and the castle abandoned. Varley 1973.

AMBERLEY, Sussex (Operates as a hotel – only accessible to guests). Manor house of the bishops of Chichester, converted into a double-courtyard castle in the late C14. The creation of the castle is related to a licence to crenellate of 1377 granted to Bishop William Rede; work was still going on in 1382. Amberley Castle has a sub-rectangular plan laid out on an E–W axis, with the outer ward to the W and the inner ward to the E, around which the earlier manorial buildings are arranged. The curtain wall incorporates three corner towers, but none projects externally, the only protrusions from the otherwise plain enceinte being two garderobe turrets (N and W), the Kitchen Tower to the N, and the gatehouse towers to the S. This gatehouse, which constitutes the principal external feature, has twin D-shaped towers flanking a central gateway with a four-centred arch. It gives access to the spacious outer ward, which was lined with two-storey domestic buildings on three sides, and on the fourth (E) side by the C14 great hall, the remains of which are incorporated into the present house. Beyond it is the inner ward, and, in the SW corner, the C13 manorial buildings. Emery 2006, 297–300.

ANSTEY, Hertfordshire (Visible from the churchyard). Motte and bailey in the grounds of Anstey Hall. Traditionally ascribed to Eustace, Count of Boulogne, who held the manor at the time of the Domesday survey. It was certainly in existence by the time of the Barons' War (1215–17), when it was strengthened. In 1218, the tenant, Nicholas de Anstey, was ordered to reduce the fortifications to their state before the war. A wet moat surrounds a large motte whose flat-topped summit extends to approximately ¼ acre. Wrapped around its eastern half is an L-shaped bailey, defined along its northern boundary by a wet ditch. Another length of ditch extends from the junction of the motte and bailey ditches on the NW. Possibly the boundary of a settlement enclosure, it heads due W for some 250ft before turning S. RCHME 1910.

APPLEBY, Westmorland (Open by appointment). Probable ringwork and bailey, the former now containing a C12 keep. The castle was in existence by 1130, the keep by 1174. Granted to Robert de Vieuxpont in 1203; inherited in 1296 by Robert, First Baron Clifford, from his mother Isabella Vieuxpont. Dismantled in 1648. Restored by Lady Anne Clifford from 1651. On Lady Anne's death in 1676 Appleby was inherited by her daughter Margaret, Countess of Thanet; Margaret's son, Thomas, Sixth Earl of Thanet, rebuilt the main residential apartments from 1686.

The town of Appleby is sited within a loop of the river Eden, and the castle lies to the E on the high ground at the neck of the peninsula guarding the landward approach. The keyhole-like plan of the main enclosure, round to the W and rectangular to the E, suggests a development from two courtyards. The enclosure is protected by a substantial ditch, except to the E where a steep scarp drops to the river. To the NW of the former W bailey another enclosure is defined by a bank and ditch and, to the S of this, a linear ditch, banked on both sides, extending to the river scarp. There are several rectangular buttress turrets around the W bailey and there were at least three round towers around the E bailey of which the best preserved is on the N side.

Access is from the N into the former E bailey. The gatehouse was built by John Clifford c.1404–22, but only the RH (W) tower survives, the LH (E) tower being an C18 rebuild. The principal medieval apartments were ranged across the E end of the E bailey, the remains being incorporated into the late C17 house. These remains suggest a N–S hall range flanked at each end by a rectangular corner tower, which may date from c.1383, when the sheriffs of Cumberland and Westmorland were charged with recruiting building workers for the repair of Roger de Clifford's castles in those counties. A suggestion that the work was done by John Lewyn is given credence by the form of the postern in the E curtain which comprises a gate with a semi-circular arch and chamfered surround recessed beneath a tall outer arch of similar form. A portcullis operated between the two, and, when raised, was exposed to view within the outer arch; an unusual arrangement but related to the entrances to the domestic ranges at Castle Bolton (qv) which are attributable to Lewyn.

The main building of the W bailey is the C12 keep (Caesar's Tower) constructed of dressed stone blocks in two phases. Built to a square plan with pilaster buttresses at the corners, it was initially three storeys high, but at a slightly later date was raised a further two storeys. The ground floor was lit by narrow loops, but the first- and second-floor windows are twin rectangular lights set beneath a semi-circular arch. These latter are of the same pattern as a window in Conisbrough Castle (qv) keep of c.1165–90. In 1651–3 the keep was repaired by Lady Anne Clifford, who built a central cross-wall and converted the interior to house a series of lodgings. Curwen 1913, 66–7, 75–80, 454; RCHME 1936; Simpson 1949; Perriam and Robinson 1998, 252–4.

ARUNDEL, Sussex (Open). Motte and two baileys, substantially rebuilt in stone over the centuries, its current appearance owing much to the C18 and C19 but containing significant medieval remains. Established c.1068 by Roger of Montgomery, later Earl of Shrewsbury, Henry I confiscated it from his rebellious son, and in 1138 it was conferred upon William d'Albini on his marriage to Henry's widow. On William's death in 1176 the castle was appropriated by Henry II who held it until 1189 and carried out building works there. The last of the Albinis died in 1243 and

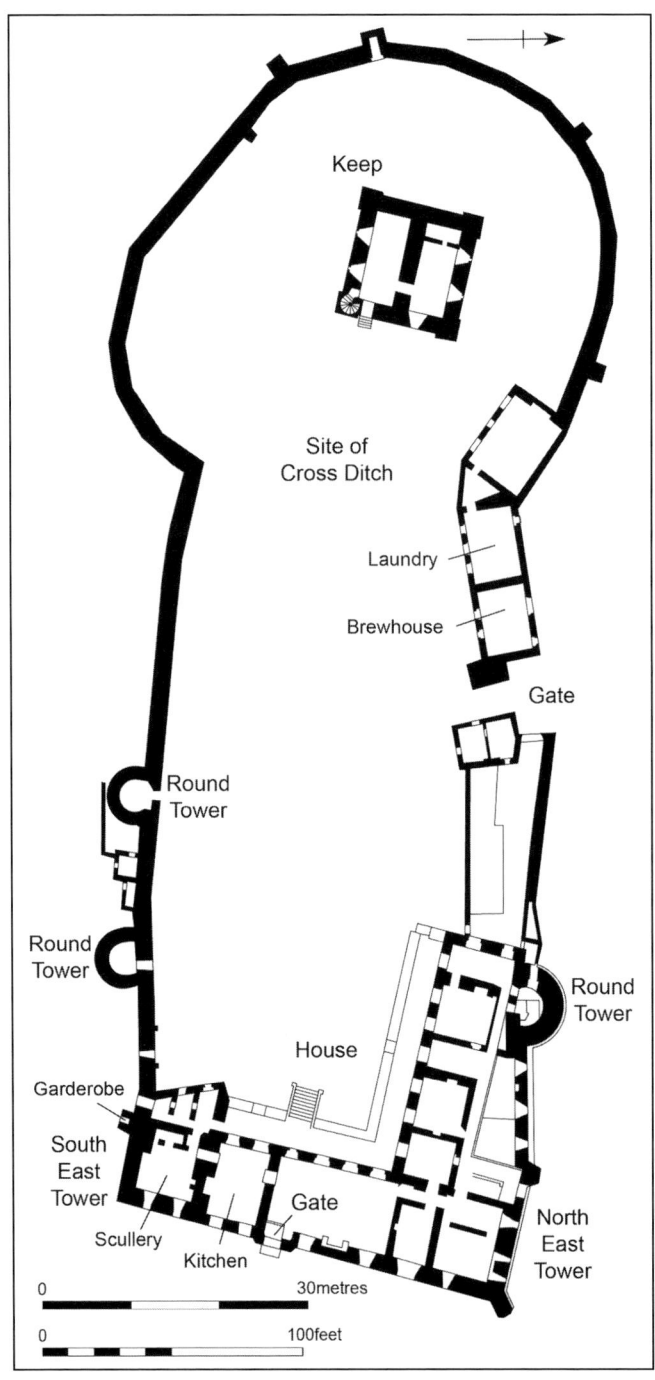

Appleby: Ground plan. After Perriam and Robinson 1998.

Arundel came to the FitzAlans whose tenure lasted until 1580. They effected substantial construction works during the latter half of the C14. After the FitzAlans came the Howards, the current owners. The Civil War, during which the castle underwent two sieges, was followed by a period of neglect until the C18. Major C18 and C19 programmes of work transformed the castle into a stately home.

The plan of the C11 castle is that of a small-scale Windsor (qv), having a similar elongated plan of upper (N) and lower (S) baileys, one each side of a central motte, the effect accentuated by the extensive C19 Windsor-like rebuilding in the lower bailey, which dominates the current approach from the S. The S front, however, also retains medieval fabric, notably a well-preserved late C12 window towards the RH (E) end, probably indicating some of the work carried out by Henry II. The medieval entrance to the castle is on the W side at the foot of the motte. First comes a late C14 barbican with twin square flanking turrets and shouldered-lintel windows, then the C11 or early C12 stone gateway with plain round arches and an early portcullis slot.

The gatehouse gives access to the alure of the motte's wing wall and thence to the C12 circular shell-keep. Probably the work of William d'Albini, the keep is now entered through a later (possibly C14) forebuilding, to the R of which is the blocked (and heavily restored) C12 gateway to the keep. Inside the shell-keep is evidence for the two-storey former apartments that lined the walls, including a C12 hooded fireplace with a rounded back of herringbone masonry. In the centre of the courtyard is the entrance to a vaulted cellar, probably C13. NW of the motte, projecting from the S curtain, another major medieval building is the Bevis Tower, its rectangular plan and diagonally projecting corner turrets reminiscent of several late C14 castles in County Durham (cf Brancepeth, Witton, Lumley); it may be of similar date. Hudson 1997, 38–51; Emery 2006, 300–4.

ASCOT D'OILLY, Oxfordshire (Private). C12 quasi-motte and bailey on the outskirts of Ascot-under-Wychwood. First mentioned in the 1150s when the manor was held by Roger d'Oilly, and probably erected during Stephen's reign. The keep was probably destroyed on the orders of Henry II *c.*1180. Prior to excavation, in 1946–7, the castle consisted of a low mound with a sub-rectangular bailey to the S containing the current manor house. Investigation of the clay mound, or motte, revealed that it had been built up in stages around the base of a square stone tower. When the keep was demolished, the mound was levelled down, but its C12 appearance would have been that of a motte capped by a stone tower. Jope and Threlfall 1959; Bond 2001.

ASHBY DE LA ZOUCH, Leicestershire (Open – EH). Between *c.*1160 and 1399 the manor of Ashby was held by the le Zouch family who gave their name to the town. During their tenure the manor house was rebuilt, and remains of the hall and crosswing survive amidst the later buildings of the castle. In 1462 the manor came into the possession of William Lord Hastings, a prominent supporter of Edward IV; it was Hastings who transformed the old manor house into a castle under a licence to crenellate of 1474, although it is evident that work had begun the previous year. The castle was probably complete by the time of Hastings' death in 1483. During the Civil War Ashby was an important Royalist stronghold, and in 1649 the castle was slighted, both the great tower and kitchen tower being partially demolished. Later in the century some of the buildings were repaired and continued to be occupied until the mid C18.

Ashby: The Hastings Tower (1474–80) from the S. Demolition of the southern half after the Civil War has revealed a doll's house-like view of the interior.

The surviving buildings comprise a tightly-planned group ranged around an inner courtyard linked by a curtain wall to the E, W and S. Contained within the N range are the great hall with chamber block (E) and service block (W), beyond which are the kitchen tower (W), and chapel (E). In the centre of the S curtain is the great tower, or Hastings Tower. Access to the castle was from the N to an outer courtyard (now mostly occupied by Manor House School), and then through the hall range, either via the hall itself or the broad passage next to the kitchen tower. There were also gardens to the S of the inner courtyard complex, the earthworks of which can still be seen.

The dominating presence and main interest of the site is the C15 work, but there are also earlier and later phases. This is best illustrated by the hall, which is a patchwork of different structural periods, the most obvious external elements being the C16 porches and C17 windows. The earliest (probably C13) fabric, however, consists of small rectangular blocks interspersed by narrow levelling courses, and can be seen externally and internally in both the hall and the W crosswing. The hall was remodelled *c.*1350 and again in the late C15, when the walls were heightened, but throughout the Middle Ages it was divided longitudinally by two stone arcades (rebuilt by Hastings) supporting its wide-span roof, their former presence indicated by two pairs of responds at the E and W ends. The E responds are C15, but the W responds are C13 and are set at a lower level, commensurate with the height of the C13 roof, but were left *in situ* and reused in the later remodelling. The contemporary two-storey W crosswing contained service rooms at ground-floor level and a great chamber above.

A passage led through the W crosswing to the C15 kitchen tower, which contains one of the most impressive castle kitchens to have survived, its great size indicative of the size of Hastings' retinue. Fireplaces survive in the N and S walls. The kitchen was 30ft high and was covered by a stone-ribbed vault of six bays. There was a residential apartment above. In the E wall a service hatch for the conveyance of food for the hall. At the SE corner is a cellar from where an underground passage led to the Hastings Tower.

Also of Hastings' time is the E crosswing or chamber block (with a good example of a C15 fireplace at first-floor level) and, attached to the SE corner, the large chapel, an aisleless three-bay structure with a three-storey W end connected at first-floor level with the E wing and linked vertically via a SW stair turret. The chapel formed the N side of what was formerly a separate courtyard in the SE corner of the castle, with an E lodging range served by four large fireplaces in the E wall.

At the SW angle of this inner courtyard is the Hastings Tower, a rectangular four-storey main block with a seven-storey turret (of equal height) projecting from the centre of the E side. The entrance (N) front survives almost intact apart from its parapet. It is a dramatic asymmetrical façade, the designer's use of massing, deep settings and bold mouldings producing emphatic contrasts of light and shade. Ground-floor entrance set within a pilaster-like projection capped by an ogee-arched and finialed niche containing Lord Hastings' arms. Long panelled polygonal bartizans are linked by three-tier corbelled machicolations to create an extravagant crown, now marred by the loss of the battlements. Best viewed from the S, the interior of the main block contained (from ground to third floor) retainers' hall, kitchen, audience chamber and withdrawing chamber or bedroom. Fosbrooke 1911; Emery 2000, 211–20; Goodall 2015.

ASHLEY (Gains Castle), Hampshire (Private). Ringwork and bailey. Possibly the castle for which William Briwere obtained a licence to crenellate in 1200. The pentagonal ringwork, which lies immediately S of the church, was entered from the W; the bailey was further W, on the opposite side of the road. There was a stone building range including a round tower on the E side of the ringwork. Renn 1973a, 94–6.

ASHTON KEYNES (Hall's Close), Wiltshire (Open access). Ringwork and bailey. Excavation of a trench across the ringwork in 1959 indicated that the bank was surmounted by a stone wall and the ditch lined with puddled clay and timber. Knocker and Sabben Clave 1958–60.

AYDON, Northumberland (Open – EH). Well-preserved late C13 manor house converted into a castle in the early C14. In 1293, the property was bought by Hugh de Reymes, a Suffolk merchant with a baronial lineage, and the current complex of buildings was probably begun by his son, Robert. In 1305 Robert de Reymes obtained a licence to crenellate his Northumbrian houses of Aydon and Shortflat (qv), an indication that the manor house was being fortified to prepare against possible Scottish incursions. Even so, in 1315 it was captured by the Scots who caused extensive damage. It was taken again in 1317, this time by English rebels, and once more by the Scots in 1346.

The castle is sited on a small promontory, demarcated by a ravine containing Aydon Burn, and forms an irregular pentagon with the main buildings at the base (S). At the N apex an apsidal-ended tower faces N towards the line of approach. A gateway within a dog leg of the NW curtain leads into the outer ward. The main period of construction was between 1280 and 1315, starting with the main residential block in the SE corner of the enclosure. This was followed first by the creation of an inner courtyard through which the buildings were accessed, and then by the outer courtyard. At some stage a middle courtyard was created in the SW corner.

The late C13 residential complex comprises a hall range, a chamber block at its E end in the form of a crosswing, and a large latrine block extending E from the crosswing. There was also an W wing (no longer extant), its roofline visible in the W gable of the hall. A simple gateway leads to the inner courtyard. The range opposite was occupied by ground- and first-floor halls, both entered from doors at the RH (W) end of the elevation, the latter from an external flight of steps (flashing grooves show that it was formerly covered and that there was a porch in front of the entrance).

The lower hall (now divided) was heated by a large fireplace, the higher-status upper hall by a brazier or open hearth. The upper room is lit by only two windows, both towards the E end where the high table would have been situated. A door in the E wall led to the private apartments which contain a massive hooded fireplace in the W wall, moved here from its original position in the E wall. There was access

Aydon from the S. From Turner and Parker 1851.

(originally the only access) from here to another high-status chamber at ground-floor level, also with an elaborate fireplace. The inhabitants of both rooms had use of the latrine block. At the W end of the hall range, beyond the courtyard, was the original kitchen; this was later moved to the range on the W side of the courtyard. Dixon and Bourne 1978; Dixon 1988; Emery 1996, 40–1.

AYTON, Yorkshire North Riding (Open). Manorial complex excavated 1958–61 of which the principal survival is a solar tower of *c.*1400. Held by the Ayton family from the C12 until 1389, when William de Ayton died without surviving male issue. Within a few years the Ayton estate was in the hands of William's son-in-law, Ralph de Eure, to whom the tower is attributed.

The three-storey tower has a plain rectangular plan; its elevations are articulated by a chamfered plinth and offsets and a moulded parapet string. Corbelled machicolations survive at the SE corner indicating the former presence of a square turret here and probably at the other angles. Western entrance with (restored) four-centred arch; on entering, a mural stair to the L (N) leads to the first floor. Straight ahead is the two-roomed basement with ribbed barrel-vault of pointed section. First, the kitchen with great fireplace in the E wall, an enlarged doorway in the dividing wall allowing access to a storeroom from which a mural service stair ascends to the first floor. The main stair gave access separately to a small northern room and a large southern room, the latter with latrine and large fireplace to the E and large windows to the W and S. How the second floor was reached is uncertain. The tower lay adjacent to a cluster of C12 and C13 domestic buildings within a rectangular enclosure. Rimmington and Rutter 1967.

BACONSTHORPE, Norfolk (Open access – EH). Late C15 quadrangular castle with C16 alterations and additions, now badly ruined. Begun *c.*1475 by John Heydon and completed by his son Henry *c.*1486. However, several subsequent construction phases point to substantial modifications in the first half of the C16. An outer courtyard was added under a licence to crenellate of 1561.

The sub-rectangular platform on which the castle is built is moated on three sides, the fourth (E) side being bounded by a mere. Approaching from the S, the track runs through the C16 outer gatehouse and thence in a straight line to the three-storey inner gatehouse, now the most prominent building of the entire complex. The moat was crossed via a drawbridge to a two-storey porch which opened to the gatehouse proper. The inner gatehouse led to the W courtyard and the principal residential accommodation. An E courtyard (to the R of the gatehouse) contained ancillary buildings. Dallas and Sherlock 2002.

BAKEWELL (Castle Hill), Derbyshire (Open access). Motte and bailey overlooking a crossing of the river Wye. A construction date in the late C12 or early C13 has been postulated. Swanton 1972.

BAMBURGH, Northumberland (Open). Large multi-period stone castle dramatically sited on the Northumbrian coast with a major C12 keep. Bamburgh has been occupied since the Iron Age, when there may have been a hillfort on the site. By the early C6 there was a residence and fortress of the Anglian kings of Bernicia here, and in the later Anglo-Saxon and early Norman period it was a seat of the earls of Northumbria. After the rebellion of Earl Robert Mowbray in 1095 Bamburgh was confiscated by the King, but in 1139 it came to Henry, Earl of Northumberland and

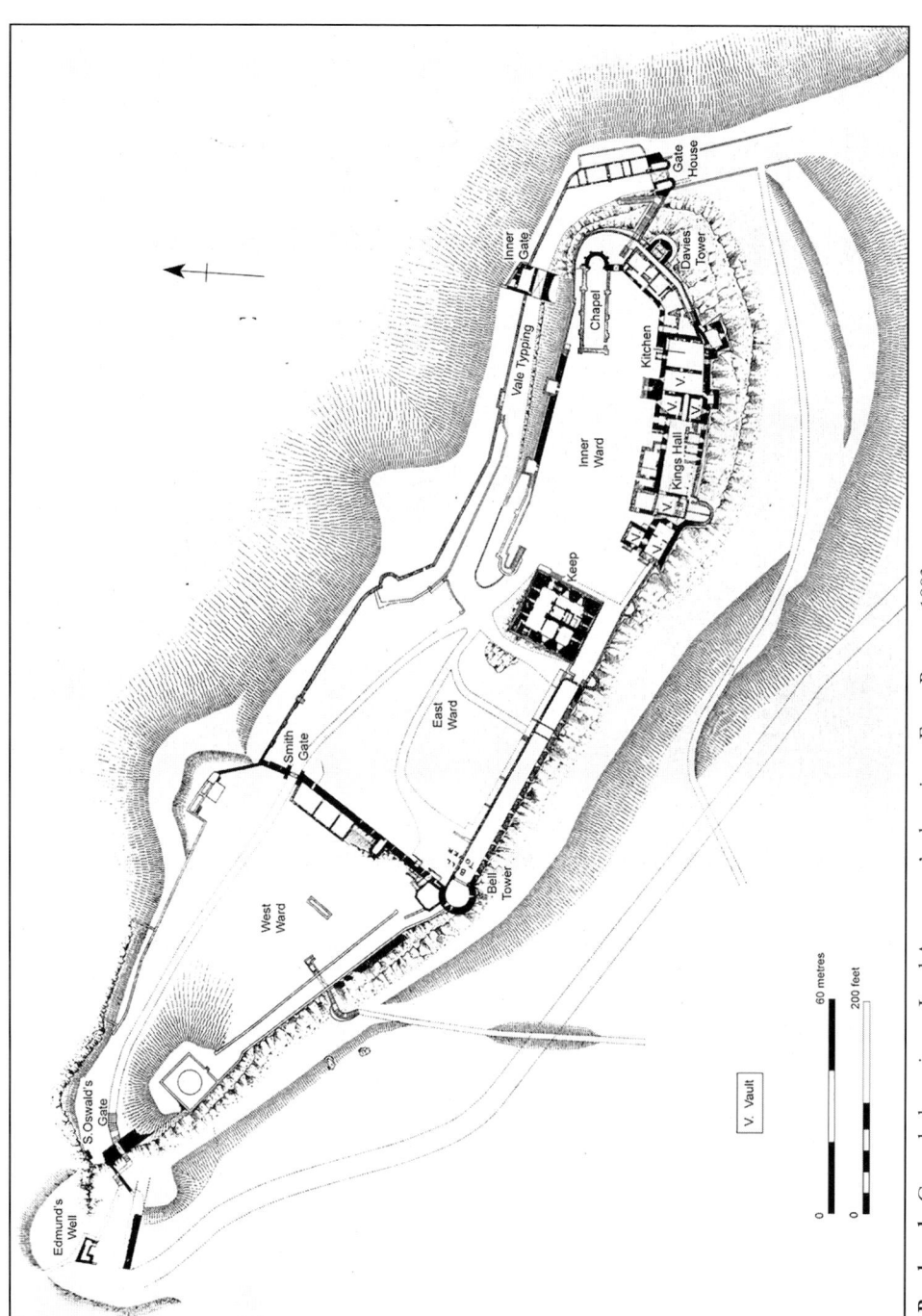

Bamburgh: Ground plan prior to Lord Armstrong's alterations. From Bateson 1893.

Bamburgh: The keep from the E.

Huntingdon, the son of the King of Scotland, who also held Carlisle (qv). Regained by Henry II in 1157 it remained a royal castle for the rest of the Middle Ages.

Henry II carried out some work, and he was very probably responsible for the rectangular wall towers of the inner ward. A good deal of building was carried out under Henry III and it may be to him that the outer gatehouse and round-fronted wall towers are owed. Repairs were carried out in the 1360s by the master mason John Lewyn, and it was probably Lewyn who rebuilt the principal domestic buildings along the N side of the inner ward *c.*1384–7. They comprised (from NW to SE) a great chamber with vaulted undercrofts, a hall with porch, vaulted service rooms (pantry, buttery, dresser and dry larder) with two chambers above, and a kitchen.

The castle was alienated from the Crown in 1610, and in 1704 was bought by Lord Crewe, Bishop of Durham, who bequeathed much of his estate, including Bamburgh, to a charitable trust. The Crewe trustee Dr John Sharp began restoration of the keep in 1757. In the early C19 the NE outer curtain was rebuilt and the ruinous great hall and associated buildings in the inner ward were restored or rebuilt. In 1894

Bamburgh was purchased by Lord Armstrong; restoration work began the following year and included the rebuilding of the great hall complex, whilst retaining the medieval fabric

Occupying the summit of a 150ft (45m) high basalt outcrop extending NW–SE for some 1,000ft (300m), the castle is divided (from NW to SE) into W, E and inner wards, the latter on the high point of the plateau. The original entrance may have been St Oswald's Gate at the NW end, but by the C12 the castle had been reorientated, with the main entry at the SE tip, as now, and a long approach along the SW flank in full view of watchers on the battlements. Four round-fronted towers along this face are C13 in origin, the best preserved being the large Bell Tower (at the junction of the E and W wards) and the Davies Tower (next to the gatehouse). The two rectangular towers are probably C12, the larger one (Muniment Tower) having been heightened in the 1380s.

After passing through a much altered and toy-like main gateway with twin C13 apsidal-ended towers, the approach road winds round to the L and along the NW side of the rock to the E ward, commanded on the L (S) by the fortifications of the inner ward and flanked on the R by the outer curtain. This route is straddled by a second gateway, a rectangular block of C12 origin, now largely C19 in character. Beyond this, on the L, are two late C12 rectangular wall towers with arrow loops on all three sides, recalling Henry II's work at Dover (qv).

Access to the inner ward was originally through a gatehouse attached to the C12 keep which dominated the entrance. The date of the keep is uncertain but was probably built for Henry I in the 1130s, perhaps by the mason Osbert. Almost square, with square corner turrets and pilaster buttresses, it sits on an unusually elaborate plinth. Also unusual is the ground-floor entrance set within a two-storey projection and giving access to a vestibule from which a mural stair led to the first floor. The original internal arrangements have been obscured by the later alterations, C12 vaulting survives over the basement and in the putative chapel on the first floor.

In the E corner of the inner ward are the ruins of the C12 apsidal-ended chapel. Otherwise, the medieval interest lies in the C14 apartments, the most significant survival of which is the great kitchen which retains three large fireplaces with pronounced segmental heads, segmental-arched window embrasures with flues in their heads (a Lewyn trait, cf. Castle Bolton and Warkworth keep), and doorways into the Muniment Tower and Small Tower. In the W wall is a large central doorway with semi-circular head flanked by two lower pointed doorways for access to the great hall and service rooms respectively (the alternation of round and pointed arches is also to be found in Lewyn's Durham Priory kitchen). There is a corresponding set in the E wall of the great hall, but the arch of the central door has been replaced. Between the kitchen and the hall are two spaces with transverse barrel-vaults, formerly divided into service rooms and passageway. Bates 1891; Bateson 1893; Goodall 2004; Time Team 2011b.

BAMPTON (The Mote), Devon (Open access). Motte and bailey overlooking a ford across the river Batherm. First mentioned in 1136 when Robert of Bampton held it against King Stephen. 50ft (15.24m) high (tree covered) motte with sub-rectangular bailey to the NE still partially defined by a ditch and counterscarp bank. Higham and Hamlin 1990; Wilson-North 1991.

BAMPTON, Oxfordshire (Private). Fragmentary remains of an early C14 fortified manor house of quadrangular form. Bampton Castle was built for Aymer de Valence, Earl of Pembroke, under a licence to crenellate of 1315. It was a large symmetrical moated enclosure with corner towers and mid-wall buttress turrets. This complex has largely disappeared and is now almost entirely represented by the rectangular gatehouse, which stood in the centre of the W front, its passage blocked and incorporated into the present house. Although the exterior is plain, inside are the richly moulded jambs of the gateways and a ribbed vault over the passage: two octopartite bays with central carved bosses. Upstairs, a C14 fireplace, the mouldings of the jambs continued around the two tiers of corbels that carry the hood. Emery 2006, 55–8; Guy 2018 19.

BANBURY, Oxfordshire (D). Concentric castle of the bishops of Lincoln, now destroyed but extensively excavated. Established in the second quarter of the C12 by Alexander the Magnificent, Bishop of Lincoln, as a ditched-around courtyard castle of trapezoidal plan with square corner towers, and a simple gateway in the centre of the S front. Rebuilt probably in the late C13 or early C14 with two concentric courtyards of pentagonal plan, each surrounded by a ditch. The outer ward had circular wall towers and a gatehouse with twin circular flanking towers. The remains of the inner ward were less well preserved, and the details are more speculative. Rodwell 1976.

BARNARD CASTLE, County Durham (Open – EH). Large multi-period stone castle on a cliff-edge site above the river Tees probably established in the 1090s by Guy de Balliol. Reconstruction in stone began *c*.1140 and was continued by the Balliols for much of the century and beyond. The Balliol tenure ended in 1296 when John Balliol, King of Scotland, was deposed and his English estates confiscated by Edward I. Barnard was granted to Guy de Beauchamp, Earl of Warwick in 1307. The male line of the Beauchamp earls of Warwick died out in 1445 and the castle came through marriage to Richard Neville, who became Earl of Warwick. After Neville was killed in 1471 Richard Duke of Gloucester (the future King Richard III) married his daughter Anne and thereby gained Barnard. Following Richard's death (1485), the castle was acquired by Henry VII and remained a royal possession throughout the C16. It was besieged in 1569 during the Rising of the North, when a deal of damage was done including the collapse of part of the outer ward curtain. In 1603 Barnard was sold and by 1630 was in the hands of Sir Henry Vane who used the castle as a source of building materials for his work at Raby Castle (qv).

Occupying some 7.5 acres, the site is an unusually large one. Aligned N–S with the Tees, it is divided into four wards: Outer (S), Town (NE), Inner (NW) and Middle (on the W bordering all three), of which only the last three are open to the public. The great gatehouse (no longer extant) led from the town on the E into the outer ward, which occupies roughly half of the castle enclosure. There was a C12 chapel here and the demesne farm, but it is now devoid of buildings apart from sections of the surrounding curtain wall.

The main access is now from the N into the Town Ward via a semi-circular-arched gate (Town Gate) of uncertain date and then the central passage of a ruined rectangular two-storey gatehouse wholly within the enclosure; it had two heated ground-floor chambers and, at the SW corner, a latrine turret serving both the ground and first-floor rooms. Also on the N side, the Dovecote Tower, in a dog-leg of the curtain and next to the Great Ditch around the inner ward; inside, its walls are lined with

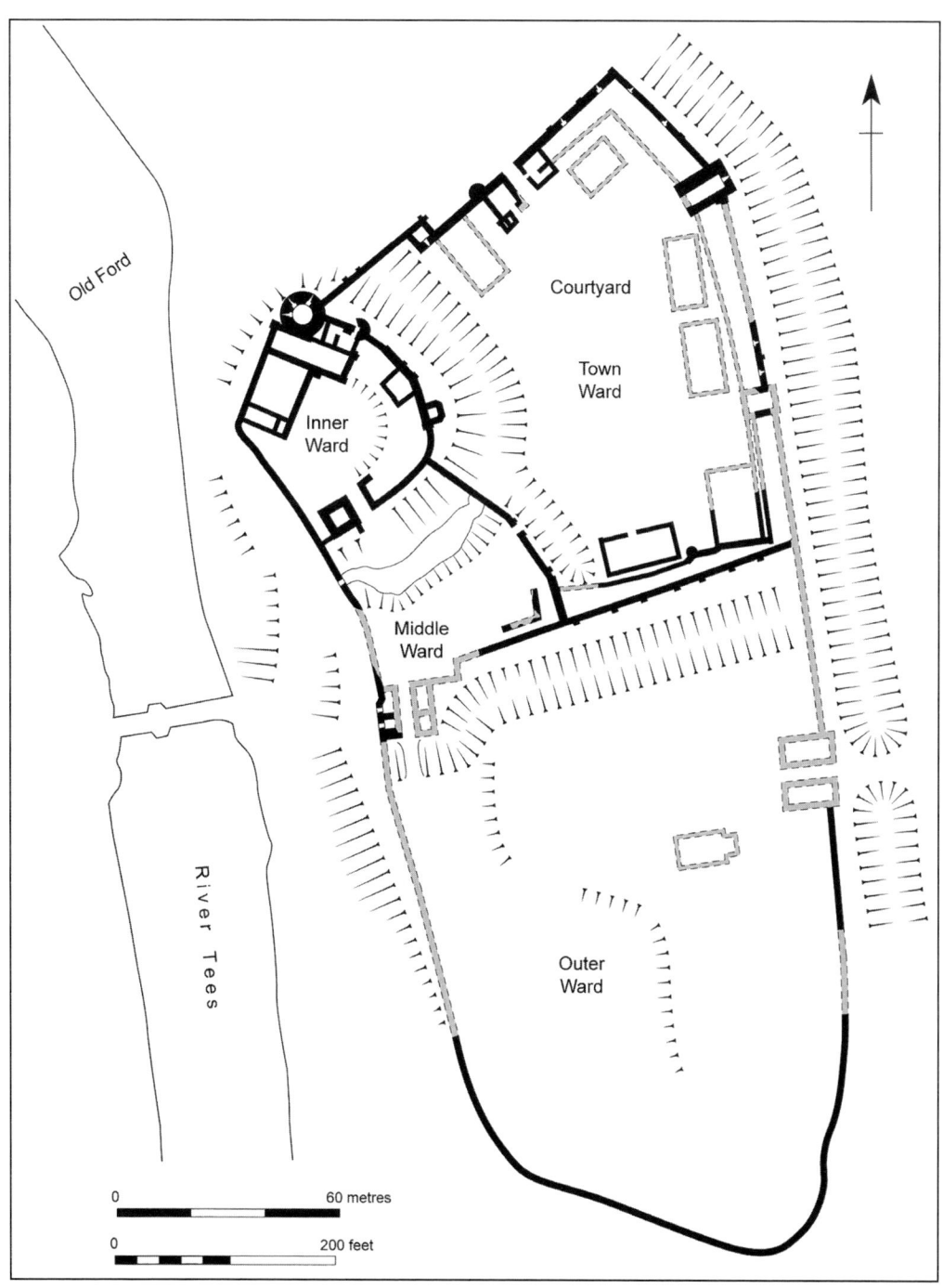

Barnard Castle: Ground plan. After Austin 2007.

nesting boxes. A first-floor doorway led from here to a now-vanished building backing onto the curtain where the profile of its double-pile roof is preserved. On the E side is the rectangular two-storey Brackenbury Tower, named after a servant of Richard III. Barrel-vaulted basement with fireplace and latrine and a staircase to the first floor. The tower is generally considered to be C12, but the latrine and stair doorways have pyramid stops, which suggest a later date. Upstairs another single room with fireplace and latrine and three fishtail arrow loops N, S and E in vaulted embrasures containing inserted (later medieval) stone benches. To the S is the stone-revetted bank between the Town and Outer Wards topped by the curtain wall. On the W side, S of the Great Ditch, there was a wet moat in front of the curtain, fed by a stream that flowed across the Town Ward and retained by a (now vanished) dam to the N of the Middle Gate.

The Middle Gate led to the Middle Ward, an area now devoid of buildings, but which served as the hub of communications between the four wards. At the SW corner are the remains of the Constable Tower, a C12 rectangular three-storey gatehouse with central passage commanding access from the outer ward. On the N side is the Great Ditch, which cuts off the inner ward. At the W end of the ditch is the arch of a buried C13 or C14 postern gate. Above this the modern bridge is on the site of a medieval bridge. Once across the ditch there is a sharp turn R (E) towards the late C13 or C14 inner gatehouse (now reduced to its foundations). It is an unusual type, consisting of an apsidal-ended tower with a gateway in the side; a sharp turn to the L (N) led to the inner ward.

The inner ward contains the principal accommodation complex. Ranged against the NW curtain is the single-storey great hall, rebuilt by the Beauchamps in the first

Barnard Castle: The Round Tower (*c.*1200) (right) and the Postern Tower (early C13) (left) from the E.

half of the C14 (note the Decorated windows in the curtain). To the L of it is the five-storey Mortham Tower, which has been raised in height twice, the final time by Richard III in the 1480s to balance the height of the Round Tower, or keep, at the other end of the complex. To the R of the hall is the two-storey chamber block, C12 in origin, but extended and altered at later periods. In the first-floor great chamber, a large oriel window was inserted in the curtain during the 1480s; on the soffit of the lintel is carved a wild boar, a heraldic device used by Richard III.

The Round Tower dates from *c*.1200, its wall being integral with that of the chamber block, an unusual arrangement that is thought to represent the rebuilding of a rectangular keep (on the site of the Round Tower) and forebuilding (on the site of the chamber block), the common wall between them having been retained as part of the redevelopment. On the E side of the tower is a rectangular single-storey annexe, its stone roof extending clockwise up and around to meet an anticlockwise extension of the chamber block wall to form a spur or broach. The only access to the tower was from the chamber block, at first-floor level, and probably from ground-floor level too. It is therefore an adjunct to the chamber block rather than an independent building. It also formed part of the defensive circuit and was provided with arrow loops on its outer face. The basement contains a well and is covered by a low domed vault; the first floor was also vaulted originally, and that may have been true of the top floor too, but confirmation or rebuttal is no longer possible from structural evidence. A few steps ascend to a mezzanine vaulted chamber housed in the annexe, then a second mural flight leads to the first-floor vaulted passage leading from the great chamber. The first-floor room was served by a fireplace and latrine, but the prominent feature is a tall round-headed opening forming a doorway to nowhere, actually an opened-out two-light window. From its embrasure a mural staircase winds anti-clockwise round the tower to the third floor.

Along the curtain towards the Town Ward are the C13 semi-polygonal Postern and Prison Towers. The former contains an inserted ground-floor passage, but probably had a solid base originally. Austin 2007; Hislop 2018 and 2019.

BARNSTAPLE, Devon (Open access). Motte and bailey within an Anglo-Saxon *burh*. Probably C11 in origin, but first mentioned in 1113 when Judhael, who formerly held the barony of Totnes, was lord of Barnstaple. After the death of Judhael's son, Alfred, *c*.1139, the castle came to his son-in-law, Henry de Tracey. It was probably during the de Tracey tenure that some rebuilding in stone took place. Barnstaple Castle is situated at the confluence of the rivers Yeo and Taw, and was consequently protected by water on the W, NW and SW sides. The bailey (Castle Green) lies to the NW of the motte, towards the convergence of the rivers. On top of the motte are the foundations of a circular tower enclosed by an outer wall. Oliver 1928; Miles 1986.

BARNWELL, Northamptonshire (Private). C13 quadrangular courtyard castle built for Berenger le Moyne, a tenant of Ramsey Abbey, *c*.1266. In 1276 the manor of Barnwell St Andrew, along with the castle, was sold to the abbey. After the dissolution of Ramsey in 1540 the manor was granted to Sir Edward Montagu, who built the adjacent manor house. About this time Leland found the castle in ruins and containing 'a meane house' of a farmer, but *c*.50 years later Camden claimed that 'of late' it had been 'repaired and beautified with new buildings' by Sir Edward. However, in 1704, it was said to be 'late demolished'.

Berenger le Moyne's builder was a master of his art, creating a simple but elegant construct with touches of originality and consistently fine detailing. It would have been a highly desirable home and a pleasure to behold. The building forms a slightly irregular rectangle aligned roughly N–S with the main gateway at the S end of the E front flanked by twin drum towers. Immediately adjacent is the SE tower, apsidal ended like the drum towers, the three together making an effective mass. Otherwise the corner towers are round, although the two at the N corners have attached latrine and stair turrets so that they form little clusters presenting pleasingly undulating surfaces to the NE and NW. Round-faced protuberances containing latrine or stair-cases are to be found in a number of C13 cylindrical keeps along the English/Welsh border, but the clustering at Barnwell is unusual and stems from a general tradition of bunched circles more common in France (eg, Houdan, Etampes) than England, although something of the kind had been used at Dover (qv) in the 1220s.

The external openings include C13 rectangular arrow loops with either one or two cross slits, and a number of C16/C17 rectangular windows. These apart, the external detailing is largely confined to the gateway which has a fine pointed arch of three orders carried on engaged and clustered half columns with moulded capitals. It leads into a barrel-vaulted passage and thence the courtyard. At the W end of the passage is

Barnwell: The clustered NE tower.

a corbel carrying the original gate arch, but beyond it the passage has been blocked and the blocking contains a narrower gateway. Here is an interesting piece of archaeology, for it is clear from an examination of the openings into the towers that this blocking is, in fact, part of a general thickening of the curtain wall, all around the courtyard, in which the (still extant) pointed arches of the earlier face were replaced by the semi-circular arches of the new work. At what date and for what purpose this work was carried out is uncertain. The round arches might suggest the C16, but the mask terminals of the hood moulds point to the C13 or C14. The basements of the towers were rib-vaulted, another fairly unusual and extravagant trait. C14 wall paintings survive in the N flanking tower of the gatehouse. Giggins 2018–19 and 2020–1.

BARWICK-IN-ELMET (Hall Tower Hill), Yorkshire West Riding (Open access). Motte and bailey within a prehistoric hillfort. First mentioned in a charter of King Stephen (dated 1142–54) confirming Henry de Lacy's possession. The hillfort encloses two hills: Wendel Hill to the N and Hall Tower Hill to the S. The castle is centred on Tower Hall Hill, where a motte was raised and the hillfort defences reused. Salter 2001, 19.

BEAUDESERT, Warwickshire (Open access). Motte with two baileys. In existence by *c*.1140, when it was held by Thurstan de Montfort, who may have been the builder. It was rebuilt in stone probably by Peter de Montfort (d. 1269) in the C13. Situated to the E of Henley-in-Arden village on a NE–SW aligned promontory known as The Mount, on which there is a linear progression along the hill of (from SW–NE) outer bailey, inner bailey and motte. The roughly oval motte is surrounded by a ditch, interrupted by a causeway to the SW, linking the motte to the inner bailey. In 2001 excavation by Time Team on the motte revealed a stone curtain, enclosing stone buildings including a hall. Salzman 1945, 45–6; Time Team 2002.

BEDFORD, Bedfordshire (Open access). Motte (Castle Hill) formerly with two baileys. Probably founded soon after the Conquest on the orders of William I to control an Anglo-Saxon *burh* as well as a crossing over the river Great Ouse. By 1086 the castle was in the keeping of the Beauchamp family. In 1215 William de Beauchamp rebelled against King John and the castle was taken from him by Falkes de Bréauté. Falkes held it until 1224, undertaking significant building operations here, but his rebellion against Henry III led to a nine-week siege and the subsequent demolition of the defences; it never seems to have recovered its status as a major fortress.

The motte is the sole element to survive above ground level, and the rest of the site is now largely built over, but historical research and archaeological excavation has confirmed something of its character and extent. The former limits of the castle are now represented roughly by Castle Lane (N), Embankment/river Great Ouse (S) and Newnham Road (E). The W boundary was between High Street and the parallel section of Castle Lane. Within this area was the motte, towards the S end of the E side. There was a bailey to the W of the motte ranged along the river containing a range of stone buildings and with a water gate to the S. A second bailey existed to the N of the motte and S bailey. Petre 2012, 9–12 and 23–51.

BEESTON, Cheshire (Open – EH) (Plate I). Unusually large C13 stone castle on the site of a prehistoric hillfort. Established *c*.1220 by Ranulph, Sixth Earl of Chester, but incomplete by the time of his death in 1232. Ranulph was succeeded as Earl of Chester by his son-in-law, John the Scot, and on John's death in 1237 his estates were seized by Henry III, and Beeston remained a royal castle until 1606. Building work was carried out periodically in the C13 and C14, but, following Edward I's conquest of Gwynedd, its strategic significance was lost and in the C15 it suffered from neglect. During the Civil War Beeston was besieged twice, and in 1646 was partially demolished.

Ranulph's castle occupies Beeston Crag, a highly visible rocky outcrop at the N end of the Peckforton Hills rising to some 500ft (152m) at its NW point. The enclosure covers an area of *c*.11 acres (4.5ha) and comprises an enormous outer ward which rises steadily to a modest inner ward at the summit. The surviving outer defences are concentrated along the E side (where they utilize the Iron Age defences) and the E end of the S side, the curtain being studded with D-shaped, mostly open-backed, wall towers, projecting wholly outside the curtain. In the centre of the E front the twin-towered great gatehouse is now largely reduced to its foundations, although a rectangular latrine turret added to it in the C14 has survived almost to full height.

From here there is a long pull up to the inner ward, which is isolated by a great rock-cut ditch from which much of the building material was obtained. It extends around the S and E sides; behind it, the inner curtain is punctuated by five D-shaped towers, including the twin towers of the inner gatehouse, but, unlike the towers of the outer defences, they project deeply into the enclosure and had a domestic as well as a military function. The gatehouse is now approached by a late C20 bridge; beneath are the remains of the C14 bridge. The inner ward towers each contained a room at ground- and first-floor levels, but no fireplace except in the SW tower at first-floor level. A well to the E of the gatehouse is some 370ft (113m) deep or more. Ellis 1993; McGuicken 2006; Liddiard and McGuicken 2007.

BELSAY, Northumberland (Open – EH). A manor house of the Middleton family rebuilt as a tower house in the late C14, with an adjoining two-storey range of 1614. The manor of Belsay was held by the Middleton family by 1270, but was forfeited in 1318, following a revolt by John de Middleton. In 1335 Belsay was granted to Sir John Stryvelyn, a veteran of the Scottish wars. He died in 1378, but the estate was held by his widow until her death in 1391, and inherited by their daughter Christiana, wife of Henry Middleton (d. 1396), the manor thereby returning to the Middleton family. A heraldic shield (no longer decipherable) on the N side of the tower formerly depicted the quartered arms of Stryvelyn and Middleton, suggesting that the tower was built after 1391. It was certainly in existence by 1415.

Originally, the three-storey tower was free-standing, its entrance to the W sheltered between two projecting turrets. These turrets, which contain accommodation, are one of the main distinguishing aspects of Belsay, setting it apart from the simpler and more prevalent rectangular block and linking it with a group of late C14 and C15 northern residential towers with one or more such wings. The other main characteristic is a set of corner bartizans, their rounded faces corbelled out from the main body of the tower. The parapets of both the turrets and the main block sit on corbelled machicolations, a defensive feature that also acts as a decorative crown. Within the main body of the tower were a ground-floor kitchen, first-floor great chamber and second-floor bed chamber. Vertical communication was via a single staircase in the SW turret. It is unlikely that the tower stood alone, and it is possible

Belsay: Tower house from the SW.

that the C17 range replaces a detached great hall. Middleton 1910; Simpson 1940; Emery 1996, 48–50; White 2012.

BENEFIELD, Northamptonshire (Private). A moated ringwork near St Mary's Church in Lower Benefield. Date of construction unknown, but in existence by 1208. It was still occupied in 1264, but in 1298 was described as an old castle, and in 1315 only as the site of a castle. The remains consist of a sub-rectangular platform moated on the N, S and W sides and an outer bank to the S and SW. Page 1930, 76–80; RCHME 1975, 18–19.

BENINGTON, Hertfordshire (In the grounds of Benington Lordship – occasional spring and summer openings). Motte and bailey with stone keep. The earthworks may date from the C11 and are perhaps the work of Peter de Valonges, to whom the manor was granted after the Conquest. Peter's son, Roger, was probably responsible for the construction of the keep in the 1130s; it was demolished on the orders of Henry II *c.*1176. A landscaped sub-rectangular mound, or motte, the top nearly one acre (0.4ha.) in extent, accommodates an early C18 house in the NW corner, and, towards the E side the stump of a C12 nearly square stone keep built of flint rubble with pilaster buttresses and a rectangular projection at its NE angle, possibly a forebuilding. The mound is surrounded by a ditch and there is a bailey bank towards the NE. Page 1912b, 73–4; RCHME 1910, 51–2.

BERKELEY, Gloucestershire (Open). Motte and bailey rebuilt in stone, traditionally the scene of Edward II's murder in 1327. Established by William FitzOsbern, Earl of Hereford probably in the 1060s. Captured by Henry of Anjou (the future Henry II) in 1153, it was granted to Robert FitzHarding by whose descendants it is retained. Rebuilt in stone during the second half of the C12. Rebuilding of the domestic apartments in the mid C14 for Thomas Third Baron Berkeley. Partial remodelling took place in the C16 including some refenestration, and interior remodelling in the 1920s.

The castle is entered from the SE via a C14 single-storey square gatehouse which leads into an outer ward. Next came a barbican with polygonal flanking towers, of which foundations survive; it led to the current C14 entrance into the bailey, a simple passageway, protected by a portcullis. The dominant building is the keep,

Berkeley: Ground plan. From Clark 1884.

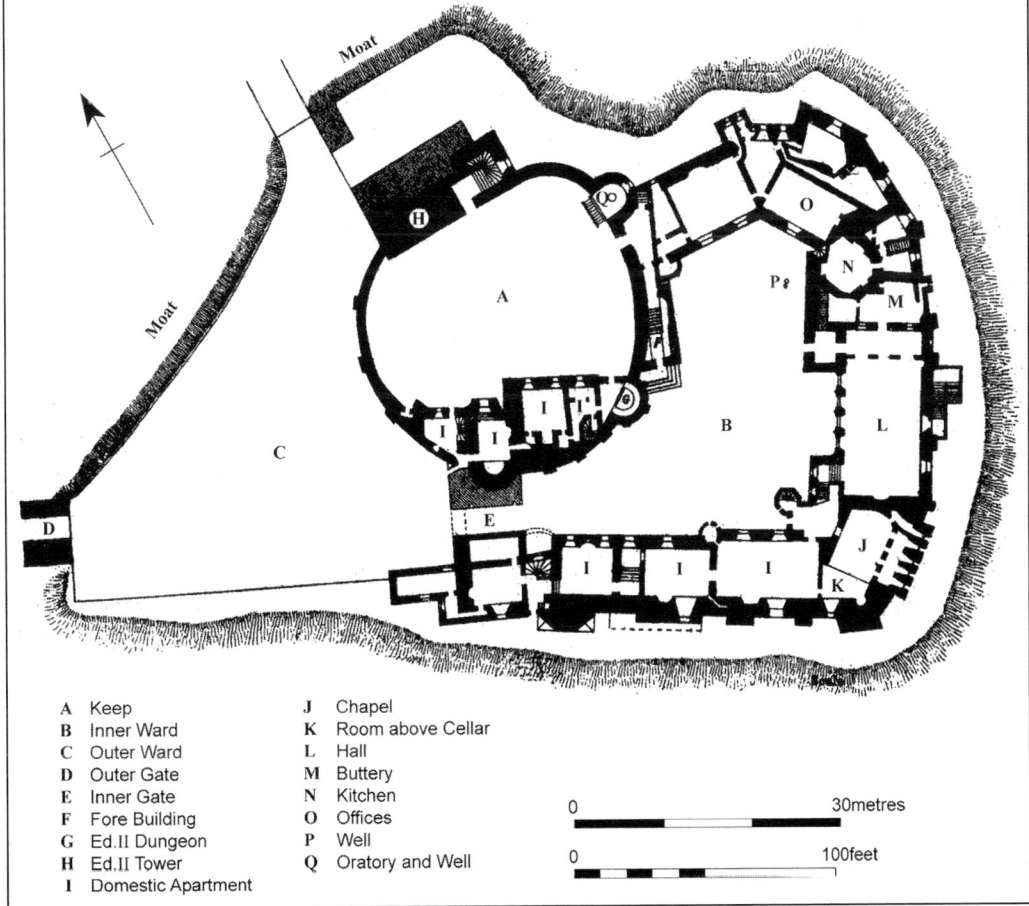

- **A** Keep
- **B** Inner Ward
- **C** Outer Ward
- **D** Outer Gate
- **E** Inner Gate
- **F** Fore Building
- **G** Ed.II Dungeon
- **H** Ed.II Tower
- **I** Domestic Apartment
- **J** Chapel
- **K** Room above Cellar
- **L** Hall
- **M** Buttery
- **N** Kitchen
- **O** Offices
- **P** Well
- **Q** Oratory and Well

a C12 stone casing and remodelling of a motte, the revetment rising above the summit of the mound as a shell-keep (cf. Farnham qv). The C12 stonework includes pilaster buttresses, three semi-circular turrets and a forebuilding on the NW side. On the N side of the motte is Edward II/Thorpe's Tower, a mid C14 addition replacing a fourth C12 turret, but rising above the battlements, and possibly acting as a prospect tower. At the top of the forebuilding stairs is the C12 entrance to the shell-keep, its one surviving shaft carved with an interlaced foliate design and topped with a foliate capital. A room over the forebuilding stairs is said to be Edward II's cell, which seems unlikely. In the SW turret is a semi-circular pit, perhaps an oubliette or more likely a floor safe. The E turret was the apse of the C12 chapel.

The C12 also witnessed the reconstruction of the curtain wall, substantial elements of which survive, but the domestic buildings backing onto it are largely C14. At the centre of the accommodation block is the great hall of the 1340s, on the site of the C12 hall and chamber block. The two-storey porch to the L (N) has a 'Berkeley' arch doorway, a polygonal form characteristic of the C14 work at the castle. It leads into the screens passage where three more such arches lead to the pantry, buttery and kitchen, Inside the hall are the restored C12 roll-moulded window embrasures on the outer side and the C14 windows towards the courtyard; the latter, like the service doors, have cusped inner arches (another Berkeley motif), and the lower lights double-cusped corbels (a type derived from Caernarfon Castle). The crowning glory is the double-pitched, eight-bay, arched-braced collar roof with side purlins, ridge piece and cusped wind braces. At the upper (S) end of the hall at first-floor level is the chapel (now Morning Room), set obliquely to the hall to achieve a more correct liturgical orientation. Begun in 1327, possibly by William Joy of Wells, it was converted for domestic use in the 1920s. In the outer wall three window embrasures with multiple cusped fringes (as in the hall); arch-braced and cambered tie beams with wall posts on bust-carved corbels, all timber components moulded. A contemporary timber gallery and private pew, which formerly stood at the W end of the chapel, is preserved in an adjacent room. Emery 2006, 58–67; Guy 2014–15a; Higham 2015, 15–25.

BERKHAMSTED, Hertfordshire (Open – EH). Motte and bailey rebuilt in stone. Probably raised for Robert of Mortmain prior to 1086. Confiscated by Henry I in 1104 following the rebellion of Mortain's son. Reconstruction in stone was probably begun during the tenure of Thomas Beckett (1155–65), then Henry II's chancellor. The fortifications were strengthened in 1215, and the following year the castle was unsuccessfully besieged by Prince Louis of France. Occupation continued until 1495.

A motte with a sub-oval bailey to the SW are surrounded by a double-ditch and bank system, an unusual and elaborate arrangement made more so by the redirection of a stream through the site to feed the ditches and so provide the basis of a moat scheme. Entry was from the S into the bailey, but the outer defences on this side have been truncated by the construction of the adjacent railway. Much of the stonework including the remains of the shell-keep and curtain wall are probably C12, but the half-round wall towers to the NW and E date from the C13. A curiosity is a series of earthwork protrusions around the N and E sides of the outer bank. These are said to be siege engine platforms, but they seem more likely to have been erected by the defenders than the besiegers. Page 1914a, 150; Remfry 2009; RCHME 1910, 97–9.

BERRY POMEROY, Devon (Open – EH). Late medieval courtyard castle substantially rebuilt in the C16 and C17. The initial builder was either Henry Pomeroy between 1446 and 1481 or Sir Richard Pomeroy between 1481 and 1496. In 1547 the castle was sold to Edward Seymour, Duke of Somerset (d. 1552). From *c.*1560 Somerset's son, Lord Edward Seymour (d. 1593), built a courtyard house within the castle. Around 1600 this house was greatly extended by Seymour's son (also Edward), a project that resulted in the loss of much of the curtain wall.

Berry Pomeroy is perched on the edge of a spur above Gatcombe Brook. The medieval remains are largely confined to the entrance (S) front. To the L (W), occupying a corner position, is the gatehouse, its twin semi-hexagonal flanking towers, angles to the fore, echoing those of the entrance to Raglan Castle in S Wales, also of the late C15. At the RH (E) end of the curtain is St Margaret's Tower, an apsidal-ended structure extending from the corner at an angle of 45 degrees.

The gateway was protected by a machicolated gallery and a portcullis, and there were gun ports in the two towers. On the first floor is a large chamber, entered from the curtain wall walk, equipped with a fireplace and a latrine. The S side is partitioned off by a stone arcade, the E end of the aisle containing an oratory with a late medieval wall painting. At the W end of the wall walk is the first-floor entrance to St Margaret's Tower from where a staircase led to the basement, also provided with gun ports. Lord Edward's courtyard house lies to the E, and the later wing to the N. Emery 2006; Kightly 2011.

BERWICK-UPON-TWEED, Northumberland (Open access – EH). Fragmentary remains of a major royal castle on the Scottish border. A C12 foundation, formerly a Scottish stronghold, Berwick was the first place to be taken by Edward I during his invasion of Scotland in 1296. The capture of Berwick was followed by a programme of strengthening the castle and fortifying the previously undefended town. Refurbishment of the defences and adaptation for artillery was carried out in the mid C16. The castle was abandoned in the early C17, and in the 1840s the railway was cut right through it and the railway station built within the former enclosure.

The castle took the form of an irregular triangle, its NE side facing the walled town, a great ditch between them, while the S side faced the river. The most extensive remnant is the southern half of the NW side and its southern continuation, the White Wall of *c.*1297, which descends to the river and the Water Tower. The other main fragment is the late C13 or C14 SE corner tower (Constable Tower), which is polygonal, as were the twin towers of the now-lost great gatehouse. Brown *et al.* 1963, 563–71.

BEWCASTLE, Cumberland (Ask permission at the farm). Small quadrangular enclosure within a Roman fort. First mentioned as a castle in 1378, as part of the estate of Sir John Stryvelyn. When Sir John's widow died in 1391 Bewcastle, like Belsay (qv), was inherited by their daughter Christiana Middleton. After Christiana's death (1421–2) the property came into the hands of the King, and it remained a royal castle for the rest of its existence and held for the King for most of that time by the Musgrave family. It was dismantled in 1641.

Set within the NE corner of an outpost fort of Hadrian's Wall, the castle utilizes the fort ditch on the outer sides, its isolation being completed by a medieval ditch on the S and W sides. On the raised platform within is a ruined stone enclosure, 87ft (26.5m) square, with a rectangular gatehouse projecting from the W front. Only the S and W curtains survive much above ground level. The castle is plain in character, with few openings in the remaining walls, and little indication of date. The gatehouse, which is not bonded into the curtain, and is therefore a later addition, is entered from the N; then there is a turn to the L (E) through a gateway in the curtain wall, said in 1892 to have had a 'flattish four-centred arch', which could suggest a date anywhere between *c*.1400 and *c*.1550. Inside, the S wall retains first-floor beam sockets and the remains of two first-floor fireplaces. Curwen 1922, 186–97; Perriam and Robinson 1998, 46–7.

BICKLEIGH, Devon (Open). Fortified manor house on the W bank of the Exe next to a river crossing and on the road between Tiverton and Thorverton. Known as Bickleigh Court until the C20. The main medieval interest is the late C14/early C15 gatehouse range, which enclosed the E side of a courtyard house. Probably built by the Courtenay family, who acquired the property *c*.1400. Altered in the C17, by the Carew family, and restored in the 1920s and 1930s.

The gatehouse forms a rectangular block with rectangular turrets at the four corners. The three-storey, two-bay front recessed between a pair of corner turrets, the LH one much restored, its upper storey entirely C20. Central four-centred gate arch of three continuous chamfered orders with flanking single-storey buttresses. Large C17 first-floor windows with four-centred relieving arches; second-floor windows of three cinquefoil-headed lights of C15 form. Gate-passage with doors to L and R, rib-vaulted in two octopartite bays. To the rear, large ground-floor windows of three trefoil-headed lights with sunken spandrels (a late C14/early C15 form). Cherry and Pevsner 1991.

BIGGLESWADE (Old Warden), Bedfordshire. Ringwork and bailey. Probably early C12. Largely disappeared on the ground but discovered by aerial photography in 1954 and trial trenched in 1962. Northern ditched bailey entered from the N and double-ditched ringwork to the N, also entered from the N. The excavation recovered early C12 pottery. Petre 2012, 70–1.

BISHOP'S STORTFORD, Hertfordshire. See **WAYTEMORE**.

BISHOP'S WALTHAM, Hampshire (Open – EH). A palace of the bishops of Winchester, evidently a fortified house in its early phase, but of greater domestic character in the later Middle Ages. A castle was established here by King Stephen's brother, Bishop Henry de Blois, in the 1130s, but probably rebuilt in the 1160s and 1170s. The palace was transformed by bishops William of Wykeham (1367–1404) and Henry Beaufort (1404–47). Substantially damaged during the Civil War, when it was held for the King.

The sub-rectangular inner courtyard, which contained the main residential buildings, was surrounded by a moat, of which only the N arm retains water. A now largely vanished gatehouse at the N end of the W side (Station Road) was the main point of entry. On the LH (N) side was a long lodging range of 1438–42, now razed apart from the N wall, the E end incorporated into a post-medieval farmhouse. Directly opposite the gatehouse on the E side of the courtyard is Bishop Wykeham's bakehouse (N) and brewhouse (S) range of 1378–81.

The focus of the bishop's accommodation was the great hall on the W side of the courtyard with services and kitchen to the N. This range of buildings was reconstructed by Bishop Wykeham, starting with the hall (1379–80) (its tall transomed windows surviving in the outer wall) followed by the services and kitchen (1387–93).

Wykeham also remodelled the C12 private apartments at the SW angle of the inner court, including the SW corner tower, which was refenestrated (and raised by an additional storey in 1406), and the S range, where the C12 N wall was retained at ground-floor level, but a new wall built in front of it to allow for a wider first-floor great chamber. The range linking the SW tower with the hall was also remodelled, being heightened by an additional storey to contain a spacious gallery between lower and upper rooms.

To the E of the hall are the fragmentary remains of the cloister built by Bishop Beaufort *c.*1440, which provided a covered link between the hall, the bishop's private quarters, in the SW angle and the chapel to the E (rebuilt by Beaufort *c.*1416); the excavated foundations of the apsidal-ended Norman chapel survive to the W of Beaufort's work.

The remains of extensive fishponds survive to the W. An outer enclosure extended around the N, S and E sides. The N side has disappeared under the A333, but otherwise, the extent of the complex, can be traced in the brick wall with occasional towers probably erected by Bishop Thomas Langton (1493–1501). Hare 1988; Wareham 2000.

BITCHFIELD, Northumberland (Private). Solar tower near Belsay (qv). The manor of Bitchfield was a property of the Middletons of Belsay, and, like Belsay, the tower probably dates from *c.*1400; a house was built against its E side in the C17, probably on the site of the medieval hall; it was restored in 1935 under W.D. Caröe. The tower is a simple rectangle rising through three storeys; the corners were formerly capped by corbelled bartizans as at Belsay. At the N end of the E wall the original pointed entrance to the tower led into the segmental-vaulted basement via a lobby, which also gave access to a staircase in the N wall, by which the first floor was reached. Hodgson and Parker Brewis 1921; Dodds 1926, 341–2.

BLENKINSOPP, Northumberland (Open to patrons of the Blenkinsopp Castle Country Inn). Remains of a fortified manor house built for Robert de Blenkinsopp under a licence to crenellate of 1340 incorporated into a C19 mansion, later gutted by fire. The character of the complex isn't entirely clear but seems to have consisted of a tower-like main block a little over 50ft (15.24m) in length, with vaulted basements, surrounded at a distance of *c.*10ft (3m) by a high curtain wall. Elements of the medieval stonework are still to be seen. Grundy *et al.* 1992, 192–3.

BLETCHINGLEY (Castle Hill), Surrey (Private). Ringwork and bailey in the grounds of Castle Hill House. The earthworks have been partially obliterated by the construction of the house and are visible only on the N and E sides. They consisted of a ringwork defined by a large ditch and inner bank and a kidney-shaped bailey extending around its N, E and W sides. Within the ringwork are the remains of an early C12 tower nearly 80ft (7.4m) square and at least two storeys in height. Malden 1912, 255.

BOARSTALL, Buckinghamshire (Open – NT). Gatehouse and moat to a house fortified by John Handlo under a licence to crenellate of 1312. The plan is rectangular with a hexagonal tower projecting from each corner, the smaller ones to the rear (SW) containing spiral staircases, while the larger ones at the front (NE) contain rooms. The C14 character of the building has been depleted by C17 refenestration and the construction of a full-height portico around and above the gateway, but the cruciform loops with oillets in the NE flanking towers are genuine, so too the segmental-arched entrance and some of the internal detailing. RCHME 1912, 57–9; Emery 2006, 70–1.

BODIAM, Sussex (Open – NT) (Plate II). The best-preserved late C14 quadrangular castle in the S of England. Erected on a new site under a licence to crenellate of 1385 for Sir Edward Dalyngrygge, a veteran of the French wars. Bodiam Castle is on a rise overlooking the river Rother and surrounded by a moat or lake; there were formerly other water features in the vicinity, including a mill pond and fishponds. Two- and three-storey ranges surround a central courtyard. The rectangular plan is enlivened by four-storey corner towers (round externally, hexagonal internally), square mid-wall turrets to the S, E and W (the S turret containing a postern) and a twin-towered gatehouse to the to the N.

The approach for visitors is from the S, which brings one first to the postern gate piercing a three-storey mid-wall turret with a machicolated parapet and a little barbican in front. There was a bridge across the moat with a drawbridge in front of the gateway. Above the entrance are the arms of Sir Robert Knollys (d.1407), Dalyngrygge's commander in France, the helm bearing a ram's head crest, the shield angled; it is flanked by two more shields no longer readable. To the R (E) a single transomed window lighting the great hall.

Continuing around the W side to the entrance (N) front, a bridge extends from the N bank to an octagonal island. Originally, however, access was from the W bank to the octagon, allowing approaching visitors to be monitored more easily. The octagon is now devoid of any superstructure but would initially have carried a building. A 45-degree about-turn gave access to a drawbridge crossing to a second island which housed the barbican, only a fragment of which survives. From the barbican there was yet another drawbridge to the gatehouse, which was further protected by a portcullis, a machicolated parapet and gun loops in the two flanking towers; two

Bodiam from the SE.

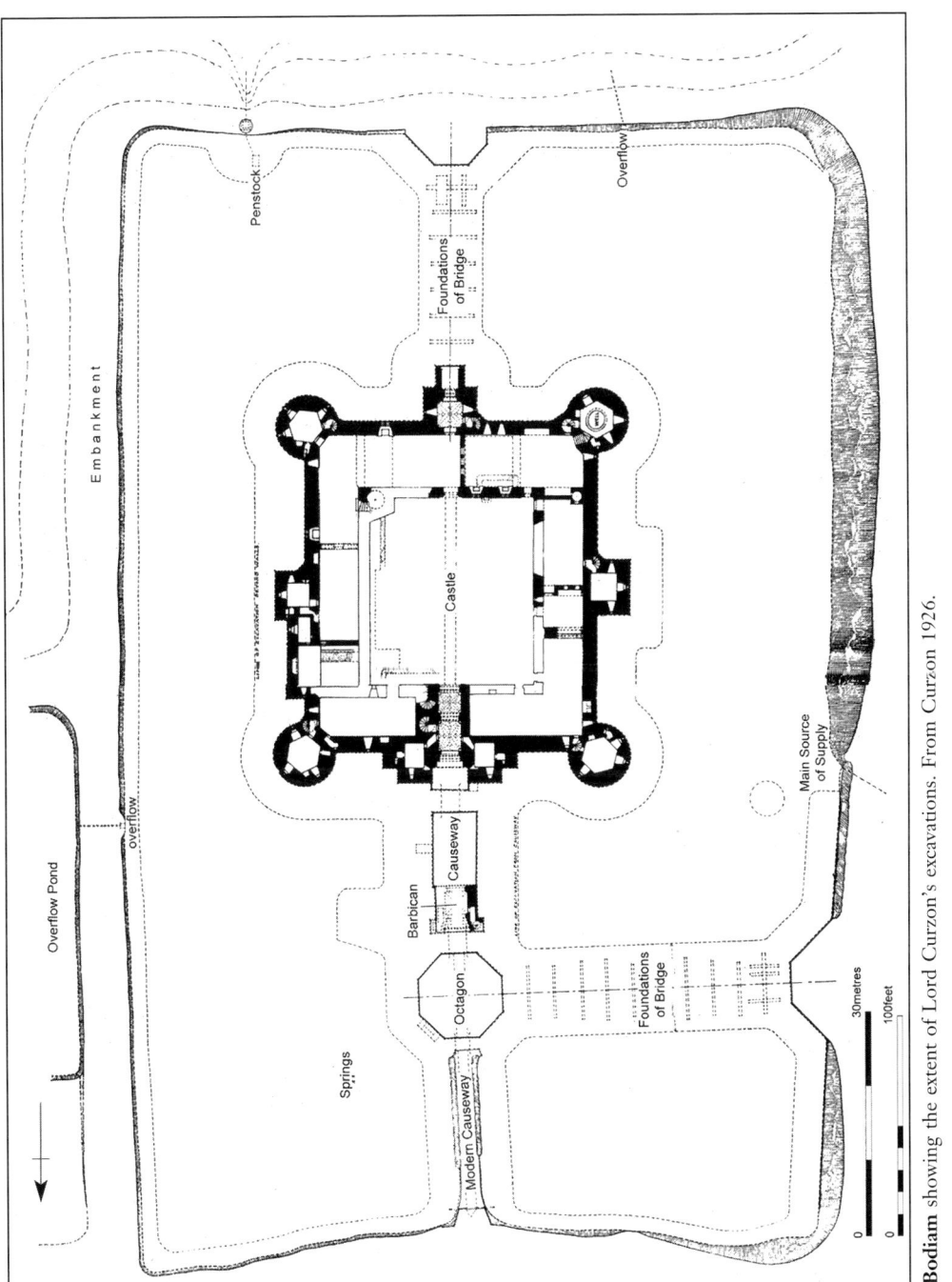

Bodiam showing the extent of Lord Curzon's excavations. From Curzon 1926.

more loops set further back were for show rather than function. Above the entrance are more heraldic shields including that of Sir Edward Dalyngrygge with his helm bearing a unicorn crest.

The gate passage has a lierne vault with perforated bosses, structural, decorative and possibly part of the defensive provisions (i.e. murder holes). On the L (E), is a doorway to a stair communicating with the upper floors of the gatehouse; a little further on a second portcullis.

Inside the castle, directly opposite the gate is the wide segmental-pointed entrance to the great hall; beyond it the screens passage leads to the postern, which is also covered by a ribbed vault. Little has been preserved of the hall, but the courtyard frontage to the R (W) of the entrance has survived. The two ground-floor windows lit the buttery, and two larger windows (of which one survives) above belong to the great chamber. To the far R (W) a doorway with a four-centred arch and a large window above it are associated with the great kitchen. Inside the screens passage are three pointed doorways leading to pantry (L), buttery (R) and kitchen (centre). In the kitchen are fireplaces in the N and S walls and a doorway leading to the remarkable well room in the SW tower, which, at ground-floor level, contains only the large well and a pavement around the perimeter.

The best accommodation was concentrated in the E range and comprised two storeys of domestic apartments over a basement. The range is now largely broken down, but retained in the external (E) wall are fireplaces and window embrasures containing stone benches, and doorways giving access to the mid-wall turret. The upper floors each contained a spacious residential suite, the upper one the most significant and entered from the great hall via a staircase. The lesser suite was entered from the courtyard. At the N end of the E range was the chapel rising through two storeys and open to the roof, its three-light E window preserved in the sanctuary, which projects beyond the curtain wall. Between the chapel and the turret is a small vestry/sacristy.

On the opposite side of the courtyard the W range accommodated a staff hall at the S end, and, next to it, another kitchen with fireplaces in the N and S walls. The N fireplace is open on both sides, both arches seemingly authentic, perhaps serving both the kitchen and the room to the N, or an oven within the N room. Curzon 1926; Faulkner 1963; Coulson 1992; Everson 1996; Johnson 2017.

BOLEBEC, Buckinghamshire. See **WHITCHURCH**.

BOLINGBROKE, Lincolnshire (Open – EH). Much-ruined stone courtyard castle built in the 1220s by Ranulph de Blundeville, Earl of Chester and of Lincoln. In the C14 it came, through marriage, to John of Gaunt, Duke of Lancaster. Gaunt's son, Henry of Bolingbroke, the future King Henry IV, was born here in 1367. During the Civil War it was held for the King, and despite weathering a siege in 1643 it was subsequently made indefensible, being described as 'demolished' in 1650.

The castle is on a level site and has an irregularly hexagonal plan. It is surrounded by a moat approximately 100ft (30m) wide. There is a twin-towered gatehouse at the N angle, and a tower projects from each of the other angles. All the towers are D-shaped except the semi-polygonal SW Tower (King's Tower), which was remodelled in 1451. The great hall was on the NE side of the bailey. To the S of the castle is a large rectangular enclosure known as the Rout Yard, which acted as a pound for stray animals. Brown *et al.* 1963, 571–2; Thompson 1966 and 1969.

BOLSOVER, Derbyshire (Open – EH). Site of a C12 castle rebuilt in the C17 partially on the medieval foundations. The medieval castle had two baileys and a great tower. The roughly oval Fountain Garden is probably the site of the inner bailey, and the keep-like Little Castle at its NW end perhaps on the site of the great tower. The Great Court, therefore, would indicate the position of the 'great bailey'. Faulkner 1961; Sheppard 2003; Drury 2014.

BOTHAL, Northumberland (Private). Stone castle notable for its monumental gatehouse. Built by Sir Robert Bertram, Sheriff of Northumberland, under a licence to crenellate of 1343. Bertram died without male issue and the castle came to the Ogle family through marriage; they held it until the beginning of the C17. The gatehouse was restored in 1830–1 when it was converted into a house and extended, a project that incorporated some architectural material from Cockle Park Tower (qv). The castle sits on a knoll above and N of the Wansbeck, the curtain enclosing a roughly oval bailey. At the N end is the three-storey great gatehouse of similar design to the inner gateway of Alnwick (qv). It has a pointed gateway of two chamfered orders recessed between two polygonal flanking towers, and a C14 pointed window at first-floor level (two trefoil-head lights with quatrefoil above, a pattern preserved elsewhere in the gatehouse.). Just below the parapet a series of heraldic shields extends across the front of the building confirming the date, and on the merlons two figure sculptures: a piper and a wild man in the act of hurling a stone. There was also an outer courtyard in front of the gatehouse with two towers: Ogle's Tower at the NW angle, and the 'Blanke' Tower. Bates 1891, 283–96; Emery 1996, 54–5.

BOURN HALL, Cambridgeshire and the Isle of Ely (Private). C11 ringwork and bailey, the castle of Picot, Sheriff of Cambridge. Circular ringwork occupied by C17 Bourn Hall, later additions to which extend over the N side of the earthwork. Inner bank and ditch, the latter formerly wet. Less visible semi-oval bailey to the E, but also banked and ditched. RCHME 1968, 21–27; Elrington 1973, 4–16.

BOURNE, Lincolnshire (Open access). Motte with two baileys. An unusual and intriguing site notable for its extensive former water defences. Mentioned 1179–81. At the SW angle of the site is St Peter's Pool, the source of the river Bourne Eau, which flows eastwards and forms the castle's southern extent. This source was tapped to feed the castle ditches which defined two enclosures, an inner bailey with a (now much diminished) motte at its S end and an outer bailey (now partly built over) extending around the N, E and W sides. The castle now lies within Wellhead Park. Salter 2002a, 46.

BOW AND ARROW CASTLE. See **RUFUS**.

BOWES, Yorkshire North Riding (Open access – EH). C12 castle with a large rectangular keep within the Roman fort of *Lavatris*. A castle was probably established at Bowes by Alan, Earl of Richmond, in the 1130s. In 1171 the Honour of Richmond was inherited by Alan's granddaughter, Constance, a minor and betrothed to King Henry II's son, Geoffrey. Bowes thus came into the hands of the King, who started to build the keep under the direction of 'Richard the Engineer', probably the Bishop of Durham's mason, Richard Wolveston. Geoffrey died in 1186 and the keep was completed by the King in 1187–8.

Bowes: The keep from the SW. 1171–88. By Richard Wolveston.

The early castle was established in the NW corner of the Roman fort, where a medieval ditch encloses a small rectangular bailey containing the keep. The main body of the keep has broad corner turrets and giant pilaster buttresses. At the E end are remains of a forebuilding that contained a flight of steps giving access to the first-floor doorway, originally the only entrance to the building. There were two main storeys and, at the E end, a gallery. Communication was via a spiral staircase in the SE turret, which also rose to the roof. A N–S wall divided the basement into two, the larger space to the E being sub-divided by an E–W arcade. This pattern was probably repeated at first-floor level. The basement was for storage, the living rooms being on the first floor. Each of the three first-floor rooms was lit by a large round-headed window. Page 1914b, 44–5; Hislop 2019.

BRAMBER, Sussex (Open – EH). Motte with two baileys. First mentioned in 1073, it was built by William de Braose as the administrative centre of the Rape of Bramber. The castle occupies a modest hill approximately ½ mile W of the river Adur. The enclosure is surrounded by a ditch and the remains of a curtain wall. It was entered from the S via a nearly square gatehouse. The gateways of this building were later blocked, and the walls raised to create a great tower of which only the W wall survives above ground level; it rises through three storeys and is the most prominent fragment of stonework in the castle. Within the enclosure a motte occupies a roughly central position. Together with its surrounding ditch (now infilled), it acted as the division between the N and S baileys. Barton and Holden 1977.

BRAMPTON BRYAN, Herefordshire (Private). Much-depleted stone castle with a good C14 barbican. First mentioned in 1295 on the death of Brian de Brampton, when there was a tower and curtilage. Around 1309 the castle came to the Harley family through marriage. The entrance to the castle was from the S via an elongated gate passage of two phases. The earlier of these, which probably dates from the later C13, was a rectangular block; it projected into the enclosure from the curtain wall. In the early C14 a grander two-storey extension with twin round flanking towers was built in front of it. High pointed gate arch recessed beneath a segmental-pointed arch, with portcullis between the two, and a higher blind arch springing from a (restored) ball-flower moulded string to create a tympanum. Cinquefoil cusped window to the

Brampton Bryan: Gatehouse from the SE.

LH tower with richly moulded surround enriched with ballflower. Remfry 1997a; Emery 2000.

BRANCEPETH, County Durham (Open – pre-booked guided tour only). Stone courtyard castle. In existence by 1216. Rebuilt for Ralph de Neville (1388–1425), later First Earl of Westmorland, probably by John Lewyn of Durham. Extensively altered 1818–21 by the then owner, Matthew Russell, under the direction of Edinburgh architect John Paterson. The work involved the refenestration of the castle, the renewal of a considerable amount of stonework, the destruction or concealment of the medieval gateway, the remodelling of much of the interior, and the construction of substantial additions.

Brancepeth Castle sits on a flat site above a precipice. The enclosure is roughly octagonal, pulled out of shape at the SW angle where the main residential accommodation was concentrated. The late C14 stonework consists of coursed and squared freestone, but a stratigraphically earlier rubble phase in the N curtain suggests that elements of the pre-existing castle were incorporated. At the NE angle is Paterson's great gateway, on the site of the medieval gateway, which was a much simpler affair flanked by two rectangular turrets of unequal size, so recalling the outer gatehouse of Raby (qv).

Brancepeth: Bartizan on the N curtain. Attributed to John Lewyn.

The main C14 apartments, at the SW angle of the castle, comprise an inventive massing of three adjoining C14 towers, projecting boldly beyond the line of the curtain and provided with diagonally projecting corner turrets. The E–W aligned Bulmer Tower came first. The other two, which are both orientated N–S, and which abut the S wall of the Bulmer Tower, are known collectively as the Neville Tower and appear to have been designed as a single building, with a common newel stair at the junction. The imposing W front of this integrated residential block builds on the massing of towers developed at Raby and recalls the three-dimensional qualities of Warkworth keep (qv).

Two other towers project from the two SE angles of the curtain: the Westmorland Tower to the E, and the Constable Tower to the S. Like the Bulmer and Neville towers they have diagonally projecting corner turrets with battlements machicolated to the sides but flush with the front, a C19 restoration of an original feature also found at Raby and Witton (qv). Emery 1996, 56–60; Hislop 2007, 30–1, 57–9.

BRANDON, Warwickshire (Private). Probably built by Geoffrey de Clinton, chamberlain to Henry I, in the 1120s, Brandon came to the Verduns through the marriage settlement of Geoffrey's daughter Lescelina to Norman de Verdun. The castle was destroyed in 1266 by Simon de Montfort's supporters. Excavation carried out in 1947 revealed the base of a great tower. Brandon Castle lies next to the river Avon, which fed its extensive water defences. Two sub-rectangular platforms towards the river probably represent the original foundation, while a much larger enclosure around the N, E and W sides may be a later addition. Of the two platforms, the larger western one contained a great tower, almost isolated by further channels; there was a central E–W block and two end wings giving an H-plan; a central latrine turret projected from the S side. The larger of the two wings (to the W) contained the base of a generously proportioned spiral staircase. Inside the main block, three sides of the space retained the facing stones, all of which appeared to have been damaged by fire, possibly signs of the destruction wrought in 1266. The keep had a number of points of resemblance to that built by Geoffrey de Clinton at Kenilworth (qv) but was roughly half the size. Chatwin 1955.

BREDWARDINE, Herefordshire (Open access). Little-understood castle on the W bank of the Wye commanding a river crossing. Described as old in 1227, it comprises a roughly rectangular bailey with a platform or mound at the S end, probably the site of a keep. Fishponds below the castle to the S and further along the bank to the S. RCHME 1931; Shoesmith 2009.

BRIDGNORTH, Shropshire (Open access to the keep). Stone castle, now mainly represented by the steeply-leaning keep. Built for Robert de Bellême, Earl of Shrewsbury, *c*.1101, it became a royal castle after his rebellion in 1102, when Bridgnorth was captured by the King's forces. Henry I probably built the keep in the 1120s. The castle was in ruins by Henry VIII's reign; the keep was blown up by the Parliamentarians in 1646.

Bridgnorth is built on a rocky promontory with the inner bailey of the castle at its S tip and the line of the outer bailey wall following the backs of the properties facing East Castle Street and West Castle Street. The North Gate, which was at the junction of these two streets with Postern Gate (a narrowed continuation of High Street), survived until 1821. Dating from the C12, the North Gate had a round arch of three

Bridgnorth: The keep from the NW. 1120s.

moulded orders. Fragments of the curtain survive here and there incorporated into later buildings.

The square keep was built across the line of Robert de Bellême's E–W aligned inner bailey wall. It was a two-storey building with a loft and an unusual roof profile descending to a central valley where the water was collected and dispersed (cf. Portchester qv). The upper room retains the jamb of an arched window towards the W and a laver, or wash basin, next to it. A lump of masonry on the N side is the remains of a forebuilding containing a staircase to a first-floor entrance. A wall stub extending from the S side denotes a division of the inner bailey; it incorporates the springing of a gate arch, and there is a portcullis groove on the (E) side, showing that this was the more exclusive area, probably housing the royal apartments. Guy *et al.* 2021–2. Time Team 2001.

BRIDGWATER, Somerset (Open access). Built for William Brewer under a licence of 1200. The only upstanding remains appear to be a length of curtain wall facing West Quay containing a water gate (between Nos 11 and 12). Baggs and Siraut 1992; Kerr-Peterson 2013; Dunning 1995, 28–30.

BRIGHTWELL, Berkshire (Private). Probable siege castle built 1145–6 by the Earl of Chester to contain Wallingford Castle. An irregular quadrilateral enclosure now containing Brightwell Manor and the Church of St Agatha, it was defined by a moat, which survives to the S and W, and by a stream to the E. In the SW is a small mound of unknown significance. Spurrell 1995.

BRIMPSFIELD, Gloucestershire (Open access). Demolished stone courtyard castle of the Giffard family next to the Church of St Michael. In existence by 1216. Destroyed in 1322 on the orders of Edward II following the rebellion of John Giffard. The remains comprise a moat surrounding an oval enclosure, earthworks denoting the sites of buildings, and elements of exposed stonework. The castle was divided into lower (W) and upper (E) wards, the outer gatehouse being at the SW angle; the upper ward contained a large rectangular keep. Dodd and Moss 1991.

BRINKLOW, Warwickshire (Open access). Motte with two baileys on the line of the Fosse Way in existence by 1130 and possibly dating from the 1060s. The substantial earthworks lie immediately E and SE of the church and comprise (from W to E) outer bailey, inner bailey and motte. Ditches surround the motte and the baileys, and the latter also have inner banks. Gardener 1904.

BRISTOL, Gloucestershire (Open access). Scant remains of a major castle at the confluence of the rivers Frome and Avon, in existence by 1088 and probably erected soon after the Conquest by Geoffrey, Bishop of Coutances. Tradition has it that Robert Earl of Gloucester (d. 1147) rebuilt the castle in stone and raised a keep. Acquired by Henry II in 1174, significant works were carried out by his grandson Henry III. Destroyed *c.*1655 and built over. The area was cleared after the Second World War to create Castle Park.

Bristol Castle occupied the E half of Castle Park, its western defences (which contained the main gateway) approximately 100ft (30m) to the E of St Peter's Church, the N side bounded by Castle Street/Newgate/Broad Weir, the W by Lower Castle Street and the S by an arm of the Avon. A western outer ward and eastern inner ward were both surrounded by a wet ditch. Elements of the curtain survive, notably to the N. Some foundations of the keep are also to be seen, on the N side of the former outer ward near the entrance from Castle Street. In the SE corner of the inner ward are the Vaulted Chambers, with two large segmental-pointed arches to the W forming a porch to the former great hall, which lay to the S, and to the King's chapel, which lay to the N. Brown *et al*. 1963, 577–82.

BROCKHURST, Church Stretton, Shropshire (Private). Double courtyard castle in existence by 1154 and possibly built by Henry II. The earthworks comprise two baileys surrounded by a ditch and counterscarp bank with a ditch between the baileys. Excavation in 1959 showed that the outer (NE) bailey had had a timber palisade and the inner (SW) bailey a shale curtain. Brown *et al*. 1963, 614; Duckers 2006, 34–6.

BRONSIL, Eastnor, Herefordshire (Private). Heavily overgrown ruins of a moated quadrangular castle probably built for Richard, Baron Beauchamp of Powick. In 1460 Beauchamp was granted a licence to empark land in Eastnor and to construct a stone tower within it, and to crenellate, embattle and provide this tower with turrets and machicolations. This is taken to refer to the castle. Approached from the NW, where a bridge crossed to a central gatehouse with polygonal flanking towers and gun loops. Octagonal corner and mid-wall towers. Broad earthen banks surround the moat and there are indications of further water features to the SE. RCHME 1932, xxvi, 74; Emery 2000, 523–5.

BROUGH, Westmorland (Open – EH) (Plate III). Stone courtyard and keep castle established *c*.1100 within the Roman fort of *Verteris*. The great tower was probably built by Hugh de Morville in the early 1170s at the behest of Henry II. When the castle was captured by the Scots the tower was partially demolished. It may have been restored by Theobald de Valoines, who was granted Brough in 1179, or by Robert de Vieuxpont, to whom it was granted in 1204. Robert Clifford obtained the castle from his aunt, Idonea de Crumbwelle, in 1308; Clifford may have been responsible for building Clifford's Tower at the SE corner and the adjacent E curtain. During the C14 the great hall, originally a single-storey building set against the E curtain, was replaced by a first-floor hall on the S side. In 1521 a fire broke out and gutted the castle; it was repaired and made habitable again by Lady Anne Clifford in 1659–62.

The Roman fort is sited at the W end of the Stainmore Pass on a bluff above Swindale Beck. The stone castle occupies the N end of the fort and is divided from the rest of the enclosure by an obliquely-sited ditch and counterscarp bank enclosing a roughly quadrilateral area narrowing towards the W end where the keep is positioned; the southern part of the Roman fort acted as an outer ward to the castle. Herringbone masonry in parts of the curtain suggest that the stone was the primary material. Entry is from the S via a gatehouse with a C12 core, to the front of which a pair of V-prowed buttresses was added in the C15. To the R (E) is Roger Clifford's Hall range, with two pointed windows containing curvilinear tracery. Beyond that, at the SE corner, is the early C14 Clifford's Tower, rounded with later rectangular latrine turret adjacent. Inside, the domestic buildings have been much reduced.

The rectangular keep has clasping pilaster buttresses at the corners and is divided horizontally by two offsets. There were three storeys below the second offset, and above that the roof, the outline of which survives inside against the E wall. Above the offset the outer walls have mid-wall buttresses to N and S and the corners were capped by square turrets. The roof was later raised, and an extra floor inserted.

On the S side a C12 window survives with shafted twin lights and tympana set beneath round arches. RCHME 1936, 50–3; Perriam and Robinson 1998, 262; Guy *et al.* 2012–13, 93–103.

BROUGHAM, Westmorland (Open – EH). Keep and courtyard castle established *c.*1214 by Robert de Vieuxpont (d. 1238) next to the Roman fort of *Brocavum* and the river Eamont. In 1268 Brougham came into the Clifford family through the marriage of Robert's granddaughter, Isabella, to the Welsh marcher lord, Roger Clifford. Their son Robert, First Baron Clifford, came into possession of his late mother's lands in 1296 and proceeded to rebuild Brougham; a licence to crenellate was issued in 1309 by which time his work was probably complete. Substantial improvements were made to the domestic accommodation by Roger, Fifth Baron Clifford, between 1373 and 1388. The castle was repaired in 1651–2 by Lady Anne Clifford, who lived and died there. It was dismantled in the C18.

Approached from the E, the castle sits on a rise above the floodplain, laid out to an irregular quadrilateral plan influenced by the positions of the river to the N and the Roman fort to the S. The unusual entrance complex, which bridges the gap between the keep (S) and N curtain, comprises an inner and outer gatehouse, separated by a courtyard but linked by a narrow building set against the curtain. The late C13 inner gatehouse came first, then the ground storey of the outer gatehouse (also late C13), then the lower part of the link block, then (in the early C14), the upper storeys of the outer gatehouse and link building were carried up together. Two phases are indicated in the E front of the outer gatehouse in the first- and second-floor windows, which show progress from a chunky Geometric style to delicately-cut curvilinear tracery.

Brougham: The C13 and C14 outer gatehouse (right) and keep of *c.*1214 and *c.*1300 (left).

Above the gateway, a C14 stone panel bearing the words 'This Made Roger', a reference to Roger Clifford's late C14 works at Brougham, repositioned here in 1848/9. Higher up, just below parapet level, corbelling for a brattice or machicolation.

The first three storeys of the square keep are attributed to Robert de Vieuxpont *c*.1214. In 1214, Vieuxpont's keep would have been old-fashioned, apparently no more advanced in style than that of Appleby (qv), and possibly a deliberate reference to it. Broad pilaster buttresses at the angles, large windows with semi-circular arches on colonettes and a forebuilding on the E side giving access to the first-floor entrance. An additional storey was added *c*.1300 by Robert Clifford, the oratory at the SE corner breaking forward on corbelling with two grotesques on the S side and an arched two-light E window with quatrefoil in the head. Long cruciform loops at the other angles both at this level and in the four truncated corner turrets above. The remains of corbelled machicolations between the corner turrets.

Initially, each floor had a single room with a latrine, and, on the upper storeys, a fireplace. When the inner gatehouse was built in the late C13 the upper rooms were linked with those of the keep, to provide more spacious accommodation, the expanded residential block culminating in the new upper storey, an interesting exercise in domestic planning whereby a central chamber with canted angles was surrounded by a mural gallery leading to a vaulted oratory in the SE angle. The plan was probably inspired by schemes in late C13 great towers in N Wales (cf. Flint *c*.1277, Hawarden *c*.1282, Caernarfon *c*.1283).

E of the keep are the fragmentary remains of the early C13 hall (later the great chamber) projecting substantially beyond the outer gatehouse. S of this, backing onto the curtain at first-floor level, is the modest late C14 great hall, its windows of two-trefoil-headed lights beneath square heads. At the lower end, occupying the SE corner, is the contemporary kitchen with plainer fenestration, then, ranged along the S curtain, the first-floor chapel, its S wall retaining piscina and sedilia and, at a higher level, two trefoil-cusped windows within square heads. At the SW corner of the enclosure the square, four-storey Tower of League containing a series lodgings served by latrine turret. On the ground floor is a fireplace with an unusual interpretation of the shouldered lintel showing affinities with Hawarden. Summerson *et al.* 1998.

BROUGHTON, Oxfordshire (Restricted opening during the summer). Fortified manor house with a late C13 to mid C14 core built by the Broughton family. About 1377 the property was purchased by William of Wykeham, Bishop of Winchester, who made some improvements to the house including a new stair to the chapel. On his death in 1404 the manor was inherited by his great nephew, Thomas Wykeham, who, in 1406, was granted a licence to crenellate; Thomas may have been responsible for rebuilding the perimeter wall and gatehouse. In 1451 the house came to the Fiennes family through marriage; in the 1460s alterations and additions were made by William Fiennes who extended the great hall to the E, built a new service block and enlarged the chamber block. The house was remodelled and added to in the later C16 and now has the appearance of an Elizabethan mansion.

Broughton is surrounded by a quadrilateral moat fed by the Sor Brook, which extends around its E and S sides. The main entrance is on the N side across a bridge (formerly a drawbridge), through a largely late C14/early C15 rectangular gatehouse. There was a second entrance through the perimeter wall at the S end of the E side. Despite the Elizabethan appearance, the medieval core extends for almost the entire length of the entrance (N) front, only the single-storey kitchen wing to the L (E) spilling beyond its lateral footprint. To the L (E) are the private apartments, breaking forward with diagonal corner buttresses; at first-floor level a C14 chapel window. R (W) of this is the hall range, its front wall set back between Elizabethan bays and wings. Internally, the principal medieval survival is in the private apartments at the upper (E) end of the hall. Here, two doorways lead into an unusual arrangement of C14 vaulted passages giving access to the undercrofts and to separate stairs to the first-floor apartments and chapel. The first-floor rooms include an antechamber, great chamber, chapel and bed chambers; there was also a third storey containing more exclusive rooms. Emery 2006, 72–80.

BUCKDEN (Buckden Towers), Huntingdonshire (Grounds open regularly). Moated palace of the bishops of Lincoln in existence by the C13. A rebuilding of the palace was begun by Bishop Rotherham (1472–80) and completed by Bishop Russell (1480–94); their work was carried out in brick. The great hall was demolished in the C17, and the rest of the house in the C19, but substantial elements of the late C15 rebuilding survive.

The palace comprised a polygonal inner ward surrounded by a moat, and an extensive outer ward to the W. The W side of the outer ward (which fronts High Street) comprises a long low stretch of a crenellated brick-built curtain wall with a rectangular single-storey gatehouse pierced by a four-centred arch. To the R (S) of it is a pedestrian gate with returned hood mould. From here there is a straight path to the inner gatehouse, a C15 three-storey building bearing the arms of Bishop Russell. Attached to the R (S) a stretch of the C15 curtain extends S and then turns to the SE to meet the C15 great tower, the principal building to have survived from this period. This is a rectangular structure with prominent octagonal corner towers, like the great tower of Tattershall (qv), another brick building of some 40 years earlier. It rises through four storeys and is lit with square-headed multi-light windows. RCHME 1926, 34–8; Emery 2000, 229–33.

BUNGAY, Suffolk (Open). Motte with two baileys rebuilt in stone. First mentioned in 1140 when it was captured by King Stephen from Hugh Bigod (subsequently Earl of Norfolk). Bigod was deprived of his castles by Henry II in 1157 but was back in possession of Bungay by 1166. However, a subsequent rebellion led to the retaking of Bungay and orders being given for its destruction in 1174. In 1294 Roger Bigod, Fourth Earl of Norfolk, obtained a licence to crenellate his *mansum* at Bungay, possibly a reference to a refurbishment of the castle.

Bungay is built on high ground with the castle on the neck of a loop formed by the river Waveney. The baileys lay to the W and SW of the motte but only the western bailey remains largely undeveloped. Architectural interest centres on the former motte, the base of which is encircled by a polygonal curtain wall with a twin-towered gatehouse, probably related to the licence of 1294. The semi-circular flanking towers of the gateway have spurred bases, a feature in vogue during the late C13. A square keep, with a forebuilding, built on the motte *c.*1150, is now reduced to its basement; a siege mine, possibly of 1174, was discovered under the SW corner of the building during excavation. Braun 1934 and 1935.

BURGH, Suffolk (Open – EH). Motte and bailey within a Roman fort. A motte which occupied the SW corner of the Roman fort, and which was still extant in the late C18, was razed in the C19, but the motte ditch was excavated in the 1960s. It is to be presumed that the greater part of the fort constituted the medieval bailey. Johnson 1983.

BURTON-IN-LONSDALE (Castle Hill), Yorkshire West Riding (Private). Motte with two baileys. Probably C12. An oval motte is associated with an almost square bailey to the W and a narrow crescent-shaped baily to the S. Excavation undertaken in 1904 suggests that the motte may have begun life as a ringwork, the centre being raised subsequently to create a motte, a process that included the construction of a circular retaining wall. White 1905.

BURWELL, Cambridgeshire and the Isle of Ely (Open access). Unfinished royal castle of Stephen's reign. One of a string of castles built by King Stephen in 1143–4 to contain the troublesome Earl of Essex, Geoffrey de Mandeville, then ensconced in the Isle of Ramsey. Mandeville attacked the castle while it was under construction, but he was shot and killed. The threat from Mandeville averted, the castle lost its *raison d'être* and building work was abandoned. Burwell Castle was laid out to a rectangular plan, material from the surrounding moat being used to raise a central platform, a process that was never completed. Foundations of a curtain wall and two stone buildings at the E end of the platform probably belong to the subsequent occupation of the site by the Abbots of Ramsey. Wright and Creighton 2016, 6–25.

BYWELL, Northumberland (Private). A Neville family castle, of which the gatehouse survives. First mentioned in 1464 and probably dating from the first quarter of the C15. Situated on the NW bank of the Tyne at a bend in the river, the gatehouse, which fronts the river, faces upstream. It is a rectangular block rising through three storeys with a central four-centred gate arch, large twin-light upper windows, a corbelled machicolation over the gateway at parapet level, and square corner turrets with octagonal caps. This last feature is an unusual one, largely a feature of County Durham (cf. Lumley qv), and probably the brainchild of John Lewyn, who owned land in Bywell, although this example probably post-dates him. The gate passage was flanked by two vaulted rooms, the western one with fireplace and latrine, probably a porter's lodge. A stair in the N wall and then the NE angle, gave access to the upper floors and roof, each with two heated rooms. Hodgson 1902, 75–8; Emery 1996, 62.

CAINHOE (Clophill), Bedfordshire (Open access). Motte with three baileys, probably established by Nigel d'Albini who held the manor of Cainhoe in 1086; the castle was probably the caput of the barony of Cainhoe, but although the barony survived into the C16, the castle had probably fallen out of use by 1272. Cainhoe Castle sits on a natural ridge, and originally consisted of the motte and W bailey. The bailey has been mutilated by quarrying but was defined by a ditch and inner bank. The S and E baileys may be later additions; the former is also ditched and banked. Petre 2012, 57–62.

CAISTER, West Caister, Norfolk (Open). A moated quadrangular castle notable for being the first brick castle in England. Begun in 1432 under the master mason Henry Wode for Sir John Fastolf, it was largely complete by 1445. Then, there were two fully moated enclosures (the dividing trench is now infilled), the outer (E) ward next to the road having semi-circular towers at the NE and SE angles, arrow loops, and a bridge and gateway on the N side. Another gate to the S gave access to a bridge leading to the gatehouse of the inner ward. The walls of both enclosures were lined with buildings, the principal apartments being in the inner ward; all have been razed to the ground except for portions of the outer walls. The W front of the inner ward retains the rectangular water gate, and at the NW corner is a slim cylindrical five-storey solar tower incorporating circular gun ports and served by a rectangular latrine turret and a polygonal stair turret, the latter rising to a height of almost 100ft (30m). The tower and adjacent curtains were provided with machicolated parapets, elements of which remain. Between the gatehouse and the tower was the great hall rising through two storeys with a great chamber above the upper end. Access from the W was via a canal called the Barge Ditch, which led into the moat via a brick archway. Barnes and Simpson 1951.

CAMBRIDGE, Cambridgeshire and the Isle of Ely (Open access). Motte and bailey built on the orders of William I in 1068 when twenty-seven houses were demolished to clear the site prior to construction. In 1284 Edward I embarked upon a major reconstruction in stone, though the project remained incomplete at his death (1307). During the C16 the castle was allowed to decay and was used as a stone quarry. The onset of the Civil War led to refortification in 1643 as an artillery fort with angle bastions, but the defences were slighted four years later. The Edwardian gatehouse was demolished in 1842. Shire Hall was built within the bailey in 1932. The castle comprised a motte (which survives) and to the N and NW of it a roughly rectangular bailey (partially preserved in the open space between motte and Shire Hall) with corner towers. Edward's great gatehouse was on the SW side facing Castle Street. Apart from the motte, surviving earthworks include a fragment of the bailey bank leading N from the motte and imprints of the N and E bastions. RCHME 1959, 304–6; Brown *et al.* 1963, 583–8.

CANTERBURY, Kent (Closed for safety reasons at the time of writing). Royal castle in existence by 1086, the main survival being the great tower of *c*.1100. Initially, the castle seems to have been built in the S angle of the city walls which have their origin in the Roman period. A mound called Dane John (known as the 'Dungeon Hill' until the C17), which occupies the angle, was probably the motte of this early castle. Excavation has located its bailey ditch towards the N. Around 1100 the focus of the castle shifted towards the W, where a sub-rectangular courtyard defined by a ditch was built just inside the SW gate (Worthgate) of the Roman defences, with the new keep occupying the SE quarter. Rectangular in plan, the great tower has projecting corner turrets and rose through at least three storeys, though only two survive. An unusual embellishment was a high and elaborately stepped plinth; the windows had shafted and chevron-moulded frames. The first-floor entrance was on the W side approached by a flight of steps and protected by a (later) forebuilding. Two E–W cross-walls (now gone) created three main internal divisions of which the outer ones were sub-divided. Spiral staircases led to the basement (W) and upper storey (NE, S and W). Internal details include unusual stepped window embrasures, and a semi-circular-arched fireplace to the N with herringbone masonry back. Bennett *et al.* 1982.

CARISBROOKE, Isle of Wight (Open – EH). Motte and bailey rebuilt in stone on the site of a possible Anglo-Saxon *burh* and enclosed by a C16 artillery fort. In existence by 1086 and probably established by William FitzOsbern soon after the Conquest, adapting the defences of the *burh*. Around 1100 the Isle of Wight was granted to Richard de Redvers (d. 1107); it was probably he who reconstructed Carisbrooke as a motte and bailey, and his son, Baldwin, who refortified it in stone (by 1136). Between 1260 and 1293 Carisbrooke was the property of the last of the de Redvers, Isabella de Forz, who remodelled the main domestic apartments and rebuilt the gatehouse.

Isabella (d. 1293) willed the castle to Edward I, after which it remained in royal ownership. In 1335–6 the gatehouse was extended and given flanking towers, and in 1380 the building was heightened. In the late C16 a major refortification of the castle was undertaken in response to the threat of Spanish invasion. Bastions were added to the two S towers, another courtyard, or 'barbican', was constructed to the E and finally (in 1597–1602) the castle was converted into an artillery fort by being enclosed within an outer curtain with bastions, erected to the designs of the Italian military engineer Federigo Gianibelli.

Entry is from the W across the outer ditch into the artillery fort, and then over the inner ditch to the castle gatehouse with its two round flanking towers. The lower storey is of 1335–6; the upper storey of 1380, with corbelled machicolations over the entrance and gun ports of inverted keyhole type in the two towers. Behind this façade is Isabella's C13 gatehouse, a simple rectangular block, retaining at the rear (E) a pair of C14 or C15 gates. The greater part of the curtain wall dates from the early C12; it encloses a roughly rectangular inner bailey, at the NE corner of which is the motte capped by a shell-keep; there were wall towers only at the two southern corners, now reduced in height and encased in the C16 artillery bastions known as 'knights'

Inside, to the R (S), is the chapel of St Nicholas of 1904, on the foundations of the medieval chapel of that name. To the L (N) is Carey's Mansion, a late C16 rebuilding of the C12 N range. At right angles to it the principal medieval residential block. Firstly, the C13 great hall, much altered in subsequent centuries and now largely lacking in medieval detail; at its N end is the now-ruined C13 chamber block. Set back to the R (S) of the hall is the C14 and C15 Constable's Lodging, again much altered, which contained the great chamber and more private rooms. To the rear (E) between the great hall and great chamber is Isabella's Chapel of St Peter dating from 1270.

The main entrance to this accommodation complex is the porch at the LH (N) end of the hall. In the rear (E) wall of the hall is a significant medieval survival: the late C14 great fireplace, with moulded surround, panelled jambs and overmantle, and behind it a C13 window blocked by its insertion. The Chapel of St Peter was converted into a stairwell in the C17, but its wall arcades survive, together with a squint in the S wall allowing a view of the altar from the great chamber. In the private chamber of the Constable's Lodging said to be Charles I's bedroom, when he was incarcerated here in the 1640s, is another C14 fireplace also with panelled jambs. SE of the Constable's Lodging is the well house, a C16 reconstruction of the medieval arrangement including a tread wheel for drawing the water. Beyond this the SE range, C14 in origin, but much rebuilt in the C19.

Finally, the shell-keep, which is C12 with later alterations and additions, the most significant of which is the addition of a gatehouse in the C14. Approached from the bailey by a long flight of steps against the N curtain, and from the curtain wall walk, which feeds into the upper part of the stair. The gatehouse is rectangular and protected by a portcullis; it leads into a C16 corridor; indeed, all the partition walls within the keep probably date from that period. On the E side is a C13 two-storey latrine turret, but this, and possibly a well on the N side, are the only signs of medieval occupation. Young 2000 and 2010.

CARLISLE, Cumberland (Open – EH) (Plate IV). Stone courtyard and keep castle on the site of a Roman fort. Established on the Scottish border in 1092 by William Rufus to restore English control in the region. Rebuilt in stone probably in the 1120s. In 1136 King Stephen granted Cumbria and Carlisle to the Scots who held it until 1157, when it was retaken by Henry II. The outer gatehouse was rebuilt in 1378–83 by John Lewyn of Durham, with timberwork by William Wright of Lancaster. In 1541–3 the castle was strengthened by the Moravian military engineer Stephan von Haschenperg. Between 1820 and 1959 Carlisle Castle was occupied by the army, a period that also left its mark on the architecture.

Medieval Carlisle occupies a promontory, with the castle on an elevated, roughly triangular, site at the northern tip, cut off from the town by an E–W orientated ditch. Behind this is the long entrance (S) front with John Lewyn's highly unusual outer gatehouse, known as de Ireby's Tower, in the centre. Rectangular main block with a kitchen tower breaking forward on the L (W) flush with the front of the square barbican, and an obliquely placed solar tower to the R (E). The kitchen tower has the base of a first-floor balcony beneath a blocked opening. At the entrance to the gate passage is the rare survival of a portcullis; wooden, clad with iron. The interior of the gatehouse was cleverly planned to contain a principal suite as well as several single-chamber lodgings. In the gate-passage the second of two doors on the L (W) gives access to an entrance hall and the stair to the first floor, flanked to S and W by self-contained chambers. Hall on the first floor of the main block with high end to the E giving access to a private chamber in the solar tower, and two-storey low (W) end formerly screened off, containing a heated chamber on each floor. The kitchen tower retains a large fireplace with broad segmental arch.

The outer ward contains several army buildings, mostly C19. In front of the inner gatehouse, within the ditch separating the two wards, are the remains of Stephan von Haschenperg's Half Moon Battery, a semi-circular fortification containing a vaulted gallery provided with rectangular outward-splaying gun ports. Above this was a breastwork, or parapet, but it disappeared in the 1820s. Next is the rectangular inner gatehouse, or Captain's Tower; C12/C13 core, remodelled in the C14 and extended in the C16. C14 segmental-pointed gate arch beneath an earlier pointed arch flanked by pilaster buttresses. At the inner (E) end a portcullis slot, and then the gateway recessed beneath a C14 outer arch with a traceried fringe of trefoil cusping with little sculptured pendants; on the lateral walls between the two arches a lovely miniature detail of brattishing, or crenellation.

In the inner ward, more army buildings, but in the E corner an octagonal C14 stair turret, which served the medieval great chamber (of which only the shell survives) and Queen Mary's Tower, which once occupied the E corner of the ward. The turret has semi-hexagonal fillets at the angles, and the sides blind curvilinear tracery bifurcated by richly moulded colonettes on corbels carved with human heads; plain oversailing parapet.

Finally, the keep, in the SW corner of the inner ward, probably dating from *c.*1120–40. Nearly square in plan with corner turrets and portcullis-protected ground-floor (altered) entrance set within a shallow projection. This led to a mural staircase communicating with the residential accommodation on the upper floors. The architectural affinities are with the keep of Bamburgh Castle (qv), and the two towers may be the work of the same master builder. The upper part of the keep was remodelled in the C16 to provide artillery emplacements; there have also been drastic alterations to

A Guide to the Medieval Castles of England

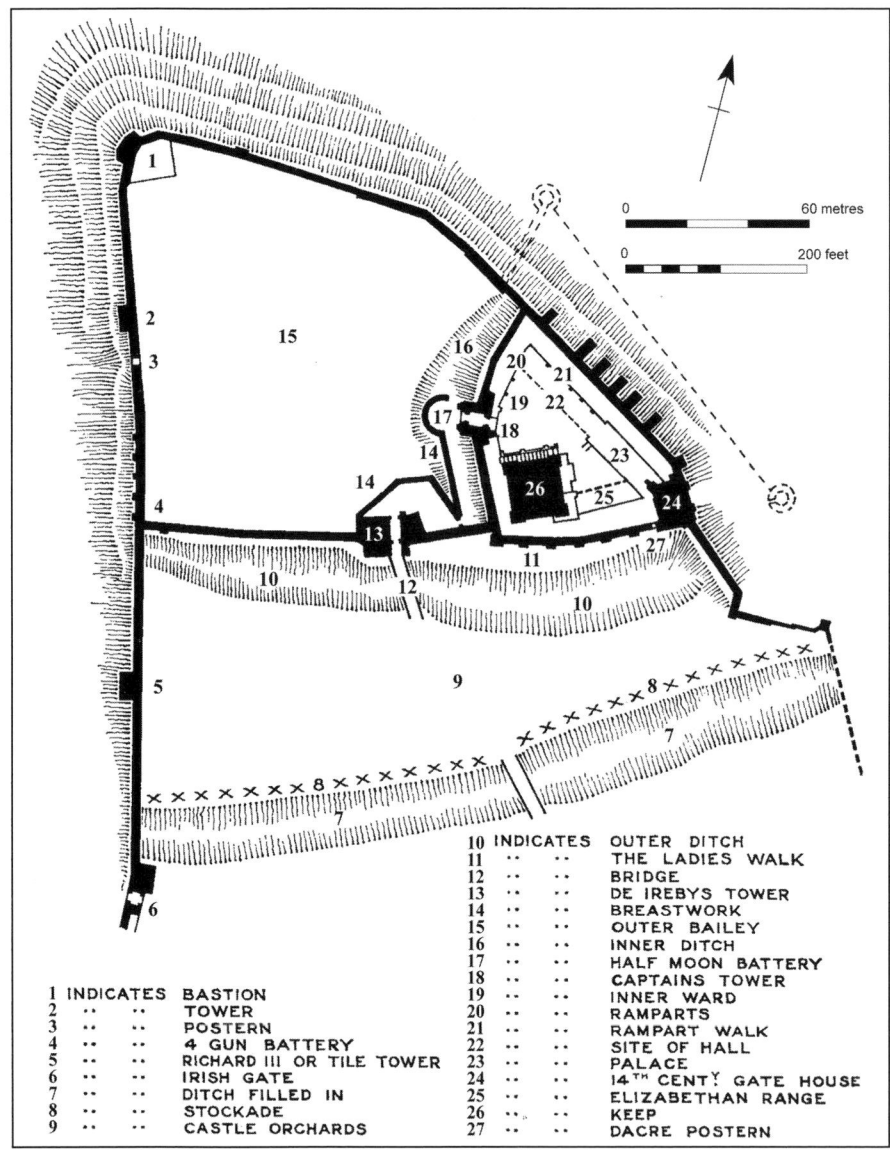

Carlisle: Ground plan. After Watson and Bradley 1937.

the interior, including the insertion of a spine wall and an extra floor, splitting the original second floor into two. The original arrangement may never be known. McCarthy *et al.* 1990; Goodall 2004.

CARTINGTON, Northumberland (Private). Fortified manor house in existence by 1415 when a *turris* was recorded here. In 1442, John de Cartington was granted a licence to 'enclose, crenellate, machicolate, and provide with towers and battlements his manor of Cartyngton'. Excavated and controversially restored for Lord Armstrong in 1887; the positioning of some of the restored details is suspect. The remains of a S courtyard with the stump of a late medieval square tower at the SE corner are entered from the W via a C17 gateway. Extending across the N side of the courtyard is a substantial residential block. This comprises a tower to the R (E) with a polygonal stair turret at the SW angle and a hall range to the L (W). An C18 drawing suggests that the tower rose through four storeys and that the corners were capped by circular bartizans. At this stage the hall range was of equal height, though whether this had always been the case is unknown. The tower dates from the late C14 or early C15; the hall range from the C15. Emery 1996, 63–5.

CASTELL BRYN AMLWG (Castle Cefn Vron), Shropshire (Private). Ringwork rebuilt in stone. Foundation date unknown but the early C12 seems probable; it may have been established to protect the Welsh border of the Clun lordship. The earthworks consisted of a ditch with inner and outer banks, the enclosure extending from N–S. Excavation undertaken in the 1960s showed that the castle was rebuilt in stone in several phases, beginning with a round tower, or keep, at the S end. Next came the curtain, and then the gatehouse at the N end. This latter had a strong resemblance to the inner gatehouse of Montgomery castle, built in the 1220s, while the round tower recalls the keeps of several native Welsh castles both in its position, straddling the curtain, and in its modest size (some 35ft D.). Alcock *et al.* (1967–8); Duckers 2006, 41–4.

CASTLE ACRE, Norfolk (Open – EH). Ringwork and bailey, the former containing the excavated remains of an interesting stone building representing the conversion of a house into a keep. The castle was built by William de Warenne (later First Earl of Surrey) probably soon after the Conquest; apart from a short period of alienation it remained in the hands of the Warenne earls of Surrey until the extinction of the line in 1347.

The very substantial banks and ditches enclose a sub-rectangular lower bailey to the S of a raised inner bailey, or ringwork. A barbican to the E of the inner bailey gives access to the E gate into the outer bailey. On the other side of the outer bailey, directly opposite the E gate, a W gate led to and from the town, which was surrounded by its own defences, elements of which survive, notably the Bailey Gate, on the N side facing Stocks Green.

Starting in Stocks Green, the Bailey Gate is a rectangular gatehouse with a high pointed gate arch flanked by a pair of round-fronted towers; it probably dates from the late C12 or early C13. There was a gate at each end and a portcullis in the centre. The gateway leads to Bailey Street, on the L (E) side of which a path leads to the W gate of the castle. Less well-preserved than the Bailey Gate, it also had round fronted flanking towers. In the gate passage, elements of the ashlar facing survive. A recess on the R (S) was probably a porter's lodge.

The massive outer bailey ramparts are probably the result of strengthening *c.*1140; they retain fragments of a stone curtain wall along the top and are breached by the E gate of which only one wall remains. The defences enclose a flat area, with earthworks in the centre denoting the position of a former building, probably a great hall.

The inner bailey has similar fortifications, also the consequence of a mid-C12 remodelling of a more modest arrangement. On the S side of the inner bailey is a rectangular gatehouse of similar date, which was approached from the lower ward via a bridge.

The principal interest of the castle lies in the building within the upper ward, which began life in the later C11 as a two-storey double-pile house with an E–W spine wall dividing the interior into two main rooms at both levels. There was a ground-floor entrance to the S and a first-floor entrance to the N. The ground floor was lit by a few narrow windows and was probably for storage; a doorway in the spine wall allowed communication between the two rooms. The upper storey has survived less well, but it contained the principal living accommodation. It retains, in the N wall, the base of a fireplace, and, in the W wall, the lower part of a window larger than those below.

Around 1140, a date that corresponds with the 'Anarchy' of Stephen's reign, a major conversion of the house was begun, in which the external walls were doubled in thickness and the openings blocked preparatory to the raising of the floor level. Then, part way through this conversion, a change of plan occurred in which the thickness of the spine wall was increased, and the northern half of the building only was raised into a tower. Coad and Streeten 1982; Impey 2008a.

CASTLE BOLTON, Yorkshire North Riding (Open). An unusually well-preserved quadrangular castle, Castle Bolton is the outstanding English example of a late medieval type, in which large-scale domestic planning was confined within a restricted compass, rising through several storeys, to create a compact, integrated castle with a custom-designed plan of sometimes labyrinthine complexity. Built for Richard Lord Scrope, steward of the household and later chancellor, it is largely a creation of the years 1378–95. Scrope's master mason was John Lewyn of Durham.

The chronology of the C14 work is based on three medieval documents: a building contract of 1378 (referring to the E range and towers and E part of the S range), a licence to crenellate of 1379, and a licence for founding a chantry in the castle chapel of 1393. These are complemented by Leland's statement that the castle took 18 years to build at an annual cost of 1,000 marks and was completed before 1399.

Mary Queen of Scots was held captive at Bolton between July 1568, when she was conducted there from Carlisle (qv), and February 1569, when she was moved to Tutbury (qv). In 1645, Bolton was besieged and taken by Parliamentarian forces; it was slighted a couple of years later and thereafter ceased to be a high-class residence. The male line of the Scropes of Bolton died out in 1646, and the castle came by marriage to John Paulet, Marquess of Winchester. It was probably he who built Bolton Hall, near Wensley, in the 1680s to replace the castle. The NE Tower collapsed in 1761. In the later C18 the W range and SW Tower (both still roofed) were occupied by two farming families.

The remains of four rectangular five-storey corner towers linked by three-storey residential ranges enclose a quadrangular courtyard. Rectangular turrets project externally from the centres of the N and S ranges. The castle accommodated eight major domestic suites centred on several halls, together with numerous individual lodgings and various domestic offices including two kitchens, a brewhouse and bakehouse. The genius of the design lies in the assimilation of the various units, a task of three-dimensional complexity that involved arranging very specific lines of communication in order to maintain a high degree of exclusivity for each residential unit. Amongst non-royal castles Bolton is the most ambitious in scale of this specialized

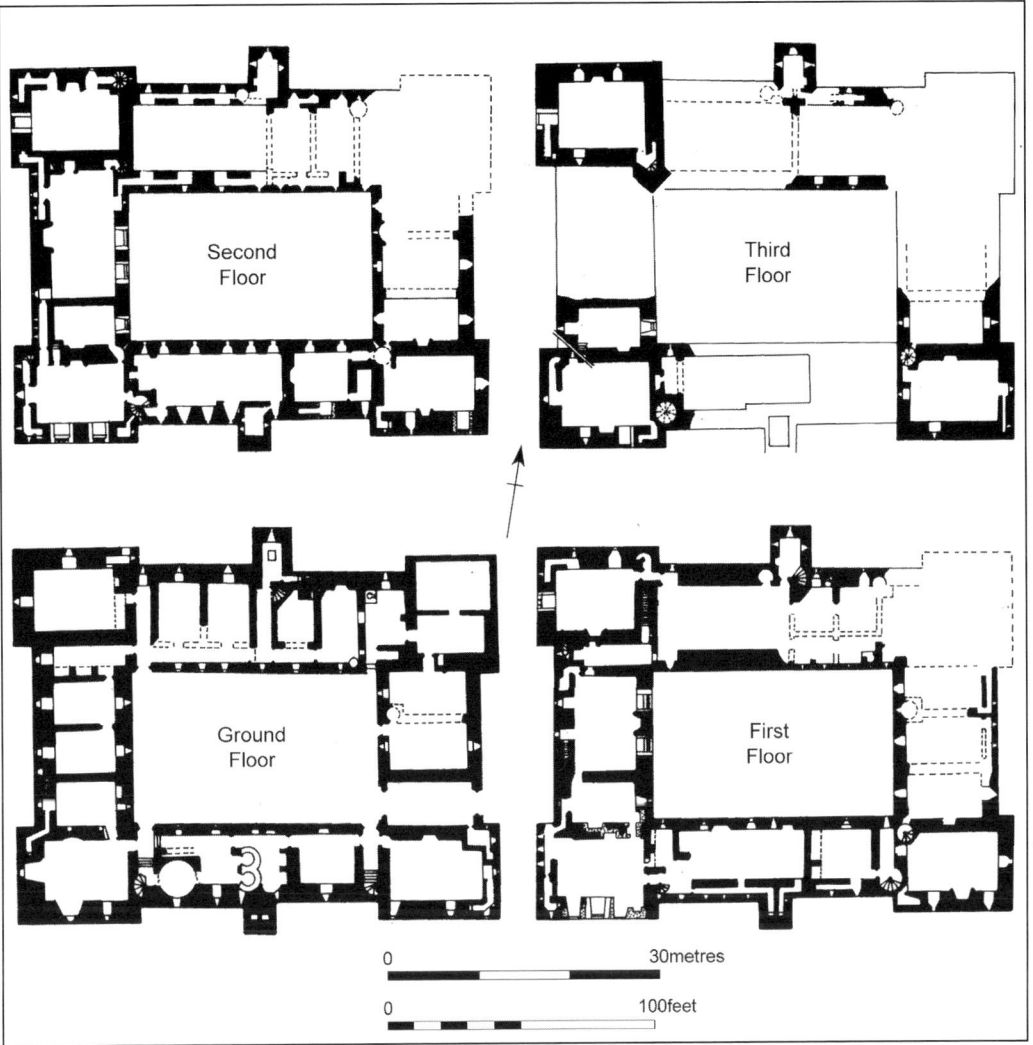

Castle Bolton: Floor plans.

type of building, and, despite the destruction of the NE tower, one of the most easily understood, owing to a high degree of survival.

A perambulation of the exterior shows that most of the primary windows were simple chamfered rectangles in three standard sizes. The other principal medieval type, which is to be found in the N, S and W elevations, is larger, with a cinquefoiled head beneath a pointed arch. Those on the N and S sides are transomed and lit the great hall and chapel respectively; those to the W denote the positions of two more private halls or great chambers. A number of post-medieval windows attest to continued occupation of some parts into the C19.

In the E range, hard up against the SE Tower, is the C14 gateway, with a high outer arch; off the passage is a porter's lodge. In the courtyard, the positions of the first-floor great hall (N) and second-floor chapel (S) are again denoted by their tall C14 windows, whereas the C16 mullioned and transomed windows locate the first- and second-floor halls of the W range. Five entrances, each with a tall outer arch and a portcullis, led into the ranges. Other noteworthy features are the machicolated squinch arches at the corners which carry diagonally placed turrets commanding the entrances, and, in the S wall, a near-vertical construction joint, showing that the western part of the range is later than the eastern part of the 1378 contact.

The approach to the great hall was via the NW entrance, down a corridor, and up a staircase to an antechamber in the N turret, the only room in the castle with ribbed vaulting. At an upper level the hall windows are linked by wall passages, and there are flues in the heads of the embrasures (a Lewyn motif) to carry off the smoke from the open hearth. Between the windows are decorated stone lamp sconces. The other (E) half of the range (now largely ruined) was occupied by service rooms at ground- and first-floor levels with staircase access between the two, and a well in the S wall extending through two storeys. There was a residential suite above. Beyond the service rooms the now destroyed NE Tower contained the first-floor kitchen, whereas the E range was divided into a series of lodgings, the details of which are now obscured by ruination and C18/C19 low-status re-occupation.

The S range basement contains the brewhouse and bakehouse, the great fireplace of the latter with two large arched openings at the back giving access to the ovens (of which only foundations survive). Behind the ovens is a trio of arches, the LH one a doorway, the others blind. This wall, which is double the normal thickness, is the dividing line between the works of the 1378 contract to the E and the later build. In the chapel, at second-floor level a broad arch at the W end carries a private pew from which the proceedings could be observed. At the E end is a (restored) piscina and, to the S, access at two levels to a turret containing accommodation for the chantry priests, the upper room with a squint.

The best accommodation was centred on the two halls in the W range, supported by apartments in the W towers. The smaller lower hall seems to have had an external entrance, now converted to a window. Both halls were heated by a fireplace (the upper

Castle Bolton: Second-floor hall in the W range (last quarter of the C14) from the S.

one restored) with corbelled lintel (larger versions of a standard type found elsewhere within the castle) and had window seats. Smaller rooms in the towers were equipped to a similar standard. Faulkner 1963; Hislop 1996a and 2007.

CASTLE BROMWICH, Warwickshire (Inaccessible). Depleted motte and bailey, its truncated remains lying between the M6 and its feeder road the A452, and now inaccessible. The castle was in existence by *c.*1171. Excavation was undertaken in 1969–70. The motte was defined by a ditch to the S, E and W, but terminating to the N, where there was a steep natural scarp. The bailey curved around its S and E sides, being protected by a ditch and inner bank, with the gateway to the SE. In the C13 or C14 the bailey was enlarged by being extended to the S. Hodder forthcoming.

CASTLE BYTHAM, Lincolnshire (Private). Motte and bailey rebuilt in stone, first mentioned in 1141 when it was held by William le Gros, Earl of York. Through marriage it came to William de Forz, Earl of Aumale, who rebelled against Henry III. In 1221 the castle was besieged and destroyed and then granted to the former tenant William de Coleville who rebuilt it. When Leland visited it in the mid C16 'great waulles of buildinge' were still in existence; substantial stone walls were excavated in 1870. Built on a spur at the E edge of the village and within a loop of the river Tham. A motte at the tip of the spur is surrounded by a ditch and outer bank; kidney-shaped bailey to the SE defined by a ditch and inner bank. Immediately E of the motte is a courtyard barbican containing a mound. Brown 1989, 76–7.

CASTLE CARLTON (Castle Hill), Lincolnshire (Private but visible from a footpath). Motte, with two baileys, of C11 or C12 origin; in existence by 1205 when it was held by the Bardolf family. The roughly circular earthwork complex is surrounded by a ditch of variable character which encloses a motte (NE), and two baileys which together take a crescentic form. There is an internal bank to the S and W, with a prominent break to the W suggesting an entrance. The two baileys are separated by an E–W ditch extending from the SW angle of the motte and aligning with the putative entrance. Wright and Creighton 2016, 26–39.

CASTLE CARY, Somerset (Open access). Probable ringwork and bailey in origin; a keep was built inside the ringwork and the defences remodelled to suggest a tower on a motte and a surrounding bailey. Late C11 in origin; captured in 1138 by King Stephen. The earthworks comprise the remains of two enclosures of which only the western side survives, in both instances consisting of a ditch and inner bank. In 1890 the foundations of a rectangular stone keep were excavated within the S enclosure; it had a forebuilding at the N end and the main body was sub-divided by a spine wall. Dunning 1995, 32–3; Leach and Ellis 2004.

CASTLE COMBE, Wiltshire (Private). A promontory site of uncertain date but usually assigned to the Anarchy, Castle Combe consists of a ringwork at the SW tip of the promontory containing the remains of a square keep, and a linear sequence of baileys extending towards the NE. It may represent the reuse of a prehistoric fortification. Creighton 2000.

CASTLE HEDINGHAM, Essex (Open). On a spur NE of the village, an oval ringwork defined by a ditch and counterscarp bank, with a quadrilateral bailey to the E, separated from the eastern high ground by a scarped ravine. Within the ringwork is a square keep probably built in the 1140s by Aubrey de Vere, First Earl of Oxford. The

Castle Hedingham: The great tower.

elevations are deceptive; although there are five levels of C12 fenestration externally, inside there were only three storeys when first built (basement and two upper floors). The third-level windows lit the uppermost floor, the twin-light windows above belonging to a mural gallery within the same room. The fifth level of fenestration is above the original roof level, and it was several centuries after the tower was built that the roof level was raised, and another storey inserted that made use of the windows. The upper windows, then, despite being the most elaborate of all, are a deceit, to suggest an upper chamber, and to enhance the aesthetic qualities of the tower.

Access to the keep is from the W at first-floor level, a flight of steps giving access to a forebuilding, of which only the base remains. Large round-arched doorway flanked by shafts with scalloped capitals from which springs a chevron-moulded arch; the entrance was secured by a drawbar and portcullis.

The first floor contained the lower hall, traversed from E–W by a segmental diaphragm arch. In the N wall is a round-backed fireplace, its arch on shafts with scalloped capitals. Narrow mural rooms or closets are entered from the window embrasures. Access to all the other levels of the tower was from the first-floor room via the newel staircase in the NW corner, though the original doorway has been blocked and the staircase is now accessed from the entrance lobby. The basement was purely for storage, but the second floor contains the upper hall, the most important room within the keep. It too is spanned by a diaphragm arch; here heavily moulded and higher than the one below, thereby allowing a semi-circular form. It acts as a proscenium arch to the inner half of the room with its tripartite arrangement of central fireplace and flanking window embrasures. These, like all the openings at this level, have chevron-moulded round arches on shafts. the room rises through two levels, the upper half containing clearstorey lighting linked by a mural gallery. It was in this impressive setting, open to the roof, that the lord, seated in front of the fire, may have received suppliants. At third-floor level, the stair turret has two doorways to S and E, giving access to the roof. On the sides of the turret are the slanting lines of the original roof, which appears to have been of pyramidal form. RCHME 1916, 51–7; Dixon and Marshall 1993a.

CASTLE NEROCHE, Somerset (Open access). An eroded but archaeologically important motte and bailey site excavated by Brian Davison in the 1960s. The castle sits on a short spur of the Blackdown Hills looking N over the Somerset Levels. The motte is at the N tip of the spur with a double-ditched bailey to the SE, the NE half of which has disappeared down the hillside. There is an outer bank and ditch to the SE and SW. Davison identified four main structural periods, the putatively earliest (Period I) being the outer bank and ditch which were assigned to the prehistoric or Anglo-Saxon era. During Period II a ditched and banked enclosure or ringwork, was built within the Period I fortifications; it represents the earliest Norman fortification of the site and might date from $c.$1067, a time of resistance to Norman rule in the SW. In Period III the ringwork was strengthened, probably by Robert of Mortain (d. 1095), by the construction of the motte and an outer ditch and bank around the ringwork. In Period IV a mound was added to the top of the motte and revetted with a stone wall raised into a shell-keep. In addition, a ring wall was built around the motte top. This phase probably dates from the first half of the C12. Davison 1972; Dunning 1995, 33–5.

CASTLE RISING, Norfolk (Open – EH). Probably established by William d'Albini $c.$1138 when he married Adeliza, widow of Henry I, and became lord of Arundel (qv); he became Earl of Sussex in 1141. The castle was built on the outskirts of an existing settlement, possibly on the site of an Anglo-Saxon manorial residence. William d'Albini's centrepiece was a great stone keep within a sub-oval enclosure, or ringwork, protected by a ditch and inner rampart and entered from the E via a stone gatehouse, which was itself accessed through a smaller ditched and banked enclosure, or barbican. A still smaller enclosure lies to the W. In the late C12 or early C13 the defences of the main enclosure were strengthened by deepening the ditch and heightening the bank, except on the W side, where the ditch material was dumped into the W enclosure to create a platform. For reasons unknown, d'Albini never seems to have finished this keep; it was only completed in the late C13 or early C14 under the Montalt lords, who acquired the castle in 1243.

Access to the castle is from the E barbican, which houses the car park. The first impression of Castle Rising is swayed by the massiveness of the main earthworks, which are at a scale emulated by few other castles. There were some stone defences too, but they were probably late in date and of poor construction; they have mostly disappeared. An exception is the C12 gatehouse, which was probably part of the primary defences. Rectangular with a central gateway, the passage was protected by a portcullis and, later in the C12, covered by a vault, as attested by a surviving corbelled respond; at some stage a short barbican was added to the front. In the gate passage, shallow wall recesses may have been for seating. On entering the courtyard, straight ahead is the keep, always the principal building, but now the only structure, apart from the foundations of an early C14 residential complex to the S of the keep, and the ruins of a late C11 church, part of the pre-castle town that was appropriated when the defences were constructed. Now hard up against the N rampart, it comprises a nave with apsidal chancel.

The two-storey keep comprises an E–W aligned rectangular block some 78½ft (24m) × 68½ft (21m) with pilaster buttresses clasping the angles and articulating the elevations. Attached to the E end is a defended staircase and forebuilding. The quality of the dressed stone and the execution of the details suggest that no expense was spared in the building's construction. Full-height shafts, set within the angles of the corner buttresses, testify to the quality of the finish, but the greatest attention has been paid to the forebuilding and staircase block, where wall arcading recalls the ornate character of the earlier keeps built by Henry I at Norwich (qv) and Falaise, which William d'Albini may have intended to emulate. A perambulation around the ramparts allows the keep to be appreciated from all sides. The showpiece forebuilding and staircase combination is directly opposite the gatehouse, and therefore the first part to be seen; the latrine and foul-water outlets are at the farther (W) end close to the rampart, and so, for the most part, kept out of sight; nevertheless, this is an interesting elevation for those interested in medieval engineer's approach to waste disposal, and not without architectural appeal.

The only access to the keep was via the forebuilding, and great care was taken to turn the approach into a memorable experience. The entrance front is crammed with masonry details: corbelling, sculpture, textured surfaces, arches and roundels all play their part in creating an emphatic entrance; not entirely successful as a decorative scheme, perhaps, but certainly an ostentatious splash that grabs the attention. The interior is less fussy but more effective in creating an impression of seigneurial power. The gate, which was secured by a draw bar, opens to a very imposing grand staircase, leading straight to the forebuilding at first-floor level, but given an enhanced perspective, and extra protection, by an intermediate gateway (roll-moulded arch on shafts with cushion capitals) giving onto a halfway landing. This gate is recessed beneath an outer arch with a 'murder hole' in the head and was also closed with a drawbar. At the top of the steps a third gateway leads into a vestibule wherein lies the climax of the approach: the entrance into the main body of the keep. Three roll-moulded orders spring from shafts with cushion capitals and bases and are interspersed with zigzag mouldings. This entrance is now blocked, but originally led into the great hall. Around 1300 the forebuilding was given an extra storey and a ribbed vault, carried on naturalistic foliate capitals.

The keep was divided into two unequal parts by an E–W spine wall. A doorway near the foot of the forebuilding stairs now leads into the narrower southern half of the basement, but originally the two spaces at this level were accessible only from above, via spiral staircases in the NE and SW angles. At first-floor level the wider northern half contained the hall and, at the W end, kitchen, service room and a pair of latrines. The southern half accommodated the great chamber and, at the E end, the chapel and its antechamber. Access to the keep is now through a forced entry into the NE stair, which opens to a mural passage broken through a series of window embrasures, which leads to the kitchen. Along the side walls, corbels in the form of sculptured heads relate to the C13/C14 refurbishment.

A doorway in the S wall of the hall allowed communication with the great chamber, but this room can now only be viewed by crossing a modern bridge across the E end of the hall, which leads to the chapel antechamber, from which a passage led across the

Castle Rising: The great staircase to the first-floor entrance to the keep (*c*.1140).

arch over the staircase. Then into the chapel itself, an engaging space, but much depleted. However, the roll-moulded chancel arch survives on demi-columns with scalloped capitals, so too do elements of wall arcading. In the W wall a segmental-arched doorway of *c*.1300 communicated with the great chamber. The great chamber itself was provided with a fireplace and two latrines. Brown 1978; Morley and Gurney 1997.

CASTLE PULVERBATCH, Shropshire. See **PULVERBATCH**.

CASTLESTEDE, Hornby, Lancashire (Private, but visible from a footpath). Motte and bailey on a rise above a crossing of the river Lune on the E side of the road to Hornby, a mile N of Hornby village, the predecessor to the C16 and later Hornby Castle. A roughly oval site with the motte to the E, a bank and ditch defines the bailey on the S side, the ditch extending around the S and E sides of the motte. In existence by 1205 when it was seized by King John from Roger de Montbegon. Curwen 1912 and 1913, 17.

CASTLETHORPE (Hanslope Castle), Buckinghamshire (Open access). Probable ringwork with later motte and bailey identified with Hanslope Castle. In 1086 Hanslope was part of the fief of Winemar the Fleming, who may have been the builder of the ringwork. His lands came to Michael of Hanslope, and then through marriage to the Maudit family *c.*1131. Hanslope Castle was destroyed by Falkes de Bréauté in 1215. In 1263 William Maudit became Earl of Warwick, and in 1292 a licence was granted to his nephew, William Beauchamp, Earl of Warwick, to build and crenellate a wall around a garden within his dwelling house of Hamslape.

The nearly circular ringwork is defined by a ditch and remnants of inner and outer banks; the earthworks are interrupted by two causewayed entrances on the W side. The Church of St James lies within the SE quadrant and the earthworks on this side have been obliterated by the churchyard. Immediately W of the church is a mutilated motte. W of the ringwork is an outer enclosure defined to the W by a long straight ditch with wide inner bank on a NE–SW alignment. RCHME 1913, 80–2; Page 1927, 349.

CASTLE TUMP, see **DYMOCK**.

CAUS, Shropshire (Private). C12 motte and bailey castle within a prehistoric hillfort, rebuilt in stone for Robert Corbet *c.*1198. Probably the successor to Hawcock's Mount. The castle is built against the southern line of the hillfort defences, enclosed to the N by a double ditch and bank system, with the entrance to the E and the motte to the W. Stone buildings including a curtain wall and a round tower on the motte are known to have existed, but little masonry is visible now. The area within the hillfort defences but outside the castle defences accommodated a borough probably from the C12.

Three-quarters of a mile due E of Caus is the ringwork known as Hawcock's Mount, which is considered to be the predecessor of Caus on the grounds that Hawcock's is a corruption of Old Caus. Probably established by an earlier Robert Corbet soon after the Conquest, the substantial earthworks comprise a moat with inner bank. Gaydon 1968, 303, 308–10; Duckers 2006, 48–53.

CAWOOD, Yorkshire West Riding (Visible from the road). Remains of a fortified palace of the Archbishops of York. Cawood was fortified under a licence to crenellate of 1272, but the existing remains date from the time of Archbishop Kemp (1425–52). These consist of the gatehouse and the attached lodging range to the E. The gatehouse communicated between the outer courtyard to the S, which remains an open area, and the inner courtyard to the N, which has been partially cleared in recent years to present an open aspect immediately to the rear of the C15 buildings. Three-storey gatehouse of brick faced with ashlar in the form of a rectangular tower with diagonal buttresses to the S and an octagonal stair turret at the NW angle. Four-centred carriage and pedestrian gateways recessed beneath a broad three-centred arch; above is a balcony, its parapet carrying a frieze of heraldic shields suggesting a date of after 1440; looming up behind it is a bay window with a crested parapet, and above that a twin-light window with square label. The slightly later two-storey lodging range to the R is articulated by stepped buttresses and has single-light windows with cinquefoil heads at the upper level. The original pitch of the roof can be seen in the wall of the gatehouse. To the N the gatehouse has an ornate first-floor oriel, and the lodging range large windows on both floors. Blood and Taylor 1992; Emery 1996, 325–7.

CHARTLEY, Staffordshire (Private, but visible from the road). Motte with two baileys partially rebuilt in stone, on a spur next to the road between Stafford and Uttoxeter. A castle of the earls of Chester from the late C11. Rebuilt by Earl Ranulph *c.*1220. After the death of his heir in 1237, the castle passed by marriage to William Ferrers, Earl of Derby. It was held by the Ferrers family until 1450. The castle earthworks consist of a linear progression (from E to W) of outer bailey, inner bailey and motte, the whole complex surrounded by a ditch and counterscarp bank, with ditches separating the motte and baileys. Only the inner bailey appears to have been rebuilt in stone. Access was via the outer bailey, across a bridge to a gatehouse at the S end of the E curtain with twin round-fronted flanking towers of which the bases remain. At the NE corner is the base of a three-quarter round tower. On the S side are more substantial remains of two D-shaped wall towers, both retaining cruciform arrow loops. The motte was capped by a cylindrical keep of which the basement remains; it had a semi-circular stair turret, a feature found in several C13 Welsh marcher castles. McGuicken 2006.

CHENEY LONGVILLE 1, Shropshire (Private). Fortified manor house to the SW of Cheney Longville village, associated with a licence of 1394 granted to Sir Hugh Cheyne. Rectangular courtyard plan enclosed by a curtain wall without towers; a moat survives to the S and W. The plain entrance (now altered) was in the short W side; it gave access to the courtyard, formerly surrounded by building ranges backing onto the curtain, elements of which survive on the S, W and E sides. The great hall and other principal apartments were on the vanished N side, now largely occupied by a C17 farmhouse. C14 details include pointed doorways and rectangular windows. Emery 2000, 525–7; Duckers 2006, 54–7.

CHENEY LONGVILLE 2, Shropshire (Private). Ringwork. Probably C11 or C12 and perhaps the work of the Saxon, Siward le Gros, who held the manor both before and after the Conquest. Situated to the NW of Cheney Longville village. Circular ditched and banked enclosure; Duckers 2006, 54.

CHESTER, Cheshire (Open). Probable ringwork and bailey rebuilt in stone. Built by William the Conqueror in 1070. Subsequently held by the earls of Chester until 1237, when the last earl died, and the King took possession. Substantial works were undertaken by Edward I who, from 1284, raised a new set of royal apartments in the outer bailey next to the great hall, and, in 1292–3, rebuilt the outer gatehouse. This latter had twin drum towers as did the inner gatehouse for which Edward was probably also responsible.

Today the medieval castle is a shadow of its former self, the outer bailey having been obliterated, its site now occupied by the C18 and C19 Shire Hall complex (now university) and forecourt (now car park). Access to the inner bailey (or ringwork) is to

Chester: Agricola Tower from the SW.

the SW of the university buildings; this entrance, and the forecourt immediately inside are on the site of the ditch between the two baileys. The C13 gatehouse, which was immediately ahead, has disappeared, but the entrance it replaced survives a little to the L, its outer portal blocked. This is the Agricola Tower of *c.*1200, the most significant medieval survival. Its former function is apparent from the rear (SW) face, where the inner portal survives. On the first floor is the chapel of St Mary de Castro.

Detached wall shafts with stiff leaf capitals carry tripartite roll and keel moulded vaulting ribs. Fragments of C13 wall paintings survive. Brown *et al.* 1963, 6-7-12; Thacker and Lewis *et al.* 2005, 204–13.

CHILHAM, Kent (Private). A castle of late C11 or C12 foundation of which the main upstanding survival is the keep which was probably raised for Henry II in the 1170s by the royal mason Master Ralph. The extent of the early castle is no longer apparent, but excavation immediately to the SE of the keep in the 1920s revealed the remains of an early hall. Henry's keep is octagonal in plan with a rectangular stair turret to the NE and an attached forebuilding the foundations of which incorporate the N end of the early hall. Henry II's slightly earlier keep at Orford (qv) probably influenced the plan. Around the tower is a later medieval curtain wall enclosing a small courtyard. Clapham 1928; Brown *et al.* 1963, 613.

CHILLINGHAM, Northumberland (Open). Quadrangular castle fortified under a licence to crenellate granted to Thomas de Heton in 1344; it seems to have been largely complete by 1348, but subsequent building phases (C16, C17, C18 and C19) tend to obscure the medieval character of the castle. Four- or five-storey rectangular corner towers and linking domestic ranges surround a central open quadrangle. The towers, for the most part, date from the C14 albeit altered and in some cases added to, while the connecting ranges are later. The C14 masonry consists of coursed and roughly dressed large blocks; the best external detail to survive is a mid-C14 two-light window on the W face of the SW tower. Inside, the basements of the towers are barrel-vaulted, those to the S with ribs. Dodds 1935.

CHIPCHASE, Northumberland (Private). Tower house linked to a C17 country house by a range of uncertain date. First mentioned in 1415, when it was held by Alexander Heron, affinities with Belsay (qv) suggest a date of *c.*1400. The tower seems to have been freestanding originally, but by 1541 had an adjoining 'manor of stonework'. The plan is rectangular with a projecting turret at the S end of the E front containing the entrance and staircase. Four storeys with chamfered plinth and first-floor offset, and a machicolated parapet carried on corbelling. Corbelled cylindrical bartizans, also with machicolated parapets, cap the four corners. A segmental-pointed entrance at ground-floor level protected by a portcullis and two draw bars gives access to a barrel-vaulted basement, evidently for storage only, and to the staircase. At mezzanine level in the turret a mural chamber giving access to a portcullis room with a loop looking E flanked by two water chutes. Poorly-lit first-floor room with hooded fireplace, perhaps staff accommodation. Above this a hall with large fireplace and large window embrasures to E and S, the former leading to an oratory with a squint, allowing a view of the altar from the hall, and the latter to a latrine. In the SE turret a small chamber with a fireplace, and in the NW angle an L-shaped room of unknown purpose. At third-floor level is another hall with fireplace, latrine and four windows in splayed embrasures of which the eastern was supplied with window seats. In the turret a kitchen with fireplace and sink. Hodgson 1897, 333–9; Emery 1996, 68–70.

CHIPPING ONGAR, see **ONGAR**.

CHRISTCHURCH, Hampshire (Open – EH). Motte and bailey, with stone keep and chamber block, commanding a crossing of the river Avon. Probably built by Richard de Redvers *c.*1100 when he was granted the manor by Henry I. The castle lies

N of Christchurch Priory and W of the Avon; its exact extent is uncertain owing to the encroachment of buildings around the periphery. Visually, it now comprises two main components: a motte surmounted by the keep, which stood on the W side of the bailey, and the Constable's House, which stood on the E side, backing onto a mill stream that follows the line of the river. The remains of the keep are fragmentary, but it was rectangular with chamfered angles and retains some large segmental-arched openings with semi-circular relieving arches over. The Constable's House of *c*.1160, which is one of the best-preserved Norman domestic buildings in England, was probably a chamber block rather than a hall. It is a two-storey structure with entrances towards the bailey (W) at both levels. The unheated basement is lit by narrow loops. A staircase in the NE corner communicated with the first floor, which was probably divided into large (N) and small (S) rooms. The former has a fireplace in the E wall, the flue rising to an unusually well-preserved cylindrical chimney, and was well lit by two-light windows to the N, E and W enriched externally by shafting and chevron-moulded arches. The unheated smaller room, perhaps a bed chamber, was provided with the luxury of a latrine turret in the C13, which discharged into the mill stream behind the house. Page 1912a, 88–90.

CHURCH STRETTON, Shropshire. See **BROCKHURST**.

CLARE, Suffolk (Open access). Motte with two baileys in existence by 1090, possibly on the site of an Anglo-Saxon residence. What remains of the castle is preserved within Clare Castle Country Park, bounded to the E by the river Chilton and to the S by the river Stour. The motte is on the western edge of the park with the upper and lower baileys to the E and NE respectively. The upper (S) bailey was bisected from E–W by the railway and the railway station built within it, though elements of the earthworks survive to N and S. The lower (N) bailey is better preserved but traversed by Station Road. A flat area between the two baileys and the Chilton may have contained gardens in the C14. Higham 2015, 38–44.

CLAVERING, Essex (Private but partly visible from the churchyard). Rectangular moated enclosure N of the church. Notable as a possible pre-Conquest castle, being tentatively identified with 'Robert's castle' of the *Anglo-Saxon Chronicle*. Clavering was held by Robert FitzWymarc, one of Edward the Confessor's Norman followers. RCHME 1916, 291–3; Brown 1989, 90–1.

CLIFFORD, Herefordshire (Private). Motte with two baileys rebuilt in stone. Probably the castle raised by William FitzOsbern (d. 1071) soon after the Conquest. By 1086 it was in the tenure of Ralph de Tosny, later coming to the Clifford family through marriage. Sited on a spur overlooking the river Wye, Clifford comprises (from E to W) a large bailey, a motte, and a small triangular bailey at the tip of the spur. Excavated remains of a stone gatehouse in a roughly central position within the inner bailey, with traces of a curtain wall extending to N and S, apparently dividing the bailey into two. The entrance consisted of a square tower and passage barbican, projecting behind and in front of the line of the curtain respectively. The barbican terminated in round turrets; a C13 or C14 date seems probable. On the motte are the remains of a shell-keep with five projecting round-fronted towers, the two eastern ones flanking the gateway which is aligned with the gatehouse in the bailey. A hall occupied the N side; this has a battered plinth surmounted by a half-roll moulding, features repeated on the NW tower (Rosamund's Tower) and found in a number of other early C13 marcher castles. RCHME 1931, 39–40; Remfry 1994a; Guy 2016–17a, 57–65.

CLITHEROE, Lancashire (Open). Natural motte and bailey on a hill S of the old town, centre of the honour of Clitheroe. It was probably established in the late C11 by Roger the Poitevin. In 1102 it was granted to Robert de Lacy and remained in the Lacy family until 1311 when it passed by marriage to Thomas, Earl of Lancaster, and in 1399 to the Crown. The craggy hill-top motte is crowned by a C12 two-storey square keep with clasping pilaster buttresses at the angles. Entry was at first-floor level via a plain semi-circular arched doorway in the centre of the N wall; it led to a tall room lit by two loops in semi-circular embrasures, but without a fireplace or a latrine. There is small mural vaulted chamber of unknown function in the SW angle. At the NW angle a spiral staircase ascended to the roof. A doorway in the S wall gave access to the wall walk of a shell wall enclosing the top of the motte, the greater part of which survives. The bailey fanned out to the SE, its former extent now partly occupied by the Steward's House (S), and the Court House (Museum). Fragments of bailey wall survive to the N and SW. Farrar and Brownbill 1911, 360–72; Adams 2005/6.

CLOPHILL, Bedfordshire. See **CAINHOE**.

CLUN, Shropshire (Open – EH). Motte with two baileys, probably built by Picot de Say in the late C11 to guard the Welsh border. It came into the FitzAlan family through marriage in the 1150s. It was probably Richard FitzAlan, First Earl of Arundel and a veteran of Edward I's Welsh wars, who raised the keep towards the end of the C13. Sited in a loop of the river Clun, which meanders around its S and W sides; the motte (a scarped natural hill) is close to the river and the baileys to the E and SE. Access was from the E via the small bailey (now a bowling green), and then via a causeway to the much larger S bailey, which was connected to the motte. On top of

Clun: Great tower looking NW from the motte.

the motte are fragments of a C13 curtain wall including two semi-circular towers on the W side. The main stone feature, however, is the great tower built onto the N side of the motte, its N wall rising from the ditch and giving an exaggerated sense of height. Three main storeys over a basement; the two upper floors being supplied with small mural rooms within the thickened northern angles. Remfry 1994b; Guy 2016–17a, 95–107; Duckers 2006, 60–4.

COCKERMOUTH, Cumberland (Private). Stone courtyard castle first mentioned in 1221, probably built by William de Forz after he received the manor in 1215. In 1323 the castle came to the Lucy family, and from *c*.1381 to the Percys when Maud Lucy married Henry Percy, Earl of Northumberland, under whom substantial re-building took place. Cockermouth Castle sits on a promontory between the rivers Cocker and Derwent enclosing a roughly triangular site, the base to the E and the apex to the W, the latter emphasised by a half-round tower. The entrance (E) front is

Cockermouth: The outer gatehouse (*c*.1385).

framed by the square Flag Tower to the L (S) and the rectangular gatehouse to the R (N), both late C14. In front of the central gateway a single-storey barbican, and above, a series of heraldic shields pointing to a date in the 1380s. The outer (E) ward has been much rebuilt, and the main medieval interest lies in the range separating it from the inner (W) ward; this was completed by the mason Roger de Barton under a contract of 1383. The high threshold of the projecting gatehouse portal indicates the difference in height between the two wards. There were lodgings to each side of the gatehouse, and, at the N end, a rectangular great kitchen tower. To the W of this, ranged along the curtain is the site of the earlier (mid to late C14) great hall and chamber block. Curwen 1911; Perriam and Robinson 1998, 90–1.

COCKLAW TOWER, West Errington, Northumberland (Private). Tower house built by the Errington family in the C15. Built of large, squared masonry, rectangular in plan and three storeys high, with a first-floor offset. Ground-floor entrance in the centre of the S end, with pointed arch made of two stones, a form that is found throughout the building. Above, at parapet level, are the corbels of a former machicolated turret. The doorway gives access to an entrance passage with doorways on the R (E) to a spiral staircase ascending to the upper floors and roof, and straight ahead (N) to the main vaulted room, lit only by a single window on the N wall, clearly for storage only. The best-appointed room is on the first floor; it has a fireplace, latrine and two-light windows with stone benches in the embrasures and a mural chamber in the S wall with trap in the floor giving access to a vaulted strongroom at ground-floor level. A doorway in the E wall served either as an external entrance, accessed via a staircase, or a means of communication with another building via a bridge. A second-floor room of similar size has a fireplace but no latrine. Knowles 1895; Emery 1996, 70–1.

COCKLEPARK TOWER, Northumberland (Private). A late C15 tower house of the Ogle family, built sometime after 1465. Tree-ring dating of the roof timbers over the main block suggest that the building was reroofed *c.*1602. Reverse L-shaped plan with short projection of the solar (N) wing towards the E containing the staircase. The main block to the S of the wing was remodelled in the late C18, an operation that included refenestration with small-pane sashes, and the main interest lies in the solar wing. On the (E) front of the stair wing is a panel containing a defaced achievement of arms, recorded in the 1820s as that of Ogle, who came into the property in 1465. In the N wall at first-floor level is a 2014 replica of the original window removed to Bothal Castle (qv) in the 1830s: two tiers of trefoil-headed lights surmounted by tracery beneath a four-centred arch with returned hood mould. Circular corner bartizans and the parapet of the N wall are carried on machicolated corbelling. The entrance is a Tudor-arched door in the E front, next to the wing. On the R (N) is the access to the spiral staircase which ascends to the first and second floors. The ground floor contained the kitchen, equipped with a large fireplace against the N wall with adjacent oven. At first-floor level, the embrasure of the restored window contains stone benches. Emery 1996, 71–2.

COLCHESTER, Essex (Open). Keep and bailey castle founded by William I on the site of the Roman temple of Claudius, the bailey roughly co-terminus with the extent of the temple precinct (Insula 22) and the keep built on top of the temple podium. The greater part of the castle is situated within Castle Park where the N and E sides of the bailey ditch are still to be seen, the southern and western extents of the bailey being represented broadly by High Street and Maidenburg Street respectively. The keep, which occupied a central position, is distinguished by being largest great tower in Europe by area, a consequence of its plan having been to a great extent determined by that of the podium.

Colchester: The apsidal-ended arm of the great tower housing the chapel from the NE.

Rectangular plan with rectangular corner turrets and, projecting from the S end of the E side, a semi-circular apse denoting the position of the chapel. The affinities of the plan are with the White Tower (Tower of London, qv), and earlier towers in Normandy (notably Ivry-la-Bataille). A high battered plinth encases the Roman vaults and rises to a chamfered offset at entrance level, above which there are two storeys; there was probably a third floor as well. The main block and the apse are articulated with pilaster buttresses. Examination of the fabric (small, squared rubble masonry alternating with levelling courses of Roman tile and ashlar quoins) reveals two phases of construction. At a height roughly equating to first-floor level, the ashlar quoins disappear, and a line of infilled battlements can be made out, indicating a hiatus in the construction programme; the threat of a Danish invasion in 1075 has been considered as a possible explanation.

The ground-floor entrance, which is in the S front hard up against the SW turret, probably dates from of *c*.1100, replacing an earlier entrance in the same position. Semi-circular arch with three roll-moulded orders, the two inner ones on shafts and capitals, and an outer arch with a moulding resembling two-tier arcading. It was protected by a portcullis and gave access to an entrance lobby now divided by an arcade; on the L (W) is the entrance to the great spiral stair housed in the SW turret; to the R (E), beyond the arcade, is a well. Beyond this, two more compartments, both entered from the N, are ranged along the S front including the sub-crypt of the chapel. The greater part of the block to the N was divided longitudinally, into one wide (W) and one narrow (E) room, a pattern that was repeated at first-floor level and possibly at the lost second-floor level too.

The larger western section is now one large space open to the roof, and occupied by the museum galleries, but was originally subdivided by a N–S arcade certainly at the lower level (where structural evidence survives) and probably at the upper levels (as indicated by the spacing of the first-floor windows in the N wall). The ground floor was primarily for storage, but the first floor contained living accommodation, perhaps a hall (W) and chamber (E). Small loops below, more frequent windows above in large semicircular-arched embrasures with long stepped sills; semicircular-arched fireplaces with rounded backs in herringbone pattern brickwork. Drury 1982; Marshall 2009–10.

COMPTON, Devon (Open – NT). Fortified manor house built in three main medieval phases by the Gilbert family. The oldest element of which we have knowledge is an early to mid C14 hall aligned E–W and occupying a roughly central position. This received substantial additions in the mid C15, including chamber and service wings at its E and W ends respectively, both extending beyond the front (N) elevation of the hall to create a forecourt, and a block of service buildings to the rear (S), arranged around a courtyard, though only the E side of this rear complex survives. In the second half of the C15 this greater complex was fortified with towers and an encompassing curtain wall, embellished by the SE corner tower. The hall was rebuilt in 1955 on the medieval foundations, where possible using existing evidence for the reconstruction of the detail.

Compton Castle is approached from the N via an outer courtyard, formerly contained by the late C15 defences, but now lacking its outer gatehouse. Stretching right across the farther (S) side of this outer court is the inner entrance front, mainly late C15, but incorporating the ends of the E and W wings (their gables peeping up behind the parapet), the position of the first-floor chapel in the W wing identifiable by its large, pointed window; the wings are now linked by a wall containing the central main gateway. This entrance is flanked by a pair of buttresses corbelled out at the top to carry a machicolated outer arch and upper storey from which a portcullis was operated. To each side is a corbelled box machicolation. Breaking forward at each end is a buttressed tower with box machicolation and an adjacent gateway, the E gate a smaller version of the main gate.

The side gates give access to the courtyard between the curtain and the domestic buildings, the main gate to a courtyard in front of the hall. The hall gives a reasonably faithful impression of the C14 building, both windows and roof being fairly authentic reconstructions of the originals, the windows suggesting a date in the first half of the century. Survival of the original fabric includes elements of the cross-passage doorways, service and staircase doorways in the cross passage and part of a staircase doorway at the upper (W) end. Better survival of doorways and fireplaces in the more private chambers of the W wing. In the northern part of the wing is the barrel-vaulted chapel, rising through two storeys, with an E window like that to the N and a cinquefoil-headed piscina. A squint in the S wall and a first-floor level two-light opening allowed occupants of the adjoining rooms to view proceedings. Another high barrel-vaulted ceiling is to be found over the kitchen which has a large fireplace extending across the E wall with associated ovens. Emery 2006, 519–22.

CONISBROUGH, Yorkshire West Riding (Open – EH) (Plate V). Two-courtyard castle with an unusual eye-catching keep, built atop a scarped natural hill *c.*1165–90 by Hamelin Plantagenet, and his wife the Countess of Surrey. The approach is from the SW, through the outer ward, a flat area at the foot of the hill now containing the visitor centre; it is defined by earthworks, but there is no visible stonework. From here a short climb to the inner ward, which was built of stone from the beginning, and which occupies the top of the hill. It is roughly D-shaped with the entrance in the centre of the bowed curtain which extends around the S, E and W sides, and which was punctuated by six solid, semi-circular towers. The entrance is prefaced by a C13 passage barbican, now in fragmentary condition, which curves around the curtain, passing one of the wall towers on the way, to end in front of the gatehouse. From this position it is possible to look down on part of the S curtain, which at some stage in the castle's history has become dislocated and slipped down the slope. The N, W and SW sides of the courtyard were lined with buildings, now mostly reduced to foundation level. The hall with its attendant service rooms and kitchen lay to the N, and the great chamber to the W. However, even when they stood to full height, none of these buildings could have detracted from the sheer dominating presence of the four-storey keep, accentuated no doubt by the strikingly original plan and comparatively small courtyard.

Cylindrical, with six semi-hexagonal buttress turrets and a steeply battered base, the form of the keep is strictly geometrical. The quality of the ashlar masonry and its detailing are superb, the work of highly skilled practitioners at the height of their powers, the ashlar blocks contrasting markedly with the slightly later rubble curtain wall by which it is abutted. The first-floor entrance on the SE side has a joggled lintel with round relieving arch and plain tympanum; above it, at second-floor level, a two-light window with a similar head and a wide mullion. Both are unadorned and in keeping with the streamlined character of the keep. The first floor is simply an

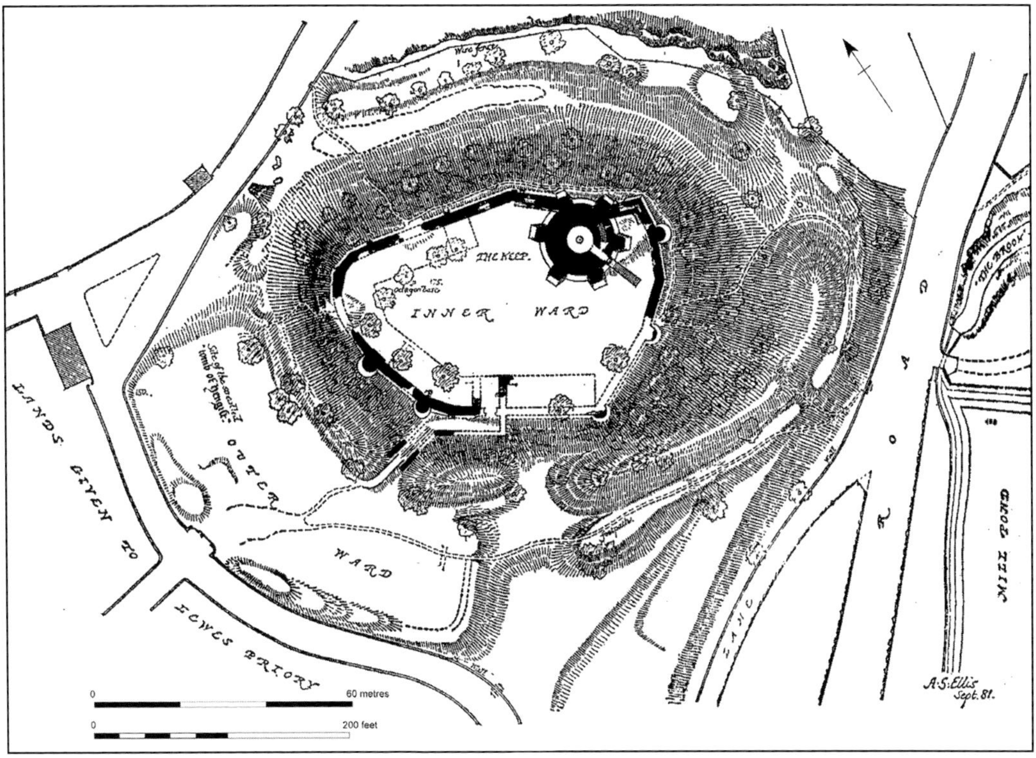

Conisbrough: Ground plan. From Clark 1884.

Conisbrough: Floor plans of the keep (*c*.1165–90). From Clark 1884.

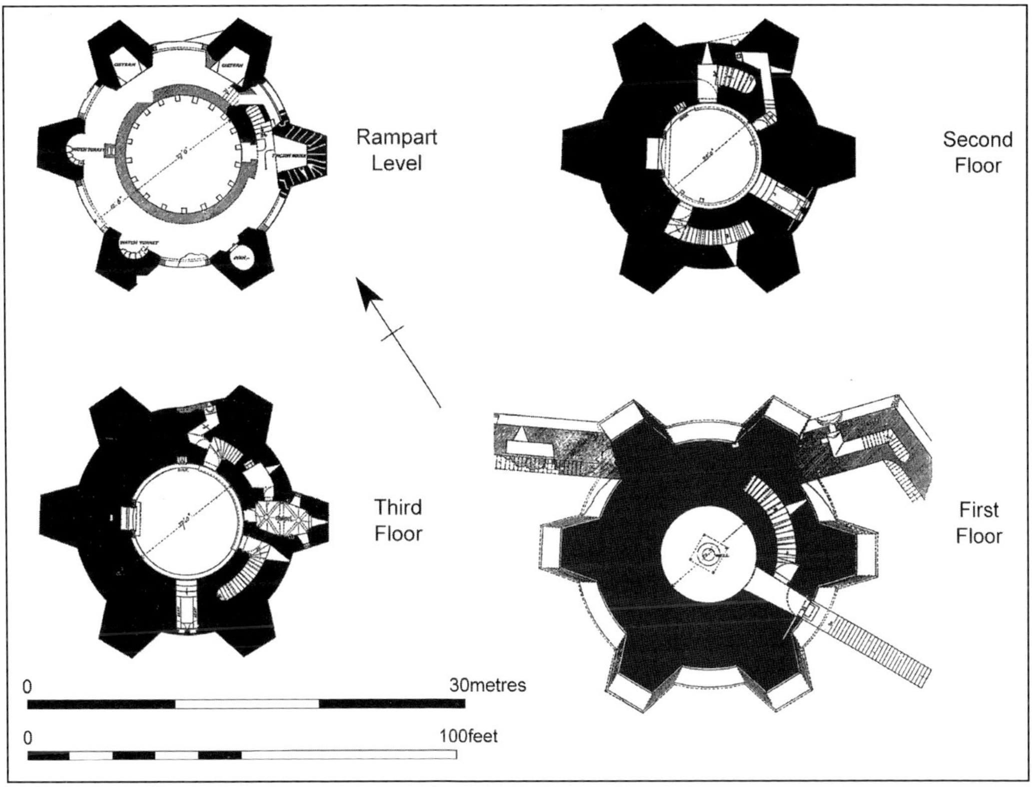

entrance hall with a circular hole in the centre of the floor allowing access to a well in the vaulted basement. Just inside the doorway a stately mural stair winds its way up to the second floor, which is where the living accommodation began.

At the top of the stairs a lobby, and then into the circular room within the body of the tower equipped with a large, hooded fireplace, a laver, or wash basin, a latrine, and window seats within the large embrasure of the window above the doorway. Opposite the entrance a doorway to another staircase leading to the second floor and another living room with similar facilities to the one below, and, in addition, a chapel housed in the E turret. This little chapel is the only space within the tower in which the sculptors have been allowed to ply their craft; demi-columns with elaborately carved capitals, chevron-moulded rib-vaulting with sculptured bosses and shafted E window with chevron-moulded arch. Trefoil-headed piscinas and porthole windows with quatrefoil cusping to N and S sides, and, to the N too, a doorway leading to a vestry also with piscina. Another stair leads to the wall walk; the current roof at this level dates from the 1990s, but in the buttresses around the periphery, are signs of domestic activity including an oven, water cistern housings and a dovecote. A smaller version of the keep was built at the Warenne castle of Mortemer, in northern France. Clark 1888, 431–53; Sands and Braun 1934; Brindle 2012; Brindle and Sadrei 2015; Davis 2015–16.

COOLING, Kent (Private). Two-courtyard quadrangular castle built for John Lord Cobham between *c.*1381, when he received a licence to 'fortify and crenellate the mansion of his manor of Coulyng', and 1385. An enamelled copper plaque fixed to the outer gatehouse proclaims the circumstances to the world: 'Knouwyth that beth and

Cooling: Ground plan. From Scott Robinson 1877.

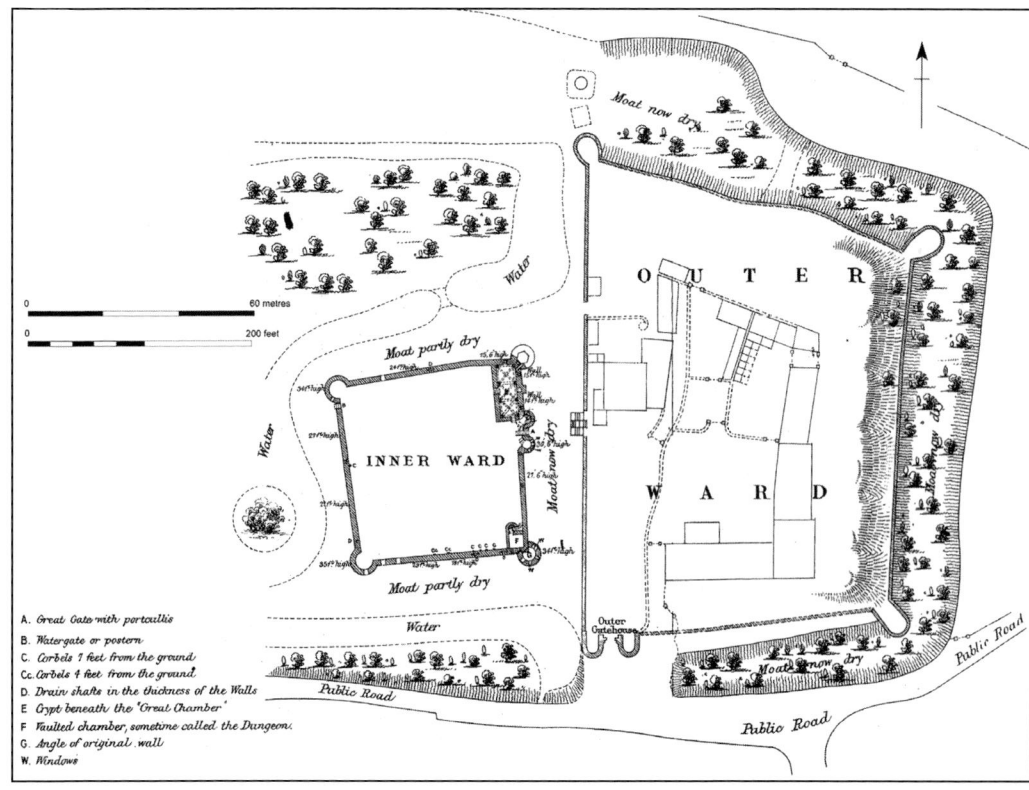

Cooling: Outer gatehouse from the SE. 1381.

schul be/ That I am mad in help of the cuntre/ In knowyng of whyce thyng/ Thys is chartre and wytnessyng'. The fortification of the manor house is said to be a response to a French raid of 1379 on the Thames estuary. The mason contractors were William Sharnhale and Thomas Crump of Maidstone who built the great gatehouse. Henry Yevele, who took measurements as a check on piecework payments, may have been the designer.

Cooling is situated on the Hoo peninsula about two miles from the Thames estuary. The castle consists of a large outer (E) ward and a considerably smaller inner (W) ward, both irregularly quadrangular with rounded corner towers and formerly moated. Entry is from the main road to the S via Crump's now-isolated great gatehouse, which stood at the W end of the S curtain. This rather squat yet striking building is dominated by its two round-fronted flanking towers with prominent arched machicolations carried on three-tier corbelling. High on the RH (E) tower, the famous plaque, and, to the R of it a circular gun port. Gateway with four-centred arch recessed beneath another four-centred arch with a portcullis groove running between them. Crenellated parapet above with a shield bearing Lord Cobham's arms on the central merlon. The remains of towers survive at the other three corners.

The better-preserved inner (W) ward was formerly approached via a drawbridge to a gatehouse in the E wall, also twin-towered with inverted keyhole gun ports, features found in the corner towers too. To the R (N) of the gatehouse, contrasting with the ragstone-faced walls elsewhere in the castle, is a fine stretch of curtain in flushwork in which knapped flint alternates with ragstone in a chequerboard pattern. This wall fronted the great chamber, which occupied the NE corner of the ward, and was evidently intended to ornament and highlight this important building. Only the basement survives; it was covered with quadripartite vaulting of which part remains. Scott Robertson 1887; Vallance 1927; Knoop *et al.* 1934; Goodall 2011, 312–14.

CORBRIDGE VICAR'S PEEL, Northumberland (Public house). Tower house vicarage interrupting the line of the churchyard wall. Recorded in 1415, it probably dates from the late C14. Built of large stone blocks, probably recycled Roman material, this rectangular tower rises through three storeys; at parapet level are the remains of square machicolated corner turrets. Ground-floor doorway with pointed arch made up of two stones only (cf. Cocklaw qv). This leads to the vaulted basement lit only by a pair of narrow loops and to a mural staircase ascending to the living accommodation. Off the first-floor landing is a stone sink; the main room at this level has a fireplace, two wall lockers, two trefoil-headed windows with seats lining the embrasures and use of a latrine just off the staircase landing leading to the second floor. The second-floor room is far more austere, the only facility being a mural recess described as a book rest. Knowles 1898; Emery 1996, 72–3.

CORFE CASTLE, Dorset (Open – NT). Spectacularly sited but badly ruined large royal courtyard castle established in the late C11 by William I and developed substantially by subsequent monarchs over the next two centuries. It may have been preceded by a Saxon royal residence, possibly the scene of King Edward the Martyr's murder in 978. The full extent of William's castle is unknown, but it certainly included the inner bailey, which occupies the summit of the natural hill on which the castle is sited, and may have taken in the whole of the later enclosed area, but apart from the 'Old Hall' in the W bailey, only the inner bailey seems to have been built in stone. Henry I built the keep within the inner bailey *c.*1105, perhaps to house Robert of Normandy who was imprisoned here, but it was King John who was largely responsible for the transformation of Corfe into a wholly stone castle and a stylish royal residence. John's work, which was carried out 1201–15, included the rebuilding of the W bailey defences in stone, upgrading the accommodation of the inner ward by raising a new courtyard house known as the 'Gloriette', excavation of the Great Ditch that isolates the inner and W baileys from the outer bailey, and perhaps the partial reconstruction of the outer bailey defences in stone. Henry III probably built the inner gatehouse in the 1240s and Edward I the outer gatehouse in the 1280s. In 1572 Corfe ceased to be a royal castle, but it was held for the King in the Civil War when it underwent two sieges. In 1646 Parliament ordered its destruction, explosives being used in its demolition. Consequently, the buildings are mere shadows of their former

A Guide to the Medieval Castles of England

selves, although the castle retains great presence owing to its outstanding topography, the soaring remains of the keep, and the dramatic signs of destruction.

Spanning the ditch between the town and castle is a stone bridge, largely C16 but retaining C13 elements. It leads to the late C13 outer gatehouse, with high segmental arch and semi-circular flanking towers. Two semi-circular corner towers to R (E) and L (W) of the gatehouse also form part of the entrance front. There is a steady climb from outer to inner gatehouse. On the way are three more wall towers along the W side of the outer bailey, but only one on the E side; this latter is the Plukenet Tower, named after a heraldic shield of Alan de Plukenet on the outer side, and therefore datable to his time as constable of the castle (*c*.1265–70); it stands at the end of King John's Great Ditch, the other end of which curves round in front of the inner (South-West) gatehouse. This gatehouse has one apsidal-ended tower to the R (E) and a three-quarter round tower to the L (W) projecting beyond the W curtain in a semi-circle like the wall towers on this side. The two flanks of the gatehouse are split asunder, and the LH (W) side has slipped a little way down the hill; this side incorporates a first-floor latrine turret which discharged outside the curtain. Then, on to the W bailey, its curtain of 1201–4 with a semi-circular tower to N and S and, at the W end, the Butavant Tower, a building of hexagonal plan. The N tower was semi-hexagonal internally, rooflines on the surviving walls show an unusual pattern of inverted

Corfe Castle: Ground plan. After RCHME 1970.

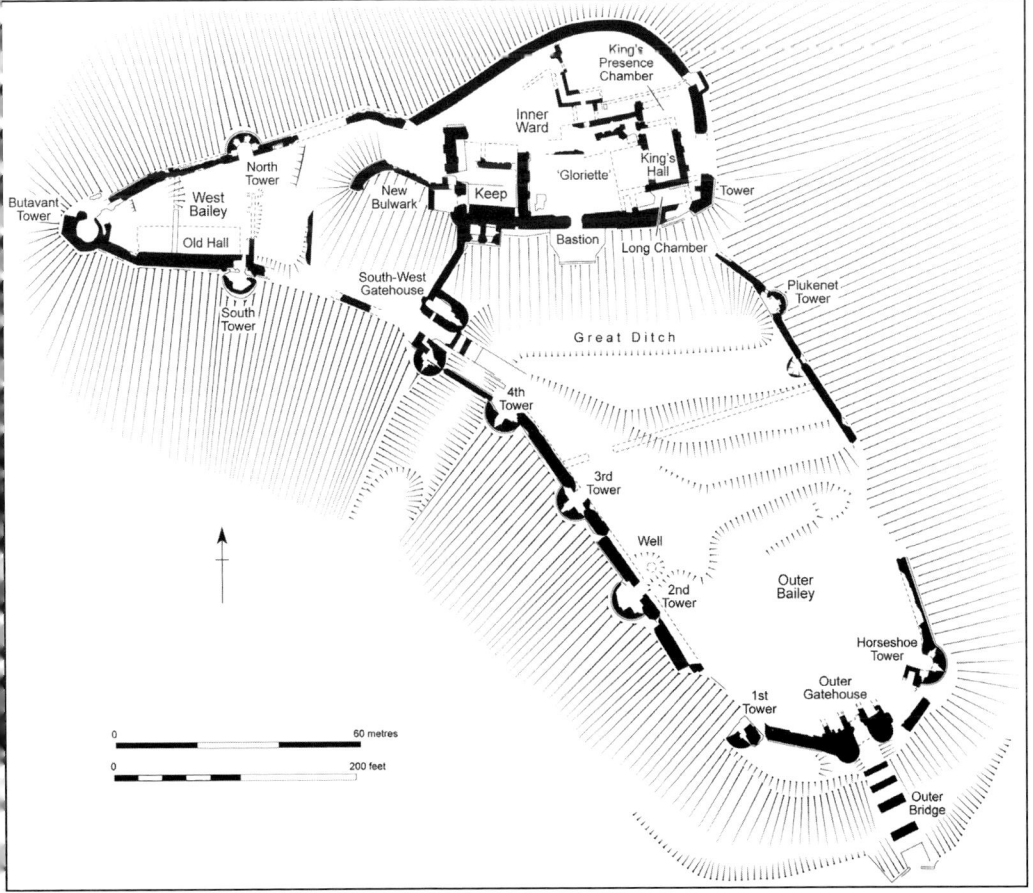

Corfe Castle from the SW.

V-shapes implying a series of drainage valleys within the walls. On the S side of the bailey is the site of the C11 Old Hall, its one surviving wall against the C13 curtain displaying herringbone masonry and blocked round-headed window embrasures.

Finally, the inner bailey, the high point of the site both literally and metaphorically. The curtain, which contains herringbone masonry, dates from the C11. Hard up against it on the S side of the bailey is Henry I's keep, perhaps built to house Robert Duke of Normandy after his capture and imprisonment in 1106–7. A rectangular building extending a good way across the bailey and dominating the approach on the N side, it was articulated by pilaster buttresses and chamfered offsets and decorated with a frieze of blind arcading around the upper stage. There is a forebuilding at the S end of the W side and an annexe on the S side projecting beyond the curtain, both slightly later additions to the main block. Within the forebuilding is a first-floor doorway with engaged shafts, tympanum and moulded round arch. Originally, there were two main floors over a basement, the second floor being divided in the C13 to create another storey just under the double-pile roof, the outline of which can be seen in the S wall, along with the second-floor offset and the inserted joist sockets and fireplace for the third floor.

The other main component within the inner ward is King John's Gloriette, which occupies the SE corner of the bailey, the main survival from this quadrangular courtyard complex being the E range, where a first-floor hall or great chamber sits on a vaulted undercroft. To the L (N) are the remains of the walls which flanked the staircase leading to the first-floor entrance. Although the porch has largely disappeared the pointed doorway survives; it has a chamfered and roll-moulded surround and a hood-mould with mutilated stops. Around it is some of the excellent-quality ashlar masonry that is a characteristic of the Gloriette. The hall, or great chamber, was lit by elegant, pointed windows also with hood-mould on sculptured stops, inside they have segmental-pointed embrasures containing stone benches. RCHME 1970, 57–78; Ashbee 2004; Reeve and Thurlby 2005.

The Rings (Cromwell's Battery). A probable siege castle built by King Stephen's men in 1139 to facilitate the investment of Corfe Castle. It lies some 400 yards (366m) from Corfe Castle, and is strategically sited to control the road from the W. It seems to have been reoccupied during the Civil War when it played a part in the final sieges of Corfe Castle, after which it took on its former sobriquet of 'Cromwell's Battery'. The Rings takes the form of a ringwork and bailey, the ditched and banked ringwork close to the road, which has encroached upon its outer defences. A gap in the defences to the SE is the entrance to and from the U-shaped bailey, this latter defended on the NE side by a bank and ditch, and on the SW and SE sides by a scarp, with elements of an inner bank. Wright and Creighton 2016, 40–8.

CRAWLEY TOWER, Northumberland (Private). Remains of a four-storey tower built of large dressed stone blocks for Sir John Heron a scion of the Herons of Ford Castle (qv) under a licence of 1343. By 1541 it was 'in greatt decaye for lacke of contynuall reparac'ons'. Now part of a larger farm complex, it formerly stood within the SE corner of roughly rectangular enclosure defined by a ditch and outer bank, of which the N and W sides are still to be seen. The tower has a rectangular plan some 50ft (15.2m) by 36½ft (11.2m). Although the S and W walls survive nearly to full height, the other two sides survive to a much lesser extent; an C18 cottage occupies the interior. C14 windows of twin lancet lights with monolithic lintels survive of the S side. Whether this was a solar tower, or a self-contained tower house, is uncertain. Dodds 1935, 408–14.

CRAYKE, Yorkshire North Riding (Private). Hilltop castle of the bishops of Durham, probably a motte and bailey in origin, with substantial C15 stone additions forming two distinct residential blocks. The earlier of the two is sited on the SW edge of the hilltop; its main component is a rectangular four-storey solar tower with floor-level offsets. There is a ground-floor entrance at the E end, and separate first- and second-floor entrances at the E end of the N side, formerly approached by a staircase. A little further to the N was the great hall; in 1441 Bishop Robert Neville began the construction of a kitchen and larder, of which the basement survives built up against the N wall of the tower; it was entered from the E and is covered by a ribbed barrel-vault. According to Leland, the second building complex, which sits on top of the presumed motte to the NE was also built by Bishop Neville. Now in ruins, it too was a tower, four storeys in height, the basements vaulted throughout, and consisting of two rectangular blocks, one containing the hall, the other containing the parlour. Emery 1996, 327–9.

CRESSWELL, Northumberland (Private). C15 or early C16 tower house. In the C18 a 'mansion' and attached chapel to the N of the tower were pulled down and a new house built on their site, attached to the tower; this house was demolished in the mid C19, but the imprint of a roofline remains on the N face. Three-storey rectangular tower with ground- and first-floor entrances towards the E end of the N elevation. Above these, at parapet level, a machicolated projection, the only traces of which are now the cut-off three-tier corbel supports immediately R (W) of the second-floor window. The barrel-vaulted basement was for storage. A broad staircase in the NE angle rises to the first floor, formerly divided into a large (E) and smaller (W) room by a timber partition. Fireplaces in both rooms and a latrine in the inner chamber. A similar configuration of rooms at second-floor level, reached by a spiral stair in the NE angle, lack fireplaces and latrine. Ryder 2003.

CREWKERNE (Croft Castle, Castle Hill), Somerset (Private). Probable site of the castle of Baldwin de Redvers, Earl of Devon, first mentioned in 1148 and sited on the top of Castle Hill approximately 2 miles to the NW of Crewkerne. Excavation by Time Team in 2011 discovered the foundations of a rectangular stone building, some 55ft × 42ft (17m × 13m) with 10ft (3m) thick walls, probably a great tower, or keep, containing a probable well, and one of three surrounding ditches indicated by geophysical survey. The pottery indicated a C12 construction date and demolition in the C13. Dunning 1995, 35–7; Time Team 2012.

CROFT, Herefordshire (Open – NT). Much-altered quadrangular courtyard castle with small cylindrical corner towers. Suggested dates for the primary structure include the late C14, mid C14, early C15, mid C15, early C16, late C16 and early C17. Unfortunately, the fabric, which is the product of a complicated building history, does not allow certainty on the matter. A house may have occupied the site since 1086 when the manor was held by Bernard de Croft, and, according to William Worcester, a Croft Castle existed by *c.*1480. In the mid C16 Leland described Croft as 'sett on the browe of a hill, somewhat rokky, dichid and waulled castle like'. These references are too vague to be of much help, but they do provide substance for the view taken here that the basic structure dates from the C15. Of the putative medieval castle only the S range and the greater part of the W range survive, albeit much altered. The earliest details are of C16 date, the N range was rebuilt in the C17 and the E range in the C18. RCHME 1934, 35–6; Croft 1949; Emery 2000, 529–30; Uhlman 1993.

CUCKNEY (Castle Hill), Nottinghamshire (Open access). Motte with two baileys probably raised during the mid C12 for the 'warlike' Thomas de Cuckney, an adherent of King Stephen during the Anarchy. The sub-rectangular inner bailey which is occupied by the church and its associated graveyard also contains a low motte at the NW corner. The inner bailey ditch lies outside the churchyard wall, and to the N and W are the remains of a double bank and ditch denoting the former existence of an outer bailey, which may also have extended around the E and S sides. Barley 1951.

DACRE, Cumberland (Private). Fortified manor house of which the main survival is a great tower. Built by one of the Dacres in the mid to late C14. The site was enclosed by a rectangular moat, of which elements remain to the W. The tower, which occupied the E half of the enclosure, has a singular plan: rectangular with boldly projecting corner turrets, diagonal to the NW and SE, square set to the NE and SW, the former containing a spiral staircase serving all floors. Curwen 1913, 269–72; Emery 1996, 204; Perriam and Robinson 1998, 182–3.

DALLY, Northumberland (Open access). C13 hall house converted into a tower house in the C14. Probably the strong house being erected by Sir David de Lindsey in 1237. The castle overlooks Chirdon Burn, a tributary of the North Tyne. It is defended by ditches to the NW and SE and by scarps to the NE and SW. The C13 house contained a first-floor hall over a vaulted basement equipped with splayed-base arrow loops. At a later date the loops were blocked, and the building was raised into a tower with turrets at three of the angles and buttresses to the two long sides. Dodds 1940, 273–80; Emery 1996, 74–5.

DANBY, Yorkshire North Riding (Private). Small quadrangular castle of integrated plan. Probably built for William Lord Latimer between *c.*1350 and 1381, and perhaps completed by his daughter Elizabeth and her husband John Lord Neville of Raby (qv). The ruins are now occupied by a farmhouse and ancillary buildings. Rectangular plan with diagonally orientated towers (of different proportions N and S) projecting from the four corners. The entrance range was on the W, the hall range to the E, and the kitchen and services in the N range. Danby's significance lies in its symmetrical plan and the part it played in the development of the quadrangular castle in England. Page 1923, 334–8; Emery 1996, 329.

DEDDINGTON, Oxfordshire (Open access – EH). Motte and bailey built on a Saxon site soon after 1066 probably for Odo, Bishop of Bayeux; it may have been the caput of his Oxfordshire lands. Rebuilt in stone by William de Chesney from *c.*1157; in decline from the mid C13, being robbed of building stone by the late C14. Now occupied by a playing field, only a remnant of the motte survives, but something of the castle's structural history was revealed by excavation in the 1970s. It began life as a banked enclosure with a motte at the E end. Still in the C11, an L-shaped stone building was constructed to the W of the motte, and later (late C11 or early C12), immediately W of this, the bailey was divided by the construction of a bank and ditch, into a large outer (W) bailey and much smaller inner (E) bailey. In the mid C12 the inner bailey received a curtain wall, which was subsequently strengthened by a gatehouse, and by a tower on the motte, by this time partly demolished. Several buildings were erected in the C13 including a hall and a chapel, and it may have been at this stage that the motte was truncated. Ivens 1984.

DEVIZES, Wiltshire (Private but visible from outside). Motte with two baileys probably raised by Osmund, Bishop of Salisbury (1078–99). Robert, Duke of Normandy, was held prisoner here from 1106. Besieged and captured by King Stephen in 1139, subsequently seized by Empress Matilda and passed on to her son, Henry of Anjou. On Henry's succession as Henry II, Devizes became a royal castle, and remained so for the rest of the medieval period. Now, the only visible remains of the medieval castle are elements of the earthworks, notably the very substantial motte and its surrounding ditch and part of the inner bailey to the E; an outer bailey, further to the E, has been engulfed by the town. There was a stone keep on the SE side of the motte and next to it an aisled hall, the foundations of which were uncovered by excavation. A C19 Gothic house known as Devizes Castle now occupies the NE side of the motte. A stone wall around the grounds of the C19 site incorporates medieval masonry. Brown *et al.* 1963, 626–8; Baggs *et al.* 1975, 237–45; Emery 2006, 627–9.

DONNINGTON, Berkshire (Open – EH). Stone courtyard castle notable for its great gatehouse, which is now the only upstanding element. Built under a licence to crenellate of 1386 for Richard de Abberbury, one of Richard II's guardians. The castle, with the exception of the gatehouse, was demolished in 1646 after a 19-month siege. Strategically situated at the junction of the London–Bristol and Oxford–Southampton roads, the castle has a symmetrical plan: rectangular with a semi-decagonal W end, four cylindrical angle towers and two square mid-wall towers (N and S). Projecting boldly from the centre of the E front is a three-storey rectangular gatehouse with cylindrical flanking towers incorporating the wall stubs of a former barbican. The towers stand on battered bases and rise through five stages articulated by offsets, the uppermost rising above the main block. There is a very strong sense of verticality. Central four-centred gate arch with moulded surround; above is a small and then a large square-framed window each with moulded hood mould returning to the sides to create a continuous string with the offsets which are themselves embellished with gargoyles. The gate passage was protected by a portcullis and doors at each end and is covered by a lierne vault. The other castle walls are reduced to their lowest courses. Page and Ditchfield 1924, 93–4; Emery 2006, 83–5.

DORSTONE (Castle Tump), Herefordshire (Visible from a footpath on the SE side). Motte with two baileys on the SW side of the village next to a tributary of the river Dore. Date uncertain but possibly of C11 origin. The motte was formerly surmounted by a shell-keep and traces of stonework have been noted in the kidney-shaped bailey to the NE. The second bailey to the SW is less well-defined. RCHME 1931, 57; Shoesmith 2009, 101–2.

DOVER, Kent (Open – EH). One of the key royal castles of England (along with Windsor and the Tower of London), and guardian of the nearest point of embarkation and arrival from continental Europe, Dover was endowed with a singular strategic and symbolic significance for the monarchs of England, who at different times also ruled large parts of what is now France. Sited on Castle Hill, a promontory above the town and harbour ending in a sea cliff, the castle was founded very soon after the Battle of Hastings; it may occupy the site of a prehistoric hillfort and an Anglo-Saxon *burh*; the Romans also made their presence felt by the construction of a lighthouse, or *pharos*, on Castle Hill and of a fort next to the harbour. In 1067 a rebellion led by Eustace, Count of Boulogne, made an unsuccessful assault on the castle, then held by the King's half-brother Odo, Bishop of Bayeux, while William was away in Normandy.

The nature of the castle's defences in its early years are unknown, but from the 1160s Henry II began rebuilding in stone, a programme of work that included a rectangular keep, a surrounding inner curtain studded with rectangular towers, and the beginnings of a towered outer curtain along the NE side. The works were under the direction of one Maurice, a leading military engineer of this period, who had previously been involved in the construction of the keep at Newcastle (qv). Henry's scheme extended into the reign of his successor, Richard I, but petered out *c.*1196. The loss of Normandy to a resurgent France in 1204 prompted King John to revive the Dover project by continuing with the construction of the outer curtain to enclose the inner bailey. This later phase, distinguishable from the work of Henry's masons by the use of round-fronted towers, included a new twin-towered gatehouse at the N end of the promontory.

John's foresight was repaid in 1216, when Dover underwent a notable siege of several months by the forces of the French Dauphin, Prince Louis. The castle was bombarded from the high ground to the N, the barbican was captured, and miners brought down one of the gatehouse towers, but the garrison under the command of the constable, Hubert de Burgh, put up a vigorous defence, the assault was repelled, and ultimately the siege failed. However, the attack had highlighted weaknesses in the castle's defences, and in the years that followed, a major scheme of repair and

A Guide to the Medieval Castles of England

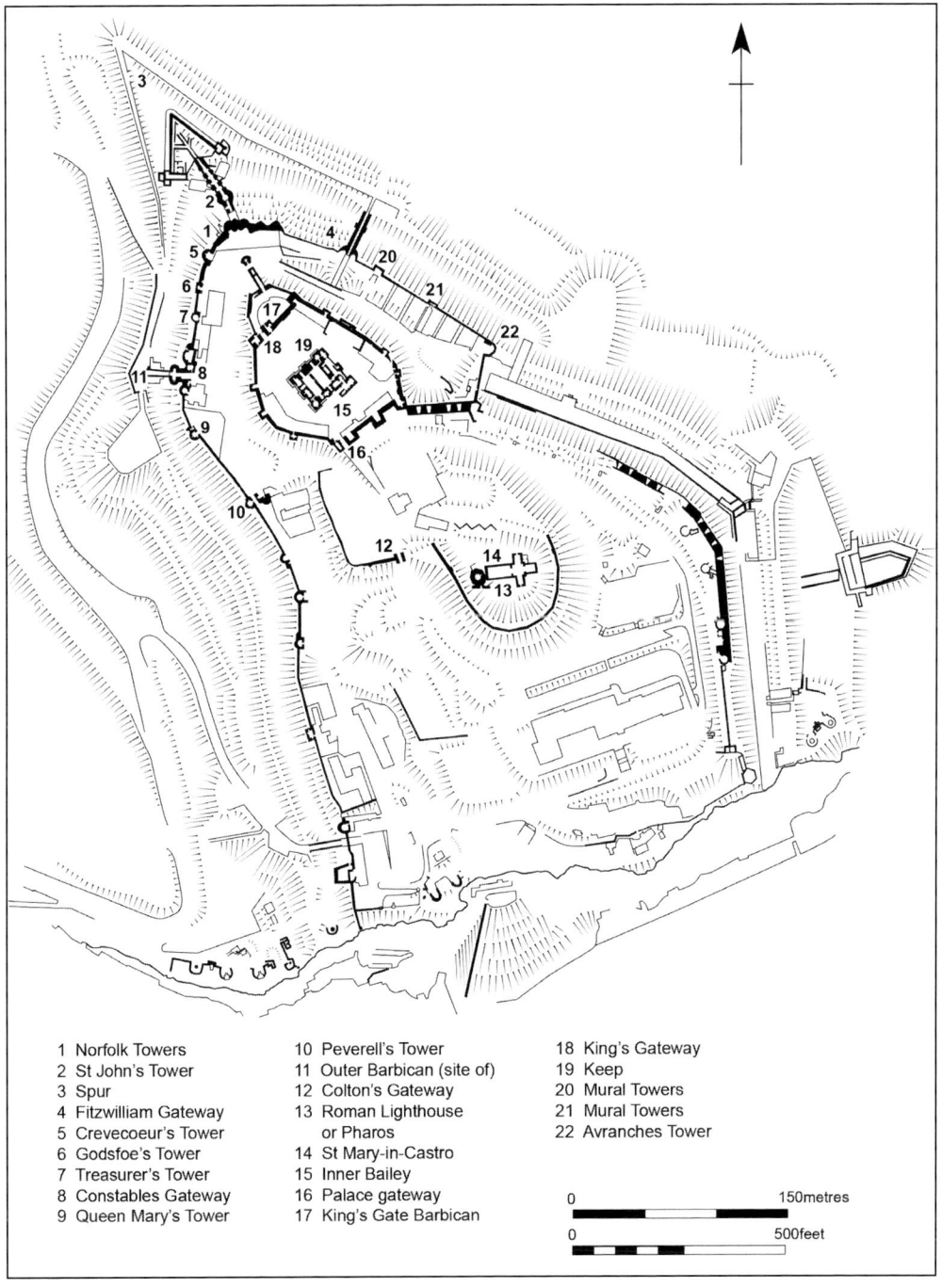

1 Norfolk Towers
2 St John's Tower
3 Spur
4 Fitzwilliam Gateway
5 Crevecoeur's Tower
6 Godsfoe's Tower
7 Treasurer's Tower
8 Constables Gateway
9 Queen Mary's Tower
10 Peverell's Tower
11 Outer Barbican (site of)
12 Colton's Gateway
13 Roman Lighthouse or Pharos
14 St Mary-in-Castro
15 Inner Bailey
16 Palace gateway
17 King's Gate Barbican
18 King's Gateway
19 Keep
20 Mural Towers
21 Mural Towers
22 Avranches Tower

Dover: Ground plan. After Code 1995.

Dover: King's Gate from the N, one of two gateways into the inner bailey (*c*.1170s–80s).

improvement was put into action. John's outer gateway, which had proved vulnerable to the besiegers, was blocked and replaced by a new outer gatehouse to the W, and the outer curtain was extended to the sea cliff. By *c*.1250 the castle was largely complete, and few later medieval alterations are now evident.

The promontory extends along a NW–SE axis (treated here as though it were N–S) and the castle defences enclose an irregularly triangular area with the apex to the N. This northern apex contained the barbican penetrated by Prince Louis' men in 1216. After the siege, the fallen tower of John's gateway was rebuilt as a solid bastion and became part of a cluster of three towers (known as the Norfolk Towers); the central one, which blocks the entrance, has a beaked front, a feature found in France and some other European countries, but in England only at Dover. A round tower (St John's Tower) was built in the ditch in front of the former gateway and beyond that a great spur was raised in the area of the old barbican to counter any future attempts to control the high ground to the N. One of the most interesting aspects of this scheme is that access to the spur was via a tunnel from the outer bailey under the old gatehouse to St John's Tower, whence a bridge extended over the ditch to the spur and into another tunnel which ended in three branches. Much of the system survives, albeit it partly rebuilt; the spur itself was remodelled in the C18. Further along the curtain to the E is the Fitzwilliam Gate, a postern flanked by two more beaked towers, under construction in 1227. It was entered across the bank and ditch by a tunnel and covered bridge.

These areas are not normally open to visitors; indeed, the greater part of the outer enceinte is inaccessible from the exterior. However, the W curtain is visible from the road and driveway, articulated (from L [N] to R [S]) by the Crevecoeur's, Godsfoe's and Treasurer's Towers. Then comes the Constable's Gate complex, and beyond it Queen Mary's Tower, and finally Peverell's Tower which marks the end of John's work. The Constable's Gate of 1221–7, which occupies the centre of this line of defence, is a singular building consisting of an outer portal, flat-faced, with rounded ends, placed in front of a D-shaped tower (supposedly one of John's wall towers reused), the top of which looms up behind the portal. This entrance is set within a cluster of round-fronted wall towers contemporary with the portal. This gatehouse was approached via the outer barbican which had its own gatehouse, now represented only by a low-walled enclosure on the outer side of the ditch.

On entering via the Constable's Gate, a turn to the R (S) takes us to Peverell's Gate, within the rear (E) projection of Peverell's Tower, which gave access to the citadel created by Henry II and John, from the southern half of the castle. The S front of the gateway is flanked on the R (E) by a round-fronted tower added by Henry III. Continuing S behind the outer curtain and then taking a path to the L and doubling back brings us to Colton's Gate, of John's time, which formed the entrance to a middle bailey. To the R (E) of this is a defensive bank topped by a wall; the bank probably dates from the 1220s and the wall from 1256; they define a horseshoe-shaped enclosure containing the Anglo-Saxon church of St Mary-in-Castro and the Roman *pharos* which was converted to serve as a bell tower. The church had fallen into ruin by the time it was restored by George Gilbert Scott in 1860–2. It comprises an aisleless nave, chancel and transepts and a crossing tower. A high-placed doorway at the W end led from a western gallery into the *pharos*.

From here it is a short step to Henry II's inner bailey, its curtain studded with truncated square towers on battered bases pierced by twin arrow loops to all three sides, an early example of a systematic approach to military engineering, which allowed volleys into the field and along the curtain wall from the comparative safety of the towers. There is a gatehouse at each end (N and S), each flanked by twin rectangular towers; the Palace Gate (S), which was probably the main entrance, has lost its barbican, but that of the King's Gate (N) survives, now approached by a ramp. In the middle of the inner bailey, surrounded by C18 and C20 buildings, is the imposing bulk of the late C12 great tower, or keep, a massive square-plan, three-storey building with corner and mid-wall turrets, exuding a sense of power, wealth and, above all, solidity.

Its entrance is on the S side via the most elaborate of all forebuildings which wraps around the SE corner and extends along the entire length of the E elevation. A short flight of steps leads N to a landing from which a door opens into the ground floor; this door, which was lockable by a bar, was probably a goods entrance, for the ground floor appears to have been mainly a storage/service area. Then, there is a right-angled turn into the forebuilding up to a first-floor vestibule (formerly closed by a door), arcaded on the E side, which also acted as the nave of a chapel, its richly decorated chancel lying straight ahead within the SE turret. A narrow mural chamber on the S side of the vestibule may have been a sacristy/vestry or a guardroom. From here, another door opened to the stairs along the E side of the building; then there was a drawbridge in front of another door, beyond which another flight of steps led to the second-floor entrance. A second-floor entrance was highly unusual, but a similar arrangement had been used by Maurice at Newcastle.

Apart from the service entrance at the base of the forebuilding, this second-floor doorway may have been the only access to the keep, leading to all levels via two spiral staircases. Within the entrance passage a doorway on the L (S) communicates with the well room, which contains evidence for an interesting example of domestic engineering. The well is at the far (S) end of the room and here is the only access to it. However, a recess in the E wall was the opening for a system of pipes allowing the distribution of water to the lower levels. A related system was installed by Maurice at Newcastle.

A cross-wall divides the main body of the tower into an outer (E) and inner (W) room, usually designated hall and chamber respectively at the two upper levels. On both floors each of these two rooms was provided with a latrine; they were situated back-to-back in the centre of the N wall and approached by mural passages. However, fireplaces do not seem to have been provided (all the fireplaces are C15 insertions), implying that heating was by braziers or open hearths; a practical-enough solution in the upper rooms, which were formerly open to the roof, so that louvres could draw off the smoke, but not so satisfactory at first-floor level, where ventilation was limited.

The second floor was at a slightly lower level than the forebuilding landing, so the hall had to be entered down a flight of steps, which is an odd feature difficult to explain, although it has been speculated that it was a contrivance for a staged entrance by the King, or other great lord, into a previously-assembled company. At the far (S) end of the upper hall there was access via a window embrasure, first to an antechamber and then to the Chapel of St Thomas Becket and an associated sacristy, lined with stone benches. The Becket chapel lies directly above the lower chapel. Like its counterpart, it is enriched with wall arcading, shafting, foliated capitals and chevron mouldings. The chapel is one of numerous small chambers at first and second-floor levels, most within the thickness of the main walls, that augment the main rooms. Their various functions are often uncertain, although several had fireplaces inserted in the C15.

To the E of the inner bailey and S of the Fitzwilliam Gate are the remains of Henry II's abortive outer curtain, a straight stretch of walling with two rectangular wall towers, but at the S end is the rather more interesting Avranches Tower, an important piece of military engineering. The tower, which is open backed, like the other wall towers, is polygonal, its several faces pierced by two tiers of multiple arrow loops to give a very wide range of fire. It is probably the first and most business-like of a small number of similarly-designed corner towers, that appear during the late C12 and early C13. Brown *et al.* 1963; Coad 1995; Pattison *et al.* 2020.

DRIFFIELD (Moot Hill), Yorkshire East Riding. See **GREAT DRIFFIELD**.

DUDLEY, Staffordshire (Open). Motte and bailey built by William FitzAnsculf and first mentioned in 1086. By *c.*1100 Dudley was in the possession of the Paynel family, and during their tenure the defences were probably rebuilt in stone. Gervaise Paynel took part in 1174 rebellion against Henry II, resulting in the slighting of the castle. Gervaise had no male heir and in 1194 his nephew, Ralph de Somery, became lord of Dudley. Ralph's son, Roger, began to rebuild the castle in 1262, obtaining a licence two years later; building work continued under his son, John. Their work included the keep, curtain, gatehouse and the main domestic range. Further alterations and

A Guide to the Medieval Castles of England

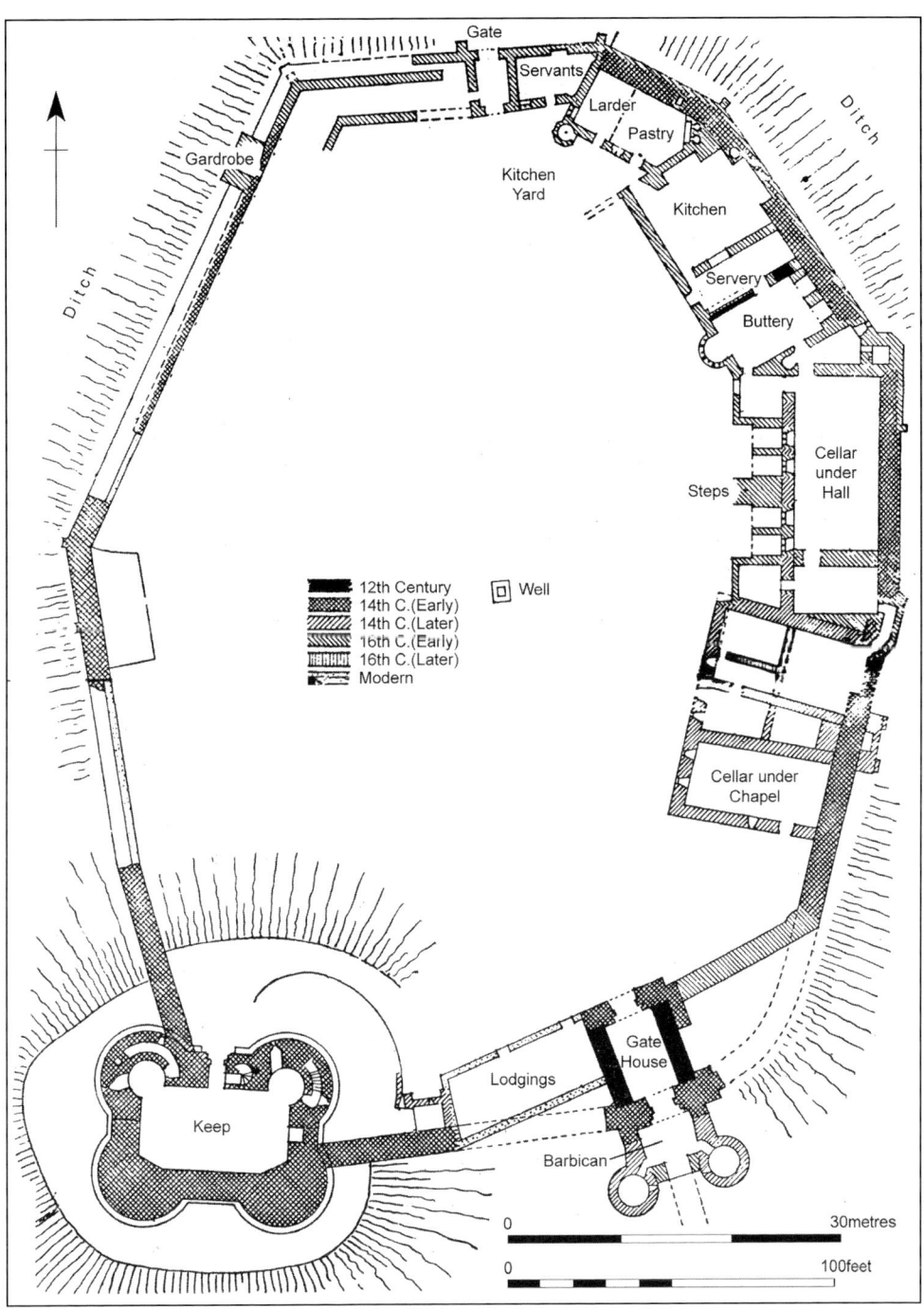

Dudley: Ground plan. From Brakspear 1914.

Dudley: The great tower from the N (*c*.1264).

additions were carried out under the de Suttons, who succeeded in 1321, including the chapel and barbican. In 1533 Dudley came into the hands of John Dudley, Duke of Northumberland, who, from 1551, proceeded to rebuild the main residential buildings to a Renaissance-inspired design supplied by Sir William Sharington of Lacock Abbey. During the Civil War Dudley was held for the King, and in 1647 Parliament ordered its demolition. Occupation continued after the war, but in 1750 a fire gutted the Sharington range, bringing an end to its use as a residence. From 1937 the castle was incorporated into the Dudley Zoo complex.

The fortress is superbly sited on the top of Castle Hill dominating the town to the S, the great-tower capped motte terminating the view along the main street (Market Place/Castle Street). The principal gatehouse is also on the S side, next to the motte: C14 barbican with round corner turrets; late C13 two-storey main block with segmental-arched gateways and bold quarter-round mouldings showing affinities with the keep. Barrel-vaulted passage, the side walls possibly C12. On the internal (N) face a first-floor window of twin trefoil-arched lights. Between the gatehouse and the motte, backing onto the curtain, is the later C17 stable block with first-floor lodgings. Immediately R (W) of this was the approach to the motte, the top of which is now occupied by the late C13 keep.

The keep is a two-storey building with four round corner towers; a similar geometrical basis underlies the plan of Clifford's Tower in York of 1245 onwards. In the centre of the N front a large portcullis-protected entrance of two continuous orders, more gateway than doorway, with large quarter-round mouldings. The main block was occupied by a single room at both levels, storage/servants' quarters below and a hall above, with rooms in the corner towers. While the keep may have been for occasional use, the principal accommodation was along the E side of the bailey, but little survives from the medieval period. The exception is the C14 chamber and chapel block R (S) of the great hall. The remaining medieval windows are rectangular with chamfered openings, except for the chapel which has a large, pointed W window and an ogee-arched S window, this latter the best medieval detail in the castle.

The remainder of the E range dates from Northumberland's C16 rebuilding. Next to the chamber block is the first-floor great hall, on the site of the medieval hall, its recessed frontage framed by square porch (L) and staircase (R) turrets. A ground-floor arcade carried a first-floor loggia, now represented only by a platform; above are the high-level windows to the hall. Next to the L (N) is the four-storey, gabled service block containing (from S to N) buttery, servery and (two-storey) kitchen with better rooms, including bedrooms, on the upper floors. A second-floor long gallery extended all along the E side of the block. There were further service rooms and upper chambers in the attached building set back to the L with octagonal corner turret. Finally, in the centre of the N curtain is the C16 postern gate. Brakspear 1914; Simpson 1939 and 1944; Hislop 2010.

DUFFIELD, Derbyshire (Open – NT). Motte and bailey, perhaps created by Henry de Ferrers (d. 1089). In the C12 an unusually large keep (now reduced to its foundations) was raised on top of the motte by the Second and/or Third Earl of Derby (i.e. between 1139 and 1190). The castle is on a knoll, the motte overlooking the valley to the E. Although the parameters of the bailey are uncertain, it seems to have lain to the W, and is now encroached upon by housing. The main interest of the site is the keep, which was nearly 100ft (9.29m) square thereby making it one of the largest keeps in England by area. The walls are 15ft (4.57m) thick, and a forebuilding projected from the W side. A cross wall (with a connecting doorway) divided the basement into two compartments of unequal size, spiral staircases at the NW and SE angles giving independent access from above. A pier base in the middle of the larger (southern) space suggests that it was sub-divided by an arcade and that this arrangement was repeated on the first floor to allow a tripartite roof. There was a well in the SW corner of the basement. Manby 1959.

DUNSTANBURGH, Northumberland (Open – EH) (Plate VI). Large stone castle on a coastal headland erected by Thomas, Earl of Lancaster. Building work began in 1313; the following year the mason Master Elias had the great gatehouse well under way, and by the time a licence was granted, in 1316, construction was probably considerably advanced. Alterations undertaken by John of Gaunt, Duke of Lancaster, during the early 1380s centred on the great gatehouse, the entrance passage of which was blocked, a new gatehouse constructed on a different site, and an inner courtyard and buildings created to the rear of the old gatehouse to create greater privacy, security and facilities for its occupants. The masons were John Lewyn (1380–1) and Henry Holme (1381–3). The castle was maintained for most of the C15, but afterwards allowed to decay.

The curtain walls enclose nearly 10 acres (4ha) but a much larger area, which included the steadily falling ground to the S, was cut off from the landward side by a series of managed artificial water features (no longer extant) to create an elongated island with the stone castle at its high point and a harbour at its southern extremity. From the harbour there was a steady climb to the three-storey great gatehouse, an arresting structure, with twin bow-fronted flanking towers, made more imposing by a pair of turrets carried above the parapet. To the R (E) of the gatehouse are three rectangular wall towers, the easternmost (Egyncleugh Tower) containing a postern.

To the L (W) is the entrance to the later C14 gatehouse complex, now partly reduced to ground level; first, a walled passage leading to a rectangular barbican, then a RH turn to the twin-towered gatehouse of 1383. Inside, on the R the wall to the inner ward built by John Lewyn in 1380; it contains traces of a former entrance, replaced (probably by Henry Holme) by one on the E side adjacent to a square corner tower. Inside, traces of buildings lining the walls include an oven in front of the blocked N entrance.

Towards the N end of the W curtain, next to a postern, is the square C14 Lilburn Tower, a visually effective two-storey residential building with prominent corner turrets. Inside the S curtain, the foundations of the Constable's House, a small domestic complex at the NE corner of the Constable's Tower arranged around a courtyard. Ashbee 2006; Oswald and Ashbee 2006; Ashbee and Oswald 2007.

Dunstanburgh: Great gatehouse from the S.

A Guide to the Medieval Castles of England

DUNSTER, Somerset (Open – NT). Motte and bailey in existence by 1086, then known as 'Torre' and held by William de Mohun. It was besieged in 1138, being then fortified by towers, walls and a rampart. In 1284, both the upper ward (the motte) and the lower ward (the bailey) appear to have been fortified in stone. The male line of the Mohuns died out in 1374, and in 1376 the right of inheritance was sold to Lady Elizabeth Luttrell, and after the death of Lady Joan de Mohun in 1404, Sir Hugh Luttrell took possession, the castle remaining with the family until 1976. Sir Hugh Luttrell built a new gatehouse and barbican to the lower ward in the 1420s. A mansion was erected in the lower ward from *c.*1617, to the designs of William Arnold. During the Civil War Dunster underwent two sieges, being first held for Parliament and then for the King. Its dismantling was ordered in 1649. In the C18 the level of the lower ward was raised, and the inner end of the Luttrell gatehouse remodelled. Arnold's house was remodelled and extended by Salvin in 1868–72.

The castle is built on a hill, the motte, or upper ward, on the summit, and the lower ward on a lower-level platform to the NE. The principal medieval survival is the gatehouse and barbican complex. This comprises a C13 NE-facing gatehouse with twin drum towers. In front of it is a square courtyard barbican, with the Luttrell gatehouse on its NW side. The Luttrell gatehouse is a three-storey rectangular residential block pierced by a gateway with heavily moulded segmental arch. On entering the barbican there is a sharp RH turn to the Mohun gateway, its RH tower encroached upon by the Luttrell building. Then through the cambered-arch gateway (retaining a pair of medieval gates), to meet a flight of steps up to the raised level of the lower ward. Other medieval buildings including towers are incorporated into the SE side of the house. Dunning 1995, 37–9; Emery 2006, 677–9; Guy *et al.* 2010–11, 126–45.

DURHAM, County Durham (Open by guided tour). Established on the initiative of William I in 1072 for Waltheof, Earl of Northumberland, but in 1076 transferred to Walcher, Bishop of Durham, whose successors held it until 1836. The following year it was transferred to the University. Durham Castle is formidably sited on a rocky hill within a long narrow loop of the river Wear, lording over the city in complementary companionship with the cathedral. The castle, which lies to the N of the cathedral across the neck of the peninsula, with the city to the N of the castle, comprises an eastern motte and a roughly triangular western inner bailey with domestic buildings ranged along the N, NE and W curtains, and a gatehouse to the S. Access to the wider fortified peninsular and thence to the castle was via the vanished N Gate which lay to the E of the motte straddling Saddler Street.

Subsequent medieval building campaigns are as follows: Bishop Flambard (1099–1128) built the lower storey of the N range; Bishop Du Puiset (1153–95) reinforced the walls and raised an upper storey known as the Constable's Hall or Norman Gallery; Bishop Bek (1284–1311) was responsible for the great hall on the W side, remodelled and extended by Bishop Hatfield (1345–81) who also rebuilt the keep on top of the motte (rebuilt 1839 by Salvin). The last medieval phase is owed to Bishop Fox (1494–1501), who created the kitchen and buttery at the SW angle of the great hall.

Later alterations and additions are considerable and have done much to damage or disguise the medieval castle. Bishop Tunstall (1530–9) added a gallery to the front (S) of the N range, a chapel to the front of the NE range and a stair turret at the junction of the two. Damaged during the Civil War, the castle was extensively refurbished by

Bishop Cousin (1660–72) who added a porch and polygonal buttresses to the front of the great hall and a stair wing (containing the renowned Black Stairs) at the junction of the N and W ranges. He also demolished the barbican and filled in part of the moat. During the latter half of the C18 the N Range was repaired and remodelled, including refenestration and internal alterations. The upper walls of the great tower were demolished in 1789 and the gatehouse Gothicised by James Wyatt in 1791. In 1839–41 Anthony Salvin rebuilt the keep for student accommodation.

The C12 gateway survives, albeit incarcerated within Wyatt's ornamental Gothick structure of 1791. Outer gateway of three chevron-moulded orders, an C18 rebuilding of the C12 entrance. On entering the courtyard, to the L (W) is Bishop Bek's great hall, built on top of the C12 undercroft, with Bishop Hatfield's extension to the L (S) of the entrance. Despite its later fittings and furnishings, the interior of the great hall is a splendid evocation of the Middle Ages, aided by the survival of John of Alverton's roof of 1350: low pitched with arch-braced tie beams, formerly decorated with cusping. At the lower (S) end of the hall are two little corbelled balconies (said to be for trumpeters) of Hatfield's time. At the SW corner of the hall is Bishop Fox's buttery with timber-framed partitions containing serving hatches with four-centred heads. Beyond this, to the S, is Fox's great kitchen made within a C12 block, with two massive brick fireplaces lining the S wall within a battlemented brick flue.

Back in the courtyard, directly in front of the gatehouse is the N range, Du Puiset's Norman gallery rearing up behind Tunstall's gallery. One of the glories of the range is Du Puiset's late C12 entrance to the N range, a sumptuous doorway of three shafted orders, formerly approached from the courtyard by a flight of steps and once in a direct line of sight from the gateway. The arches of this heavily moulded piece are encrusted with chunky bands of repeated motifs, with smaller-scale mouldings at the divisions. It is an extravagant and eye-catching introduction to Du Puiset's hall, though the interior was altered in the C16. The other remarkable aspect of the N Range is the Constable's Hall, or Norman Gallery, on the upper floor, which contains, along the interior of its S wall, towards the courtyard, an inventive chevron-moulded arcade of columned window embrasures alternating with pairs of smaller blind arches containing stone benches. The columns are detached from the walls and sit on the ends of the benches.

Adjoining the N Range to the E is the Chapel Range, which contains another architectural treasure: the late C11 chapel, at undercroft level. The chapel is aisled, the groin vaulting supported on six round columns with volute capitals and square abaci and responds on the four walls. The columns are richly decorated with a variety of low-relief carvings.

Finally, the keep. Essentially a C19 building but retaining some medieval fabric and built on the old foundations. As rebuilt by Hatfield in the C14 it was an irregularly octagonal shell-keep with buttress turrets at the angles, domestic apartments lining the walls and a courtyard at the centre. John Lewyn, described in 1368/9 as 'the bishop's mason', may have been involved. A possible model is the Round Tower at Windsor (cf.), as remodelled in 1353–7. Page 1928, 64–91. Emery 1996, 76–81.

DYMOCK (Castle Tump), Gloucestershire (Private). Motte and bailey first mentioned in 1148–54 when it was granted to William de Braose by Roger, Earl of Hereford. Situated in Dymock parish 1½ miles to the SE of Dymock village and next to a Roman road (B4215), which cuts through the bailey. The bailey lay to the S of the motte. Salter 2002b, 20.

EARDISLEY, Herefordshire (Private but a track lies immediately S of the site). Motte and bailey and associated earthworks. A *domus defensabilis* existed here at the time of the Domesday survey, when the manor was held by Roger de Lacy, but the castle was first mentioned in 1183. From the mid C13 Eardisley was in the hands of the Baskervilles; it was burnt out during the Civil War. This is a little-understood earthwork complex of which the most recognizable elements are a motte with a bailey to the E, probably kidney shaped, though the form has been obscured by the filling in of some of the ditches; a surrounding moat was fed by a millstream to the N. There are two further moat enclosures immediately to the W, both moated, and apparently related to the castle. Page 1908a, 236–7; RCHME 1934, xxix, 52–3.

EATON SOCON (Castle Hills, The Hillings), Bedfordshire (Private). Earthwork complex on the W bank of the river Ouse on the site of a Saxon cemetery. Probably raised by the Beauchamps or Geoffrey de Mandeville in the mid C12. The earthworks comprised a horseshoe-shaped enclosure defined by a ditch, its open side towards the river, and, within it, two rectangular ditched and banked platforms linked by a causeway. Petre 2012, 62–3.

ECCLESHALL, Staffordshire (Private). Fortified manor house of the bishops of Coventry and Lichfield. In 1200 King John granted Bishop Muschamp a licence to crenellate. Rebuilt by Bishop Langton *c*.1310, but badly damaged during the Civil War and the medieval fabric is now very much depleted. A house was built within the enclosure in the 1690s. Situated on the S bank of the river Sow, which fed the moat, and approached from the S across a C14 bridge, the castle formed a symmetrical quadrangular enclosure with the main apartments on the E side, between two nine-sided corner towers, of which one survives, the main remnant of Langton's reconstruction. Maddison 1993, 68–70.

EDLINGHAM, Northumberland (Open access – EH). Probably begun soon after 1296 by William Felton who built a two-storey, three-cell hall house with polygonal corner turrets. Subsequent (C14) additions include the construction (or reconstruction) of the defended enclosure, and the addition of a solar tower to the S side of the hall house. Most of the buildings have been demolished but the tower survives, and the plans of the other stone buildings have been recovered by excavation.

The irregular quadrilateral courtyard was entered from the NW via a rectangular gatehouse fronted by a passage barbican. The remains of the hall house are directly opposite; in front of it is the foundation of an external staircase that led to the upper storey and the principal living accommodation, the general layout of which is probably reflected at ground-floor level, where there were three rooms within the main block: a central hall (later subdivided) entered from the courtyard, a kitchen to the W, and a chamber to the E. There was an additional, storeyed, accommodation block attached to the E end.

The three-storey tower, which dates from the mid C14, was accessed from a chamber at the lower end of the first-floor hall through a passage link, internal communication being via a staircase housed in an adjacent turret. The quality of workmanship is high, even in the basement, where the vault was carried on heavy chamfered ribs, a technique extended to the window embrasure, in which the ribs are

Edlingham: Solar tower (*c*.1350) from the W with the ruins of the hall house (*c*.1300) to the left.

carried shaft-like down the walls. However, the greatest care (and expense) has been concentrated on the first-floor room, which boasted a large fireplace with an elaborately joggled lintel (now largely disappeared) carried on figure-carved corbels, and a high pointed ribbed vault, also with figure corbels that allowed clearstorey lighting in the E and W ends. Fairclough 1982, 1984, 1992.

EGREMONT, Cumberland (Open access). Motte and bailey rebuilt in stone. Established *c*.1120 by William de Meschines overlooking a crossing of the river Eden. Rebuilt in stone later in the later C12 and C13 including the erection of a shell-keep on top of the motte. Damaged by the Scots in 1315. By 1578 the castle is reported to have been in ruins except for a chamber used as a courthouse, which functioned until 1789. The shell-keep suffered partial collapse in the C18 and has since disappeared entirely. The main gatehouse at the SW angle is a rectangular tower with segmental-arched gateway recessed beneath an outer semi-circular arch. The vaulting of the passage has gone, but the columnar responds remain. To the L (N) of the gatehouse in the W curtain is a stretch of herringbone masonry representing the primary phase of stonework. The bailey was separated from the motte by a ditch, now infilled. Beyond the ditch, on the motte, is the early C13 great hall with large pointed windows, and, to the L (W), a semi-circular-arched doorway with a portcullis slot approached by a bridge across the ditch. An unusual feature is a continuous string carried over the windows as dripstones and decorated with a repeating twin-leaf motif like half a dogtooth moulding. Curwen 1913, 134–7; Turnbull and Walsh 1994; Perriam and Robinson 1998, 102–3.

ELLESMERE, Shropshire (Open access from Castlefields). Motte and bailey. In existence by 1138, but generally considered to have been established by Roger de Montgomery, Earl of Shrewsbury, in the late C11. Built on a ridge to the SW of the lake known as the Mere, the remains comprise a motte to the W (at the junction of Sandy Lane and Church Hill) separated by a ditch from a sub-rectangular inner bailey to the E delineated on the N and E by a ditch and counterscarp bank. The motte has been carved from a natural mound and subsequently levelled to create a bowling green. Brown *et al.* 1963, 645–6; Duckers 2006, 73–5.

ELMLEY, Worcestershire (Open access). Ringwork to the S of Elmley Castle village on Bredon Hill within the defences of a prehistoric hillfort. In existence by 1216 by which time it was a seat of the Beauchamps. Ditched and double banked sub-oval enclosure aligned N–S with E and W entrances, the hillfort defences enclosing potential outer baileys. Within the ringwork the partial foundations of a rectangular building, probably a keep. Still habitable in 1528 but in ruins some ten years later. Page and Willis-Bund 1913, 339–40, and 1924, 431–3.

ELSDON (Mote Hills), Northumberland (Open access). Ringwork and bailey considered the best earthwork castle in Northumberland. Probably built by Robert de Umfraville in the early C12 as the caput of the Liberty of Redesdale. The substantial and well-preserved earthworks occupy a N–S aligned spur and comprise two massively-banked enclosures separated by a ditch, the ringwork occupying the S end of the spur. It was probably replaced by Harbottle Castle (qv) in the mid C12. Hunter Blair 1944 and 1947.

ELY (Cherry Hill), Cambridgeshire and the Isle of Ely (Open access). Motte and bailey raised by William the Conqueror in 1071. Situated at the S end of the cathedral precinct just inside Ely Porta. Sub-rectangular bailey to the SE of the motte. Pugh 1953, 28–30.

EMBLETON TOWER, Northumberland (Private). Fortified rectory in the form of a tower adjacent to the churchyard. Probably a former hall house of 1332–41 converted into a tower *c.*1395. Elongate plan some 40ft × 20ft (12.19m × 6m) now forming the SE wing of a much larger house. Two main phases of stonework are evident, the ground storey of rubble and the two upper floors of ashlar, suggesting the late C14 conversion from an earlier house. The tower has been refenestrated, but a number of small medieval loops survive here and there. The basement is divided by a cross-wall and covered by two transverse barrel-vaults; generally, however, the interior is much altered, and its medieval character considerably obscured. Bateson 1895, 80–2.

ETAL, Northumberland (Open – EH). Stone courtyard castle associated with a licence to crenellate of 1341 granted to Sir Robert Manners. Sited on the E bank of the river Till, the castle was roughly rectangular, orientated NE–SW facing NE with the gatehouse at the E angle and a great tower at the W angle. Rectangular gatehouse, the segmental-pointed gateway recessed between two flanking towers of unequal width, a type also found at Raby (qv) slightly later in the C14. Above the gateway Manners' heraldic shield and helm, and over that a window with curvilinear tracery compatible with the date of the licence. A first-floor doorway in the RH tower and stone toothing on the faces of both towers are evidence for the former existence of a barbican. On either side of the gate passage is a porter's lodge, one equipped with a fireplace, the other with a latrine; the vaults of both are carried on heavy transverse ribs, a familiar feature of mid C14 castles in the N. The technique was also used in the four-storey great tower, a building of rectangular plan, with a rectangular entrance turret now reduced to its foundations. The entrance was at ground-floor

Etal: Gatehouse (c.1341) from the E.

level; it opened to a lobby and then a portcullis-protected passage leading straight ahead to the vaulted basement and (on the R) a doorway to the staircase and the living accommodation above which consisted of two storeys of large central rooms appointed with fireplace, latrine and mural chambers and an unheated uppermost chamber with a latrine. Of the S corner tower only the ground storey survives, and of the curtain only the SE side is upstanding. Vickers 1922, 460–71; Nelson 2013.

EWYAS HAROLD, Herefordshire (Private). Possibly the castle established by Osbern Pentecost (Pentecost's Castle of the *Anglo-Saxon Chronicle*), which was in existence by 1052. After the Conquest Ewyas Harold was refortified by William FitzOsbern (no relation), Earl of Hereford (d. 1071) and granted to Alfred de Marlborough (possibly the nephew of Osbern Pentecost), who was tenant in chief in 1086. By 1100 the castle was in the possession of Harold FitzRalph (d. 1057), from whom it takes its name. The castle occupies a spur overlooking Dulas Brook, a tributary of the river Dore; it consists of a circular motte with a kidney-shaped bailey to the E; an outer bailey lay to the S. Page 1908a, 237–8; RCHME 1931; 63–4.

EWYAS LACY, Herefordshire. See **LONGTOWN**.

EXETER (Rougemont), Devon (Private event centre – exterior only). Stone courtyard castle founded by William the Conqueror in 1068 on a rocky eminence (Rougemont, from the reddish colour of the rock) in the N corner of the Roman city wall which provided the defences to the NE and NW. A roughly square enclosure was created by the excavation of a ditch and bank to the S, and the construction of a stone gatehouse which is now the main interest of the castle. There was also an outer bailey, no longer extant, but confirmed by historical and archaeological evidence. The approach is from the SE along Castle Street, the early gatehouse standing immediately to the L of the current entrance. Its (blocked) semi-circular arched gateway, with attached shafts and cushion capitals, is recessed within a short barbican with high open arch. Above the gateway is a pair of windows with triangular-arched heads, a familiar characteristic of Anglo-Saxon construction. The curtain walls cresting the bank to L and R contain herringbone masonry suggestive of an early date; certainly, they seem to have been in existence by 1136 when the castle was besieged by King Stephen; archaeological evidence suggests they replaced a timber palisade. Brown *et al.* 647–9; Blaylock and Higham 2021.

EYNSFORD, Kent (Open – EH). Stone courtyard castle probably established by William de Eynsford in the late C11 on an Anglo-Saxon site. In 1261, the inheritance of the last de Eynsford lord, including the barony of Eynsford, was divided equally between his two sisters, and through them came to the Kirkeby and Criol families. In 1307 the Kirkebys sold their share to a judge called William Inge and five years later the castle was attacked and damaged by the Criols and another family called Lese who also had a claim to the de Eynsford estates. This episode seems to have brought an end to the castle as a noble residence. The roughly oval enclosure, which is sited on the E bank of the river Darent, is surrounded by a curtain wall of flint and a moat. There was a rectangular gatehouse at the SE angle largely within the curtain. The main castle building, which was built over a probable Anglo-Saxon structure, was a C11/C12 hall with chamber block of which only the undercrofts remain. In front of the building are the remains of a substantial stone staircase, which led to a porch and thence into the first-floor hall. Rigold 1971; Rigold and Fleming 1973; Horsman 1988.

FARLEIGH HUNGERFORD, Somerset (Open – EH). Ruinous quadrangular courtyard castle of the late C14, to which an outer ward was added in the C15. Built by Sir Thomas Hungerford, Speaker of the House of Commons (1377), who in 1369 purchased the manor of Farleigh Montfort (later Farleigh Hungerford). In 1383 Sir Thomas was pardoned for having crenellated his manor house of Farleigh Montfort without permission. It is to be assumed that by this time the inner ward was complete, and that construction had begun in the 1370s. An outer ward was added to the S by Sir Walter, First Baron Hungerford *c.*1430–45.

Irregularly polygonal outer bailey with two round towers and E and W gateways, of which the former survives to full height; it is a square block with the Hungerford emblem of a sickle above the gate and the Hungerford coat of arms above the first-floor window, inserted there by Sir Edward Hungerford (d. 1522). The main point of interest in the outer ward is the much-altered C14 chapel of St Leonard, the former parish church, commandeered as the castle chapel when the outer ward was built around it, a replacement being provided a quarter of a mile to the S in 1443. A NE chapel was added by Sir Thomas to house his tomb; Sir Walter refenestrated the chapel *c.*1440 (compare the E window with that of the parish church) and commissioned wall paintings. Inside is the chest tomb of Sir Thomas and his wife with recumbent effigies enclosed by a C15 wrought iron screen; remains of wall paintings including an over life-size St George. E of the chapel, extending outside the line of the curtain, is the Priest's House of 1430, built to accommodate the priests serving the chantries established by Sir Walter for his father and later himself.

Sir Thomas' quadrangular castle to the N had a twin-towered gatehouse in the centre of the S front and four round corner towers, the northern ones with attached latrine turrets. The only parts to retain much height, however, are the two southern towers, the SW had at least five storeys and the SE at least four. Extending across the courtyard from E to W are the remains of the principal residential range comprising hall, chamber block (E) and kitchen and services (W). It is probable that this range represents the existing manor house that Sir Thomas fortified. This, together with other divisions split the castle into a number of separate areas or courtyards. Wilcox 1980; Dunning 1995, 57–8; Emery 2006, 553–7; Guy *et al.* 2010–11, 34–47.

FARNHAM, Surrey (Open [keep only] – EH). Castle of the bishops of Winchester, recorded as having been built by Bishop Henry de Blois in 1138. A trench excavated across the motte in 1958–9 revealed that a conical motte was built around a stone tower base, rising 30ft (9.14m) above the medieval ground surface and containing a central well shaft. Subsequently, the motte was encased in stone and its surface area expanded. The exact chronology cannot be verified, but the tower base was rendered and probably predates the motte rather than being contemporary, and it has been suggested that Bishop Henry was responsible for fortifying an existing country house, of which the tower formed part, rather than initiating building at Farnham. The castle was probably demolished *c.*1155 on the orders of Henry II and reconstructed in the late C12.

The castle comprises the encased motte, or shell-keep, a triangular bailey to the S of the motte, and an outer bailey enclosed by a late stone curtain with occasional rectangular wall towers which encompasses the entire site. Access to the outer bailey is on the SW side where there is a much altered and disguised gatehouse with twin polygonal flanking towers; exposed C15 brickwork and earlier stonework to the rear. The S front of the bailey is dominated by the brick tower porch raised by Bishop Waynflete in the 1470s; to the R (W) is the C13 kitchen; behind and to the L (E) is the late C12 great hall, elements of its blocked S arcade visible in the existing elevation. At the NE angle of the hall within the E range is the C13 bishop's camera.

The encasing wall around the motte has a high battered plinth, pilaster buttresses, four rectangular turrets and a rectangular gate tower to the SE, this latter approached via a stone staircase from the wall walk of the inner bailey. At the top of the steps is a segmental-arched gateway within a central recess, suggesting a pair of flanking towers. Inside, in the centre of the open area, a rectangular 'flange' built over the buried tower was probably constructed to accommodate a well house. Thompson 1960 and 1967; Riall 2003; Emery 2006, 337–9; Higham 2015, 45–53.

FEATHERSTONE, Northumberland (Private). Remains of a fortified manor house incorporated into a largely C19 country house. The medieval elements comprise fragments of a mid-C13 hall house within the W range, and more substantial remains of a C15 four-storey solar tower at the SW angle. The main medieval features of the hall are a C13 pointed doorway re-set in the E wall and a re-set two-light window in the W wall, unlikely to be earlier than 1350 and more likely to be C15. The tower, at the SW angle of the greater complex, is L-shaped, allowing a series of two-room suites. The main block has a square-set NW angle turret and a diagonally-set NE turret, the former containing a spiral staircase. There was ground-floor entry from the hall giving access to the barrel vaulted basement and the stair to the residential floors above, now considerably altered. Hodgson 1840, 356–7; Gibson 1926; Emery 1996, 93–4.

FILLONGLEY, Warwickshire. **Castle Hills** (Private, but visible from the road). Ringwork and bailey to the NE of Fillongley village, the probable centre of the manor known as Old Fillongley in the 1280s, held by the Marmions of Tamworth Castle (qv) and their successors from the early C12 until *c*.1400. Ringwork defended by a ditch and inner bank, the former probably fed by the stream which flows down the W side of the castle. Slightly raised rectangular bailey to the SW. Salzman 1947, 69–71.

Castle Yard (Open access). Ringwork and bailey to the S of Fillongley village. By 1235 the manor was held by the Hastings family. In 1301 a licence to crenellate the manor and town of Fillongley was granted to John, First Baron Hastings, a former competitor for the Scottish throne. This grant may relate to a reconstruction of an existing castle in stone. The roughly triangular site is defined by two streams to the E and W converging at the northern apex of the site, and by a bank and ditch to the S. A roughly oval ringwork towards the N end of the site was surrounded by a stone curtain, now largely disappeared. Salzman 1947, 69–71.

FOLKESTONE (Caesar's Camp, Castle Hill), Kent (Open access). Ringwork with two baileys, part excavated by General Pitt-Rivers in 1878. A castle was in existence by *c*.1137. Situated on the top of Castle Hill 1.75 miles NW of Folkestone. A bank encompasses the roughly oval site, except towards the W. Within this outer bank an oval ringwork occupying the summit to the SW, and a large bailey to the NE and E, are each enclosed by a ditch and inner bank. To the NW, between the outer defences and those of the ringwork, is a much smaller bailey separated from the E bailey by a bank and western ditch. The entrance was at the NE corner of the E bailey. Amongst the finds of the 1878 excavation was a silver penny of King Stephen (1135–54), but also prehistoric and Romano-British artefacts, suggesting that the castle might occupy an earlier occupation site. Page 1908b, 115–18.

FORD, Northumberland (Private). Quadrangular castle built under a licence to crenellate of 1338 granted to Sir William Heron. Two years later the manor house of Ford was described as being 'enclosed with a high embattled wall'. In 1515 Ford was occupied and then burnt by the Scots, and although repairs were carried out the buildings of the castle were described as decayed in 1541. The N range of the castle was rebuilt as a mansion in the later C16, and there have been several subsequent building campaigns in the C17, C18 and C19.

The medieval castle consisted of four rectangular corner towers linked by a curtain wall. Small square towers to the S, a larger square tower to the NW, and an elongated rectangle to the NE some 70ft by 30ft (21.3m by 9.14m). The unusual proportions of this latter tower suggest that, like a number of other Northumbrian towers, it may have originated as a hall house, which will have predated the castle. To what extent the walls were lined with buildings in the medieval period is uncertain, but the main apartments were probably along the N side, being swept away by, or incorporated into, the C16 rebuilding. What survives from the medieval period are the two western towers: the King James Tower (N) and Cow Tower (S) and stretches of the W and N curtains, all much altered, in addition to some fragments of the NW tower at the E end of the N range.

The King James Tower, which is attached to the W end of the later house, rises through five storeys; it has a barrel-vaulted basement carried on unchamfered ribs, and a ground-floor room entered from the E. The four-storey Cow Tower is smaller; it too has a vaulted basement carried on ribs and entered from above via a trap. A highly unusual feature is the recessed uppermost storey, in the manner (though not the form) of the near contemporary Caesar's Tower at Warwick (qv). Vickers 1922, 369–425.

FOTHERINGHAY, Northamptonshire (Open access). Motte and bailey best known as the scene of the trial and execution of Mary Queen of Scots. Possibly established *c*.1100 by Simon de Senlis (also St Liz), Earl of Huntingdon and of Northampton, but first mentioned in 1212. On the death of Marie de St Pol, Countess of Pembroke, in 1377, Fotheringhay was granted to Edmund of Langley (later Duke of York) who rebuilt the castle, including, according to Camden, a keep (presumably on the motte) in the form of a fetterlock (i.e., D-shaped); he was probably responsible for enclosing the early castle within an outer bailey. Sited on the N bank of the river Nene, the earthworks of the original castle survive as a rectangular bailey with a motte at the W end, the complex circumvented by a moat on three sides and by the river on the fourth. Less well-preserved is the outer bailey, which encompassed the motte and bailey on the landward sides, and which was also surrounded by a river-fed moat. RCHME 1975, 43–6.

FRAMLINGHAM, Suffolk (Open – EH). A castle of the Bigods on an Anglo-Saxon settlement. In existence by 1157 when it was confiscated by Henry II. Returned to Hugh Bigod in 1165, but, owing to his rebellion in 1173, the King ordered the

Framlingham: Ruins of the chamber block and its well-preserved C12 chimneys.

destruction of the castle's defences. It was Hugh Bigod's heir, Roger, who set about rebuilding the castle in stone from *c.*1190; the Bigods continued to hold it until 1306.

A roughly oval inner courtyard is surrounded by a stone curtain and outer ditch, a crescentic outer bailey (also ditched) lies to the S and E, and an embanked (and formerly walled) rectangular lower courtyard to the W, beyond which is a lake known as the Mere, now considerably diminished, which protected the site on this side. The current entrance is from the S into the outer bailey, the drive making a beeline for the gateway to Hugh Bigod's stone-walled inner ward, the high point of the castle, both topographically and architecturally. The curtain is polygonal in plan, made up of a series of straight lengths in the local flint and septaria rubble stitched together with ashlar quoins; projecting from it are thirteen mostly rectangular open-backed towers.

Apart from the lack of a great tower, the best comparisons are with the slightly earlier royal castles of Orford (qv) and Dover (qv). Arrow loops are to be found in the parapets of the curtain and towers and a concentration of twin loops at courtyard level in the curtain between the gatehouse and SE corner tower. This tower is exceptional in that it is five-sided, so allowing a greater field of fire. Another anomaly is the western tower, an elaborately-defended postern which extends across the ditch, and which linked with the (now largely vanished) curtain around the lower court.

The gatehouse is simply another rectangular wall tower containing a gateway. There was a small barbican in front and a stone bridge, remnants of which survive. The current gate arch and the achievement of arms above date from the early C16, but the C12 arch to the rear of the entrance survives: it is triangular and made up of joggled voussoirs of the same form as those used in the entrance to Orford Castle keep (qv). Within the courtyard the only building is the C17 and C18 Poor House, on the site of the medieval great hall and incorporating some medieval masonry. Directly opposite is the site of the chamber block, which predated Roger Bigod's reconstruction, one wall being incorporated into the curtain, thereby protecting two remarkably well-preserved C12 chimneys. Continuous wall-walk through the towers via round-arched doorways. Sockets for shutter hinges survive in some of the embrasures. Coad 1971; Renn 1973b; Plowman 2005; Stacey 2009.

GAINS, Hampshire. See **ASHLEY**

GIDLEIGH, Devon (Private). Solar tower, part of an otherwise vanished residence. Possibly built by Sir William Prouz (1280–1316). The building consists of a two-storey N–S aligned main block, with a polygonal stair turret at the SE corner, and the fragmentary remains of a N wing of equal height. The only entry was via the stair turret, which has a ground-level doorway, and which leads to the first floor. Access to the basement was from this upper level via a mural stair. The basement was covered by a ribbed barrel-vault and was evidently for storage; the first floor was provided with a fireplace and access to an inner chamber within the wing. Emery 2006, 565–6.

GILLING, Gilling East, Yorkshire North Riding (Private). Late C14 great tower incorporated within a country house. The tower was built either by Thomas de Etton senior (*fl.* 1316–80) (who in 1374 was granted a licence to enclose a park at Gilling) or, more probably, by his son, Thomas de Etton junior (*fl.* 1349–1402). It is a very substantial three-storey building, 79½ft × 72½ft (24.23m × 22m), disguised by C16 remodelling and C18 additions; the only part of the interior to have retained its medieval character is the basement. This has a central E–W passage with a doorway at each end, one (W) pointed, the other (E) four-centred with a portcullis groove and embellished with a series of shields bearing the Etton arms. Just inside the W doorway is a wide mural staircase (now blocked), apparently the main medieval access to the first floor. To each side of the barrel-vaulted passage are three vaulted rooms entered via four-centred doorways. The rooms to the S are each furnished with a latrine, and the centre chamber with a fireplace; those to the N have no facilities, but the E and W rooms each have access to a mural stair. This floor seems to have housed staff quarters and storage space; the service stairs hint at a similar level of complexity to Warkworth Castle keep (qv). Bilson 1906–7; Emery 1996, 337–9.

GILLING EAST, Yorkshire North Riding. See **GILLING**.

GLEASTON, Lancashire (Private, but visible from the road). Quadrilateral stone courtyard castle in existence by 1389 and probably built for Sir John and/or Sir Robert de Harrington *c.*1340–50. It succeeded Aldingham Castle (qv) as the centre of the manor of Aldingham by the C14 but was abandoned as a manor house in 1458 and allowed to decay: when John Leland saw it in the mid C16 he described it as a ruin. Aligned N–S with four rectangular corner towers varying in size, and a square turret in the centre of the W front. At the N end of the W curtain is the gateway, a simple opening apparently undefended except for the gate. The adjacent three-storey NW tower was a great tower, or keep, and much bigger (92ft × 53ft [28m × 16.15m]) than the other three corner towers. L-shaped plan, the W end outside the curtain extending further S than the remainder. Ground-floor entrance, the interior at this level divided longitudinally into three rooms. Latrine shaft at the NW corner serving all three floors. The NE tower has largely disappeared, but the two S towers are more complete. Curwen 1913; Perriam and Robinson 1998, 382–3.

GODARD'S, Kent. See **THURNHAM**.

GOODRICH, Herefordshire (Open – EH) (Plate VII). Stone quadrangular courtyard castle on a bluff overlooking the river Wye, taking its name from Godric Mappa, who held the manor of Hulla at Domesday. In 1138 Goodrich was transferred to Gilbert de Clare, Earl of Pembroke (d. 1148), who probably built the keep. Gilbert's heir, Richard (Strongbow) de Clare, died in 1176, when his children were minors, and his estates were taken into the hands of the King. Strongbow's son died before he came of age, but his daughter, Isabella, married William Marshal who was subsequently given the earldom of Pembroke and Goodrich Castle. The male line of the Marshals came to an end in 1245, and in 1247 Goodrich was granted by Henry III to his half-brother, William de Valence (d. 1296), who married William Marshal's granddaughter Joan. It was under William de Valence (from *c*.1261), and possibly his son Aymer (d. 1324), that Goodrich was largely rebuilt. During the Civil War the castle was besieged and bombarded by the Parliamentarians who brought down the NW tower and did considerable damage to the N range.

The line of approach is from the S, the castle coming into plain view as the track skirts around the substantial rock-cut ditch that forms the outer defence work to the S and E. From here, the most notable features of this compact but powerful-looking fortress can be seen: the keep in the centre of the S range; the two southern angle towers, both cylindrical and rendered more distinctive by prominent spur buttresses, those of the SE tower exaggeratedly high, those of the slightly later SE tower, squat; examples of the former are repeated on the gatehouse block situated at the NE corner. The track leads across a subsidiary ditch to a half-moon barbican, an arrangement based on the Lion Tower of 1275–85 at the entrance to the Tower of London. Then, a right-angled turn across the main ditch via a stone causeway. The rather unusual gatehouse block has a large apsidal-ended flanking tower to the L (S) housing the chapel and only a little cylindrical corner turret to the R (N) containing a porter's lodge. A single flanking tower of this type is also found at William de Valence's outer gatehouse of *c*.1258 at Pembroke Castle in S Wales, which may have influenced the design.

The gate passage is protected by a drawbridge, two gates and two portcullises; on the RH (N) side is a doorway to a mural passage leading to the porter's lodge (E) and a latrine (W). So, into the courtyard, the greater part of which is surrounded by residential ranges backing onto the curtain, formerly connected by pentices. In the rear wall of the gatehouse is the C15 W window to the chapel, and, next to it, the C13 doorway with triangular arch, an unusual form, but the dominant type at Goodrich.

Inside, the polygonal sanctuary retains a piscina and sedile to the R (S) of the altar and an aumbry, or cupboard, to the L (N). Within the nave, large window embrasures to N and S. At the SW corner of the gatehouse block a semi-octagonal turret leads to the E curtain wall walk and upper rooms of the gatehouse, firstly a residential chamber over the chapel with large, hooded fireplace and window; secondly, the room over the gate passage from where the portcullises were controlled: note two portcullis slots in the floor and a pair of recesses in the E wall which housed the winding mechanism for the outer portcullis.

S of the gatehouse block is the site of the single-storey E range, which, in the C13, contained a hall, the large fireplace of which survives in the curtain wall together with the external windows, the embrasures of which contain seats. At the N end a stair descends to a storage room under the chapel, and at the S end, which was probably partitioned from the hall, three doorways lead into a latrine turret. The adjacent SE tower contains high-quality residential rooms in the two upper storeys with fireplaces and window seats.

Next is the keep, of c.1145, the oldest of the stone buildings, a square three-storey tower with pilaster buttresses. First-floor entrance of two shafted orders with scalloped capitals, now blocked with a C14 window and replaced by the current four-centred arch doorway at ground-floor level. C12 second-floor windows to N and W.

To the E of the keep is a prison, and to the W the site of the kitchen. This latter is immediately adjacent to the great hall in the W range, their doorways next to each other. In the W wall of the hall is a large fireplace and three tall windows with stone benches in the embrasures. Smaller windows to the E above the roof of the former pentice. Between the windows and fireplace two lines of corbels, the upper ones doubled, supported the ends of tie beams (upper) and braces (lower). In the S wall four doorways at various levels leading into the SW tower. The basement was for storage, the first floor contained the pantry and buttery, and the second floor a heated chamber with latrine. Beneath the tower are the foundations for an earlier smaller round tower, possibly indicating a change of plan during the course of construction.

At the other (N) end of the great hall an inserted doorway gives access to and from the N range porch, which, together with the NW tower, comprised the solar block, the lord's more private apartments. Now in a ruinous state, the most prominent aspect of this block is a two-storey, two-bay arcade that divides the range into a small W room and a large E room. At courtyard level the former contained a vestibule entered from the porch while the latter was probably the great chamber. A staircase descends from the porch to the basement, another large room of uncertain function, but containing in its S wall a trefoil-headed basin supplied by pipe and emptied via a drain. A door in the N wall leads into the outer ward, which contains the foundations of the C17 stable block that was destroyed by the Parliamentarians in 1646. Faulkner 1963; Ashbee 2005; Shoesmith 2014.

GREAT CANFIELD, Essex (Private). Well-preserved motte and bailey of uncertain date but first mentioned in 1214. Circular motte immediately SE of the churchyard with horseshoe-shaped bailey to the S, with inner and outer banks, the whole complex surrounded by a moat system. Arms of the moat extend towards the E suggesting a second bailey, now the grounds of Canfield Hall. A dam extends NE to the river probably part of the water management system connected with the moats. RCHME 1921, 91–2.

GREAT DRIFFIELD, Yorkshire East Riding (Open access). Motte and bailey built in the C11 or C12 on a C4 Roman occupation site. The manor was held by Earl Morcar before the Conquest but was in royal ownership by 1086. In 1210–12 nearly £600 was spent on 'the work of the king's houses of Driffield', which were probably within or close to the castle. Motte with ditch, the motte partially demolished in the 1850s. Brown *et al.* 1963, 923–4.

GREAT SOMERFORD, Wiltshire (Visible from the churchyard). Motte W of the Church of St Michael and All Angels, overlooking a crossing of the Avon. Excavation in 1811 revealed a stone building with walls 2ft (0.6m) thick containing a door and two semi-circular arched windows, possibly the remains of an early (i.e., C11 or C12) church or chapel. Godard 1930; Crowley 1991, 194–204.

GREYSTOKE, Cumberland (Private). Fortified manor house of William Lord Greystoke who was granted a licence to crenellate in 1353. The current house which was rebuilt in the C18 and C19 incorporates the remnants of one C14 rectangular tower at the N end, and another more complete towards the S, set at an oblique angle to the surrounding buildings. This latter contains a barrel-vaulted basement carried on unmoulded transverse ribs. Elements of a linking W wall survive within the house. Curwen 1913, 205–6; Perriam and Robinson 1998, 186–7.

GROBY (Castle Hill), Leicestershire (Private). Motte and bailey partly destroyed by the construction of the A50, which lies immediately N. In existence by *c.*1174 when it was captured and subsequently destroyed on the orders of Henry II following the revolt of its then owner Robert de Beaumont, Earl of Leicester. Groby came to the Ferrers in 1279, remaining in the family until 1445, when it passed into the hands of the Greys through marriage. Excavation of the motte in 1962/3 and 2011 (by Time Team) revealed that it was built up against a stone building, probably a keep, of uncertain date, although the C12 seems probable. The building incorporated a basement reached by a mural staircase. A number of trenches dug in the bailey to the SW of the motte recovered evidence for an early C14 residential complex. Time Team 2011a.

GUILDFORD, Surrey (Open access). Motte and bailey next to the river Wey. A late C11 origin seems probable but the first mention dates from 1173–4 when it was a royal castle. The bailey lay to the S and E of the motte, but there is a degree of uncertainty about its extent. However, part of the W curtain survives along Quarry Street, including elements of the great gatehouse of 1256 (next to the museum), notably its segmental-pointed outer portal known as Castle Arch. Through here, and then into Castle Gardens at the back of the museum, are the remains of the late C12 royal apartments, and a little further to the N, along the boundary of the gardens, a wall representing the gable end of the great hall.

The most significant surviving element, however, is the motte and its buildings. Firstly, the remains of a polygonal shell-keep probably dating from the C11. In the early C12, the nearly square keep was built into the E side of the motte; initially a two-storey building containing basement storage and first-floor living accommodation. The walls were raised later in the C12 (the position and form of the original crenellations have been very effectively picked out in render), when clasping and mid-wall pilaster buttresses were added. In the C16 an upper floor was inserted within the existing walls and the keep reroofed.

Rubble walling with bands of herringbone masonry, pierced by C12 round-arched twin-light windows recessed beneath an outer arch, and simplified C16/C17 versions in brick. The first-floor entrance in the centre of the W front has a slightly pointed head; it leads into the main room, formerly open to the roof, which was lit by three two-light windows. Doorways lead to three mural chambers; that in the SW angle is L-shaped and contains the chapel (in the S wall) and antechapel (in the W wall), the latter retaining along the outer wall C12 blind arcading with columns and capitals, a feature that formerly continued along the wall of the chapel itself. A passage led from the N window embrasure to a spiral staircase in the NW angle, which rose to the parapet. Alexander 2006.

HADDON HALL, Nether Haddon, Derbyshire (Open). Fortified manor house of the Vernon family continuously maintained for nearly 600 years, but despite being the product of an accretive development, it remains more than anything else a good example of a late medieval castellated house. The Vernons had a dwelling here by 1170; some twenty-five years later, Richard Vernon was granted a licence to strengthen his house at Haddon with a 12ft-high wall without crenellations. Be that as it may, the medieval complex as it exists today is the product of two principal building periods, the first dated to the C14 and represented by the upper court, the second to the C15 and the construction of the lower court. The only recognizably earlier work is in the chapel, formerly the parish church of Nether Haddon, which incorporates vestiges of late C11 or C12 fabric.

The upper court is the work of Richard Vernon, who in 1330 obtained a licence to enclose a park at Haddon. Architectural details suggest that the work was done before he left for the Holy Land in 1357. The building of the lower court has a more elongated chronology, being underway by 1427, by which time the parish church of Nether Haddon was in the process of being converted into the castle chapel (the date is inscribed on the E window), and continuing in stages into the C16. Between 1535 and 1565 Sir George Vernon created a long gallery on the S side of the upper court. Sir George was the last of the Vernon lords of Haddon, and in 1565 the estate came through marriage to the Manners family who have held it since that time. Their contributions to the house include the refacing in stone of the late C15 Earl's Apartment in the lower court, the remodelling of the Long Gallery, the partitioning of the C14 upper chamber block and construction of a new staircase turret on the north side of the hall, and the creation of a new set of lodgings on the N side of the upper court. A conscientious programme of restoration was undertaken in 1920–32.

Sitting on an elevated site above the river Wye, the castle comprises a rectilinear block orientated NE–SW (but for ease of understanding treated here as if it were E–W). The buildings are grouped around upper (E) and lower (W) courtyards separated by the C14 great hall range. The C14 gatehouse is at the N end of the E range, but with the construction of the lower courtyard, including a new gatehouse at the W end of the N range, the house was reorientated. Thus, the approach now leads to the late C15 NW gatehouse, a four-storey rectangular tower pierced by a gateway, with lodgings above. Moving into the lower court, to the R (W) is the late C15 W range, which contained lodgings at two levels, and to the L (E) the hall range fronted by a broad terrace and approached by steps. Straight ahead is the chapel with a large C15 three-light chancel window and octagonal belltower; breaking forward next to it is the Earl's Apartment.

The chapel comprises a two-bay aisled nave with a chancel of equal length, aligned with the cardinal points and askew to the main orientation of the lower court. The S aisle is an addition of *c.*1200; the central cylindrical column of the arcade is of this date, but the scalloped capital was much disfigured when the arches were rebuilt in the C14. In the mid C13 the aisle was widened and is now lit by lancet windows of that date. The narrower N aisle dates from the C14, though it may replace an earlier one. Above the arcades are elements of C15 wall paintings. The chancel was rebuilt in the early C15 and given large three-light windows with square heads and a pointed five-light E window. The walls are embellished with a C15 painted repeating pattern. High up in the N wall is the doorway to the former rood loft, and at the E end a C15 piscina. Above the stone altar is an ill-fitting reredos made up of nine C15 alabaster panels depicting the Passion of Christ; it was imported in the 1930s. Mostly C17 timber fittings, perhaps incorporating elements of the rood screen.

Back in the lower court, projecting from the front of the great hall are a three-storey porch (L) and a broad chimney stack, both C15 additions. To the R (S) of the stack is one of the C14 hall windows: two-centred arch with two lights and quatrefoil in the central spandrel. To L and R of the hall, chamber blocks break forward. In the RH (S) crosswing is the C15 eight-light window of the parlour; above it is the late C16 window of the great chamber. The porch gives access to the cross passage with four C14 doorways on the L (N) leading (from W to E) to buttery, kitchen passage, pantry and staircase to the first-floor chamber. To the R (S) a C15 timber screen divides the passage from the hall. The gallery linking the two chamber blocks is a C16 insertion, and the roof dates from the C20 restoration, but the window seats and fireplace are authentic. At the lower end, the kitchen passage leads to a (now covered) courtyard, its extent marked by two opposed segmental-arched doorways on the line of the passage. Beyond the former courtyard is the C14 kitchen (a similar arrangement existed at Raby), now a low-ceilinged room but formerly open to the roof. In the outside (N and W) walls, two great segmental-arched fireplaces.

The main medieval survival in the upper court is Peveril's Tower, the main gatehouse to the castle before the building of the lower court. Essentially a two- and three-storey rectangular block with a central gateway, comparable to a number of late C14 gatehouses (eg Cockermouth, Whorlton) were it not for the central tower, set back from the front of the gatehouse and looking like an afterthought, which adds an incongruous element to an otherwise conventional building. Although the gatehouse has largely been refenestrated, a rectangular loop at ground-floor level may be original. Above the four-centred gateway is a row of double corbels for a (now vanished) machicolated parapet. Inside the gate passage two doorways with four-centred arches and ogee apexes, unusual but possibly C14. Faulkner 1961; Hartwell *et al.* 2016, 413–25; Emery 2000, 383–9.

HADLEIGH, Essex (Open – EH). Ruined stone enclosure castle built on a spur overlooking the Thames estuary for Hubert de Burgh to replace Rayleigh (qv) as the caput of the honour of Rayleigh. A licence to crenellate was granted in 1230, although work may have begun in the 1220s. The castle was seized by the King in 1239 and substantially rebuilt by Edward III in the 1360s. At the same time Edward was constructing an entirely new castle at Queenborough (qv) on the opposite side of the estuary. Hadleigh Castle was built to an elongated polygonal plan aligned E–W with the gateway towards the W end of the N curtain. The gateway was preceded by an

Edwardian barbican with round corner turrets, of which the drawbridge pit and a fragment of walling survive. Next to it was Edward's High Tower, or great tower, which straddled the curtain. Edward also built a new domestic range backing onto the S curtain and rebuilt the E end of the castle including the two round wall towers that now form the main visual attraction of the site. These towers contained lodgings, equipped with fireplaces and latrines. Brown *et al*. 1963, 659–66; Drewett 1975; Alexander and Westlake 2009.

HALLATON (Castle Hill Camp), Leicestershire (Open access). Motte and horseshoe-shaped bailey on a hill to the NW of Hallaton village. The bailey lies to the NW of the conical motte; it has an inner bank, with a gap to the NW denoting the entrance; both motte and bailey are surrounded by a ditch and counterscarp bank. On the NE side of the motte is a sub-rectangular enclosure or platform, probably a later addition. Creighton 1997.

HALTON, Cheshire (Open – interior via The Castle public house). A stone courtyard castle in the village of Halton, now part of greater Runcorn. First mentioned in 1146, but possibly late C11 in origin. In 1194, Roger FitzEustace, lord of Halton, inherited the Barony of Pontefract (qv) and took the name of Lacy. The last of the male line, Henry de Lacy, Earl of Lincoln, died in 1311, his estates being inherited by his daughter Alice, wife of Thomas, Earl of Lancaster, by which means they were to become part of the Duchy of Lancaster, and, from 1399 onwards, Crown property. During the Civil War it was held by Parliamentarians and Royalists in turn, but finally captured by Parliament in 1644 and dismantled.

The plan of inner (SW) and outer (NE) wards is suggestive of a motte and bailey, the inner ward occupying the high point of the rock and separated from the outer ward by a rock-cut ditch. The approach road leading from the S ends in front of The Castle public house, the former C18 courthouse that stands on the site of the gatehouse built in the 1450s by the royal mason John Heley. Old illustrations show a monumental piece with twin polygonal flanking towers. To the L (W) of the pub is the inner ward, on the NW side of which is the best surviving section of medieval masonry, incorporating two long cruciform loops with round oillets top and bottom, probably C14. A little further to the L (N) of these is the rectangular N tower, which stands at the end of the dividing ditch. The rest of the curtain has been much rebuilt. McNeil and Jamieson 1987.

HALTON, Northumberland (Private). Fortified manor house, of which the main surviving component is a solar tower of *c*.1400. Towards the end of the C13 the manor house was burnt, probably in the Scottish incursions of the late 1290s. Some defensive provisions were in place in 1382 when Halton was raided by a party of Northumbrians, being described as a house and fortlet. It was burnt by the Scots in 1385 but appears in 1415 as the *Turris de Halton*. Halton was rebuilt in the late C17, the main range of this date being built against the E faces of the solar tower and an adjoining range to the N which links the tower to the fragmentary remains of a late C13/early C14 hall. The four-storey tower was entered from the N, at ground-floor level, via a porch or forebuilding (no longer extant); the four-centred doorway is unlikely to date from much before 1390. Original trefoil-headed windows survive in the two uppermost storeys to the S and E; the angles of the tower are capped by corbelled bartizans (cf. Belsay and Chipchase). The entrance leads into a mural vestibule, from which there is access to the barrel-vaulted basements, and to a stair in the E wall ascending to the first floor. Vertical access continued via a spiral stair in the SE angle. Bates 1891, 311–22; Craster 1914, 395–413; Dixon and Bourne 1978.

HANLEY CASTLE, Worcestershire (Private). Site of a castle built by King John *c*.1206–12 some 600 yards S of the church, just N of Mere Brook which marks the parish boundary. In 1216 it was granted to Gilbert de Clare, and, after the de Clare line came to an end, to Hugh Despencer. During the 1320s Edward II paid for substantial works at the castle under the direction of royal carpenters Robert de Glasham and Richard de Felsted, including the excavation of a great ditch and the construction of a peel, or palisade. No buildings survive above ground level, but the castle is said to have had four towers and a keep in the NW corner. There are, however, remains of a moat which enclosed a sub-rectangular area, now a field. Page and Willis-Bund 1924, 93–6; Brown *et al.* 1963, 667–9; Toomey 2001.

HANSLOPE, Buckinghamshire. See **CASTLETHORPE**.

HARBOTTLE, Northumberland (Open). Motte and bailey partially rebuilt in stone. Established soon after 1157 by Odinell de Umfraville on the orders of Henry II, it replaced Elsdon (qv) as the caput of the Liberty of Redesdale. Captured by the Scots in 1174 and 1318 and destroyed in 1320. Rebuilt later in the C14, being reoccupied by 1390. Building was in progress in 1432, and further work was carried out during the C16. The motte, which lies to the S, is partly surrounded by a crescentic bailey and separated from it by a ditch. Extensions of the ditch define the bailey, which was also defended by an inner bank. Rebuilding in stone was confined to the motte and the W half of the bailey. The former was given an irregularly polygonal shell-keep; a wall was built from N to S across the bailey, continuing up the motte, and a curtain wall erected around the W half. At the N end of the E wall was a square wall tower, and on the edge of the motte ditch, a gateway between the two halves of the old bailey. The entrance was protected by a portcullis, and a turning bridge within a passage barbican. The upstanding stonework on the motte contains C16 gun loops. Dodds 1940, 472–87; Crow 2004.

HAREWOOD, Yorkshire West Riding (Private). Fortified manor house, attributable to William de Aldeburgh who was granted a licence to crenellate his manor house of Harewood in 1366. On a sloping site above the river Wharfe, the building is aligned NW–SE (described here as if it were N–S). Architecturally, Harewood is related to the near-contemporary tower houses of Northumberland, notably Langley (qv) and Haughton (qv), both evolutionary developments of the hall house, each of which comprises a main block with a number of corner turrets. At Harewood, the two-storey main block (which contains the hall) is augmented by four corner towers (five storeys to the S, four storeys to the N, the NE tower containing the entrance) and a four-storey combined service and chamber block to the N, incorporating the NW tower. Structural anomalies suggest that the N block preceded the main block, and that the NW tower came later still, though these phases result from changes of plan during the course of construction, rather than different building campaigns.

Good-quality ashlar masonry with chamfered plinth and offsets. The corbels of a machicolated parapet survive at the S end. Generally plain fenestration, the windows mostly rectangular, the larger ones with mullions and transoms and moulded

Harewood from the SE.

surrounds. Exceptions are the chapel windows on the second floor of the entrance (NE) tower. Firstly, N and S, twin trefoil-arched lights with surmounting quatrefoil beneath a pointed arch. Secondly, a three-light E window with shield-shaped tracery echoing two flanking heraldic escutcheons. These latter bear the arms of Edward Balliol (L), erstwhile claimant to the throne of Scotland (of whom Aldeburgh was a follower), and those of Aldeburgh himself (R). Above the window a panel bearing the Aldeburgh motto '*vat sal be sal*' (what shall be shall). Below the E window a rather plain pointed entrance secured by a drawbar and a portcullis; inside the rib-vaulted porch a more elaborate inner doorway with moulded surround, the hood mould terminating in sculptured heads, led into the screens passage of the lower hall giving access to the kitchen and service rooms to the R (N) and to the hall. The lower hall was heated by a fireplace at the upper (S) end and retains stone side benches. On the W side of the former dais is an elaborate buffet with cinquefoiled fringe and ogee finial. Above is the upper hall, with a fireplace not only at the S end, but also in the E wall. In the towers and N block, many chambers with fireplaces and latrines. This kind of tightly planned and complex interior is related to a small group of castles in northern England associated with John Lewyn (cf. Castle Bolton, Lumley, Warkworth, Wressle, etc). Emery 1996, 339–44; Dennison and Richardson 2012.

HARTSHILL, Warwickshire (Private, but visible from the road). An under-researched motte and bailey on a ridge to the W side of the village. The circumstances of its foundation are obscure, but the manor was a property of the earls of Chester, and by the early C12 was held by the Hartshill family. Motte to the N, engulfed by the adjacent wood, and walled bailey to the S in the form of an irregular pentagon, both ditched around. The walls are pierced by cruciform arrow loops with circular oillets, probably C14. The chapel backed onto the bailey N wall and in the NE angle; similarly making use of the curtain are the ruins of a C16 house. Salzman 1947, 131; Wilson 2016, 2017a and 2017b.

HASTINGS, Sussex (Open). Motte and bailey on the site of an Iron Age promontory fort. Probably the castle raised by William the Conqueror in 1066 and depicted on the Bayeux Tapestry. A tower, most likely a keep, was built by Henry II in the 1170s. Substantial repairs were carried out in the 1220s. The inner bailey of the castle occupies the W end of the promontory, isolated by a rock-cut ditch. Its odd shape results from the loss of a large area to the S, owing to erosion of the cliff. The motte is at the NE corner of the bailey, of which it is now an integral part and no longer a distinct entity. Indeed, the top of the motte is now divided by the C13 curtain wall which survives on the NW and NE sides but has disappeared to the S with the collapse of the cliff. The main gatehouse, which occupies a roughly central position in the NE curtain, has twin D-shaped towers. There was an outer bailey to the NE defined by a ditch. Barker and Barton 1978.

HAUGHLEY, Suffolk (Private, but the motte and moat are visible from the village). Motte and bailey. Probably built by Hugh de Montfort who held Haughley in 1086. In 1163 it became a royal castle and in 1173 was destroyed by opponents of Henry II. Conical motte of impressive dimensions rivalling that of Thetford (qv), with off-centre summit producing a more precipitous outer (N) scarp. Bailey to the S with an inner bank, separated from the motte by a ditch, the whole complex surrounded by a moat. Traces of earthworks, including a moat, in the vicinity of the castle suggest an encompassing outer ward containing the church to the S of the bailey, and probably other elements of a settlement. Page 1911, 598–600.

HAUGHTON, Northumberland (Private). Former courtyard castle of which the main survival is a great tower converted from a hall house. Haughton was first mentioned as a castle in 1373, but the manor house that forms the core of the current tower was probably raised by the Swinburne family *c.*1280. As first built, it was a first-floor hall house with buttresses on all sides, four rectangular corner turrets rising above the main block and a (possibly three-storey) E bay containing the more private rooms. The first-floor entrance was at the W end of the S front (its internal face is still visible). Access between the ground and first floors was via a staircase in the W wall, and from the first floor upwards by means of a spiral stair in the SW turret. Probably in the early C14, as a response to deteriorating security on the northern border, the house was fortified by raising it into a tower, with the addition of an extra storey carried on a series of giant machicolated arches erected on the tops of the buttresses. Later in the C14 the walls were strengthened by infilling the arcades. Dodds 1940, 203–20; Simpson 1951; Emery 1996, 97–100.

HAWCOCK'S MOUNT, Shropshire. See **CAUS**.

HAW HILL, Morpeth, Northumberland. See **MORPETH**.

HEDINGHAM, Essex. See **CASTLE HEDINGHAM**.

HEIGHLEY, Staffordshire (Private). Stone courtyard castle built *c.*1220–40 for Henry de Audley (d. 1246), a follower of the Earl of Chester. The castle occupies a rocky promontory, which provides protection on the N and E sides, while the S and W sides were protected by a rock-cut ditch, the material from it being used to construct the walls in the manner of Alton (qv) and the Earl of Chester's Beeston (qv). Like both these castles, Heighley had a gatehouse with twin round-fronted flanking towers. The site is heavily overgrown, and the standing remains are fragmentary. Cantor 1966; Salter 1989, 21.

HELMSLEY Yorkshire North Riding (Open – EH). A property of Robert of Mortain, who may have built the first castle. By *c.*1122 it was in the hands of Walter Espec, whose lack of a male heir brought it to the Ros family in the 1150s. The greater part of the stone castle was built between 1191 and 1226, during the lordship of

Helmsley: The East Tower from the S.

A Guide to the Medieval Castles of England

Robert de Ros, the work perhaps extending into the lordship of Robert's son, William. Improvements were made to the domestic accommodation in the C14, and during the course of the C16, when the castle was held by the Manners family, Helmsley was remodelled and the residential accommodation much improved, a process that impacted on the medieval fabric. In 1644 the castle was surrendered to Parliament after a two-month siege and subsequently slighted.

Built on a sandstone ridge and forming a sub-rectangular site orientated NW–SE (described here as if it were N–S), the castle is surrounded by two ditches separated by a great rampart. The ditches were moats, fed from the N by a tributary of the river Rye. The main approach was from the S via an outer bailey. Facing it across a ditch is the front of the mid C13 S barbican, with (formerly open-backed) D-shaped towers at the two angles and flanking the gateway. The gateway now looks rather odd, owing to the addition of a C16 portal which, visually, pushes the towers into the background. The portcullis-protected gate passage was remodelled in the C16. So, into the barbican, which is traversed by the inner ditch, within which are the drawbridge abutments and mid C13 additions to the now ruinous S gate of *c.*1200. The inner abutment contains posterns or sally ports giving access to the ditch.

Through the gateway, directly in front is the E Tower, or keep, which straddles the E curtain, though only the inner (W) half has survived the C17 slighting. This tower is notable for its apsidal E prow, a most unusual and striking form. The tower rises through four storeys, as evidenced by the fenestration in the E wall. Originally, however, there were only two storeys: a basement lit by narrow loops carrying a vault on a central pillar, and a tall main floor open to the roof, lit by three lancet windows to the W, and above them a single lancet just below the ridgeline. In the C14 the tower was heightened, the old roof removed, a stone vault built over the first floor (remains of which are visible within the W window embrasures, which were encroached upon) and two additional storeys squeezed in above. The sequence can be seen quite clearly inside, where the original roofline is preserved. In concert with the heightening of the tower a pair of impressive corner turrets was added, rising above parapet level and corbelled slightly proud of the wall surface, the sides framed by prominent fillets.

The E Tower was a trophy piece that endowed prestige, but the main residential block was centred on the great hall, which lined the W curtain. Now only footings remain, but the service rooms can be made out at the S end together with the adjacent kitchens. At the NW corner of the hall, at a step in the W curtain, is the rectangular W Tower, a solar tower of *c.*1200, originally of three storeys, but given another floor in the C14, and substantially altered in the C16 including refenestration and alteration of the floor levels. The most unaltered part is the basement, which retains its original doorway and barrel-vault on large, chamfered ribs. N of the W Tower is the chamber block, heavily remodelled in the C16; extending E from it are the foundations of a long gallery.

Through the N Gate, to the thoroughly ruined N front: central gateway with D-shaped flanking towers and round corner towers at each end, the LH (E) tower with a semi-circular protrusion, or turret (cf. Barnwell, Longtown, Chartley). On the N side of the inner ditch is the N barbican, less elaborate than the S barbican, with only the gatehouse in stone, the sides of the flanking towers carried back as shield walls to the E and W right across the rampart. Kenyon 2017.

HEREFORD, Herefordshire (Open access). Motte and bailey, the remains of which are SE of the Cathedral next to the river Wye. A castle had probably been built at Hereford by 1051 by one of Edward the Confessor's Norman favourites, possibly his nephew Ralph, Earl of Hereford from 1052. When Leland saw it *c*.1540 it was on the brink of falling into ruin, but he considered it had been 'one of the fairest, largest and strongest castles of England.' The motte survived into the C18; its site is now occupied by Redcliffe Gardens. The kite-shaped bailey which fanned out towards the SE is now represented by Castle Green. The adjacent Castle Pool formed the N arm of the moat which connected with the Wye. Brown *et al.* 1963, 673–7; Shoesmith 1980 and 2009, 144–62; Whitehead 2007.

HERSTMONCEUX, Sussex (Open). Built by Sir Roger Fiennes under a licence to crenellate of 1441, Herstmonceux is one of an exclusive but significant group of C15 brick-built castles (see also Caister, Kirby Muxloe and Tattershall). Analogies with Eton College, which was under construction contemporaneously (1441–61), may point to the involvement of the King's master mason, Robert Westerley, who was overseeing work at Eton from 1441. In the C18 the castle was gutted and abandoned in favour of nearby Herstmonceux Place, and only restored as a home in the first half of the C20. The castle is now occupied by the Observatory Science Centre.

Herstmonceux is a symmetrical quadrangular courtyard castle with polygonal towers at the corners and three to each elevation; the castle is enclosed on three sides by a moat. There is a twin-towered main entrance in the centre of the S front, and a single towered postern gate in the middle of the N front, very much as at Bodiam (qv) with the compass points reversed, though Herstmonceux is a rather larger building. The standard C15 window is a single rectangular light with a transom.

The architectural high point of the castle is the grand three-storey main gatehouse in which a four-centred gate arch is recessed beneath a high outer arch of similar form. Between the two is a large transomed first-floor window of two cinquefoil-headed lights framed by the two vertical slots for the drawbridge counterbalance beams. Above the outer arch a stone panel bearing the arms of Sir Roger Fiennes is flanked by two twin-light transomed windows. The towers to either side of the gate, though polygonal in the lower storeys, become circular at second-floor level where they are corbelled out over the lower stages. All three stages carry ashlar-framed cruciform loops with oillets, and beneath the lowest stage of loops is a line of circular

Herstmonceux from the SE. From Turner and Parker 1859.

gun ports. Continuous corbelled and arched machicolations carry the crenellated parapet, the merlons of which are pierced by further cruciform loops. Behind the parapet, rising above each tower, is a round turret adding a modicum of height, without necessarily improving the prospect.

Apart from the gatehouse range, the buildings now extending around the central courtyard date from the C20. They occupy the sites of the medieval ranges, but in the C15 the central area also contained buildings, for instead of a single courtyard, the accommodation was arranged around four courtyards, three of them fringed by cloisters. Amongst the buildings in this central area was the great hall which bordered the N side of the largest of these courtyards. Emery 2006, 343–55.

HERTFORD, Hertfordshire (Open access to the grounds). Motte and bailey on the SE bank of the river Lea probably established by William I soon after 1066, though the first record of building works dates from the 1170s, at which time the curtain wall around the inner bailey may have been raised. The one recorded siege was in 1216, when the castle was captured by Prince Louis of France. In 1360 Hertford was granted to John of Gaunt, soon to be Duke of Lancaster, and, as part of the Duchy, returned to the Crown in 1399. Lancaster set about improving the domestic accommodation in 1380, when a contract was drawn up with the royal carpenter William de Wintringham for the construction of 'certain new houses, chapel and other enclosures', which were to be of timber on stone foundations. These apartments are probably the ones that appear on the E side of the inner bailey on a C16 plan of the castle. They include an aisled hall on one side of a courtyard, and further N, an arrangement of buildings around a cloister. A new great gatehouse of brick was added by Henry VI during the 1460s under the master mason William Hull and master carpenter Thomas Norman. This is now the principal survival from the medieval period.

A small motte lies to the N next to the river Lea with an irregularly polygonal bailey extending towards the SE enclosed by a curtain wall, remains of which survive to the NE and SE. This complex was enclosed by a moat which joined the Lea at both ends. There was an outer bailey to the SW and an outer moat extended around the entire castle as far as the Lea. The inner gatehouse is on the SW side and was formerly approached across the moat from the outer bailey. Although the moats have gone, the outer bailey remains as gardens. The C15 gatehouse is now accompanied by C18 (R) and C20 (L) brick extensions, and was refenestrated in the C18 with Gothick windows, but once these distractions are dismissed from the mind, together with the Gothick porch, which covers the medieval gate arch, we can appreciate the stately character of Henry VI's gatehouse. Built in red brick laid to English bond and framed by polygonal corner turrets, it rises through three storeys with an arcaded corbel table at the wall head and crenellated parapet. The other remains of the medieval castle include a decapitated flint-built polygonal tower at the S angle of the inner bailey, flanking a pointed gate arch, and elements of the flint-built inner curtain. Brown *et al.* 1963, 677–81; Zeepvat and Cooper-Reade 1994–6; Emery 2000, 256–8.

HEVER, Kent (Open). Quadrangular moated courtyard castle S of the river Eden. In 1271 Stephen Penchester (see Allington, qv) obtained a licence to strengthen his manor house of Hever with a wall of stone and lime and to crenellate it in the manner of a castle. Over 100 years later, in 1383, a second licence was granted to the then owner, John Lord Cobham (then building Cooling Castle [qv]). It is not apparent that anything of Penchester's castle survives within the current fabric, and Hever is generally considered to be a late C14 building, albeit much altered. Modifications were begun by the Boleyns, who acquired the property in 1462, and they culminated in the restoration by William Waldorf Astor in 1903–7, during which the interiors were refurbished, Astor also built an extensive complex of cottages and outbuildings to the N of the castle. The medieval castle was formerly closer to the Eden, which fed the moats, but the construction of the Astor buildings to the N necessitated altering the course of the river, and in the process, widening it.

Lord Cobham's castle is approached from the S. The main feature of the entrance (S) front is a massive central gatehouse rising through three storeys, its size accentuated by the diminutive square corner towers which frame each end of the frontage; it's an odd arrangement, but evidently a deliberate confection to emphasize the gatehouse, which takes up one whole side of the courtyard. The off-centre gateway is set between stepped buttress turrets linked at parapet level by arched machicolations on corbelling. The buttresses are decorated with blind two-tier panelling beneath gablets. Further decorative panelling exists over the entrance and above it is a single gun loop of inverted keyhole type. Additional defensive features are to be found in the gate passage, which was protected by three portcullises and two pair of doors; the rib-vault is pierced by murder holes. Emery 2006, 355–7.

HINTON WALDRIST, Berkshire (Private). Probable motte and bailey next to the church of St Margaret, now the grounds of a private house. The earthworks comprise a ditch (of which only the SW and NW arms are visible), defining an enclosure, or bailey, of uncertain extent, and, on the SW edge of the ditch, a flat-topped mound, or motte. Excavation in 1939 suggested an early C12 date; the excavators argued that it was erected during Stephen's reign (1135–54). Gardener and Jope 1940.

HOLDGATE, Shropshire (Private). Motte and bailey built by Helgot (from whom Holdgate takes its name) who held the castle in 1086 as the caput of his barony. Helgot's grandson died without leaving a son, and *c.*1200 the barony passed to the Maudit family who held it until 1258, when it was alienated to Richard, Earl of Cornwall, and held of him by the Knights Templar. In 1284 Holdgate was acquired by Robert Burnell, Bishop of Bath and Wells, and owner of Acton Burnell (qv). The castle lies NE of the church and comprises a large motte with a roughly square bailey to the NE, generally ill-defined but retaining scarping around the N, NW and NE. The triangular platform on which the Norman church is built is considered to be a second bailey. Stonework remains on top of the motte suggest the former presence of a keep; a C13 D-shaped tower on the NW side of the bailey, attached to a post-medieval farmhouse, is usually attributed to Burnell; it has ground-floor level arrow loops and first-floor level narrow rectangular windows. Duckers 2006, 84–9.

HOLLINSIDE, County Durham (Open access). Ruined C13 and C14 fortified manor house built on the edge of a slope overlooking the river Derwent. Aligned NE–SW facing SE (hereafter N–S facing E). Hall with attached chamber and service wings projecting E either side of the recessed entrance. A tower carried on a high arch thrown between the wings was built over the recess; the tower has largely gone but the arch remains and is now the most remarkable aspect of the building. Comparisons have been drawn with the entrance to Lumley Castle (qv) of *c.*1390, though perhaps the Moot Hall, Hexham, is a more apposite analogy. On the S face a C13 first-floor pointed window of two lancet lights beneath a circle. Hugill 1979, 55–6.

HOPTON CASTLE, Shropshire (Open access – EH). Mostly known for its great tower. The manor of Hopton was occupied by the Hopton family by 1165, with whom it remained throughout the Middle Ages. The origins of the castle are unknown but architectural detailing of the tower suggests a construction date for that particular component in the late C13/early C14. Garrisoned for Parliament in the Civil War, the castle was besieged, damaged by artillery, captured, and the garrison put to death. The tower stands near the centre of a complex of earthworks comprising three baileys: an irregularly-shaped NE enclosure, containing the tower, a small inner bailey to the W of the tower and an L-shaped bailey to the S and E. These enclosures were moated around with water from two streams which extend around the S and E sides of the castle. The tower itself, which is set upon, or rather within, a low mound, is rectangular, the main body some 45 ft × 37 ft (13.7 m × 11.2 m), with a square turret at each corner, that to the SW much larger than the others. The pointed ground-floor entrance is in the N side at mound-top level and must have been approached by a flight of steps; coping stones over the doorway denote the pitch of the former porch roof. Inside there were two principal storeys, each containing a heated main room with associated intra-mural chambers including latrines. Curnow 1989; Duckers 2006, 90–2; Time Team 2010.

HORNBY, Lancashire. See **CASTLESTEDE**.

HUNTINGDON, Huntingdonshire (Open access). Motte with two baileys built by William the Conqueror in 1068 on the N bank of the river Ouse to control the Ermine Street crossing. In the C12 Huntingdon came to the kings of Scotland through marriage, and in 1173, when William the Lion supported Prince Henry in the rebellion against his father Henry II, Huntingdon was besieged and destroyed and seemingly not rebuilt. Both the motte and the two baileys have suffered by being cut through by the railway. Kidney-shaped bailey to the E of the motte enclosed by a ditch and inner bank, and larger W bailey of similar plan demarcated by a scarp. The earthworks appear to have been modified in the C17 by the construction of a gun emplacement on the motte. Remains of a motte on Mill Common, some 400 yards to the W of Huntingdon Castle, may be the siege castle erected by Henry II in 1173. Page *et al.* 1932; RCHME 1926, 149–51; Brown *et al.* 1963.

HUNTINGTON, Herefordshire (Private). Motte with two baileys rebuilt in stone near the Welsh border. Date uncertain, but in existence by the 1220s when it became the seat of the barony of Kington (qv) under Reginald de Braose, lord of Bramber, Brecknock, etc. In 1244 it came by marriage to the Bohun family. Motte with oval inner bailey to the NNE, both enclosed by a ditch around the N, S, and E sides and by a berm along the steeply scarped W side; a counterscarp bank followed the ditch. The entrance to the inner bailey (marked by a causeway across the ditch) was on the E side via the semi-oval outer bailey, which extends towards the N. There are some masonry remains including fragments of a stone curtain and a semi-circular wall tower. The outer bailey is demarcated by a ditch to the N and E and also has an eastern entrance directly opposite the inner gateway. RCHME 1934, 75–6; Remfry 1997c; Shoesmith 2009, 168–70.

HUTTONS AMBO, Yorkshire North Riding. See **HUTTON COLSWAIN**.

HUTTON COLSWAIN, Huttons Ambo, Yorkshire North Riding (D). Site of a fortified manor house taking its name from one Colsweinus, who held the manor in the C12. Excavation by M.W. Thompson in the 1950s revealed two medieval phases. Firstly, a C12 lightly defended triangular enclosure with a timber hall. Secondly, a more heavily defended, sub-rectangular enclosure with substantial ditch and inner bank, within which the C12 hall was rebuilt, partly in stone. At the E end of the N side a stone causeway crossed the ditch to a gateway, equipped with inner and outer gates. Thompson 1957.

HYLTON, County Durham (Open – EH). Stone courtyard castle of which only the great gatehouse and the chapel survive above ground level. Built for William Lord Hylton *c*.1395–1405. Major alterations, including refenestration and internal remodelling, were effected in the C18, when the gatehouse became the core of a classical house. Restored to a C14 appearance in 1869. Taken into guardianship in 1950 and consolidated as a ruin over the next 20 years.

The gatehouse is an imposing self-contained residence of rectangular plan, the main block rising through three stories. Most of the fenestration dates from 1869, but the cinquefoil-headed form is derived from primary examples discovered during the

Hylton: The great gatehouse from the W.

restoration of which one or two survive. The gateway (narrowed in 1869) is recessed between a pair of square turrets linked at parapet level by an arched machicolation. Just below the arch is a display of heraldic shields which, together with further devices on the E front, provide the date range for the castle. The entrance and corner turrets are capped by octagonal battlements carried on triangular-shaped stones laid across the corners, and the parapets are carried on corbelled machicolations. This entrance arrangement derives from the slightly earlier Lumley Castle (qv), very probably a work of John Lewyn.

To the rear (E) a broad central turret (formerly containing the gate arch into the courtyard) bears the arms of Lord Hylton and the white hart of Richard II. Topping the corners of the main block are circular bartizans (cf. Tynemouth Priory gatehouse [qv]). Morley 1976 and 1979; Time Team 1995.

INKBERROW, Worcestershire (Open access). A castle was in existence at Inkberrow by 1216 when, under the tenancy of William Marshal, Earl of Pembroke, it was repaired. In 1233 was seized by the King from William's son, Richard, and the order given to destroy it. The site of the castle is represented by a rectangular moat on Millennium Green, some 350ft (106.7m) NE of the church. Page and Willis-Bund 1913, 421–3 and 1924, 428.

KENDAL, Westmorland. **Castle Hill** (Open access). Ringwork and bailey of uncertain date, rebuilt in stone. Built on a ridge to the E of the medieval town centre, the earthworks consist of a nearly circular ditch with counterscarp bank to the S, and traces of a ditched rectangular bailey to the N. From this latter there was access to the main gatehouse of the ringwork, now vanished, although a C16 sketch depicts twin cylindrical flanking towers. To the E of the entrance are the remains of the C14 first-floor hall on a vaulted basement, with a rectangular tower at its NE angle. On the NW side is a C12/C13 cylindrical tower half-in and half-out of the curtain, with a corbelled latrine in the angle with the curtain. Then, to the W, a C12/C13 solid half round tower, and, to the S, another rectangular tower, closing a space caused by a staggering of the two adjoining lengths of curtain. Curwen 1908, 84–102, and 1913, 145–9; RCHME 1936, 122–4; Perriam and Robinson 1998, 348–9.

Castle Howe (Open access). Motte and bailey built *c*.1092. Situated on a spur about 200 yards W of Highgate. Motte to the W with irregularly triangular bailey to the E. Curwen 1913, 30–1; RCHME 1936, 122; Perriam and Robinson 1998, 335.

KENILWORTH, Warwickshire (Open – EH). One of the great English castles, established by Henry I's chamberlain, Geoffrey de Clinton, in the 1120s, probably with royal financial backing; it is likely that de Clinton was responsible for the keep. The water defences that were to be a notable feature of the C13 castle were in existence by the later C12. In 1173/4, on the death of another Geoffrey de Clinton, Kenilworth was taken into the hands of the Crown and remained in royal ownership until 1253. This period probably witnessed the completion of the stone defences. Simon de Montfort, to whom the castle was granted for life in 1253, is also recorded as having fortified the castle, possibly a reference to the outwork known as 'The Brays', which protects the main approach from the SE. After de Montfort was killed at the Battle of Evesham in 1265 his supporters ensconced themselves in Kenilworth, undergoing a six-month siege the following year. In the later C14 John of Gaunt, Duke of Lancaster, remodelled the inner court, where he created a palatial

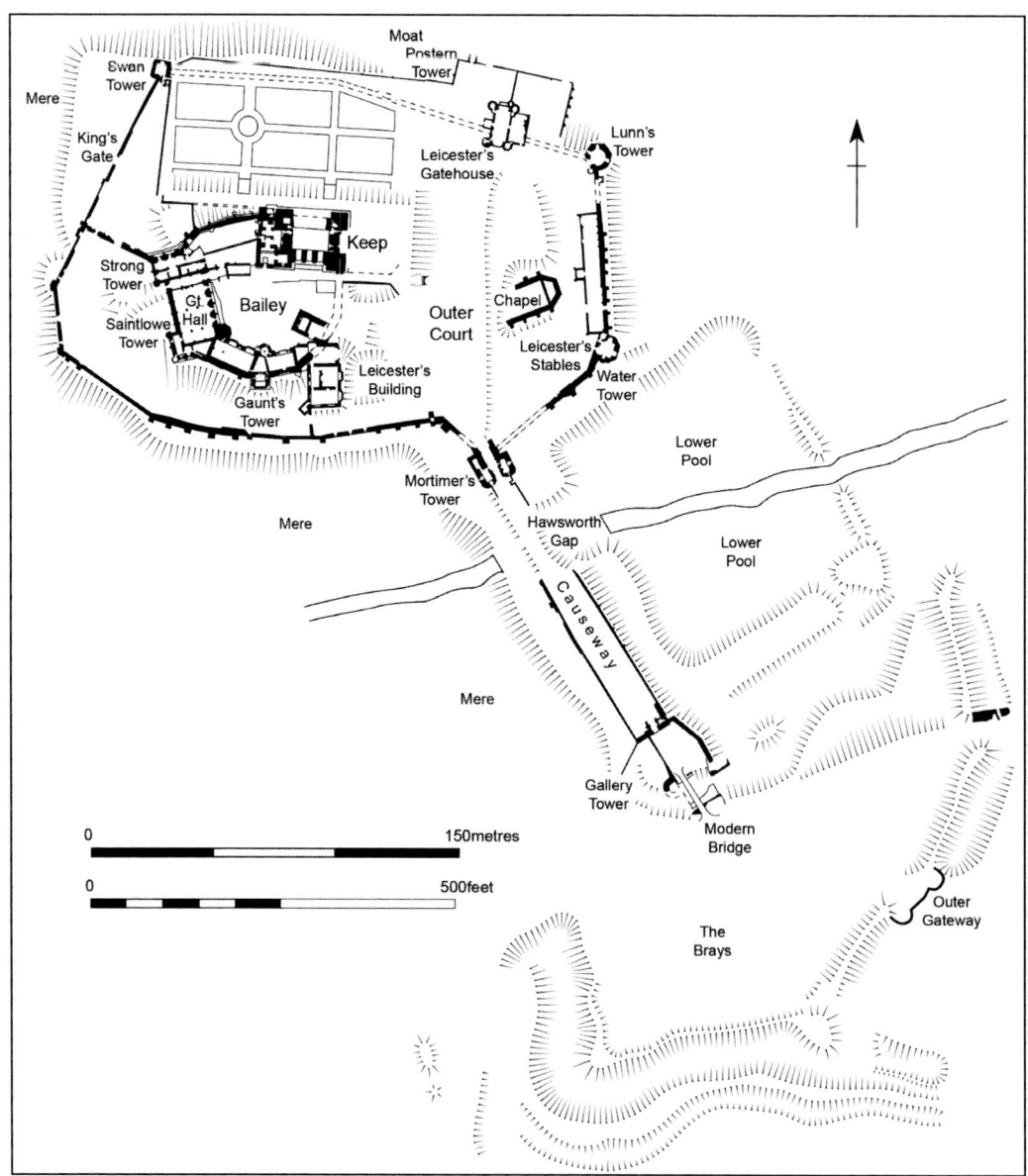

Kenilworth: Ground plan. After Thompson 1977.

residence under the direction of the royal craftsmen, Henry Spenser, mason, and William Wintringham, carpenter, both of whom had worked at Windsor (qv). The last great building period was that of Robert Dudley, Earl of Leicester, who in the 1570s constructed a large new N gatehouse, built a lodging tower known as 'Leicester's Building' attached to the inner court, and remodelled the keep.

Kenilworth is built on a low sandstone hill, near the confluence of two streams which were utilized to feed a moat to the N and E, the Mere, an artificial lake that protected the castle to the S and W, and the Lower Pool to the SE. The access road to the castle is via the Brays, a courtyard barbican enclosed by a curving ditch and inner bank, and formerly entered via a SE gateway with rounded flanking towers. A bridge led from The Brays (now the castle car park) to the Gallery Tower, of which stonework traces remain below the level of the present bridge. This led onto the Tilt Yard, a causeway and dam dividing the Lower Pool on the R (E) from the Mere. At the far (N) end of the Tilt Yard is Mortimer's Tower, the castle's S gateway. The boldly projecting round-fronted flanking towers with cruciform loops are in fact a C13 extension (probably one of King John's improvements) of a C12 rectangular gatehouse, remains of which lie to the rear.

From here, the castle can be circumperambulated. Following the path around the S and W sides, which faced the Mere, the curtain is relieved only by buttresses, the first tower after the gatehouse being the square Swan Tower at the NW corner, a much-altered structure of probable C14 origin. Then a long stretch of garden wall, which replaced the demolished N curtain, breaking forward towards the E end in front of Leicester's Gatehouse of 1570–5, which looms up behind it on the site of the old N gatehouse. Leicester's Gatehouse is rectangular with prominent octagonal corner turrets following the late medieval tradition; the gateways in the short sides were blocked and an extension added to the LH side when the building was converted to a house after the Civil War. Then, at the NE corner, the rather interesting early C13 Lunn's Tower, a three-storey cylindrical building, its outer face articulated by broad pilaster buttresses and originally pierced by two tiers of recessed arrow loops with fishtail bases. Next to the S, at the junction of the moat with the Lower Pool, is the early C14 Water Tower; polygonal on a square base, the corners rising as pyramidal buttresses, an apparent adaptation of the squat 'spur' principle that occurs at Alnwick (qv) in the early C14. Cruciform arrow loops with oillet terminals, and old fashioned-looking first-floor windows of two lights beneath a pointed outer arch.

Kenilworth: The keep from the SE.

A Guide to the Medieval Castles of England

So, back to Mortimer's Tower and through to the outer court. Here, built against the E curtain, is Leicester's Stables, in fact built by his father, the Earl of Northumberland, *c.*1550. Timber-framed with decorative panels, on a high stone base with a tall gabled porch. Formerly lofted, it is now open to the roof. Immediately R (S) of the stables is the Water Tower, the canted sides of the upper storey being carried on squinch arches; both rooms were heated and equipped with a latrine. To the L (N) of the stables is Lunn's Tower with polygonal interior. In front of the stable building are the partial foundations of Thomas of Lancaster's chapel of between 1314 and 1322; they show the E end with its polygonal apse.

Now for the highlight of Kenilworth: the inner court, which occupies the highest point of the castle. Viewed from Leicester's Stables, the former entrance (E) front is flanked by the C12 keep to the R (N) and by Leicester's Building of 1571 to the L (S), which are sited at the NE and SE angles respectively. The inner court was formerly surrounded by a ditch. The gateway was adjacent to the keep and approached by a causeway across the ditch; its portcullis groove is still to be seen in the fragment of curtain still attached to Geoffrey de Clinton's keep (Caesar's Tower). The keep is a substantial two-storey building with a high plinth stepping up to a raised ground-floor level, pilaster buttresses, and very prominent corner turrets, these latter being the defining aspect of the tower. The building may have been heightened in the late C12/early C13 when the arrow loops with their wide fishtail bases were added, together with the upper windows of the SW turrets; both openings have double-splayed surrounds, like the openings of Lunn's Tower. Some of the original recessed round-arched windows survive, but much of the fenestration is owed to the Earl of Leicester's remodelling of 1570, in which some of the C12 windows were opened out, and mullioned and transomed windows inserted. Entry to the keep was through a forebuilding at the W end, with entrances at ground- and first-floor levels, the latter via a staircase. Leicester removed the stair and created a grand arcaded entrance gallery leading both to the keep through its original ground-floor doorway, and to the formal garden in the outer court. The main body of the keep contained a large room on each floor connected by a spiral stair in the NE corner, both levels having access to a well in the SE corner. The C12 window embrasures survive, semi-circular at ground-floor level and segmental above, the latter taller, reflecting the greater height of the upper room and its superior status.

The W side of the inner court was occupied by the great hall, rebuilt for John of Gaunt in the 1370s. Associated with this, lining the curtain to the W of the keep, were the kitchens, which were rebuilt at the same time. Only fragments remain, including indications of three large fireplaces along the curtain, and a fourth, with associated bread oven, at the E end. Service rooms were in the Strong Tower at the N end of the hall, including (at first-floor level) the pantry and buttery. Gaunt's hall was also at first-floor level; an external staircase (the foundations of which can be seen next to the keep forebuilding), led to a porch at the lower (N) end of the hall; a remnant of its base survives in front of the entrance to the basement. The porch was balanced at the upper (S) end of the hall by the surviving polygonal bay, or oriel, window. Otherwise, the main features of the range are its very large hall windows with four-centred arch heads and Perpendicular tracery.

Inside, the walls of the basement retain responds for rib-vaulting which was supported by two rows of columns. In the hall above, two fireplaces survive opposite one another in the side walls; formerly there was also a triple fireplace in the S wall to warm the backs of the diners at the high table and a smaller one in the bay window. The hall fireplaces and windows are sumptuously decorated, both incorporating heavily moulded surrounds and panelled jambs. Between the window heads are chases for the former roof trusses. A doorway in the W wall gives access to the external elevation, a symmetrical frontage, the hall recessed between a pair of quasi-towers, the Saintlowe Tower to the R (S) and the Strong Tower to the L (N), each with octagonal corner turrets and the unusual feature of a central triangular buttress, a form reflected in the buttresses of the hall on this side. The higher status of the Saintlowe Tower (which formed part of the private apartments) is denoted by its large traceried windows as opposed to the plain rectangular lights of its counterpart at the lower end of the hall.

At the upper end of the hall, lining the S curtain, were the (now largely destroyed) main residential apartments. These were entered via the oriel and contained sequentially more private rooms: a great chamber, inner chamber, and finally a bed chamber. At the junction of the first two rooms, the externally projecting Gaunt's Tower contained latrines at two levels. Opposite this on the courtyard side are the remains of another polygonal oriel window. The apartments were remodelled by Leicester, when he added his new four-storey lodging tower at the E end of the range. Salzman 1951, 153–8; Thompson 1977; Emery 2000, 399–408; Morris 2011 and 2015.

KILPECK, Herefordshire (Open access). Motte with several baileys W of the church. Later C11. The motte is accompanied by an outer bailey to the S and a crescent-shaped inner bailey to the E. There is a third enclosure to the W, and a fourth was noted to the NW in the 1930s, though this is no longer apparent. On top of the motte are the remains of a C12 polygonal shell-keep incorporating a fireplace. RCHME 1931, 158–9. Shoesmith 2009, 174–88; Higham 2015, 60–3.

KINGERBY, Lincolnshire (Private). Ringwork with two baileys, now the grounds of early C19 Kingerby Hall. In existence by 1216 when the castle of Peter d'Amundeville was burnt by the forces of King John. Two years later Henry III ordered its complete destruction, but occupation of the site continued. At the centre of the castle remains is a roughly circular ringwork comprising a raised platform within a moat. Earthwork remains of two baileys to the E and W meeting to the S of the ringwork. Salter 2002a.

KINAIRD'S FERRY, Lincolnshire. See **OWSTON FERRY**.

KIRBY MUXLOE, Leicestershire (Open access – EH). Moated quadrangular castle begun for William Lord Hastings in 1480 on the site of an existing manor house, but never completed. Hastings was executed in 1483, but work continued in a desultory fashion until the end of 1484. The master mason was John Cowper, who was concurrently undertaking the reconstruction of Tattershall church, some 100 miles away. Kirby Muxloe is a brick-built castle, its walls enlivened by dark blue headers forming diaper patterns against the more uniform red. Existing remains are the moat, platform, gatehouse and W tower, but the castle foundations show there were to be four corner towers, each with a stair turret and a latrine turret, and mid-wall turrets on all but the (NW) entrance front, where the gatehouse occupies the centre. Intended as a three-storey structure, this now only rises through two. Octagonal turrets at the two corners with attached latrine turrets. Circular gun ports at ground-floor level. Hastings' initials appear in blue brick above the gateway and there are further symbolic patterns to either side. The W tower survives to full height and contained a

Kirby Muxloe: The rear of the gatehouse.

series of lodgings and low-level gun ports. In the centre of the courtyard are traces of the foundations of the former manor house. Thompson 1913–20; Goodall 2015.

KIRKOSWALD, Cumberland (Private). Fragmentary remains of a quadrangular castle begun by Humphrey Lord Dacre, on whose death, in 1485, it was described as 'newly built'. His son Thomas Lord Dacre (d. 1525) 'did finish it and mote it about with great change'. Kirkoswald Castle was gradually dismantled between $c.1610$ and $c.1630$, some of the materials being used for the repair of Naworth Castle (qv). A roof with cambered tie beams in Lord William's Tower at Naworth is believed to have come from Kirkoswald. The castle was entered from the W. There were three corner towers, that to the NW possibly a great tower with diagonally-projecting turrets (cf. Dacre qv) to the three external angles, of which one (SW) survives almost to full height. Otherwise, the masonry remains are minimal, although the surrounding ditch can be traced. Curwen 1913, 150–3; Perriam and Robinson 1998, 124–5.

KNARESBOROUGH, Yorkshire West Riding (Open). Royal courtyard castle first mentioned in 1129/30 occupying a cliff-faced promontory on the E bank of the river Nidd. Substantial works were carried out by King John in 1203–12 including major ditching operations, to isolate the promontory and deepen the natural defiles to the N and S. In the early years of the C14 Edward I carried out a programme of repairs and reconstruction. Royal interest in Knaresborough increased under Edward II, who between 1307 and 1312 caused a new great tower (the King's Tower) to be constructed under the master mason Hugh of Titchmarsh. The initiation of work on the King's Tower coincided with the granting of the honour of Knaresborough to Edward's favourite, Piers Gaveston, and it has been suggested that the tower was intended to bolster Gaveston's prestige. In 1644 the castle was besieged and captured by Parliamentarian forces and subsequently slighted.

Apart from the partially demolished great tower, the remains are fragmentary. The E ditch has been largely infilled and the curtain has to a great extent disappeared, although its path is denoted here and there by the remains of a few solid D-shaped wall turrets, and, at the S end, by the twin flanking towers of the outer gateway, of similar form and ashlar faced; on the N side it was straddled by the keep. Roughly triangular in plan, the castle was divided into an inner and outer ward by a N–S wall extending from the SE angle of the keep, where there was a gateway between the two enclosures, still surviving in part.

The keep itself was rather unusual, having a semi-polygonal plan, its canted prow projecting outside the curtain wall, and round turrets to the N and SW. Now greatly diminished by its partial demolition, it was once a palatial residence of peculiar originality comprising three storeys over a cellar. The elaborately vaulted cellar and main ground-floor room were entered separately from the S, while the main approach to the first floor was via an elegant mural staircase (now largely vanished) beginning within the vicinity of the gateway between the wards and extending through the E side of the keep. It led to an antechamber and then into a hall, or audience chamber, with a western dais (its position indicated by a great arched recess) served by a fireplace at the N end and by an enormous pointed window at the S end. There was a chamber above, though almost nothing remains. Dixon 1990.

KNEPP, Sussex (Accessible by footpath from the Knepp Castle Estate walkers' car park). Hunting lodge established by the Braose family within the barony of Bramber (qv). It was forfeited by William de Braose in 1208 and so came into the hands of King John. The castle was repaired in 1210 and 1214. John ordered its destruction in 1216, but Henry III returned it to the Braose family. Sub-oval enclosure defined by a ditch and counterscarp bank, within which is a large natural mound or motte. On top is a wall, apparently the remains of a keep, with pilaster buttresses at the one surviving angle and a first-floor entrance. Hudson 1986, 111–12.

KNOCKIN, Shropshire (Private). Probable motte and bailey immediately E of the church, first mentioned in 1165 when it was held by Guy le Strange, who, according to tradition, was the builder of the castle. Tree-covered low rectangular motte (or possibly a raised inner bailey) to the W, with an L-shaped outer bailey to the E and N, the eastern section containing the former rectory. The site is bounded by streams to the E and W. Salter 2001, 48; Duckers 2006, 93–5.

LANCASTER, Lancashire (Open). Built on a hill within a loop of the river Lune, and on the site of a Roman fort, Lancaster Castle, which is most notable for its great square keep, was probably founded by Roger de Poitou $c.$1092 as a ringwork. Roger was probably also responsible for the construction of the keep between $c.$1092 and 1102, when he rebelled against Henry I, and his English possessions were seized by the Crown. King John did some work here in the early C13, which may have included rebuilding the enceinte in stone. In 1267 the Lancaster estate was granted to Edmund Crouchback (later First Earl of Lancaster). Tree-ring dating of the timbers suggest that a refurbishment of the keep was carried out under John of Gaunt, Duke of Lancaster, probably in the 1380s. In 1399, when Gaunt's son was elevated to the throne as Henry IV, the Duchy of Lancaster estates came to the Crown. In 1402 Henry IV initiated a major building programme at Lancaster, which included the construction of a new gatehouse (second only to the keep as one of the main interests of the castle). Some demolition was carried out after the Civil War to render the castle untenable. Subsequently, Lancaster contained the county gaol, and remained a gaol until 2011.

Starting at Henry IV's great gatehouse, at the junction of Castle Park and Castle Hill, an easily achieved perambulation around the castle walls via Castle Hill/St Mary's Parade (E), St Mary's Gate (N), Castle Parade (W) and Castle Park (S), gives an idea of the extent, though it should be noted that most of the current enclosing wall lies forward of the position occupied by the medieval curtain. However, the few landmarks are instructive. First, the C14 Well Tower (or Witches' Tower) on St Mary's Parade, a large rectangular residential building, its front now nearly flush with the prison wall, but formerly projecting almost entirely outside the curtain. A little further on, looming up behind the walls, the great tower, or keep. Then, on the W side, the late C18 Shire Hall complex, its orientation following that of the great hall, and incorporating its medieval basement, which was set against the curtain wall. At the S end is Adrian's Tower, which stood at the SW corner of the castle; its medieval character has been lost through refacing in ashlar, but its circular plan suggests a C13 date, and it may be part of King John's improvements.

So, back to the monumental gatehouse on Castle Hill, one of the best-preserved buildings of its type in England, maintaining not only much of its original external appearance, but also its primary timberwork. Its impact is accentuated by the steep rise of the approach, the three-storey building has a central pointed entrance of two moulded orders recessed between semi-polygonal flanking towers pierced at ground-floor level by cruciform loops with basal oillets. Above the gate a niche is flanked by two heraldic shields, both depicting the royal arms as configured in 1406–22. Within the niche is an 1822 statue of John of Gaunt (then thought to be the builder of the gatehouse); Henry IV is more likely to have been the original subject. The building is crowned by a machicolated parapet breaking forward on continuous corbelling, and its verticality and three-dimensional quality is accentuated by a pair of watch turrets sticking up behind the parapets of the flanking towers.

In the soffit of the outer arch are two 'murder holes', and beyond the portal, in front of the gate arch proper, a portcullis. Then the gateway of two hollow-chamfered orders with segmental-pointed arch and squat, dogtooth-like ornamented capitals, shaped in sympathy with the arch and jamb moulding. Inside the gate passage is evidence that the C15 builders incorporated elements of an earlier gatehouse. The roughly coursed masonry of the side walls contrasts with the ashlar of the exterior, and may be contemporary with a series of corbelled vaulting responds with foliated bases, short filleted shafts, and octagonal capitals dating from *c.*1200.

To the rear of the gatehouse, on the LH (N) side, a C13 round stair turret has been adapted to serve the new building; it has a C15 square upward extension. There are also two doorways on the RH (S) side which give access to staircases leading to the upper rooms. At second-floor level is a row of C15 two-light traceried windows with square heads and labels providing clearstorey lighting to the rooms at this level; just below these a row of plain rectangular windows indicates a second-floor corridor from which the rooms were accessed.

The ground storey was entered from opposed doorways at the inner (W) end of the gate passage. There is a ground-floor guard room on each side, the S side equipped with mural latrine, the N side with a doorway formerly giving access to the berm in front of the (now vanished) medieval curtain. Both rooms, in common with all the upper rooms, retain their original flooring, consisting of massive arched-braced tie beams supported by wall posts set on corbels. Tree-ring analysis suggests a felling date of *c*.1404 for the timbers. The tripartite division of the ground floor is repeated on the upper floors. An interesting feature over the outer (E) end of the gate passage is a narrow portcullis chamber, entered from the N room, complete with portcullis and lifting mechanism. Above this is the second-floor corridor, running between N and S staircases. At this level the timber roof structures survive, very similar in construction to the flooring, the cambered tie beams supporting a pair of purlins and a ridge piece.

Regarding the Well Tower (Witches' Tower) on the W side of the castle, tree-ring analysis of timbers therein suggests an earliest felling date of 1265 (but the tower is more probably a C14 construction), and refurbishment in the late C14/early C15. Unpretentious courtyard (W) elevation with three entrances, the (pointed) LH one set within an oblique deflection of the wall which denotes the line of the lost medieval curtain. The central doorway has an ogee arch made from two stones, while the head of the RH one is a late rebuild. The replacement windows of the upper rooms appear to be set beneath medieval relieving arches. In essence, there are three storeys above barrel-vaulted basements; the upper two storeys are equipped with latrines and were intended as high-class domestic accommodation.

Finally, the three-storey keep, which occupies the high point of the site. It is *c*.80ft (7.4m) square and 70ft (21.3m) high, although the uppermost storey is a late medieval addition. Ghosts of the original battlements can be seen in several places just below the level of the third-floor windows. Archaeological recording suggests that the early keep was completed in two main building phases, the large stone blocks of the ground and first floors giving way to smaller stones above. Above that is the more regular masonry of the late medieval heightening. Pilaster buttresses clasp the corners and occupy the centre of each face, those to E and W marking the position of the spine wall dividing the interior into two equal parts. Only the N and E elevations are largely unobscured by adjoining buildings. Here, a number of C11/C12 windows survive with semi-circular arches on nook shafts with cushion capitals.

The entrance to the keep was at the W end of the S front, at first-floor level, but is now blocked from view by the late C18 Debtors' Wing; other doorways are later insertions. Owing to considerable alteration, and the masking of the walls with plasterwork, the interior is for the moment imperfectly understood, but in its primary form comprised two storeys: a basement which was probably for storage, and first-floor residential apartments, which may tentatively be identified as hall (S) and chamber (N).

An E–W line of heavy timber posts on stone pads divides the S basement and supports the first-floor bridging beam; arched braces extend from the posts to the beam; dendrochronology suggests that the timbers were felled in the 1380s. Three reset nail-studded prison cell doors at the W end of the basement have also been given late C14 dates. Also in the later medieval period the hall was divided horizontally by the insertion of an upper floor, with wall posts and arched braces supported on inserted stone corbels; a felling date range of 1379–1404 is indicated. Guy 2014–15b and 2016–17b.

LANGLEY, Northumberland (Hotel open to guests only). First mentioned in 1365, all that remains of the castle of Langley is the mid C14 great tower probably built for Thomas de Lucy (d.1365) of Cockermouth, sometime after the Battle of Neville's Cross of 1346. Following the death of Thomas' son, Anthony, in 1368, the Lucy

Langley: Perspective and ground plan. From Turner and Parker 1853.

estates were inherited by Thomas' daughter Maud, and through her marriage to Henry Percy, Earl of Northumberland *c*.1381, became a Percy property. By 1541 the tower had lost its roof and floors and was little more than a shell. In 1882 it was purchased by Cadwallader Bates, who restored it as a home.

Sited on a triangular spur between Langley Burn (E) and its tributary Deanraw Burn (NW), the great tower is aligned roughly N–S, facing E. Rectangular in plan, with four corner towers projecting E or W, the main body rises through four storeys, and the towers one storey higher. The N and S ends of the building are articulated by buttresses capped with restored round bartizans, based on surviving evidence, and there is a large entrance block, hard up against the SE tower extending the full height of the central block. A notable feature of the central block is a collection of large traceried windows on all four sides above ground-floor level; despite the restoration of tracery, these, for the most part, appear to replicate the primary fenestration.

The entrance was protected by a portcullis and led first to the staircase from which the upper storeys were reached, and then to the ground floor. The first four storeys all comprised a large central space, and, opening off it, four chambers in the corner towers. At all four levels the central space was provided with at least two fireplaces; there were also fireplaces in the tower chambers from second-floor level upwards. Apart from the uppermost storey, the SW tower was given over to latrines, two at ground-floor level and rows of four at first-, second- and third-floor levels. It's a highly unusual arrangement, implying large numbers of occupants and more redolent of a monastic community. The only instance of more private provision is a single latrine in the NW tower at second-floor level. Bates 1885; Emery 1996, 110–14; McNeill and Scott 2018.

LAUNCESTON, Cornwall (Open – EH). A motte and bailey the subject of a major research excavation between 1961 and 1983. Probably founded by Brian of Brittany *c*.1068; acquired by Robert, Count of Mortain *c*.1075, who created the motte and bailey design. Between 1140 and 1175 the castle was held by Reginald, Earl of Cornwall, an illegitimate son of Henry I, and an adherent of the Empress Matilda. Some stone buildings were probably raised by Reginald, including the shell-keep on the motte and the S gatehouse. Major changes were carried out during the tenure of Richard, Earl of Cornwall (1227–72), including the construction of the curtain wall, the re-fronting of the S gatehouse with twin flanking towers, the construction of a stone great hall in the bailey, the fortification of the motte steps with a gate tower and side walls, the remodelling of the motte top by the construction of an encircling mantlet, the provision of a new gatehouse to the shell-keep, and the raising of the cylindrical keep known as the High Tower. It was Earl Richard's programme which defined the character of the castle as it is known to us today.

The starting point is the two-storey S Gatehouse on Western Road, probably C12 in origin and rectangular in plan, but now fronted by a pair of C13 solid drum towers, and these by a C14 passage barbican. The entrance was protected by a portcullis and the upper storey reached via an external staircase. The C13 curtain wall, of which elements survive on both sides of the gatehouse, is plain without interval towers, although a tower formerly existed at the SE angle. There is also a gatehouse on the N side of the bailey, which gave access from the town, and where the constable of the castle was lodged. The C13 N Gatehouse is rectangular, its E end pierced by a gate passage. Now only a single storey in height, the constable's lodgings would have been in an upper storey. In the SW corner of the bailey are the excavated foundations of a group of buildings, the largest of which is the N–S aligned C13 great hall. To the S, separated by a yard, is its associated kitchen, a square building next to the S curtain. E of the kitchen a smaller hall-like building; sockets within the walls are interpreted as postholes for members supporting the roof structure: a kind of cruck construction has been envisaged.

The C13 approach to the motte was across the motte ditch (now via a modern bridge) and through a C13 gate tower with a rounded prow towards the W. From here there was a climb up a flight of steps (on the site of the modern steps) enclosed by side walls and roofed. On the motte top there are only vestiges of the C13 mantlet and gatehouse, but traces of the latter's portcullis slot survive. The gate to the roughly circular C12 shell-keep was secured by a draw bar, and on the LH (W) side of the gate passage is a doorway to a mural staircase which led to the wall walk; there is little indication of the C12 internal arrangements, but beam sockets in the external face of the two-storey High Tower show that in the C13 the space between the tower and the shell wall was roofed over to create a covered passage, or ambulatory, around the tower. Access to the High Tower is on the W, where a well-preserved doorway with segmental-arched head leads into a mural entrance lobby giving access to a ground-floor room devoid of facilities, its door barred from the outside, and to a doorway to a mural staircase ascending to a first-floor lobby. From the lobby, a second flight of stairs rose to the roof, a doorway to the E led to the wall walk of the shell-keep over the roof of the ambulatory, and a doorway on the W led to the first-floor room, which was provided with a fireplace and large window with embrasure seats. Despite the limited accommodation in the keep, the C13 motte complex must have been something of an architectural spectacle, with its elevated position and tiered arrangement of concentric rings. Saunders 2006.

LAVENDON, Buckinghamshire (Private). Motte with three baileys, in existence by 1192 and probably founded by the Bidun family. The motte comprises a low platform, which was ditched around, now partly built over with farm buildings. There is an embanked sub-rectangular bailey to the NW of the motte, and a larger rectangular bailey to the NE with an entrance to the SE. In line to the NE of this larger bailey is a third enclosure, also rectangular and of comparable size. RCHME 1913, 163–4; Page 1927, 380, 387.

LEEDS, Kent (Open). Laid out on two islands within a lake, Leeds Castle presents a delightful aspect, making it one of the most memorable of England's ancient strongholds, even though the medieval remains are somewhat disappointing and their chronology uncertain. A castle was certainly in existence at Leeds by 1139, and an origin in the late C11 or early C12 is probable. Acquired by Edward I in 1278, it was extensively remodelled during the tenures of his two queens, Eleanor (until 1290) and Margaret (from 1299). Edward II granted the custody of Leeds to Bartholomew de Badlesmere, an act which led indirectly to the only siege of the castle when, in 1321, Queen Isabella was refused entry by Bartholomew's wife, and her followers were fired upon, resulting in several deaths. The King returned with an army, captured the castle and sent Baroness Badlesmere to the Tower.

Three causeways allowed the castle to be approached from the N, SE and SW, the three routes converging on a courtyard barbican isolated from the outer bailey by an arm of the lake. At the end of the northern causeway the way is blocked by the C13 castle mill, a continuation of its N wall pierced by a segmental-pointed gateway giving access to what is effectively an outer barbican. From here and the other two causeways there is a bridge to the inner barbican, which was also enclosed in stone. Then, across the lake to the outer gatehouse, a single rectangular tower, pierced by a segmental-pointed arch within a rectangular recess for a drawbridge and holes for the lifting chains. Over the entrance are corbelled machicolations carried on two flanking buttresses. Attached ranges to L (N) and R (S) falling back arrowhead fashion. The C13 alterations also include the curtain wall which surrounds the outer bailey punctuated by round fronted towers. Inside, there is little of medieval interest. On the R (E) is the C16 Maiden's Tower, a large rectangular residential block. Straight ahead, occupying the far end of the island, is an early C19 mock Tudor range.

Finally, across another bridge to smaller, apsidal-ended island, which houses the 'Old Castle', or 'Gloriette', a residential block built around a courtyard, probably C13 in origin, but much rebuilt and reordered internally. The main survival from Edward's time are the chapel windows, two high pointed lights of *c*.1290 with twin shafts and moulded arches. Tipping 1921, 201–19; Brown *et al.* 1963, 695–702.

LEICESTER, Leicestershire (Open access to exterior only). Motte and bailey, rebuilt in stone, established *c*.1068 by Hugh de Grentmesnil in the SW corner of the Anglo-Saxon town next to the river Soar. Hugh's son Ivo joined Robert de Bellême's 1101 rebellion, and, as a consequence, Leicester Castle was destroyed or damaged. Subsequently, Ivo's lands were granted to Robert de Beaumont, Count of Meulan, later First Earl of Leicester (d. 1118), who built the church of St Mary le Castro in the castle bailey; his son Robert 'le Bossu', the Second Earl (d. 1168), was responsible for rebuilding the great hall and extending the church, and perhaps also for rebuilding the defences in stone. In 1173 the Third Earl, Robert 'Blanchmains', joined the rebellion of Prince Henry, and the King ordered the demolition of the castle, an action which, in view of the hall's survival, may have been confined to the defences. Later, the castle came to Simon de Montfort, and after he was killed, to Edmund Crouchback; subsequently it became a Crown property as part of the Duchy of Lancaster. Much building work occurred in the early C15, including the reconstruction of the curtain wall.

The early castle consisted of the motte with a bailey to the N and NE, its truncated area now represented by Castle Yard, but to judge from a section of the ditch excavated to the N of the S gate, formerly included the area now occupied by the church and churchyard of St Mary le Castro. The castle boundaries were rearranged in the later medieval period and formalised in the reconstruction of the curtain wall. Thus, the church of St Mary le Castro was divided from the castle, while an additional bailey (the Newarke) was created to the S with the foundation of the Hospital of the Annunciation *c*.1330.

The Newarke extended as far S as the Mill Lane/Bonners Lane line and is now largely occupied by De Montfort University. What survives is the early C15 Magazine Gateway facing E onto Oxford Street/Vaughan Way. It is a square three-storey block, wholly domestic in character, with carriage and pedestrian entrances under four-centred arches, rectangular mullioned windows with square hood moulds, and round corbelled bartizans at the angles. At the rear, a single wide carriage arch. Through the gateway into the Newarke; on the R is Castle View straddled by the Turret Gateway of *c*.1422, the conduit between the Newarke and Castle Yard, the nucleus of the Norman bailey. The gateway consists of a modest square tower pierced by a portcullis-protected four-centred gate arch. Further along the Newarke is the entrance to Castle Gardens and access to the motte, approximately 30ft (9m) high, its spacious summit the result of lowering to make a bowling green.

The main entrance to the castle is immediately adjacent to the N side of the church off Castle Street, the driveway leading to it extending through the site of the former barbican. On the L is the much-rebuilt St Mary le Castro, vestiges of the Norman church visible at the W end and in the reset N doorway. It was a long aisleless rectangular building with no narrowing of the chancel. Robert le Bossu extended the chancel when the church became collegiate in the mid C12. More C12 work is visible inside, including wall arcading. The gateway in its current form, with jettied timber-framed upper storey, probably dates from 1444–5. It gives access to Castle Yard at the heart of the Norman Castle. Here, the noteworthy structure is the great hall, its roof looming up behind a late C17 brick façade. It is a most significant building, some 84ft × 58ft (25.6m × 17.6m), stone-built with timber arcades, but much altered and now largely enclosed with later buildings. A date of *c.*1150–60 is probable on dendrochronological and stylistic grounds. Fox 1944–5; Alcock and Buckley 1987.

LEWES, Sussex (Open). Notable for having two mottes (cf. Lincoln qv), Lewes Castle was founded soon after the Conquest by William de Warenne, a veteran of Hastings, William I's Chief Justiciar of England, and, from 1088, Earl of Surrey. His descendants held it until 1347 when the direct line of descent came to an end. The defences were reconstructed in stone *c.*1100. In 1264, John, the Seventh Earl, fought with Henry III at the Battle of Lewes, within sight of the castle, and in 1265 at the Battle of Evesham in which Simon de Montfort was killed. It was shortly after this, in 1266, that efforts began to erect walls around the town. Headquarters of the Sussex Archaeological Society since 1850.

The castle is built on a promontory to the N of the High Street immediately within the bounds of the former walled town and constitutes part of the defensive circuit. Orientated NE–SW, it has a motte at each end of the bailey. Brack Mount (NE), the earlier of the two (now isolated from the rest of the site by a lane called Castle Precincts), has a view of the river Ouse crossing some 500 yards to the E, and was no doubt situated for this purpose. Now, it is bare of buildings but was formerly crowned with a shell-keep. Excavation in 2001 revealed a well lined with chalk blocks, very probably of medieval date.

Encroachment of the town onto the bailey means that only the SW part of the castle is generally accessible to the public, but thoroughfares traversing through and around it allow a greater degree of visibility to the rest of the site even though there isn't a great deal to have survived above ground level. The exception is a stretch of curtain wall, containing courses of herringbone masonry, following the line of Castle Ditch, which links Brack Mount with Castle Gate.

Castle Gate leads to the barbican of *c.*1330–50, an imposing three-storey flint tower, its presence accentuated by the rising approach. Segmental-pointed gate arch, the passage protected by two portcullises; long round angle bartizans on rectangular bases and stepped and moulded corbelling, a feature derived from the Gate-next-the-Sea, Beaumaris, Anglesey, of 1295 onwards; first-floor cruciform loops with oillet feet; the parapet between the bartizans carried on corbelled and arched machicolations. At the NW angle to the rear is a circular stair turret and two short walls

Lewes: The gatehouse from the SW.

linking the tower to the Norman gatehouse, originally a rectangular tower projecting inwards though now only the outer gate arch survives.

Castle Gate continues through the bailey, but only the area to the W is maintained by the Sussex Archaeological Society for visitors. Here, the main attraction is the sub-oval Norman shell-keep on top of the motte, to which two semi-polygonal towers were added *c*.1300. The encircling wall to the N and NE has largely disappeared, whilst that to the S and SW survives. The two towers each have a lower room entered from motte top level and an upper room reached from the wall walk. Excavation within the shell-keep has revealed foundations of buildings lining the walls. A good view from here across the town and the castle. Godfrey 1929; Salzman 1940, 19–24; Higham 2015, 72–8.

LEYBOURNE, Kent (Private). Courtyard castle, possibly C11 or C12 in origin, but under reconstruction in 1260 when Roger de Leybourne was ordered to cease work on its defences. Building was in progress again in 1266 with the King's blessing, the royal mason Robert of Beverley supplying stone for the project. Formerly surrounded by a ditch, the western half of which is traceable, and which suggests a roughly circular enclosure. The medieval stonework is largely C13, and the most conspicuous element is the great gatehouse, which faces NE. This has twin flanking drum towers pierced by long cruciform arrow loops set beneath relieving arches, and large rectangular windows at first-floor level. The RH tower has an attached round-fronted turret, the juxtaposition of the two akin to configurations at Barnwell Castle (qv), also of the 1260s. Deeply recessed between the towers, the portcullis-protected gateway was set beneath a high machicolated arch, and between the two is the slot of a water chute designed to dowse fires in front of the gateway. Amidst the ruins is a house of 1930. Ludlow 2021–22.

LIDGATE, Suffolk (Open access). Traditionally, Lidgate was the manor of Reginald Sanceler, who gifted it to the abbey of Bury St Edmunds in the time of Abbot Baldwin (d. 1097); the castle itself may date from the late C11. The earthwork complex is usually described as a motte and bailey, but it is one of unusual character in that the 'motte' is square and more like a platform than a mound. It is surrounded by a ditch (formerly a moat) except for a gap in the centre of the S side, which gives access from the bailey. This is L-shaped: rectangular, but for a narrow arm extending along the E side of the motte. The W side of the bailey contains the church. It too was enclosed by a ditch, now largely encroached upon. Other features include a rectangular enclosure to the N of the motte, an earthen bank along its W side, and that of the motte and a semi-circular moat to the E. It is probable that some of these structures post-date the original castle. Page 1911, 600–1.

LINCOLN, Lincolnshire (Open). Founded by William the Conqueror in 1068, in the SW quarter of the Roman upper town. A major figure of the C11 and early C12 was Lucy, latterly Countess of Chester, a thrice-married Anglo-Norman heiress with large estates in Lincolnshire, and the supposed builder of the castle's Lucy Tower. In 1140 the castle was taken by Lucy's son, Ranulph, Earl of Chester, but taken back by King Stephen a few years later. Henry I appointed Robert de la Haye as constable, a position that became hereditary. In 1311 the castle came to Henry de Lacy, Earl of Lincoln, and thence to his son-in-law, Thomas, Earl of Lancaster, ultimately becoming part of the Duchy of Lancaster. In the C18 and C19 the main use of the castle was as a prison, some of the buildings of which remain.

The castle forms an irregular quadrangular facing E towards the Cathedral, and it is possible to make almost a complete circuit of the enceinte along the existing road system. There are large banks to all except the S side, though the ditches have been infilled. To the S there are two mottes, one crowned by the shell-keep known as the Lucy Tower, and a smaller one at the SE corner bearing the Observatory Tower. The

Lincoln: The outer gateway.

use of herringbone masonry suggests that the curtain wall is early, possibly as early as the C11. There are Norman gates to the E and W.

The rectangular E Gate breaks forward from the curtain, its Norman gateway now hidden by a large, pointed gateway, above which is a pointed prow squeezed between a pair of C14 circular bartizans. There was formerly a passage barbican before the gate, under construction in 1224–5, its two walls terminating in circular turrets, their positions now marked out on the pavement. Originally, the E and W gates were similar in character, but the E gate (which can be viewed from Union Road) retains its Norman appearance with plain semi-circular arch, and the remains of a barbican in front. At the NE corner is Cobb Hall (viewable from St Paul's Lane), a C13 round-fronted wall tower with plain loops.

One of the attractions of Lincoln Castle is that it is possible to make a complete circuit of the wall walk and enjoy the views over the city and surrounding countryside, most notably the Cathedral. Such a circuit also allows an inspection of the Lucy Tower and the Observatory Tower. First, the Lucy Tower, which has an irregular polygonal plan with pilaster buttresses at the angles and a NE entrance within a projection of the wall, like the two gateways: a plain semi-circular arch on imposts. To the SW is a postern with segmental-arched head. At each of the two junctions with the curtain is a small square turret containing a chamber, that to the E with a latrine. The interior of the shell-keep was used as a cemetery for prisoners. Finally, the Observatory Tower on the SE motte: a two-storey rectangular building of Norman origin having been extended to the E in the C14, so giving the tower a new façade, the centre recessed between square turrets. In the C19 a round observation tower was raised on top of the S turret. Lindley 2004; Higham 2015, 79–95.

LITTLE WENHAM HALL, Suffolk (Private). Fortified manor house of which the main surviving component is a predominantly brick-built chamber block of *c.*1280, in all likelihood the work of Master Roger de Holebrok, who acquired the estate in the early 1270s. The house stood within an enclosure of uncertain extent, at least partially enclosed by a moat, which survives to the S and W. The L-shaped solar block comprises a two-storey N–S aligned main range with a three-storey chapel tower extending from the E side. A stair turret lies in the angle between the two components and the angles of the building are marked by clasping buttresses (except at the SW – see below). The rooms are lit by lancet loops at ground-floor level, and by large pointed windows of twin cinquefoil-headed lights and Geometric tracery above; the chapel has a three-light E window in the same vein.

A number of structural anomalies centre on the SW corner: the absence of the characteristic corner buttresses, discontinuations of the plinth and string course on the S and W sides, and two sets of ground- and first-floor doorways, one to each side. Although there have been alterations, all these entrances may be original. There are different ways of interpreting these features, but the absence of buttresses, plinth and stringcourse at this angle suggest that there was an attached building or buildings here; a great hall has been postulated. It is generally agreed that the first-floor entrance on the W side was the principal entrance to the building, but whether this was from the hall or an external staircase is disputed; on the whole, the former seems more probable. The southern doorways are generally interpreted as the entrances from the chamber block to a now-vanished latrine turret, but they appear to face outwards, and the lower doorway was barred from inside the tower.

Within, the ground storey of the main block is covered with three bays of quadripartite vaulting with stone ribs and brick webbing; the lack of facilities suggests a storage space. At the N end of the E wall is access to the chapel tower (also rib-vaulted), and to the staircase rising to all the upper levels including the roof. The first-floor great chamber has a fireplace on the W side, replaced in the C16. The entrance to the chapel is a chapter-house-like composition of central door and flanking (shuttered) windows of two lancet lights and plate-traceried trefoil, all three with hood moulds. The chapel has quadripartite brick vaulting with stone ribs, the wall ribs incorporating very early examples of wave moulding. In the base of the S window embrasure is a trefoil-headed sedile, and, communicating with it, to the E, a matching piscina. Opposite the piscina is an aumbry, and to either side of the E window a bracket for an image or a sconce. Martin 1998; Emery 2000, 119–24.

LLANCILLO, Herefordshire (Open access). Motte of unknown origin with ditch and counterscarp bank. On the top, stone remains suggest the former existence of a shell-keep. Shoesmith 2009, 201–2.

LONDON, TOWER OF, London and Middlesex (Open) (Plate VIII). The castle was founded *c.*1066 within the SE corner of the Roman city walls, and the White Tower, or keep, from which the complex takes its name, was begun in the late 1070s and completed *c.*1100. Major works were carried out under Richard I from *c.*1190 including the excavation of a ditch connecting with the Thames and the raising of a stone curtain. A major reconstruction and expansion of the castle was carried out during the reign of Henry III, mostly 1220–50, when the Roman wall was demolished, a new line of defence established further to the E, and the inner curtain wall mostly rebuilt. Further fortification was undertaken by Edward I in 1275–85, including the completion of the inner curtain, the construction of the outer curtain, which created the outer ward (reclaimed from the Thames on the S side), and beyond it the excavation of the great moat. His master mason was Robert of Beverley and his water engineer for the moat Walter of Flanders. As completed by Edward I, then, the Tower of London comprised inner and outer courtyards arranged concentrically with a moat around the N, E, and W sides, and the Thames to the S. The White Tower occupied a central position within the inner ward and immediately S of it was the innermost ward. The main landward entrance was at the S end of the E side and the main water gate (St Thomas' Tower) in the centre of the S front. Essentially, this arrangement survives.

Access to the Tower of London is still via Edward's SW entrance complex, an elongated route approached from the N, where a fortified bridge crossed an arm of the moat into a half-moon shaped barbican known as the Lion Tower. The excavated base of the bridge can be seen within the (now dry) moat, the slots for the counterbalance beams of the drawbridge clearly visible. Of the barbican only the E wall is exposed, though the curving line of its semi-circular plan is picked out in the pavement. From here, there was a right-angled turn across another drawbridge to the Middle Tower, the gatehouse at the outer end of the bridge across the moat, which in turn leads to the Byward Tower at the inner end. These two gatehouses are of similar design, rectangular with bold circular flanking towers at the outer angles, the Byward Tower, as the principal gatehouse, rising higher. The Middle Tower has been substantially refaced with Portland stone, but the Byward Tower retains more of its medieval fabric. Both had arrow loops in the towers, two portcullises either side of the gate, and murder holes in the vault. A rare survival is one of the Byward Tower portcullises, which may be original to the C13 gatehouse, although the lifting mechanism was remade in the C17.

Through the gatehouse into the S arm of the outer ward, built on land reclaimed from the Thames by Edward I's men. Just inside the gateway is Richard the Lionheart's Bell Tower of *c.*1190, polygonal up to first-floor level, but cylindrical above, and occupying the SW corner of the inner ward. The Bell Tower is one of an exclusive group of late C12/early C13 polygonal corner towers pierced with multiple arrow loops, the best known of which is the slightly earlier Avranches Tower, Dover (qv).

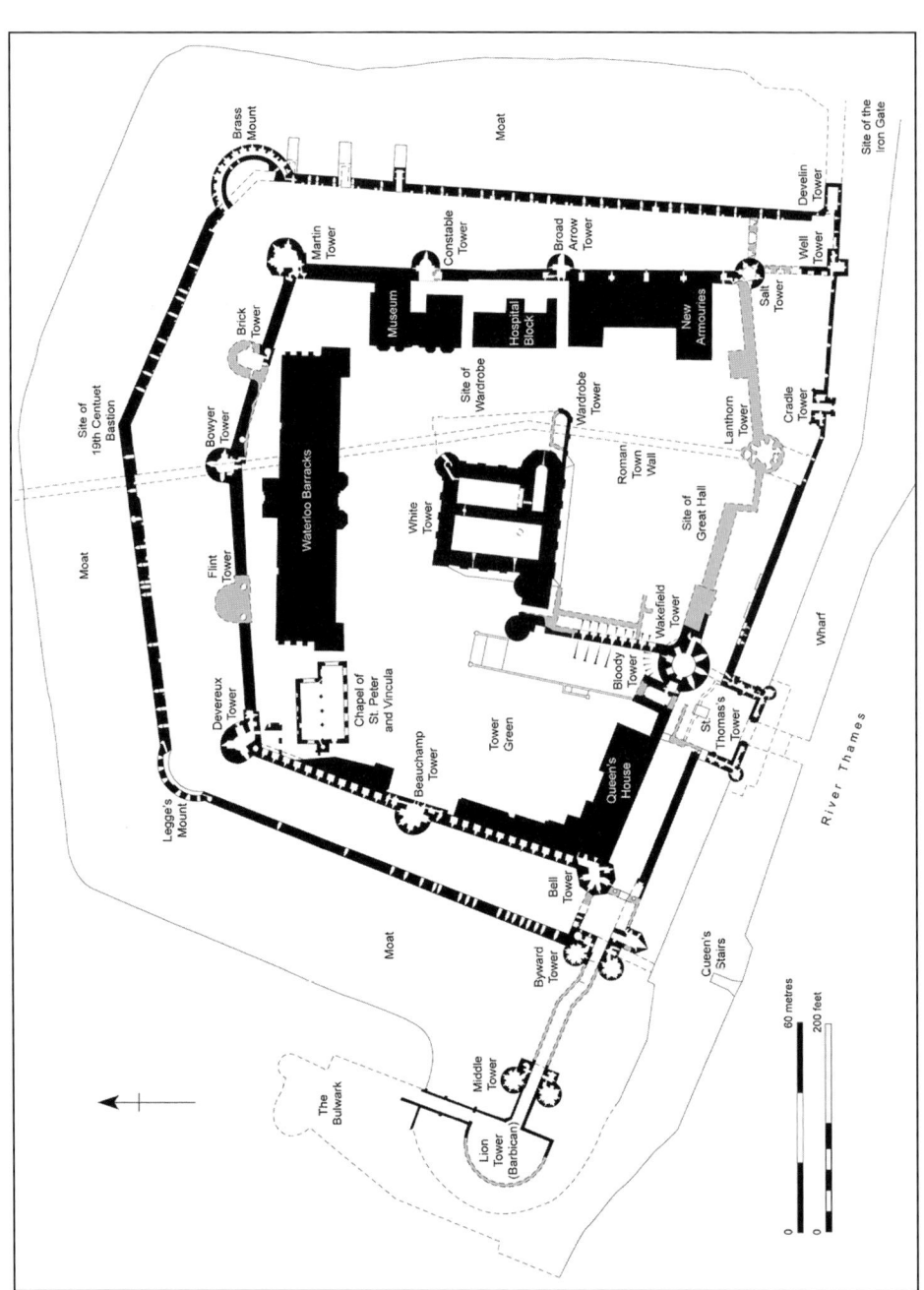

Tower of London: Ground plan. After Brown and Curnow 1984.

Inside, at basement level, is a high pointed ribbed vault dividing the W half into four bays, each corresponding with an arrow loop embrasure.

Next is the back of St Thomas' Tower, containing the water gate, or Traitor's Gate, as it became known, which was begun in 1275. The front, flanked by twin narrow round towers, can be viewed from the Wharf. Boats entered through a wide segmental-pointed gate into the harbour, or basin, within the tower; the lower storey is backless, the N wall of the upper storey being carried on an extraordinary segmental arch, made up of joggled voussoirs, with a span of *c.*65ft; a marvellous piece of C13 engineering.

St Thomas' Tower stands directly in front of the Bloody Tower, which incorporates Henry III's water gate of the early 1220s, left high and dry following Edward's expansion into the Thames. At that stage the gate passage was extended into the inner ward and the building raised into a tower; the first floor was rebuilt in the 1360s; a third storey was added in the early C17. These phases are clearly visible in the stonework. To the R (E) of the Bloody Tower, and projecting boldly from the curtain to command the old water gate, with which it is contemporary, is the Wakefield Tower, a great two-storey round tower forming part of the royal apartments within the innermost ward. Entering the Bloody Tower gate passage, there is a porter's lodge on the R (E) within the curtain wall; here too is the tower's glory: the elaborate vault over the gate passage built by the master mason Robert Yevele in 1360–2. So, into the inner ward. On the R (E), extending from the Wakefield Tower, are the remains of the innermost curtain wall, also of the 1220s, pierced by a continuous line of closely-set loops. It terminates at the SW corner of the White Tower, where the Cold Harbour Gate gave access (from the N) to the innermost ward. Only the foundations of this gatehouse remain but show the entrance to have been flanked by two round towers.

Despite being the oldest surviving building of the complex, the White Tower, or keep, remains the architectural climax. It has a rectangular footprint with an apsidal projection from the S end of the E elevation denoting the position of the chapel, and a round stair turret at the NE angle. The origins of this unusual plan are to be found in Normandy (eg, Ivry-la-Bataille, Pithiviers); the contemporary great tower of Colchester (qv) was based on a similar scheme. Four storeys, with corner turrets rising above the parapet, elevations articulated with pilaster buttresses and blind arcading above the second-floor windows. Originally, there were three storeys, most of the tower being roofed just above the level of the blind arcading, with only the chapel block rising higher. The windows at third-floor level lit a mural gallery extending all around the building. Of the windows themselves, nearly all have been replaced and many enlarged, but the positions are for the most part authentic.

The building was entered from the S, at first-floor level, via an external staircase (later enclosed within a forebuilding). A mural entrance lobby leads into the main room, which occupies the western half of the building. The eastern half contains a smaller rectangular room (N) and the crypt of the apsidal-ended chapel. This pattern of division is repeated on the second floor. Access to the basement, which was largely for storage, and to the second floor, was solely from the staircase in the NE turret. Other than in the chapel, signs of domesticity are to be seen in the provision of fireplaces and latrines, suggesting a two-room residential suite on each of the two main floors. Of these, the upper suite appears to have been the more prestigious of the two, with larger windows, more latrines and access to the chapel from both the other rooms.

The chapel itself is the architectural highlight of the building. Nave and chancel in one with a continuous arcade and a tribune, or gallery, above the aisles and ambulatory carried on groin vaulting; plain barrel-vaults over the main body and tribune. Round-columned arcade with square abaci; most of the capitals bear a tau-cross motif on each side and triangular stylized leaf forms effecting the transition from column to abacus. Stilted arches over the narrower openings around the apse.

From the second floor, stairs rise not only from the SE angle but also from the NE and NW, all giving access to a mural gallery that, with the tribune of the chapel, which it communicates with, extends all around the uppermost storey. Originally, however, it was an external feature, its inner openings looking onto the roof. About 1490, the roof was raised, and the third floor created. The staircases continue from this level to the parapet.

Within the inner ward most of the buildings date from the C19 and C20. One of the exceptions is the chapel of St Peter-ad-Vincula, a church of medieval origin (in existence by 1240) but rebuilt *c.*1520 and restored in the late C19; it is the resting place of two of Henry VIII's unfortunate wives, Anne Boleyn and Katherine Howard, and of Lady Jane Grey.

The rest of the double enceinte is largely inaccessible to the public but can be viewed from outside the castle, working clockwise from the pedestrian precinct outside the W entrance (W), Tower Hill (N) and Tower Bridge Approach (E). Edward I's outer curtain is characterized by numerous arrow loops and by two round-faced corner bastions: Legge's Mount (NW) and Brass Mount (NE), akin to features in the near-contemporary Welsh concentric castles of Caerphilly and Harlech (also built for Edward). There is an even greater profusion of loops in Edward's W inner curtain, in the centre of which is the semi-circular Beauchamp Tower, probably on the site of a gatehouse raised by Henry III, which collapsed in 1240. Henry's surviving work begins at the NE corner with the Devereux Tower behind Legge's Mount and continues all along the N and E sides to the Salt Tower at the SE angle. Impey and Parnell 2006; Impey 2008b.

LONGTHORPE TOWER Northamptonshire (Soke of Peterborough) (Open – EH). A C13 manor house fortified by the addition of an early C14 solar tower, probably by Robert de Thorpe, steward to Peterborough Abbey. The three-storey tower is attached to the NE corner of the N–S aligned former manorial chamber block. Originally, the ground and first floors of the tower were entered independently from the chamber block (to which there is no public access), but admittance is now from the E through an inserted first-floor doorway. The vaulted ground floor is devoid of facilities and was probably for storage. The first floor houses the principal chamber, which is also vaulted and equipped with a fireplace and a latrine. A stair in the S wall ascends to the second floor, probably a bed chamber, which was also provided with a latrine corbelled out from the S wall. The principal interest of Longthorpe tower, however, lies in the extensive C14 paintings which adorn the walls, vault and window embrasures of the first-floor chamber, and which constitute one of the most complete and therefore significant medieval schemes to have survived in a domestic building. Serjeantson *et al.* 1906; Emery 2000, 272–4, Impey 2014.

LONGTOWN (Ewyas Lacy), Herefordshire (Open access – EH). C11 castle of the de Lacys within an Anglo-Saxon *burh*, itself a refortification of a Roman fort, probably by Earl (later King) Harold Godwinson during his Welsh campaign of 1055. Walter

Plate I. **Beeston**: Inner gatehouse from the SW.

Plate II. **Bodiam** from the NW.

Plate III. **Brough**: Gatehouse and great tower from the SE.

Plate IV. **Carlisle**: Outer gatehouse of 1378–83 by John Lewyn.

Plate V. **Conisbrough**: Keep from the W.

Plate VI. **Dunstanburgh**: Lilburn Tower from the S.

Plate VII. **Goodrich** from the SE.

Plate VIII. **London**: Western entrance with the Middle Tower in the foreground and the Byward Tower in the background.

Plate IX. **Ludlow**: Main residential block with central great hall recessed between the Solar Block (*left*) and Great Chamber Block (*right*).

Plate X. **Norwich**: Keep from the SW.

Plate XI. **Old Wardour**: The gateway flanked by doorways to adjacent rooms, from within the inner courtyard, *c*.1391.

Plate XII. **Rockingham**: The gatehouse from the E.

Plate XIII. **Sheriff Hutton** from the E.

Plate XIV. **Warkworth**: Great tower from the S.

de Lacy may have established the castle within the Anglo-Saxon *burh* soon after the Conquest; it was rebuilt in stone by Gilbert de Lacy *c.*1150–60. After the failure of the Lacy male line, in 1241, Longtown declined in importance, and by 1328 was in ruins.

The earthworks comprise a rectangular enclosure surrounded by a ditch and inner bank with a motte at the NW angle. This enclosure is now divided by the main road through the village, the E half (known as Castle Green) is given over to pasture, while the W half contains the stone castle. A holloway within the inturning of the bank, in the centre of the S side, may represent the main entrance to both sides of the enclosure. Access to the W half is now from the road into an outer bailey, where only a short stretch of walling on the E side is now visible. The stone curtain around the inner bailey, however, is more complete, particularly that of the entrance (S) front. The gateway is a quite a simple affair comprising a narrow round-arched entrance flanked by a pair of solid round-fronted towers.

The main architectural interest lies in the keep, the plan of which has been laid out with geometrical precision: a circle with three half-round turrets protruding from the circumference, their centres forming an equilateral triangle. The S turret (destroyed) housed the spiral staircase; the other two were solid, but strategically sited in front of a fireplace (NE) and latrine (NW). The two-storey tower has a high battered plinth, the stone heavily robbed, and a string course at the level of the roof. Three large (formerly two-light) windows with semi-circular relieving arches light the lower storey; the voussoirs of the N window arch bear carved decoration, and are probably rejects from another building project, reused here only for structural purposes. Only a couple of single loops illuminate the upper storey; also at this level, hard up against the NW turret, is a corbelled latrine outlet. The destroyed entrance, which was next to the S turret, gave access to the ground floor chamber, apparently the main room, which contains a fireplace and a wall cupboard in each of the three window embrasures. Cook and Kidd 2020.

LUDGERSHALL, Wiltshire (Open access – EH). Ringwork and bailey probably built by Edward of Salisbury, Sheriff of Wiltshire, in the late C11, perhaps on the site of an Iron Age fort. By 1103 Ludgershall was in the possession of the Crown, and during Stephen's reign the castle was held by John FitzGilbert, the father of William Marshal, who soon switched his allegiance to the Empress Matilda. King John carried out work here in the early C13, and Henry III made considerable improvements, including the construction of a new hall in 1244–5. From the later C15 it was allowed to decay and by the mid C16 the buildings had been largely razed.

The castle consists of a northern and southern enclosure, both double-ditched and banked, but only poorly preserved to the S. At the centre of the complex is a working farm, and this part of the castle is therefore inaccessible, but the northern enclosure, where the main residential buildings were located, was excavated in 1964–72, revealing a long and complex building history. The excavated lower courses of the domestic buildings are exposed to view; the one building to remain standing is a small rectangular tower at the NW angle of the complex. From here the outer bailey curtain begins again, extending all the way to the E gate, interrupted by a single rectangular wall tower on the E side. Ellis 2000.

LUDLOW, Shropshire (Open) **(Plate IX)**. A major marcher castle first mentioned in 1139, Ludlow was probably founded by Water de Lacy (d. 1085) in the late C11. So far as we know, it was a stone castle almost from the outset, but was probably confined

Ludlow: Chapel of St Mary Magdalene (*c*.1150) from the SW.

to the current inner bailey, the large outer bailey being added in the mid to late C12, perhaps around the same time that the inner bailey gatehouse was converted into a keep. Attributing these early works to individuals is problematic, though it is a reasonable assumption that Gilbert de Lacy was responsible for the construction of the Chapel of St Mary Magdalen *c*.1150 (see below). Mortimer's Tower, an early C13 gatehouse to the outer bailey, is to be attributed to the last Lacy lord, another Gilbert (d. 1241). Ludlow was inherited by Gilbert's daughter Maud, wife of Geoffrey de

Geneville (d. 1314), who began the reconstruction of the main residential block in the inner bailey. Subsequently, the castle came to the Genevilles' granddaughter, Joan, wife of Roger Mortimer of Wigmore (qv), who probably completed the reconstruction of the main apartments by building the Great Chamber Block and adjacent lodgings.

Mortimer was created Earl of March in 1328, and Ludlow became the caput of the earldom. In 1425 the Mortimer lands passed to Richard, Duke of York, and thence to his son Edward (King Edward IV from 1461); it was probably Edward who remodelled the keep, perhaps owing to damage inflicted by the Lancastrians in 1459. As a royal castle, Ludlow became the headquarters of the Council of the Marches. Under the presidency of Sir Henry Sidney (1560–86), part of the Mortimer additions to the domestic accommodation was rebuilt and another set of lodgings constructed within the inner bailey for the accommodation of the judges who presided over the Council's courthouse within the castle. The abolition of the council in 1689 left and the castle without a *raison d'être* and it was allowed to decline. Its acquisition by the Earl of Powis in 1771 arrested its decline and was the major factor in its subsequent preservation.

The old centre of Ludlow is sited on a bluff, with the castle on its NW edge, forming a roughly square enclosure, the early inner bailey occupying its NW angle. Although the NE quarter is private land, and not generally accessible, the exterior of the castle can be circumperambulated by paths. Facing the main gate, on the E side, to the L (S), the curtain wall follows a straight course to the SE corner and is relieved only by a short stretch of preserved battlements, At or near the corner there was once a round-fronted tower, and a little further along the S side a rectangular tower, though both have vanished. About mid-way along the S curtain, the battlements begin again and continue around the SW corner.

Towards the W end of the S curtain the path is diverted through an C18 opening into a walled-off section of the outer bailey and out through another opening in the W curtain. On the N side of this little enclave are the remains of St Peter's Chapel, dating from the 1320s, and converted into the courthouse of the Council of the Marches in the C16, when a western extension was added. N of this, projecting from the W curtain, is the three-storey Mortimer's Tower, early C13 and D-shaped. Built as a gateway, the entrance in the front of the tower is now blocked. It's a highly unusual form, though paralleled at Dover (Constable Tower, early C13) and Aberystwyth (1277).

Further N, the W outer curtain abuts the Oven Tower (wholly within the line of the curtain) of the C11 inner bailey. Beyond that are the rectangular Postern Tower, and, at the angle, the NW Tower, with the little Closet Tower abutting its S side. The NW Tower adjoins the C14 solar within the inner bailey. Further along, the N curtain is pierced by the C14 great hall windows, then comes an impressive latrine tower added in the C14, after which are the windows of the Tudor Lodgings and then the C11 Pendover Tower at the NE angle of the inner bailey.

From here, a long stretch of N and E outer curtain, broken only by a single C11 rectangular tower, brings us back to the E gateway, a simple rectangular affair, formerly approached by a bridge across the (now infilled) ditch, and giving access to the outer bailey. Inside, adjoining the gatehouse to the S, is a range of C16 buildings backing onto the curtain wall, and containing (from N to S) the porter's lodge and prison of 1552, and the stables of 1597. In the SW corner of the outer bailey the N and

E walls of St Peter's Chapel/Courthouse can be seen. N of that is Mortimer's Tower, a C16 window within the blocked gateway. Access is now from the adjacent doorway to the spiral staircase at the NE corner. The former gate passage is covered by a C15 octopartite rib-vault and contains a C17 fireplace, but evidence for its former function is to be found in the remains of portcullis grooves and door rebates within the former portal. In the C13 there were two upper floors, the first floor residential with fireplace and latrine, the second floor with access to the curtain to the S.

Now for the inner bailey, its C11 quarter-circle curtain terminating in the Oven Tower (W) and Pendover Tower (N) and isolated from the outer bailey by a rock-cut ditch. The main feature of this frontage is the three-storey keep next to the present entrance. The original gateway, however, was through the keep, then a great gatehouse. Though this earlier entrance is now blocked, its arched form can be discerned on the S face of the building. The S front of this building is a façade insofar as it disguises a narrowing of the tower inside the curtain, to give a T-shaped plan. It has been suggested that the wider frontage is an addition, part of a C12 encasing and strengthening of the gatehouse, to create a keep, a theory that seems to be corroborated from excavated evidence to the rear (N) of the building. Above the former gate arch is a string course, then two C12 windows, a rather plain round-headed lancet to the R (E) and a more elaborate one to the L (W) within a shafted outer surround. Between them is a vertical line of later windows, the one breaking through a second string course, above which the tower has been heightened or rebuilt.

The current C13/C14 segmental-pointed gateway next to the keep sits beneath a larger two-centred outer arch, the gate passage now extending through the Judges' Lodgings of 1581, which line the inner curtain, recognizable from the outside from their mullioned and transomed windows and two surviving gables. Above the gateway are the arms of Sir Henry Sidney, President of the Council of the Marches, who built the lodging range.

The interior of the keep is accessed from the inmost bailey, isolated by a C13 wall from the inner bailey. Excavation has shown that the keep once extended further to the N but was truncated and remodelled on a smaller footprint in the C15 to create a four-storey building, the upper rooms with fireplaces. The ground storey contains the former gate passage, both sides of which retain elements of late C11 arcading: plain round arches on shafts bearing scalloped capitals embellished with simple volute and linear designs. Above is the barrel-vault, inserted in the C12, pierced by murder holes. Access to the upper floors is now a spiral staircase reached from the E via a C15 doorway with a four-centred arch and continuous moulded surround.

Standing alone on the E side of the inner bailey is Chapel of St Mary Magdalene of *c*.1150, the only castle chapel with a circular nave, a form based on the Church of the Holy Sepulchre in Jerusalem and favoured by the military orders associated with the crusader states. Gilbert de Lacy, who became a Knight Templar in 1158, was probably the builder. Although the greater part of the nave survives, the chancel has been reduced to its foundations. Stubs of the side walls, the scar of a former stone vault, and the profile of a pitched room are, however, preserved on the wall of the nave. The chancel was square in plan with a polygonal apse.

W doorway of two orders; only one of the shafts remains, but all the scalloped capitals survive, with textured upper faces; chevron and billet-moulded outer arch. Inside, the walls are lined with shafted arcading, in which alternating chevron-and roll-moulded arches spring from scalloped capitals with carved upper faces. The climax of the interior is the rather magnificent chancel arch: three shafted orders with sculptured scallop capitals and arches, the latter bearing (from W to E) chevron and billet mouldings, roll mouldings, and an all-over repeating pattern of saltires.

Ranged along the NW curtain is the main residential block, the two-storey Great Hall range recessed between two three-storey wings: the Solar Block to the L (W) and the Great Chamber Block to the R (E), an effective if slightly asymmetrical massing of the three components. The Great Hall and Solar Block date from *c.*1280–1310, the Great Chamber Block is a little later. There are a few C16 insertions: Solar Block undercroft window, Great Hall undercroft central doorway and Great Chamber Block first-floor windows, but otherwise the openings appear primary.

The first-floor Great Hall has two large transomed windows with cusped Y-tracery; a third (central) window was blocked with a fireplace in the C16, but its rear arch can be glimpsed through the small C16 window and seen to better effect inside. To the L (W) is the large, pointed entrance, up a flight of steps to a landing. A substantial porch seems to have been planned, as evidenced by toothing on the adjacent Solar Block, and (less visibly) on the hall, and by a second-floor doorway (later made into a window) in the E wall of the solar, which must have been intended to access such a building. A door also led to the Solar Block from the hall stair landing.

The hall door now opens to a viewing platform at the level of the former floor. In the W wall are four doorways, the southernmost a C16 insertion, but the other three, side by side at the N end of the wall, are primary: the northern one gave onto a spiral staircase ascending to the second floor of the Solar Block; its twin, led to the first floor of the Solar Block, and perhaps, via some no longer apparent route, to service rooms in the undercroft. The third opening, which is larger than the others, communicated solely with the passage of the second doorway, only later being broken through to the Solar Block.

In the hall itself, the middle S window is readily visible in spite of being blocked by a C16 fireplace; all three N windows survive. Evidence for the character of the roof is to be found the corbelling projecting from the side walls: a closely set upper tier probably for carrying the wall plates into which the feet of the rafters were set, and a more widely spaced lower tier to support bracing for the tie beams.

The Solar Block contained large, heated chambers at all three levels, the upper ones of superior character, the rooms of the open-backed NW Tower and the Closet Tower forming annexes. The Great Chamber Block was similarly arranged, but with the advantage of access to a new latrine turret, containing two chambers on each storey, and presumably serving contemporary apartments to the E, later replaced by the C16 Tudor Lodgings, which now occupy this position. These comprise another three-storey residential block with a main division; the upper floors were reached from the round stair turret which protrudes from the S front. Hope 1908; Shoesmith and Johnson 2000.

LUMLEY, County Durham (Hotel – open to guests only). Quadrangular castle representing a development and formalizing of the plan adopted at Castle Bolton (qv) of *c.*1377–96. Probably built by John Lewyn for Ralph Lord Lumley after 1384; Lumley obtained licences to crenellate from Bishop Skirlaw (1389) and from the King (1392). Heraldic sculpture over the outer gateway suggests that the castle was completed by 1399. Around 1570–80 John Lord Lumley remodelled the courtyard elevations and made some internal changes; further alterations were made from 1721 to the

A Guide to the Medieval Castles of England

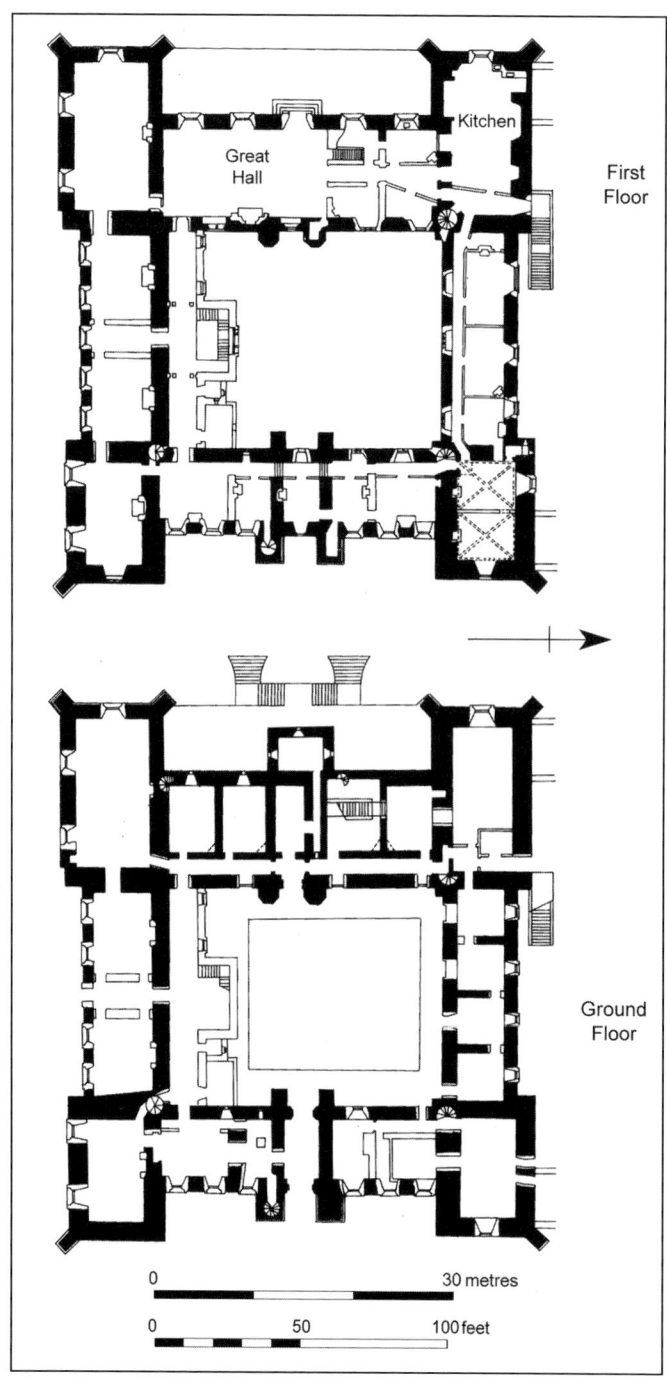

Lumley: Floor plans.

design of Sir John Vanburgh, including the creation of a Baroque W front, the refenestration of the external elevations with sash windows, the construction of a new staircase wing on the courtyard side of the S range, and the remodelling of the principal apartments. The C18 improvements have masked the C14 internal layout, particularly in the S range and towers.

Two- and three-storey ranges define a rectangular courtyard, and a taller three- or four-storey tower projects from each corner. As at Castle Bolton, the ground storey was vaulted, but here at Lumley was largely residential. The W range contained the first-floor great hall and its attendant services; the kitchen was in the NW tower, and the chapel in the NE tower. The best apartments were in the S range and towers, but this is the most altered part of the castle.

Diagonal buttresses capped by octagonal battlements project from the W angles of the W towers, and from the outermost angle of each of the E towers. The battlements are stepped up towards the corner turrets and buttresses. Communication between floors was by means of newel stairs in the inner angle of each corner tower. A square turret projected from the centre of the W front; its stump is now buried beneath the C18 terrace. The main gateway, in the centre of the E range, is flanked by square turrets with octagonal battlements like the angle buttresses, an arrangement found at Bywell (qv) and Hylton (qv). Above the gateway are carved six achievements of arms, and at parapet level, the recess between the turrets is spanned by a machicolated gallery carried on a segmental arch with multiple cusping, now much decayed.

A tunnel-vaulted gate passage leads into the courtyard. Directly opposite, in the centre of the W range, is the inner gateway, flanked by a pair of semi-octagonal turrets, and protected by a portcullis, operated from the lower end of the great hall. To the L, next to the C18 stair wing, is the only one of the C14 great hall windows to survive; pointed with Perpendicular tracery, the ultimate source for the design probably Winchester College of c. 1387, the same pattern being used in the dormitory of Durham Priory of 1398–1402 (Walter Skirlaw, Bishop of Durham between 1388 and 1406, was previously Bishop of Winchester).

A lobby just inside the entrance gives access N and S to two arms of a corridor extending along the E side of the range, and W to a vaulted compartment. On the N side of the latter is a doorway to a narrow, E–W aligned, mural corridor, with a squint or observation hatch at the E end commanding the N–S passage, and a porter's lodge at the W end within the former W turret. Otherwise, the ground floor of the range contains four single-chamber lodgings equipped with fireplaces and latrines. A staircase linked the S room with the upper end of the hall; another linked one of the northern rooms to the first-floor services.

The main route of access to the first-floor great hall is uncertain, owing to the reconstruction of the first-floor services, but was probably via the N section of the E corridor and the staircase in the NW tower. In the great hall itself two C14 window embrasures survive on the E side. Each has a segmental rear-arch, and a continuous roll-moulded surround. One of the window embrasures was converted into a fireplace in the C16, suggesting that the C14 hall was heated by an open hearth or brazier, with the smoke being conveyed through flues in the heads of the windows, a Lewyn speciality, as at Bamburgh (kitchen), Castle Bolton (great hall) and Warkworth (keep hall). The first-floor great kitchen in the NW tower rises through two storeys and retains two C14 fireplaces. The chapel is covered by two bays of quadripartite rib-vaulting. Hislop 1996b and 2007; Emery 1996, 117–21.

LYDBURY NORTH, Shropshire. See **LOWER DOWN**.

LYDFORD 1, Devon (Open access – EH). Lydford Castle probably dates from 1195 when a 'strong house' to accommodate prisoners was built in the town. In 1239 Henry III granted it to his brother Richard, Earl of Cornwall, who remodelled the castle; from 1337 it has been part of the Duchy of Cornwall. The upstanding remains, which lie N of the church, appear to comprise a motte surmounted by a stone keep with a rectangular bailey to the NW defined by earthen banks and outer ditches on the NE and SW sides and by a valley to the NW. This appearance is somewhat misleading in that the 'motte' is actually a revetment piled up against the base of the stone tower. This occurred in the C13, following Richard of Cornwall's acquisition, and was accompanied by the partial demolition and raising in height of the late C12 prison, the ground-storey remains of which were buried within the revetment or 'motte'. The entrance to this early building must have been at first-floor level, for there is no doorway at ground-floor level. Access, then, was from above although the details are uncertain. The interior was divided by a cross-wall into a large SW room containing a well, and a much smaller NE room with a doorway between the two. In the C13 reconstruction two storeys were added, both of which maintained the cross-wall division. Entered from the top of the mound at first-floor level, a mural stair leads from the portal to the second floor. These upper storeys were equipped with latrines. Saunders 1964 and 1980.

LYDFORD 2, Devon (Open access – EH). Ringwork to the SW of the church on the tip of the promontory on which the town is built. Defended by a ditch and shale-revetted bank which was constructed over early C12 pottery. Saunders 1964 and 1980.

LYMPNE, Kent (Hospitality and conference venue accessible only to guests). Fortified house of the archdeacons of Canterbury on the edge of an escarpment, next to the Church of St Stephen, with views across Romney Marsh. A N-facing, largely C14, hall and chamber block incorporates an earlier square tower at the E end. A round-ended tower was added to the W end in the C15. In 1906 it was sold to F.J. Tennant, brother-in-law of the future Prime Minister, Herbert Asquith. Tennant proceeded to restore the castle and build a house next to it under the direction of Sir Robert Lorimer.

Facing the N front the two-storey porch is on the L (E), its E wall abutting the earlier tower, which, in the C14, contained the kitchen at ground-floor level, and a chamber above; two service rooms were built to the S of the tower, of which one survives. To the R of the porch, three large pointed two-light windows, with mid-position transoms, and later C14 style tracery; two light the hall, the third illuminates the parlour. The chamber over the parlour has a crown-post roof. Beyond the parlour bay are two small rooms of uncertain date and function, though the S wall of the southern one (now truncated) contained latrine chutes. To the S of the complex are the lower courses of a curtain wall. Emery 2006, 369–70.

LYONSHALL, Herefordshire (Private). An enigmatic site NE of the church first mentioned as a castle in 1209. Before the Conquest, the manor was held by Harold Godwinson and at Domesday by Roger de Lacy; it is possible that de Lacy established the castle in the late C11. However, it is a moot point as to whether the whole earthwork complex is of one date. By the second half of the C12 it was tenanted by the Devereux family. The castle was alienated in 1301 but returned to John Lord

Devereux in 1388 and remained in the family's possession for the rest of the Middle Ages and beyond.

A roughly circular moated platform, or ringwork, occupies the SW corner of a larger, sub-rectangular, enclosure the W side of which is moated and which gives the appearance of being an interloper into an earlier earthwork. A smaller adjoining enclosure to the N, now containing farm buildings, continues the western defensive line, and is perhaps contemporary. The inner bailey, or ringwork, contains, towards its N edge, the stump of a circular keep, and was enclosed by a curtain wall, parts of which survive, notably the N side, where the wall is configured as two semi-polygonal prows, one of which is designed to shadow the keep. Dating evidence is lacking and the overgrown nature of the site makes interpretation difficult. RCHME 1934, 142–3; Shoesmith 2009, 218–20; Guy 2016–17, 120–25.

MARMION TOWER, Yorkshire North Riding. See **WEST TANFIELD**.

MARSHWOOD, Dorset (Private). Little is known of the origins and development of Marshwood Castle. First mentioned in 1215, Edward III gave orders for its repair on behalf of his son Lionel, Earl of Ulster, in 1357. It was a quadrangular enclosure defined by a moat, now largely infilled, and an inner bank, of which traces survive to the N. In the SE corner is the base of a rectangular stone keep. Also traces of a ditched and banked outer enclosure to the S, E and W, containing on the W side the site of the chapel of St Mary. RCHME 1952, 156–7.

MAXSTOKE, Warwickshire (Private, but there is usually an annual open day). A symmetrical courtyard castle built for William Clinton, Earl of Huntingdon, under a licence of 1345, Maxstoke is the expression of an ideal in which martial, domestic and aesthetic considerations converge in a harmonious design that soothes the nerves, lifts the spirits and excites the imagination. Part of the charm is in the water-filled moat that surrounds the little island, part in the human scale of the building and its inherent homeliness, but most of all in the high quality of the design and workmanship. The plan is rectangular with boldly projecting octagonal corner towers and has been planned and laid out with scrupulous accuracy and proportionality. For instance, the width of the NW tower (Lady Tower), which is larger than the others, amounts to one-sixth of the length of the castle, while that of the other towers is one-sixth of the width of the castle. Such instances are a measure of the attention to detail that underlies the design of Maxstoke and accounts for its visual appeal. Similar qualities of planning can be discerned in Stafford Castle keep of 1348, just 30 miles away, which was built by the master mason John of Burcestre (Bicester).

The entrance is to the E, where the gatehouse forms the striking centrepiece of a formal front, being linked by a low curtain wall to squat three-storey corner towers. In the case of the gatehouse itself, the emphasis is on verticality; it rises twice as high as the curtain and is flanked by narrow octagonal towers. A perambulation of the castle's surrounding berm allows an appreciation of the C14 workmanship: twin-light transomed windows with monolithic trefoiled ogee heads, the chapel W window with its Decorated tracery, moulded parapet strings interspersed by gargoyles, moulded crenellation caps and decorative chimney stacks, all provide evidence for the presence of a team of skilled artisans.

Having noted also, that in addition to its extra width, the Lady Tower is also higher than its counterparts, back to the gateway. The segmental-pointed entrance was protected by a portcullis, and there are murder holes in the soffit of the portal arch, in this instance the outlets of water conduits for dowsing fires against the gate. After these defensive measures, the gate passage is covered by a beautiful ribbed vault with sculptured bosses, a decorative feature, certainly, but also practical in its fireproof qualities. So, into the courtyard, now more spacious than in the C14, owing to the disappearance of much the domestic accommodation that lined the walls. However, the most important residential block, the W range, which contains the hall, great chamber and chapel does survive in great measure, encased behind a later frontage. Alcock *et al*. 1978; Hislop 1993.

MEPPERSHALL (The Hills), Bedfordshire (Private). Motte and two baileys, possibly one of the castles besieged by King Stephen in 1138. The motte and baileys are arranged in a linear sequence from W to E and surrounded by ditches; both baileys have inner banks, except for the side towards the motte. Petre 2012, 67–9.

MERDON, Hampshire (Private). Ringwork and bailey built within a prehistoric hillfort in 1138 for Henry of Blois, Bishop of Winchester. Destroyed by Henry II *c*.1155 but continued in use as a bishop's palace until the later C14. The ringwork lies to the N, close to but entirely within the hillfort defences, whereas the bailey breaks through the S side of the hillfort, so obscuring the line of the earlier earthworks on this side. Both ringwork and bailey are enclosed by a ditch and inner bank much greater in scale than the earthworks of the hillfort. The ringwork had a stone curtain, of which traces remain, and, on the N side, a stone tower, probably a keep. Cole 1994.

METTINGHAM, Suffolk (Private). Built under a licence of 1342 for Sir John Norwich, a veteran of the Scottish and French wars, Mettingham is a two-courtyard moated site like the later C14 castles of Scotney (qv) and Cooling (qv). The approach is from the N, the conspicuous height of its central gatehouse contrasting with the low curtain, in this respect reminiscent of its close contemporary, Maxstoke (qv), despite being much plainer in architectural character. A segmental-pointed, portcullis-protected gateway is recessed between a pair of turrets of unusual design, squared to the front and inner sides, but canted on the outer sides. There were internal towers at the two northern corners and an internal mid-wall turret to the W. It was in the outer court that the hall complex was situated, and there is access from here across a dividing moat into the inner court, which was probably mostly garden. Also accessible from the outer court, but occupying the NE angle of the inner court, is a third moated enclosure, containing the remains of domestic buildings ranged around a central courtyard. In the C16 this was known as the 'olde castell' and may represent an earlier manor house incorporated into the mid C14 castle. The surviving elements comprise two towers on the S side and the remains of an outer wall pierced by openings against which apartments were formerly ranged. Emery 2000, 124–6.

MIDDLEHAM, Yorkshire North Riding (Open – EH). **William's Hill**, ringwork and bailey on a ridge ¼ mile SSW of Middleham Castle, built in the C11 or C12 by one of the lords of Richmond. The remains consist of the ringwork defined by a massive bank and ditch entered from the SE, and a less-well defined SE outer bailey entered from the E, its ditch partially retaining water.

   Middleham Castle. It was probably Robert FitzRanulph who built the keep in the 1170s. When Robert's grandson, Ralph, died in 1258 without a male heir, Middleham was inherited by his daughter Mary. Her marriage to Robert Neville brought

Middleham from the NW.

Middleham into the possession of what was to be one of the most powerful families in northern England. Mary's grandson, Ralph Neville (d. 1367), was one of the leaders of the English army which, in 1346, inflicted a decisive defeat on the Scots at the Battle of Neville's Cross near Durham, and who subsequently began the construction of Raby Castle (qv). His son, John (d. 1388), continued with the work at Raby, rebuilt Brancepeth (qv) and built an entirely new castle at Sheriff Hutton (qv). In 1397 John's son Ralph (d. 1425) was created First Earl of Westmorland. When, in 1399, Henry Bolingbroke claimed the throne of England he was backed by Westmorland, and during the rebellions that occurred in the early part of Henry's reign, Westmorland played his part in destroying the power of the Percy family, his main rivals in the North, thereby making himself pre-eminent amongst the northern nobility. It was probably he who remodelled Middleham in the late C14/early C15, greatly enlarging the accommodation in the process.

The castle takes the form of a slightly irregular rectangle with three rectangular corner towers, and one round tower (the Prince's Tower) at the SW angle. A number of latrine turrets project from the curtain and the N, S and W walls are lined with domestic buildings. The plan of this enclosure bears a general resemblance to Castle Bolton (qv), some 10 miles to the NW, but the element that marks it out as having much earlier origins is the C12 keep, which occupies a central position, looming above the curtain wall and its towers and dominating the entire complex. The keep is generally dated to the 1170s which may point to the date at which William's Hill was abandoned in favour of this lower-lying site. Nevertheless, much happened subsequently to create a patchwork of different building periods, although the use of the same local limestone rubble throughout is responsible for a high degree of unity of appearance and makes the task of separating one phase from another a little more difficult.

The earliest part of the enceinte is generally dated to *c.*1300, though the dating evidence is far from overwhelming. Some windows with shouldered lintels in the SE tower could be of that date, but generally the fenestration is sparser and less diagnostic. The curtain wall is characterized by pilaster buttresses their sandstone ashlar contrasting with the limestone rubble of the walls, and with a little step near the top. They rise to about one third the height of the curtain, implying that the early curtain was quite low. The walls were raised in the C14/C15 when the single-storey domestic ranges were given an upper floor. A row of buttresses along the S front may have been built to contain the extra load. A cinquefoil-headed window in the S curtain looks late C14 (cf. the hall and chapel windows at Castle Bolton (qv) of *c*.1377–95); the upper windows of the N front are more likely to be C15.

The main point of entry was formerly on the E side, where the foundations of a rectangular tower are still to be seen. This was replaced *c*.1400, when the NE corner tower was raised in height and converted into a gatehouse. It is a three-storey tower, the inserted entry glaringly obvious from its yellow sandstone ashlar construction. The windows of the uppermost storey are cinquefoil-headed single lights with sunken spandrels; above are the corbelled machicolations of the former parapet, an embellishment that became popular in the North towards the end of the C14, but which had been used at a slightly earlier date at the Neville castles of Raby, Sheriff Hutton and Brancepeth. Statues of armed figures found during clearance of the site probably adorned the battlements as they do on the outer gatehouse of Raby. The large, pointed gateway, which was protected by a portcullis, leads into a rib-vaulted gate passage, the ribs springing from corbels carved with faces.

Passing through the gatehouse the visitor is confronted by the overpowering presence of the great tower, a rectangular building with corner turrets, and latrine turrets to S and W. It is one of the larger English keeps by area, though originally it only had two storeys. Access was at first-floor level, through a (now-vanished) forebuilding set against the E wall, where the modern steps now stand. However, breaches in the walls now allow ingress to the ground floor from outside. The keep was divided longitudinally by a cross-wall into an E and W compartment, the larger E room further divided by a central N–S arcade of which the column bases remain. Covering the W bay was a type of groin vaulting. These ground-floor areas, which were devoted to cooking and to storage, were linked by two doorways in the spine wall. At the S end of the building the spine wall contained two large back-to-back fireplaces for cooking. Communication between the floors was solely via the spiral staircase in the SE turret.

The spiral stair and the external steps on the E side give access to a modern viewing gallery within the great hall, which occupied the entire E bay to the R (N) of the entrance. At the S end, to the L of the entrance, was access to a latrine turret and two to the main staircase in the SE turret. Just below the sills of the S windows is an integral basin, the better-preserved of a pair that drain through the wall. At the upper (N) end of the hall doorways led into an oratory housed within the NE turret (not accessible to the visitor) and into the W bay (only visible from ground level), which contained the great chamber (N) and smaller inner chamber (S), each served by a fireplace and a latrine.

Attached to the E side of the forebuilding and extending right across the courtyard to the curtain wall, are the remains of a three-storey chapel tower added *c*.1250. The uppermost storey, which contained the chapel, was once entered from a porch at the top of the forebuilding stair. At ground level a passage passed through the building from N–S to allow communication between the two sides of the divided courtyard. Emery 1996, 368–72; Kenyon 2015.

MIDDLETON STONEY, Oxfordshire (Private, but the earthworks of the castle can be seen from the parish church, which lies within the park). A castle in Middleton Park, probably of mid C12 origin, but first mentioned in 1215 when King John ordered the Sheriff of Oxford to convey the castle to Richard de Camville, heir to his recently deceased father Gerald. It appears that Richard then took part in the opposition to King John, and as a result the order was given for the castle to be destroyed the following year. There is no record of it having been refortified.

The earthworks consist of a mound encompassed by a ditch, with a nearly square bailey to the W, bisected by the drive to Middleton Hall; this bailey was defined by a ditch and counterscarp bank, now only visible to the S and W. There is a second bailey to the E, seemingly pre-Norman in origin, demarcated by ditch, inner bank and counterscarp bank, much disturbed by quarrying. The mound was built around a large stone building, either a hall or keep, aligned NW–SE with corner turret buttresses extending from the long sides. The E turret contained a latrine shaft. Rahtz and Rowley (1984).

MILEHAM, Norfolk (Open access to the main earthworks S of the road). Major motte and bailey complex on the S side of the B1145 probably raised by the FitzAlans and first mentioned in 1153; it was described as decayed in 1302. A motte and a kidney-shaped inner bailey to the N of it are surrounded by a ditch, and then by an embanked circular enclosure or outer bailey. On the opposite (N) side of the road is a rectangular enclosure, probably coeval with the motte and bailey, to give absolute control over the thoroughfare. Brown 1989, 158, Cushion and Davison 2003, 173–5.

MISERDEN, Gloucestershire (Private). Motte and bailey in Miserden Park, of C11 or C12 origin, certainly existing by 1146 when it was surrendered by its lord, Robert Musard, to King Stephen's forces. The castle was abandoned sometime between 1266 and 1289, being replaced by a manor house on the site of the present house of Miserden Park. Situated on a rocky spur within a loop, and next to a crossing of the river Frome, the castle is defended by outer banks and a substantial ditch cutting across the neck of the spur, and then the motte, beyond which is the bailey. Excavations have revealed a shell-keep and a gatehouse. Herbert 1976, 50.

MITFORD, Northumberland (Open access). Motte and bailey partially built in stone, probably in existence by 1138 when Mitford was described as the *oppidum* of William Bertram. By 1327 it was in ruins, having been burnt out, probably by the Scots. The castle lies to the S of the Wansbeck occupying a sub-elliptical hill partly circumvented by the Park Burn which winds its way round the S and E sides on its way to the river. Ditches on the W and E sides may have been intended to accentuate the defensive qualities of a wet landscape. The motte is positioned centrally on the W side and the rest of the hill is divided into two wards by an E–W wall, but only the S bailey had stone defences. The motte carries the remains of a shell-keep inside which a pentagonal great tower was raised *c.*1200; of this tower only the vaulted basement remains, divided by an axial wall. Hunter Blair 1937, 1944 especially 116–70, and 1955.

MONTACUTE, Somerset (Open access – NT). C11 motte and bailey sculpted from a natural hill (St Michael's Hill), the work of Robert, Count of Mortain. About 1102 William of Mortain founded a Cluniac priory at Montacute, the castle being amongst the endowments, after which it lost any military significance. No medieval buildings survive, and the hill is now topped by an C18 folly. The motte constitutes the scarped hilltop. On the W side is a ditch and counterscarp bank, and beyond that, extending around three-quarters of the mound, is a very broad terrace; a bailey extends across the fourth (SW) quarter and projects down the hill. Dunning 1995, 40–2.

MONTFICHET'S TOWER, London and Middlesex (D). Vanished castle in the City of London. First mentioned *c.*1136, but possibly built in the late C11. During the C12 it was held by the eponymous Montfichet family of Stansted Mountfichet Castle (qv). Given to the Dominicans in 1275 as a site for the construction of Blackfriars. The castle was situated in the SW quarter of the walled city set against the W wall; the extent of the site is broadly represented by Ludgate Hill (N), Carter Lane (S), Ludgate Broadway (W) and Ludgate Square (E). Excavation in the 1980s revealed a series of ditches and pits. Watson, B. 1992a and 1992b.

MORTHAM TOWER, Yorkshire North Riding (Private). Fortified manor house of the Rokeby family, probably C14 in origin, replacing an earlier house destroyed by the Scots following the Battle of Bannockburn. The principal surviving medieval element is a late C15 solar tower. Sited on a spur S of the Tees and W of its tributary the river Greta, the manor house was approached from the S. A gateway with a four-centred arch breaks forward from a low crenellated curtain and leads into a courtyard surrounded by buildings on the other three sides. The N range may incorporate the remains of the medieval hall with chamber block to the W. The ashlar-built solar tower, at the NW corner of the courtyard, is rectangular, with an obliquely-set stair turret at the NE angle rising to parapet level. To the E and W (i.e., towards the courtyard) the first and second floors have square-headed two-light windows with cinquefoiled-headed lights and returned hood moulds. Above the second-floor room an oversailing attic storey with bartizans, all of different plan, corbelled out from the NW, SW and SE angles. Surmounting the tower and replacing the medieval battlements is a cresting with large rectangular openings. The tower is entered at ground-floor level via the stair turret. Each of the main storeys contained a single room with fireplace and latrine; the proportions expand as the tower rises. Emery 1996, 380–2.

MORETON CORBET, Shropshire (Open access – EH). Stone castle of the Toret family now dominated by an Elizabethan S range. The castle was built or rebuilt in the late C12, probably by Bartholomew Toret (d. 1235), the last of the male line. His heiress, Joanna, married Richard Corbet of Wattlesborough (qv) whose son (another Richard) inherited Moreton. Around 1596 a major remodelling of the castle was initiated by Sir Andrew Corbet (d. 1578) and continued by his son Robert (d. 1583), whose death brought the scheme to an end.

The medieval work is of large, squared blocks, like the keep of Wattlesborough. Curtain wall with battered plinth studded with rectangular towers of slight projection. An essentially C13 rectangular gatehouse to the N with pointed-arch gateway, refurbished in 1579 (datestone above the gate arch) by Sir Andrew Corbet, who inserted the large first-floor window. Large portcullis groove of semi-circular section. The ruined keep, or solar tower, is attached to the W curtain, its ground plan almost identical to that of Wattlesborough keep. At first-floor level a large, formerly hooded, fireplace dominates the N wall. It has engaged flanking shafts of semi-octagonal section with foliate capitals, apparently waterleaf derivatives, which support the projecting ends

Moreton Corbet from the N.

of two massive blocks, deeply embedded in the wall, carrying the lintel. It has the appearance of being an insertion, but at what date that occurred is open to question.

The S range carries dates of 1576, 1578 and 1579; two storeys and attic on moulded plinth with applied Doric (ground-floor) and Ionic (first-floor) orders, and entablature. The nine-bay front is articulated with slightly projecting centre and end bays, the latter retaining dutch gables. Large mullioned and transomed windows, and a small doorway next to each of the two end bays. Remfry 1999; Salter 2001, 60–2; Duckers 116–19.

MORPETH, Northumberland. **Haw Hill** (Open access in Carlisle Park). A castle of the de Merlay family established in the C11. It occupied a ridge to the N of the present Morpeth Castle and took the form of a motte and bailey, with the motte at the E end and the bailey towards the W. Excavations in 1830 uncovered C12 masonry fragments and the foundations of a rectangular building. This castle was captured and may have been destroyed by King John in 1216. Salter, M. 1997a, 80.

Morpeth Castle (Landmark Trust holiday let). Morpeth Castle is thought to have been a replacement for the castle on Haw Hill, which lies some 200m to the N. It is uncertain whether the new castle was built by the de Merlays, or by their successors the Greystokes, who gained Morpeth through marriage in the C13. In the late C15 the castle came to the Dacres by the same means. By 1596 it was in a dilapidated state. A map of 1604 depicts a great tower within the inner ward, possibly a schematic record of a now-lost building. During the Civil War it was held for Parliament, badly damaged during a siege, and subsequently part demolished. The gatehouse was restored as a residence in 1858–60.

The upper ward is sub-rectangular, entered directly via a gatehouse at its NE corner, and enclosed by a curtain wall, elements of which remain. There was a sub-triangular outer ward to the W; stone foundations on its W boundary probably belong to a great barn. The main feature now is the C14 gatehouse, a rectangular three-storey building with post-medieval roof and attic storey. In the centre is a four-centred gate arch, unprotected by a portcullis; the large two-light windows above are C19, but may represent an original form. A particularly striking feature is the corbelled machicolation that supports the external parapet extending around the corners, which are surmounted by turrets with canted outer corners.

Four-centred barrel-vault over the gate passage and four-centred doorways from it into the flanking guard rooms, each of which is equipped with a fireplace. Access to the upper rooms was via a first-floor doorway on the S side; from the entrance lobby a spiral staircase ascended to the second floor and roof. The first floor was divided into two rooms each with fireplace and latrine; the second floor was served by a latrine, but there is no surviving evidence of heating or division.

There is some doubt about the usual attribution of the gatehouse to William Lord Greystoke. His dates (1342–59) seem a little early for some of the details, which would fit more comfortably with the late C14. William's successor, Ralph Lord Greystoke (d. 1418), may therefore be a more likely candidate. Perhaps the tower said to have been built by William was the great tower depicted on the C17 map. Ryder 1992; Emery 1996, 121–2.

MOUNTSORREL (Castle Hill), Leicestershire (Open access). Site of a late C11/early C12 castle of the earls of Chester first mentioned *c*.1152 when it was transferred to the Earl of Leicester. Destroyed by Henry III in 1217. The castle was sited on a rocky crag overlooking a crossing of the river Soar. The earthworks are heavily disturbed by quarrying. Wright and Creighton 2016, 105–16.

MOUNT THOROLD, Northamptonshire and the Soke of Peterborough. See **PETERBOROUGH**

MULGRAVE, Lythe, Yorkshire North Riding (Both sites are in Mulgrave woods on the Mulgrave estate). **Foss** (Open to walkers on Wednesday, Saturday and Sunday). Ringwork on the edge of a cliff overlooking Barnby Beck said to be founded *c*.1072 by Nigel Fossard. It was protected by a ditch and, to the N, by a counterscarp bank. It was replaced by Old Musgrave Castle. I'Anson 1913, 348–51.

Old Mulgrave Castle (Open to walkers on Wednesday, Saturday and Sunday). Old Mulgrave Castle is situated on a ridge between two eastward-flowing streams. It comprises a multi-period walled enclosure of sub-rectangular plan with projecting rectangular tower at the E end, and latrine turret to the NW. It is entered from the W via a gateway with solid, round-fronted flanking towers dating from the late C12 or C13. Occupying a roughly central position within the courtyard are the remains of a great tower, or keep, nearly square with rounded corner towers. It is usually dated to *c*.1300 but has been much altered with the insertion of large mullioned and transomed windows. The medieval details that survive suggest a C13 or C14 date, as do those of the E tower. Page 1923, 390–3.

MUNCASTER, Cumberland (Open – restricted hours during the winter). The seat of the Pennington family from the C13. The main visible survival from the medieval castle/manor house is a much-altered rectangular solar tower at the SW angle of the present mansion. Remaining details are few, but the tower may date from the C14, as has been suggested. Vaulted basement, and spiral staircase at the NW angle. Curwen 1913, 308–9; Perriam and Robinson 1998, 107.

MYDDLE, Shropshire (Private). Scanty remains of a quadrangular castle created by John le Strange of Knockin, who was granted a licence to crenellate his dwelling house at 'Medle' in 1308. In the mid C16 John Leland found it 'veri ruinus'; it was damaged by an earthquake in 1688. Interpretation is largely based on a description from memory of Richard Gough in his *History of Myddle* of 1700 (published 1875) and limited (unpublished) excavation in the 1960s. There was a moated outer ward to the E with a gatehouse at the NE corner (part of the moat was still extant in 1879). The entrance to the inner ward, which was also moated (still containing water in 1879), was in the centre of the E front. Inside, ranges of apartment lined the walls; the hall probably occupied the W side. The main relic of this castle is the remnant of a stair turret which stood at the NE angle of the hall (from which it was entered) and the NW angle of the courtyard. It retains a moulded trefoil-headed doorway. Remnants of the curtain also survive. Gough 1875, 27–9; Duckers 2006 119–21.

NAFFERTON, Northumberland (Private). Enclosure castle that Philip de Ulecotes, Sheriff of Northumberland, was engaged in building in 1218. A complaint by Richard de Umfraville of Prudhoe (qv) prompted the King to order the cessation of operations and destroy what had already been built. Further instructions for demolition were issued in 1221, after Philip's death. In the C15 or early C16 the site was reoccupied with the construction of a tower house. The site, which lies N of the A69, next to Whittle Burn, approximately two miles NW of Prudhoe Castle, consists of the remains of a rectangular embanked enclosure with later tower house at the SW angle. Excavation in the 1960s showed that although the castle was of timber initially, work had begun on rebuilding it in stone. The site is associated with the folk ballad of Lang Lonkin. Dodds 1926, 254–62; Harbottle and Salway 1960; Harbottle *et al.* 1961.

NAPPA HALL, Askrigg, Yorkshire North Riding (Private, but visible from footpath). Fortified manor house probably built between *c.*1470 and 1500 for Thomas Metcalfe, Chancellor of the Duchy of Lancaster. E–W aligned S-facing single-storey hall range with attached end towers. Four-storey solar tower at the upper (W) end of the hall, and three-storey tower at the lower (E) end. Square-headed windows throughout with returned hood moulds and cinquefoil-headed lights. Those in the W tower diminish in size in ascending order. Two-centred entrance at the lower (E) end into a cross-passage. Interior substantially altered. Emery 1996, 382–3.

NAWORTH, Cumberland (Private). In 1333 Ralph Lord Dacre was granted a licence to strengthen and crenellate his house at Naworth, which occupies the W end of a low but precipitous spur at the confluence of two streams. Here, Dacre created an irregular quadrilateral courtyard castle with a square tower (Dacre Tower) projecting from its SE angle. The great hall was rebuilt against the N wall in the early C16, but by the 1580s the castle was much decayed. It was restored and transformed into a mansion in the early years of the C17 but was largely gutted by fire in 1844 and the following year restored under the direction of Anthony Salvin. What survives from the C14 are the curtain walls of large squared and coursed blocks, and the lower parts of the Dacre Tower and Lord William's Tower at the NE angle. The approach was from the E, but the principal entrance was on the S side next to the Dacre Tower. Ferguson, 1878–9; Donaldson-Hudson 1956–8; Curwen 1913, 213–18; Perriam and Robinson 1998, 166–7.

NEROCHE, Somerset. See **CASTLE NEROCHE**.

A Guide to the Medieval Castles of England

NETHER STOWEY, Somerset (Open access). Motte with two baileys in existence by 1154. Built by Alfred d'Epaignes, who held the manor in 1086, or one of his successors, possibly his son-in-law Robert de Chandos (d. 1120). The castle came to the Columbers family through marriage, and, in 1342 to the Audleys, with whom it remained until 1497, by which time it may have been abandoned.

The motte, which has been scarped from a natural mound, was surrounded by a ditch and counterscarp bank, and surmounted by a rectangular keep, the foundations of which were exposed to view in the C19. This tower was divided by a spine wall and the two divisions by transverse walls. A projection at the SE corner may have been a forebuilding. The two baileys lie to the NE and SE, contiguous with one another, being divided by a ditch. The greater (SE) bailey is defined by a bank and ditch, while the NE bailey (which is on higher ground) is protected by scarping. Dunning 1981 and 1995, 43–4.

NEWARK, Nottinghamshire (Open). Enclosure castle of the bishops of Lincoln built *c.*1130 for Bishop Alexander 'the Magnificent' on the site of an existing, possibly C11, fortress on the E bank of the Trent. Alexander's castle was remodelled in the late C13/early C14 when the W curtain was moved closer to the river and new domestic apartments ranged along it; improvements were made to the accommodation in the C15. In the C16 the castle came to the Crown and was leased out, and in the early years of the C17 significant alterations were undertaken by Lord Burghley. Newark was held for the King during the Civil War and subsequently slighted by Parliamentary order.

The best view of the castle is from the opposite side of the river, from where the C13/C14 W front can be viewed in its entirety. Characterized by polygonal towers/turrets and horizontal banding created by judicious use of masonry in two different colours, this front was strongly influenced by Caernarfon Castle in north Wales (begun 1283). The wall was built against the cliff face, courtyard level being denoted

Newark from the NW.

by a prominent chamfered offset just below the lower tier of large windows. At wharf level, two features of note are, to the L (N) the watergate, and to the R (S) two arched latrine outlets.

The main courtyard buildings comprised two halls and chamber blocks ranged along this frontage. In the centre was the great hall lit by two high pointed windows, one each side of the Middle Tower. To the R (S) of the great hall a smaller two-light window, its sill at a higher level, denotes a first-floor chamber above the service rooms. To the L (N) of the great hall was the bishop's hall also lit by high pointed windows, of which one survives, the position of the other being taken by a late C15 oriel; beneath the hall a line of small rectangular loops indicates the presence of an undercroft. Hard up against the corner tower was a two-storey chamber block, now with large C15 windows. A number of mullioned and transomed windows relate to the C16 alterations.

On the N side, set back from the road (there was probably an outer bailey), is Bishop Alexander's great gatehouse of *c*.1130, a large rectangular building with a semi-circular arched gateway between large buttresses (now fronted with C19 rock-faced ashlar), the high threshold formerly approached across the moat by a bridge. The gatehouse was largely faced with ashlar, still extant over the entrance but otherwise extensively robbed. C16 windows over the gateway, but the shapes of the blocked C12 first-floor fenestration they replaced can still be seen. Unvaulted gate passage, and on the R (W) a little porter's lodge and stone benches on both sides.

Inside the castle, a stair turret on the E side of the gatehouse gives access to the upper rooms. The largest of these, which lies to the S, rose through two storeys to the roof, and was lit by large windows to the E and W, and by a wheel window to the S at a higher level. Although the function of this space cannot be confirmed, both chapel and audience chamber have been suggested. To the N of this room, outside the line of the curtain, was a smaller chamber with three large windows to the N, suggesting that it might have been a viewing chamber, and a curiously contrived route to a latrine within the N curtain via an external timber gallery overhanging the W wall of the gatehouse, now vanished apart from the beam sockets.

Of the riverfront range, only the external wall survives; the other walls were of timber; the roof line is preserved on the wall of the NW tower. However, the undercroft of *c*.1300 is still intact, being entered from the watergate stairs. It is divided into eight groin-vaulted bays by a central row of octagonal columns and rectangular wall responds supporting round arches. This was a storage chamber, well-situated for receiving goods brought via the watergate. It could also be entered from the great hall by means of a staircase at its S end. Marshall and Samuels 1997; Marshall 1998.

NEW BUCKENHAM, Norfolk (Private but the exterior can be circumperambulated and the key can be applied for at the King's Stores, King Street). Ringwork and bailey, the former containing the remains of what is considered to be the earliest cylindrical keep in England. Built *c*.1140 by William d'Albini, who, in 1138, married Adeliza of Louvain, the widow of Henry I, and was created Earl of Sussex. His new foundation replaced the castle now known as Old Buckenham (qv), which lies some 1½ miles to the S. Circular ringwork with moat and substantial inner bank; the bailey lay to the E, interposed between the ringwork and the town, which was laid out at the same time. Access to the ringwork was via the bailey through a gatehouse now buried beneath the bank, a consequence of a remodelling resulting in a new entrance

New Buckenham: Stump of the round keep (*c*.1140).

and bailey to the W. The stump of the keep, which lies to the S of the old gatehouse, is built of flint rubble in an area with a dearth of freestone and a consequent tradition of round church towers. Unusually for a C12 great tower, it was entered at ground-floor level. Apart from being the earliest cylindrical keep it is also one of the largest with an external diameter of nearly 70ft (21.3m). This explains the central cross-wall, a feature well known in rectangular keeps as a means of facilitating flooring and roofing, but almost entirely absent from those of circular plan, which are generally of a more manageable size. Renn 1961; Rigold 1980; Brown 1989, 58–60; Remfry 1997.

NEWCASTLE UPON TYNE, Northumberland (Open). Founded in 1080 by Robert Curthose, eldest son of William I, on the site of the Roman fort of *Pons Aelius*. In 1095 the castle was captured by William Rufus from the rebellious Earl of Northumberland, Robert Mowbray. From 1139 the earldom of Northumberland, including Newcastle, was held by sons of the Scottish king. Henry II brought it under the control of the kings of England again in 1157, and in 1171–8 he raised the keep, a project that was under direction of his master mason, Maurice, who was later to work at Dover (qv). The great gatehouse (the Black Gate) was rebuilt by Henry's grandson, Henry III, in 1247–50. To our great good fortune, these two significant pieces of well-dated and interesting architecture have survived, whereas much of the castle has vanished. Now they form two incongruous islands within an area that was radically transformed during the C19, not least by the construction of two railway viaducts, one of which cuts right across the castle, missing the NW corner of the keep by a whisker and separating it from the gatehouse; in circumstances such as these it is not easy to envisage the extent and layout of the medieval castle. However, it was a

A Guide to the Medieval Castles of England

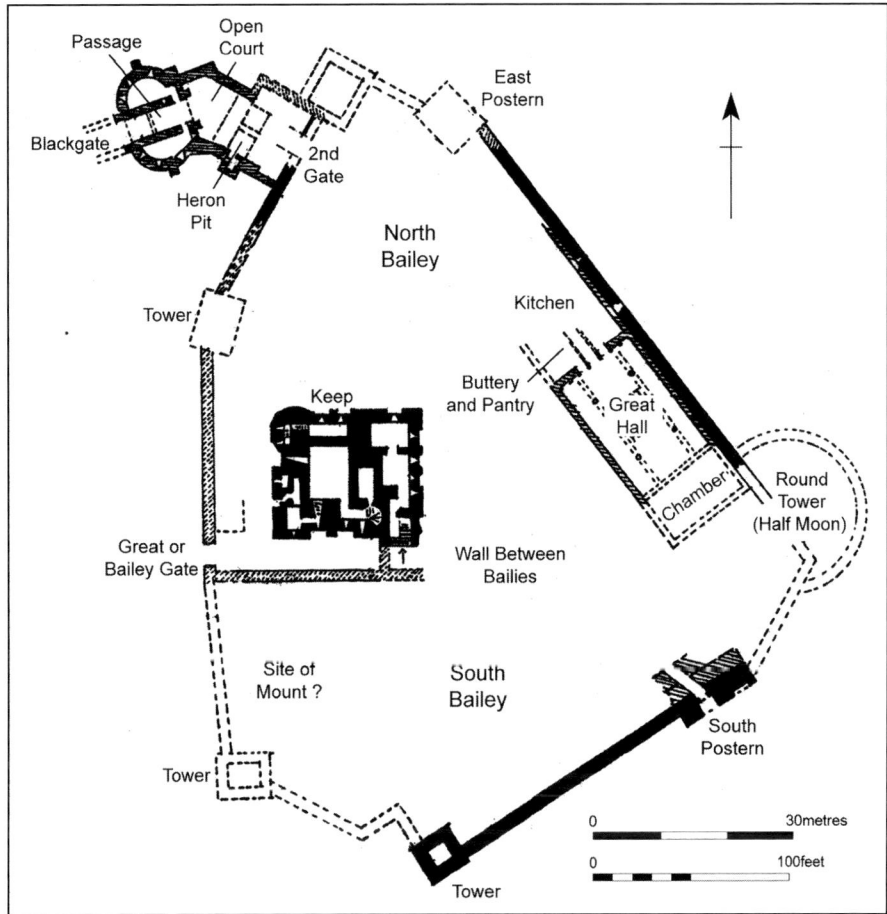

Newcastle: Ground plan. From Knowles 1926.

sub-triangular enclosure established on a spur above the river Tyne, with the base towards the SE and the apex towards the N. On the SE side it was protected by the steep river escarpment, and on the NE side by a ravine (The Side). The spur was cut off from the land to the W by the excavation of a great ditch, which extended in front of, and due S from, the Black Gate, which itself lies immediately W of the N apex.

Starting on St Nicholas' Street in front of Henry III's Black Gate we are presented with one of the most unusual of English castle gatehouses. Thrust well forward of the curtain is a barbican-like extension to the C12 gate. Influenced by the Constable's Gate at Dover (qv) of some 20 years earlier, the outer gate tower takes the general form of the Dover portico in resembling two D-shaped towers placed back-to-back. Here at Newcastle, instead of a plain flat front, the centre of the building breaks forward on a pair of buttresses flanking the gateway, an arched recess formerly rising above first–floor level. On each side of the gateway is a row of three arrow loops with fishtail bases, and in each buttress an image recess, now devoid of statues. The tower

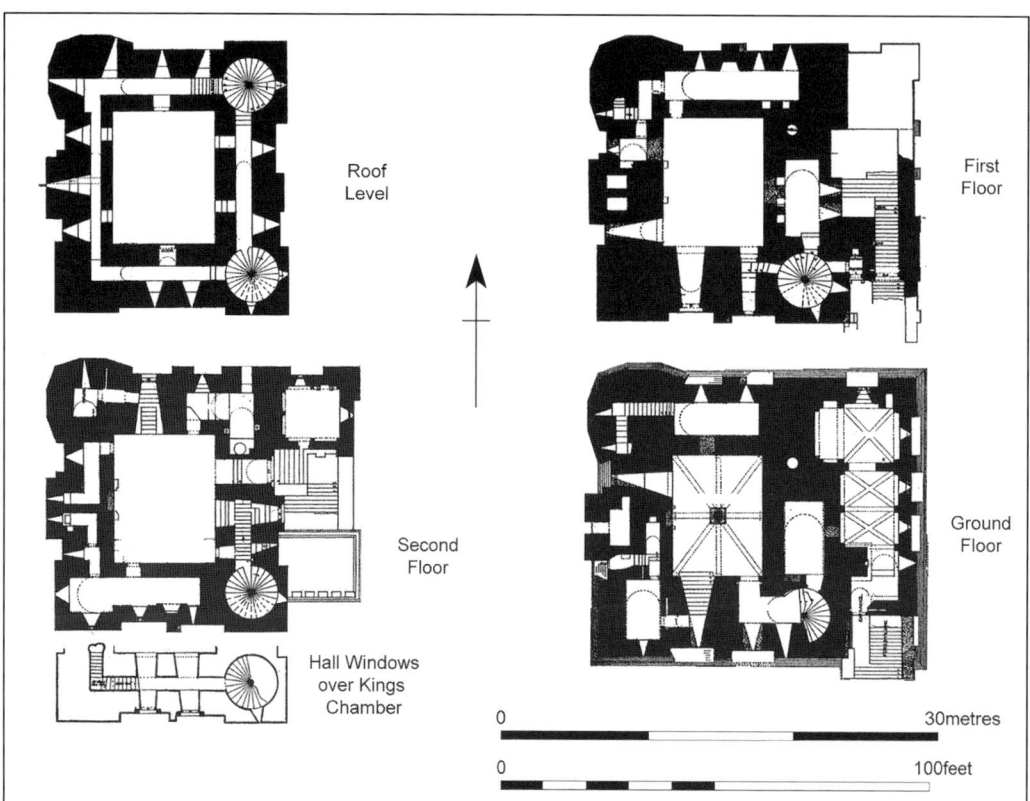

Newcastle: Floor plans of the keep. After Knowles 1926.

rises through four storeys, but the upper half was largely rebuilt in the C17. Inside the vaulted gate passage was a portcullis and gate and, on each side, two trefoil-arched recesses containing stone benches, and a pointed doorway leading to a pair of rib-vaulted guardrooms.

Beyond the tower is a yard, then come the fragmentary remains of a second gatehouse; it was a rectangular building standing proud of the curtain and containing a drawbridge pit. So, into the castle enclosure now largely an open space divided by the viaduct. Through the viaduct arch, the main residential block was on the LH side set against the NE curtain, its site now occupied by the former Council Offices. On the R (W) is the keep some 30ft from the site of the W curtain. To the S of the keep, a wall divided the enclosure into a N and S bailey. Further along on the LH (NE) side, past the Moot Hall, which also encroaches on the castle, is Castle Steps, which descends through the S postern, a rectangular C12 gateway projecting from the remains of the S curtain. The gateway comprises two semi-circular arches, the RH (NE) one blocked, the LH one containing a deeply recessed pedestrian entrance.

Back up the steps to the keep, a square tower with square corner turrets, except at the NW angle which, unaccountably, has an irregularly polygonal profile. On the E side there is a large and elaborate forebuilding, entered from the S, containing a steep staircase ascending to second-floor level. To the L (W) of the staircase a doorway leads to the substantially restored chapel, which occupies the ground floor of the forebuilding and comprises a two-bay nave and single-bay chancel; double-shafted wall arcades with water-leaf capitals; quadripartite rib-vaulting decorated with chevron (nave) and pellet (chancel) mouldings. Despite the N–S alignment of the forebuilding, the orientation of the chapel is liturgically correct, with the altar to the E, as evidenced by the position of a piscina in the S wall. The rising staircase allows for a higher vault in the chancel than in the nave.

The first stage of the staircase rises to a gate tower with a segmental-arched gateway beneath a semi-circular arch on shafts with cushion capitals. Above, and to the L (W), is a narrow doorway to a little chamber containing a cistern; corbels below the doorway suggest it was linked to the W curtain by a timber walkway. Straight ahead, at the top of the stairs, another tower contains a single room above the chapel, having arcaded walls, perhaps a waiting room, before continuing up more steps to the entrance to the keep. A second-floor entrance, as here, is very unusual, but the device was repeated by Maurice at Dover. The much-restored doorway is highly decorated with much inventive deployment of chevron-inspired mouldings, the inner order incorporating a repeated leaf motif.

The entrance passage leads into the main second-floor room, a hall-like room covered by a C19 barrel-vault, with clearstorey lighting from a mural gallery that extends all around the keep, making the room exaggeratedly high. Originally, however, the roof began below gallery level and the hall was less ungainly in its proportions, though still of impressive height. This room was the hub of communication within the keep. From it the other storeys were accessed via the main staircase in the SE angle; a second staircase in the NE corner leads to the battlements. No fireplace seems to have been provided, so the room must have been heated by an open hearth or brazier(s). A doorway in the W wall led to a latrine, and one in the N wall to the well chamber, the only place in the building from which the well could be drawn. Wall recesses contain pipe holes by which the well could be conveyed to the basement and to a cistern in the forebuilding. Another mural chamber in the S wall known as the 'King's Chamber' has a fireplace and access to a latrine.

There is a lesser residential suite at first-floor level with a smaller main room and a private room in the N wall known as the 'Queen's Chamber' with a fireplace and access to a latrine in the W wall. Between the Queen's Chamber and the latrine, a staircase descends to a vaulted room immediately beneath the Queen's Chamber which is lit by a pair of loops in the N wall but with no other facilities. In the E wall, now communicating with the main room but formerly entered only from the SE staircase, is a vaulted chamber, probably a storage room. Down to the ground floor, first another vaulted storage room under the upper one, and then a passage to the main space, the 'Garrison Room', which is covered by an octopartite rib-vault supported on corbelled responds and a central column with scalloped capital. From the S window embrasure, a passage leads first to a vaulted chamber, the door to which was barred from the inside, then to a latrine, and to a postern in the W wall, probably a goods entrance. Longstaffe 1860; Knowles 1926; Harbottle and Ellison, 1981; Brindle 2013.

NEWCASTLE UNDER LYME, Staffordshire (Open access). Motte and bailey in existence by *c.*1149, when it was granted to Ranulph, Earl of Chester. The appellation suggests that it may have been a replacement for an earlier castle, possibly at Trentham. In 1267 Henry III granted it to his son Edmund, Earl of Lancaster, and it later formed part of the Duchy of Lancaster. Excavation has confirmed that the castle was built on a raised platform and surrounded by a large pool created by the damming of neighbouring streams. The visible remains comprise a truncated motte within

Queen Elizabeth Park on the SW side of Silverdale Road, and the remnants of a stretch of ashlar walling at the S end of John O'Gaunt's Road at its junction with Silverdale Road. This latter is thought to have been associated with the entrance to the castle. The bailey (which was built over in the C19) lay to the NW of the motte. Jenkins 1963, 11–15.

NEWNHAM, Kent (Private). Undocumented motte and bailey comprising a low mound surrounded by a ditch with a bailey to the SW. The E side of the site is partly built over by the adjacent farm. Excavation in 2012 revealed a steep-sided ditch some 14ft (4.5m) deep around the mound, and, on top of the mound, the foundations of a flint-built structure some 91ft (8.5m) square with rounded corners. A projection on the E side corresponded with the position of a round-backed fireplace inside. A square projection at the W end of the N side may represent the base of a porch. Jardine-Rose 2012–13.

NORHAM, Northumberland (Open access – EH). Ringwork and bailey rebuilt in stone. Castle of the bishops of Durham built in 1121 by Bishop Ranulph Flambard on the Scottish border. Destroyed by the Scots in 1138 and rebuilt by Bishop Hugh du Puiset between 1157 and 1170, including a major reconstruction of the keep by the Durham mason, Richard Wolveston. The gateway was rebuilt in 1408, and the keep remodelled in the 1420s. Severe damage inflicted by a Scottish bombardment in 1513 necessitated substantial rebuilding over the next decade and beyond. The accession of James I in 1603 removed the castle's significance as a border fortress and it was allowed to decay.

The castle sits on a small promontory above the river Tweed, its two wards defined by a pair of concentric curving ditches, the outer ditch now partly occupied by the modern road. The main approach was from the village to the W which leads to the West Gate, the C12 core of which comprises a simple rectangular tower containing a vaulted passage; it was enlarged towards the W in the C15 and given a barbican. There was a second entrance to the S (Sheep Gate), of which the arch remains; it may have communicated with an outer enclosure to the S. Most of the visible stonework belongs to the C16 reconstruction, including three gun embrasures in the N curtain.

The main survival from the medieval period is the keep, which occupies the SE corner of the inner ward. This incorporates three main construction phases, including the remains of Bishop Flambard's two-storey great tower of 1121, which is represented by part of the inner (NW) section of the basement. Bishop du Puiset extended the building to the SE, cutting back and refacing the original SE wall, which became a partition wall, and adding an additional storey at the SE corner to contain a chamber. In the 1420s the rest of the keep was raised to the same height. Hunter Blair 1932–4, and 1944 especially 137–41; Dixon and Marshall 1993.

NORTH ELMHAM, Norfolk (Open access – EH). Fortified manor house converted from the former cathedral of North Elmham by Bishop Henry Despenser, who in 1381 had played a major part in putting down the Peasants' Revolt in these parts. Despenser obtained a licence to crenellate his manor house here in 1387. The church was retained but converted for domestic use; it lies within the SW corner of a sub-rectangular enclosure defined by a wide ditch. Further protection was provided by an inner ditch around the N and E sides and an inner bank (partly removed). The main entrance to the manor house was on the S side, at first-floor level; it was flanked by two semi-circular towers of which the LH (W) one was a re-used Anglo-Saxon stair turret. Inside, there was an undercroft at church ground-floor level and the main apartments were above on inserted floors. The hall and services were in the nave, the chamber block occupied the transepts and crossing and the services the narthex. Rigold 1962–3.

NORWICH, Norfolk (Open) (Plate X). Probably raised by William I in the 1060s, Norwich Castle comprised a motte and two baileys. Between *c*.1095 and *c*.1120, a programme of improvement was underway, a project that included the strengthening of the defences and the construction of a great tower, or keep, on top of the motte. There was a bailey to the S of the motte, part of its extent now represented by Castle Gardens; another bailey lay to the NE. However, the upstanding remains are now largely represented by the motte, and particularly the great tower, which is one of the most significant keeps in England.

The stone keep was instigated by William II *c*.1095, though not completed until *c*.1115 owing to a hiatus in construction, possibly attributable to the King's death in 1100. Innovatory aspects include a central spine wall in contrast to the asymmetrical arrangements of earlier keeps, and the provision of an elaborate forebuilding, by which the first-floor entrance was accessed via a grand staircase, a seminal feature that was to become the vogue for buildings of this class. The keep presents a splendid spectacle perched high on the motte, a pleasingly proportioned cube, its walls articulated by pilaster buttresses, the intervening panels covered above basement level with tier upon tier of blind arcading. Such an extravagant decorative scheme is unparalleled in castle architecture, but similar arcading is to be found on the contemporary Norwich Cathedral, suggesting perhaps that the same architect may have been responsible for both; certainly, a comparison of the masons' marks has shown that the two buildings were served by the same stone cutters.

The present appearance of the keep dates from the 1830s, when it was refaced in Bath Stone ashlar, replacing both the flint rubble of the ground-storey panels and the Caen stone ashlar of the buttresses and upper walls. However, pre-restoration drawings suggest that the medieval pattern of arcading was replicated rather than altered. The current entrance through the C19 Great Gatehouse leads to the late C20 replacement for the medieval staircase which ascends to the forebuilding (Bigod's Tower) at the N end of the E front. At first-floor level, Bigod's Tower formed a loggia-like porch with an arcade of large windows to the E. Although the porch may have been replaced, the greater part of the large and ornate doorway to the keep survives: plain round arch within two moulded orders springing from shafts with carved capitals; around the inner order the upper part of each voussoirs bears an individual carving in relief and the lower part takes the form of an embryonic beakhead. To the R (N) of the doorway is a smaller blind arch, and over both a big outer arch, to create a very emphatic introduction to the interior.

The first floor has been very substantially altered, but although more than one theoretical reconstruction of the original layout has been published, some essentials are agreed upon. The main entrance gave access to the great hall, which occupied the greater part of the keep to the N of the E–W cross wall. On the S side of the cross-wall the chapel occupied the SE corner with the ante chapel to the N and a chamber to the E, all three rooms entered separately from the hall. Less certain is the arrangement at the W end of the tower, which contained additional rooms, including, at the

NW angle, a kitchen. In the W wall a series of four communal latrines provided accommodation for thirty-two occupants at any one time. There were only two main storeys, but a gallery extended around all four sides of the keep and provided clearstorey lighting for the hall and other rooms. At the time of writing, Norwich Castle keep was closed and undergoing a major internal remodelling. Heslop 1994; Dixon and Marshall 2002; Drury 2002; Popescu *et al.* 2009.

NOTTINGHAM, Nottinghamshire (Open). Established by William the Conqueror in 1067/8, Nottingham Castle was built on a sandstone ridge above the river Trent, a position of considerable natural strength. The S end of the ridge was isolated by a deep rock-cut ditch, which, together with scarping, effectively created a motte, known subsequently as the upper bailey. To the N of this was the middle bailey, and to the E a much more extensive enclosure, which, in a truncated form, became the outer bailey. The defences of the upper and middle baileys were probably rebuilt in stone in the 1170s and 1180s. A great tower, or keep, was in existence by 1188, probably the rectangular tower on the N side of the upper bailey shown in John Smythson's 1617 plan.

In 1191, while Richard I was on crusade, Prince John seized the castle and was only forced to relinquish it in 1194, when Richard returned and captured the outer bailey by assault. The damage inflicted on the outer bailey defences was repaired by King John, and from *c.*1252, under Henry III, the fortifications were rebuilt in stone, further work being carried out *c.*1290 by Edward I.

One of the most dramatic episodes in the history of the castle is Edward III's *coup d'état* against Roger Mortimer and Queen Isabella, in which an armed party led by Sir William Montagu and his men entered the castle via a passage in the rock. Traditionally this has been identified with Mortimer's Hole, a postern leading from Brewhouse Yard, at the foot of the rock, to the upper bailey, although recent research favours a different entrance which communicated with the middle bailey. Numerous works were undertaken during Edward III's long reign, though nothing much has survived.

In the 1470s substantial works were carried out by Edward IV, who remodelled the middle bailey creating a range of stone and timber-framed lodgings against the N curtain in conjunction with a large new semi-octagonal tower (Richard's Tower), effectively a great tower, at the NW angle. It was the last notable project of the medieval period. After the Civil War, the castle was slighted and following the Restoration of 1661 the Duke of Newcastle cleared the ruins and built a mansion on the site of the upper bailey.

Little survives of the medieval castle, the most prominent remnant being the lower part of the outer gatehouse of *c.*1252–5. Medieval fabric survives to just above the outer gate arch, but much was hidden when the walls were largely refaced in the C20. Thankfully, this exercise did not include the gateway itself; segmental-pointed and recessed beneath an outer arch of similar form, it is flanked by twin drum towers and was protected by a portcullis. In front of the gatehouse, the medieval bridge is supported on a single segmental-pointed arch; a drawbridge operated between the bridge and gatehouse. To the R of the gatehouse the outer curtain has entirely disappeared, but, to the L, the lower courses survive together with the stumps of Edward's Tower and the SE corner tower (both visible from Castle Road). At this point the curtain turns towards the E and continues as far as the upper bailey.

Elements of a curtain wall also survive on the N side of the middle bailey, including the stump of the C13 three-quarter round NE corner tower (the Black Tower) and the base of Richard's Tower, excavated in the 1970s. The gatehouse to the middle bailey has gone, but the bridge abutments remain, the present arch replacing the gap that was spanned by a drawbridge; excavation of the W abutment revealed the presence of a pit into which the inner end of the bridge descended when raised. The construction of Newcastle's mansion resulted in the clearance of the medieval remains of the upper bailey, except at subterranean level, where man-made caves survive, notably King David's Dungeon, which probably dates from the C13, and the adjoining Romylowe's Cave. Drage 1989.

NUNNEY, Somerset (Open access – EH, exterior only). Imposing and picturesque moated tower house on the old road between Frome and Shepton Mallet, built under a licence to crenellate of 1373 by local worthy Sir John de la Mare, who was knighted in the same year. Bombardment of the castle by the Parliamentarians in 1645 punched a hole in the entrance (NW) front of the main block, and in 1910 the greater part of the wall collapsed. Between 1927 and 1930 the site was cleared by the Office of Works, and the building consolidated as a ruin.

The castle is sited on the NW bank of Nunney Brook, which fed the moat, and at a crossroads, its NE–SW axis broadly reflecting the line of the Frome–Shepton Mallet road. The main block of the tower is rectangular and large round towers project from the corners. A near parallel for the outline plan is the great tower of Dudley (qv) of c.1267, but the general concept of a self-contained residence with rectangular range and projecting corner towers is shared with the keep of Stafford (qv) of 1348 and several northern English fortified halls and their derivatives, e.g., Dally (qv), Tarset (qv), Edlingham (qv), Haughton (qv), Langley (qv).

There were four storeys, the towers being the same height as the main body; a continuous parapet carried on corbelled machicolations extended all around the building; the towers had tall conical spires and the main block a steeply pitched roof that rose high above the parapet. The entrance is an unobtrusive ground-floor doorway with four-centred arch at the LH (NE) end of the much-depleted NW front. It led directly into the ground floor, and from the entrance lobby a mural staircase ascended to the first floor. No internal partitions survive, and only the broad parameters of the internal plan can be reconstructed, but the kitchen and services appear to have been at ground-floor level, a hall at first-floor level heated by a fireplace on the SE wall and served by latrines in two of the towers. Twin fireplaces at second- and third-floor levels probably denote a division into an outer and inner chamber on each storey of the main bock; there were further fireplaces and latrines in some of the tower chambers. Rigold 1956; Dunning 1995, 63–5; Emery 2006, 604–7.

OAKHAM, Rutland (Open). The repute of Oakham Castle rests almost entirely on its late C12 aisled great hall, a building remarkable as much for its survival as for its architectural character. Oakham was a royal manor at the time of the Domesday Survey but came into the possession of the Ferrers family in the C12; it was Walkelin de Ferrers (d. 1201) who was responsible for the construction of the great hall, a tour de force of domestic art and architecture at a time of transition from the Romanesque to Gothic styles.

The castle occupies a position at the heart of the town, between Station Road (N), Market Place (S), Burley Road (E) and Church Street (W). A roughly square bailey is

Oakham: The great hall from the SE. From Turner and Parker 1851.

defined by a bank (and formerly by a moat) capped by a depleted curtain wall, with a couple of round-fronted towers at the SW corner and the supposed remains of a motte at the SE angle. A second, broadly rectangular enclosure to the N, known as 'Cutt's Close', was an outer bailey. A widening of the moat between the two contained fishponds.

Access is now via Castle Lane, a narrow road leading from the Market Place terminating in front of a C17 gateway which leads into the main bailey. Straight ahead is the great hall, immediately recognizable as an aisled structure, the roofs of the main body and aisles being sharply defined as separate entities. Regularly disposed along the S front are a central door and four two-light windows, which contrast with the four-bay rhythm of the internal arcades, a disparity made possible by building in stone rather than timber. All is not what it seems with this front, for the doorway was originally at the RH (E) end of the frontage, having changed places with a window in the C18 or C19. The round-arched door contrasts with the pointed heads of the two-light lancet windows. All the openings were flanked by shafts with foliate capitals, set within dog-tooth mouldings. The jamb shafts of the windows have gone, though the capitals remain.

In the E gable end are two blocked doorways (beneath two inserted windows), and in the RH (N) aisle, just one jamb of a third doorway, all three of which formerly communicated with a lean-to service block of timber-framed construction. There was a similar wing at the W end, though the communicating door is now only visible from inside. The apex of each gable is decorated with a sculptured finial and the doorway is flanked by two reset sculptures, just the tip of a metaphorical iceberg of carver's art that ornaments the interior.

The entrance gave access to the E bay of the aisled hall, but this was no through-passage as became the norm in medieval halls, for there is no opposing doorway in the N wall. In the E wall, the three blocked service doorways, two pointed and one (N) round arched. Above the N door is a first-floor doorway, which must have been reached by a stair, giving access to a garret in the end block. These are mundane matters, for the main architectural interest lies in the two great arcades, unusual in a domestic setting for being built in stone. Round arches with dog-toothed hood moulds are carried on round columns with crocket capitals; sculptures adorn the tops of the capitals and the responds in the end walls. The current roofs dates from the C18, but structural and dendrochronological analyses have revealed numerous re-used C12 timbers with an estimated felling date range of 1160–85, which probably came from the original structure. Clough 1981; Hill 2013; Time Team 2013.

ODIHAM, Hampshire (Open access). Keep and courtyard castle raised by King John in 1207–12 within a loop of the river Whitewater. In 1216, towards the end of John's reign, French troops under the Dauphin, Prince Louis, descended upon Odiham and laid it to siege; despite the deployment of siege engines its thirteen-man garrison held out for over a week. In 1236 Henry III granted the castle to his sister Eleanor, who subsequently married Simon de Montfort, a tenure ending in de Montfort's death at the Battle of Evesham. In 1275 Edward I gave it to his wife Queen Eleanor, subsequent recipients being queens Margaret (1299), Isabella (1327), Philippa (1330), Anne (1382), Margaret (1454) and Elizabeth (1464) but by the end C15 the castle had probably fallen into irretrievable decay.

A moated quadrilateral platform contains the remains of a stone keep. A second platform to the SE has been truncated by the Basingstoke Canal. The main interest lies in the three- or four-storey octagonal keep, one of a small number of polygonal great towers constructed during the late C12 and early C13. It was built of flint rubble faced with ashlar, the latter now largely disappeared; excavation has revealed that it was surrounded by a circular moat and that the first floor was supported on a central column. A rectangular sump or well within the building has been dated to the 1240s. Allen and Stoodley 2010.

OKEHAMPTON, Devon (Open – EH). Motte and bailey established by Baldwin de Brionne, Sheriff of Devon (d. 1090), before 1086. In 1173 Okehampton came, through marriage, to the Courtenay family, earls of Devon from 1276. The castle was largely rebuilt under Earl Hugh (d. 1340) who also enlarged the associated deer park. The Courtenays held Okehampton until 1539, when John Courtenay, Marquis of Devon, was executed and his estates confiscated by the Crown. Thereafter, the story is one of decline.

The castle is built on a steep-sided, NE–SW orientated spur next to the river Okement, approximately a mile SW of the village of Okehampton. The motte is to the SW, and the approach from the NE where, just off the road, are the remains of the rectangular outer gatehouse. The LH side of the frontage still stands two storeys high, is pierced by tiers of putlog holes and retains a jamb and arch springer of the gateway. This leads into a long passage barbican which climbs up the hill to the rectangular inner gatehouse. Adjoining the inner gatehouse to the L is a latrine turret with a stone tile roof, which served a range of domestic apartments in the bailey. The gate passage was formerly covered by a rib-vault and retains chases for the now-vanished columnar responds. On the RH (NW) side is a lobby or guard room with a corner staircase giving access to the great hall and, formerly, to the room above the gateway. The great hall, a single-storey building open to the roof, backs onto the NW curtain. The principal entrance was from the bailey into a cross passage, with a staircase at the far (NW) end, and two doorways to the L (SW) leading to kitchens and buttery respectively. At the upper (NE) end are the remains of a dais on which the high table stood, and along the NW wall, indications of a stone bench. Above the buttery was a heated chamber. Hall and buttery were under the same roof; chases in the two end walls reflect the character of the timber trusses which formed part of the framework. Beyond the buttery are the ruins of the extensive kitchen complex. On the opposite side of the bailey is a two-storey, three-room range of lodgings with three ground-floor and first-floor chambers served by two latrine turrets, the better-quality upper chambers heated and provided with large arched windows.

Next to (SW of) the lodgings is the chapel, entered from the bailey via a porch. The liturgical E end is lit by two pointed and traceried windows; a trefoil-headed piscina also survives. On the SE side a narrow space probably served as a two-storey vestry/lodging for the priest attendant on the chapel. Adjoining the chapel to the SW is another two-storey lodging dating from the late C14/C15 and built on the site of the infilled motte ditch.

Thus, we come to the motte: raised on the high point of the spur and surmounted by a two-phase keep, it exudes a dominating presence that pervades the entire complex and provides a fitting climax to the inclined nature of the site. Facing the bailey is Baldwin de Brionne's C11 square keep, now badly mangled, but a strangely preserved finger of masonry above the entrance (the remains of the NE stair turret), rising nearly to full height, gives an idea of the greater impact that the tower must have had when complete. The turret and doorway date from a partial rebuilding of the keep, which occurred when a large extension was built to the W. This latter doubled the size of the keep and allowed slightly more sophisticated accommodation. The E doorway served both phases of the enlarged tower, the two halves linked by a ground-floor doorway; there was probably a similar relationship at first-floor level, giving an inner and outer room. The upper chambers were residential, the lower probably for storage. Higham 1977; Higham and Allan, 1980; Higham *et al.*, 1982.

OLD BUCKENHAM, Suffolk (Private). The predecessor of New Buckenham (qv), the castle site is represented by a moated rectangular enclosure. It was abandoned as a castle *c.*1146 when William d'Albini, Earl of Sussex, and Queen Adeliza, his wife, founded an Augustinian priory on the site, the materials from the castle to be used in the construction of the priory.

OLD HOLLINSIDE, Co. Durham. See **HOLLINSIDE**.

OLD SARUM, Wiltshire (Open – EH). Very soon after the Conquest William I caused a castle to be built here, at Anglo-Saxon *Searoburg*, within an Iron Age hillfort. The new castle, and the area between it and the remodelled prehistoric defences, were to become the inner and outer baileys respectively. In 1075, the See of Sherbourne moved to Sarum and a cathedral was built within the outer bailey. Bishop Roger (1107–39), who was granted the castle by Henry I *c.*1130, built himself a courtyard house within the inner bailey, similar to a complex he had established at Sherbourne Castle (qv). Roger also enlarged the cathedral and began the construction of a curtain wall on the inner bank of the outer bailey defences. In 1139 the castle was confiscated by King Stephen, and subsequently remained in royal ownership. In 1220 the seat of the bishop was transferred to New Sarum (Salisbury), and the construction of the present cathedral began; the cathedral at Old Sarum was left to decay. After the C14, the castle itself was neglected, and in 1512 Henry VIII gave permission for the stone to be carted away.

The outer defences of Old Sarum comprise a ditch with inner and outer banks, while the main E gateway and subsidiary W gateway were protected by barbicans, now represented by mounds outside the entrances. In the NW quarter of the outer bailey, the foundations of the cathedral comprise an C11 nave, early C12 transepts and choir, and mid to late C12 W towers. The cloisters were to the NE with the bishop's palace on the N side.

The inner ward, which takes the form of a low mound, or motte, surrounded by a ditch, is approached from the E across a modern bridge on the site of its medieval predecessor. All the buildings of the inner bailey have been reduced to their lower courses or foundations, and of these it is the flint rubble core that survives, though the former presence of ashlar facing stones is attested by surviving patches. The gatehouse was a rectangular tower with a central passage, a drawbar cavity on the S side marking the position of the outer gate. Straight ahead (W), forming part of the enceinte, is the stump of rectangular great tower or keep, in existence by 1130, divided by a transverse cross-wall, with a later turret at the SE corner. NW of this is Bishop Roger's split-level courtyard house, the S and E ranges with undercrofts, the single-storey W and N ranges containing hall and great chamber respectively. A tower at the NE corner contained the kitchen. Latrine turrets extend from the W side of the tower and the E side of the E range. McNeill 2006.

OLD WARDEN, Bedfordshire. See **BIGGLESWADE**.

OLD WARDOUR, Wiltshire (Open – EH) (Plate XI). An exquisitely designed courtyard castle built for John Lord Lovel of Titchmarsh (qv) under a licence of 1393, possibly by William Wynford. The plans of the outer and inner wards are both based on a regular hexagon. Although the current curtain wall dates from the C16, excavation has shown that it represents a rebuilding of the medieval curtain, suggesting that the plan dates from the C14. The reconstruction of the curtain preceded the 1570s remodelling of the inner ward by Robert Smythson. The work involved the replacement of a good deal of medieval architectural detail, although enough survives to allow an appreciation of the building's medieval character. More serious is the loss of the SW and W ranges, casualties of the Civil War. In spite of all, however, the sheer quality of the architecture shines through, delivering an intense visual impact.

Externally, the details are mostly Smythson's, but these barely detract from the power of the (NE) entrance front. It is framed by a pair of projecting towers, between them the first-floor hall with two tall, pointed windows containing the remains of tracery. Parapet level is marked by a C14 string course carved with fleurons, and carried round the one surviving bartizan at the SE corner. Several surviving C14 details in the courtyard including a tripartite arrangement of gateway and flanking doors, the former pointed and the latter four-centred, reminiscent of a cross-passage ensemble; above them a pair of hall windows reflecting those at the front. A giant Smythson archway shows the way to the hall; above the staircase a C14 ribbed vault. The stair led into a screens passage; four-centred service doorways survive in the SE and NE walls (the latter to a service stair). Emery 2006, 658–65; Girouard 2012.

Old Wardour: Inner ward from the NE.

ONGAR, Essex (Private). Motte and bailey in existence by 1157 when it was held by Richard de Lucy. The flat-topped motte with kidney-shaped bailey on its W side are both surrounded by connecting moats. The bailey has an inner bank with a break in the centre denoting the entrance from the town. Extending from the NW angle of the bailey is a stretch of the town defences, comprising a moat and inner bank. Gould 1900; Round 1900; RCHME 1921, 53–4; Powell 1956, 159–62.

ORFORD, Suffolk (Open – EH). Royal castle built by Henry II in 1165–73. It comprised a keep surrounded by a curtain wall studded with rectangular towers and pierced by an eastern gateway. Today only the keep remains amidst a complex of earthworks, but this is one of the most interesting great towers in England and evidently the work of a highly accomplished architect. A near contemporary of Conisbrough Castle keep (qv), it has the same combination of geometrical precision, bold massing and technical virtuosity that characterizes its northern counterpart.

The three-storey keep has a faceted exterior, giving the impression of a polygonal plan, though geometrically it is based on a circle, and has indeed a circular interior. At regular intervals around the circumference of the tower, giving the impression of holding it firmly in place like the arms of a drill chuck, are three rectangular turrets extending through six storeys, the uppermost rising above the tower and entered from the roof. Attached to the side of the E turret is a three-storey forebuilding reaching a little over half-way up the tower. Like the later castle of Framlingham (qv), 12 miles to the NW, Orford was built of the local septaria rubble (formerly rendered) with limestone ashlar plinth, quoins and dressings. Details include two-light round-arch windows with chunky convex quadrant surrounds for the main rooms and, on the W side, four arched latrine outlets.

Orford: Great tower from the SW.

The entrance is at first-floor level, via a staircase formerly enclosed within a porch. Go through a triangular-arched gateway (with joggled voussoirs and portcullis slot) into a vestibule, then a quick turn to the L, prefaced by a splendid triple-order round arch springing directly from the LH wall, splaying out to the R and terminating on sculptured responds, which display an extraordinary rendition of trumpet capitals, the 'trumpets' hollowed out to resemble a line of linked inverted omegas. They seem to be from a different world than the conventional scalloped and cushion capitals elsewhere in the keep. From here, two more triangular-arched doorways lead to the main tower containing a single well-lit living room with a fireplace, twin latrines, and access via window embrasures to a kitchenette in the W turret, and a small chamber in the N turret. A staircase entered from the window embrasure to the L of the fireplace ascends to a second little chamber in the N turret.

The E turret houses the generously-proportioned main staircase, its mortared vault carrying the imprints of the medieval centring planks. It descends to the basement, essentially a storage area with a central well, mural sink and drain, and vaulted recesses in the N and W turrets. Back up the staircase, past the first floor to a mezzanine level, a passage leads to the chapel in the forebuilding, and then to a vestry or priest's chamber in the W turret equipped with a latrine. The little chapel has wall arcading, all round arches again with colonettes and scalloped capitals; the sanctuary recess contains the remains of a stone altar, a piscina and aumbry.

A little further up the staircase a passage leads to the main second-floor suite, similar to that on the first floor, with a central room, fireplace, a kitchenette in the W turret, another small chamber in the N turret and a latrine entered from the window embrasure to the L of the fireplace. Two closets, possibly for storage or close stools, flank the window embrasure to the R of the fireplace. An interesting feature at this level is a line of corbels extending around the central room; these were supports for the roof timbers. Angled chases cut into the wall above the corbels show that the rafters were set at an angle of 65 degrees. At a higher level, to the L of the fireplace a doorway to an isolated chamber in the N turret shows that there must have been a timber gallery behind the rafters to allow access to it. The route was from the main staircase, along a mural passage from which a second doorway (also visible in the main room) opened. At the end of this passage a room with a sunken floor within the W turret has been interpreted as a cistern. Finally, continuing up the main staircase to the roof, there are two more turret rooms, one containing an oven. Brown *et al.* 1963, 769–71; Brown 1964; Heslop 1991; Brindle 2018.

OSWESTRY, Shropshire (Open access). A late C11 motte and bailey castle built by Reginald de Bailleul, Sheriff of Shropshire, though now only the motte remains visible. Excavation on top of the motte in 2015–19 revealed, on the W side of the mound, the lower courses of a N–S aligned rectangular ashlar-built structure with a splayed base, probably a keep. A metalled surface was uncovered on the S side. There seems to have been a spiral staircase within the SW angle. To the E of the keep was a second rectangular stone building on an E–W axis with a doorway in the S side. Salter 2001, 64; Duckers 2006, 122–6.

OVER STOWEY, Somerset (Private). Like Nether Stowey (qv), a manor of Alfred d'Epaignes in 1086. An 'old castle' existed in the later C12. Its remains lie to the N of the hamlet of Over Stowey, the main feature being a large flat mound, so far unexcavated. Dunning 1981 and 1995, 44–5.

OWSTON FERRY (Kinaird's Ferry), Lincolnshire (Open access). Motte and bailey. Probably late C11. Repaired by Roger de Mowbray in 1173 in association with his rebellion against Henry II. In the aftermath of the revolt the castle was slighted and never rebuilt. In the C13 the Church of St Martin was built inside the bailey. The motte lies to the SE of the church; the northern extent of the bailey is represented by the curving line of Church Street. A pair of broad banks, which curve around the sides of the motte, the ends nearly but not quite meeting to the S, seem to have extended around the bailey as well. Salter 2002a, 58.

OXFORD, Oxfordshire (Open). Motte and bailey built in 1071 by Robert d'Oilly, the first custodian, at the behest of William I, to control a crossing of the river Isis and the Anglo-Saxon *burh*. It remained a royal castle throughout the Middle Ages. The chapel of St George was built within the enceinte in 1074. In 1142, in an attempt to capture the Empress Matilda, King Stephen laid siege to the castle, but after three months Matilda effected a daring escape and took flight to Wallingford (qv). The castle was besieged again in 1216, when it was attacked by the rebel barons, but this time was relieved. A garrison was maintained until 1322, but thereafter, the buildings were allowed to decay. By 1230 the castle contained a gaol, and this became one of its principal functions. From 1786 the gaol was rebuilt; it was enlarged in the mid C19. The County Hall was built within the precinct in 1841; this and the prison buildings remain, albeit converted, and are now the dominant components of the site.

Not a great deal remains of the medieval castle, the main surviving components being the motte, which lay at the NW end of the bailey, and St George's Tower which occupied a position on the W curtain. The extent of the bailey, which was entered from the SE, is broadly represented by Paradise Street (SW), Castle Street (SE) and New Road (NE). To the SE of St George's Tower, a round tower terminating a wing of the prison block, is on the site of a medieval wall tower.

The motte is now devoid of upstanding superstructures, but it was formerly surmounted by a tower of decagonal plan, apparently a shell-keep with stone apartments surrounding a central courtyard; elements of the foundations survive. Also preserved is a subterranean well chamber of hexagonal plan with an C13 rib-vault carried on corbels. St George's Tower is of greater interest as it is considered to date from before the Norman Conquest; it may have been a *burhgeat*, or gate tower, associated with the Anglo-Saxon *burh*, incorporated into the castle in 1071. The tower seems to taper towards the top owing to a series of six offsets. All four sides of the uppermost stage are pierced by infilled round-arched windows, the blockings containing cruciform loops. The projecting stair turret at the SE angle is a C12 addition. One other area of note is the crypt of the former chapel of St George, which abutted St George's Tower. Though the chapel was demolished in 1794, the crypt was rebuilt, incorporating the C11 columns, squat with massive capitals. Munby *et al.* 2019.

PAN CASTLE, Shropshire. See **WHITCHURCH**.

PEAK, Derbyshire. See **PEVERIL**.

PEMBRIDGE CASTLE, Welsh Newton, Herefordshire (Private). Not the better-known village of Pembridge in the N of the county, but Pembridge Castle near Welsh Newton, in the far SW corner of Herefordshire. However, both are connected with the Pembridge family, who took their name from the village and gave it to the castle.

The medieval remains are predominantly C13 but slighting during the Civil War and substantial reconstruction in 1913–15 have hindered interpretation.

The castle is quadrangular and formerly entirely surrounded by a moat. The late C13 great gatehouse, at the E end of the S front, has two round-fronted flanking towers, the RH one largely rebuilt. When Thomas Wakeman visited Pembridge in the 1850s he found the gatehouse reduced to a single storey and the RH tower much smaller in diameter than its partner; now they are of equal size. At the W end of this front is a four-storey round corner tower, sometimes described as a keep but only 25 ft (7.6m) in diameter. There is a solid small round buttress at the NW corner, and another solid buttress at the NE angle, in the form of a quarter circle. Squinch arches, perhaps machicolated, extended across the angles at parapet level to support bartizans; it's an idiosyncratic arrangement and something of a mystery.

A long (33 ft [10m]) vaulted gatehouse leads into the courtyard. The main residential block probably abutted the SW round tower to the N, ranged along the W curtain, its position now occupied by a C17 house. The C17 kitchen and what was probably another service room back onto the S curtain. In the NW corner is the C17 chapel which sits on a C13 vaulted undercroft. RCHME 1931, 250–2; Shoesmith 2009, 276–80.

PENDRAGON, Mallerstang, Westmorland (Private, but visible from the road). C12 great tower within earthworks. Perhaps built by Sir Hugh de Morville (d. 1202), one of the assassins of Archbishop Thomas Becket, but first mentioned in 1228. Revitalized by Sir Robert Clifford under a licence to crenellate of 1309. Burnt by the Scots in 1341. Restored by Lady Anne Clifford in 1660 but dismantled in the 1680s.

The castle sits on a spur above the river Eden, defended to the N by a curving ditch, and otherwise by scarping of the hillside. Within the enclosure are the depleted remains of a stone keep some 65 ft × 59 ft (19.8m × 17.9m) square with wide pilaster buttresses at the angles, now only partially rising above ground-storey level. At the SW angle is a latrine turret, a later addition set diagonally. Next to it in the S wall a large first-floor window with semi-circular arch. A slight projection of the wall in the centre of the N front contains the ground-floor entrance, which was protected by a portcullis. To either side of the mural entrance lobby a doorway gives access to a spiral staircase; the W doorway is round arched, the S doorway has a flat lintel; both are probably of Lady Anne's time. Apart from containing the staircases, the walls, some 12 ft (3.6m) thick, accommodate a room at each of the four angles. Curwen 1913, 120–4; RCHME 1936, 163–4; Perriam and Robinson 1998, 300–1.

PENRITH, Cumberland (Open access – EH). Quadrangular castle built to the SW of the town largely by Ralph Neville, First Earl of Westmorland, who was granted the manor of Penrith in 1396. The castle faces NW (treated here as N for ease of description), and the remains consist of a roughly 130 ft (12m) square enclosure with a central courtyard surrounded by domestic ranges. Projecting from the curtain are a number of mid-wall and diagonal corner buttress turrets, and two large square towers: the mid-wall Bishop's Tower to the E, and the Red Tower at the E end of the N front. Hard up against the Red Tower is the main gatehouse. The Red Tower, gatehouse, and indeed the domestic ranges surrounding the courtyard, are structurally later than the curtain wall and Bishop's Tower, which appear to be the earliest surviving elements. How much later is a matter for conjecture.

Two rare features suggest a connection with John Lewyn of Durham. Firstly, the two surviving buttress turrets with parapets corbelled out to the sides (cf. Raby [qv] and Brancepeth [qv], both Neville castles); secondly, a machicolated octagonal wall head turret at the SE corner supported on triangular stones placed across the corners of the building (cf. Lumley [qv] and Hylton [qv]). Also, the parapet of the curtain wall was carried on corbelled machicolations, another characteristic of the two Neville castles. The N front is now dominated by the Red Tower, the N wall of which still rises through three storeys. The adjacent gatehouse had a central portcullis-protected entrance and two flanking rooms, including a porter's lodge. At the inner end of the passage is the early drawbarred gateway and beyond it a passageway through the N range, making for quite an elongated entrance. There was also a postern gate on the S side of the Bishop's Tower secured by a draw bar, with a portcullis at the inner end of the passage through the E range. Emery 1996, 237–9; Perriam and Robinson 1998, 212–13; Perriam (2008).

PENWORTHAM, Lancashire (Open access within St Mary's churchyard). Motte and bailey on a cliff overlooking the river Ribble, in existence by 1086. The end of the spur on which the castle is situated is cut off to the S by a ditch, which also separates it from the adjacent church. The motte occupies a hillock, with the bailey towards the N. Excavation of the motte in 1856 revealed three phases of construction: firstly, 11ft (3.3m) below the summit, was a 'rude pavement of boulders' and the remains of a timber building with a truncated central post; above these remains, some 7ft (2m) below the top of the motte, was a second pavement, but no signs of habitation; the mound had then been raised to create the existing motte. Thornber 1856–7.

PETERBOROUGH (Mount Thorold, Toot Hill), Northamptonshire and the Soke of Peterborough (Private). Motte some 350ft (100m) N of the cathedral, within the grounds of the Old Deanery. Probably the castle recorded as having been built by Abbot Thorold in the late C11. Serjeantson *et al.* 1906, 406.

PEVENSEY, Sussex (Open – EH). Best remembered as the first place in England to be fortified by William the Conqueror, whose invasion force landed here in 1066, Pevensey Castle has a much longer history, being built within the existing defences of the Roman fort of *Anderitum*. Established in the 290s, *Anderitum* occupied a peninsula extending eastwards into Pevensey Bay, an extensive natural harbour of great strategic significance. The landscape is now much changed, the bay has been reclaimed from the sea, and Pevensey lies a mile from the coast, so that the former coastal fortress has been left high and dry and its original purpose is no longer readily apparent.

In 1067 Pevensey was granted to Robert of Mortain, who during the rebellion of 1088 held Pevensey against William II. The garrison endured a six-week siege, before surrendering owing to lack of supplies. In 1106 the castle was appropriated by Henry I, who may have built the keep. Pevensey was besieged again in 1147, when it was held against King Stephen; its capture was again the result of supply failure. In 1246 Henry III granted Pevensey to Peter (later Count) of Savoy, lord of Richmond, and uncle of Queen Eleanor; Peter rebuilt the defences of the inner bailey in stone, and in 1264 successfully resisted a siege by Simon of Montfort. After Peter died, in 1268, Pevensey came to Queen Eleanor, who carried out extensive repairs in the 1280s under the mason, Master Simon, a programme which probably included the heightening of the gatehouse. Yet another siege took place in 1399 when the constable took the part of Henry Bolingbroke (soon to be Henry IV) against King Richard II and held out successfully.

The Roman defences enclose an irregular oval area, a highly unusual layout for a Roman fort, but one that was related to the form of the peninsula. The walls were faced with small masonry blocks, of two different types of stone, which, combined with tile bonding courses, were so contrived as to produce a decorative pattern of horizontal bands. The landward approach to the peninsula is from the W, which leads to the site of the Roman W gate, set between two solid D-shaped towers, which, unlike the gate, survive. Interval towers of similar type project from the walls.

In the SE corner of the Roman enceinte is the medieval inner bailey, enclosed by a moat. The curtain and its three D-shaped wall towers date from the mid C13, but the gatehouse, which has twin drum towers, is earlier, the first two storeys probably dating from the 1190s, thus making it a very early example of its type. The uppermost storey was added in the 1280s. There are few buildings within the bailey, but the remains of fireplaces and corbels for roof timbers show that it was tightly packed with buildings backing onto the curtain wall.

Set against the E wall of the Roman fort, and incorporating its fabric, is the much-reduced keep, a most unusual and little understood building probably built by Henry I (reigned 1100–35). The rectangular main block is conventional for the early C12; not so the three solid apsidal-ended turrets of bold projection with which it is augmented. Two are close together on the W side, the third projects N from the NW corner. It is uncertain whether they are part of the original design or additions to it. Porter 2020.

PEVERIL (Peak), Castleton, Derbyshire (Open – EH). Peveril is one of the most dramatically sited of English castles, perched on top of a steeply rising promontory looming over the little town of Castleton to the N and defined by two precipitous ravines to the E (Cavedale) and W (Peak Cavern Gorge). This is the E or inner bailey; there was also a W bailey, on the opposite side of Peak Cavern Gorge, linked to the E bailey by a timber bridge, an arrangement reminiscent of Tintagel (qv), another castle in which the untamed character of the setting adds a frisson of romance to the appreciation of the architectural remains.

The name of the castle is derived from its founder, William Peverel, a follower of William I, who had established his castle here by 1086. It was one of the handful of early Norman castles to be built in stone from the outset. Acquired by Henry II in 1155 it became, in addition to being the caput of the honour of Peveril, the administrative focus and a hunting lodge for the royal forest of the Peak. It also gave the King a stronghold in this remote area, where there were silver and lead mining interests at stake. Henry's main legacy here is the keep, probably of the 1170s, but he may also have been responsible for a hall, the E gate and a rectangular tower that was added to the N curtain. A new hall was built *c.*1250. In 1372 Peveril became part of the Duchy of Lancaster but seems to have been neglected from that time onwards.

The only approach to the E bailey is now from Castleton whence a path zigzags up the hill, past the N curtain, which contains areas of herringbone masonry typical of the C11, to the C12 E Gate, of which only one jamb and the springing of an arch remain. This gives access to the E apex of a triangular sloping site with the keep at the SW angle and the great hall close to the NW corner. The medieval S curtain has largely disappeared but traces of two towers, round and semi-circular, remain. Along this side too are the footings of at least two buildings, firstly an E–W orientated

Peveril: The great tower (*c*.1170s) from the E.

structure containing herringbone masonry, possibly a chapel, and secondly, traces of a larger range, possibly the C12 hall. This brings us to Henry II's square keep at the high point of the castle, a rather plain building but faced with good-quality ashlar, now much robbed, although sizeable portions remain on the less accessible SE and SW faces. There were two storeys: a basement storage room and a first-floor reception room equipped with a latrine corbelled out on the entrance front, but outside the curtain wall. Access was at first-floor level through a round-arched doorway, and vertical communication via a spiral stair in the S corner.

Descending from the keep northwards along the side of the C11 W curtain (note the herringbone masonry) brings us first to the foundations of a W range, probably domestic, backing onto the curtain, and then to footings of the C13 hall range, which stands clear of the N curtain. At the W end of the hall is the hearth and column bases of a fireplace that heated the dais where the high table stood.

Although there is now no link between the E and W baileys the latter may be visited independently on foot by walking up Cave Dale to the E of the castle and cutting back along the ridge on the W side of the vale. Eales 2018.

PICKERING, Yorkshire North Riding (Open – EH). Well-preserved motte with two baileys, rebuilt in stone in several phases. The royal castle was probably established during William the Conqueror's subjugation of northern England in 1069–70. At first a timber castle, except perhaps for the hall, rebuilding in stone began in the late C12 with the curtain wall of the inner ward. Henry III probably built the shell-keep on the motte in the 1220s, and in 1267 granted the castle to his son Edmund, Earl of Lancaster. After the execution of Edmund's son, Thomas of Lancaster, in 1322, Pickering returned to the Crown, the defences of the outer ward being rebuilt in 1323–6 under Edward II, probably in response to a Scottish invasion of Yorkshire in 1322. Pickering was restored to the Lancasters in 1326 and thence to the Crown again in 1399, when Henry Bolingbroke, the Lancaster heir, became King Henry IV. During the C16 the castle was allowed to fall into disrepair.

Built on a headland, the castle is cut off from the high ground to the E and S by a ditch. The crescentic outer bailey is also enclosed by a bank, and on this is the curtain wall of 1323–6 studded with four rectangular towers: from L (W) to R (E), Mill Tower, Gatehouse, Diate Hill Tower and Rosamund's Tower. In front of the outer gateway are the remains of the side walls of a barbican with access to a wall walk from a doorway in the curtain. At the back of the barbican is the partially-blocked pointed gate arch.

On entering the outer bailey, one is confronted by the conical motte built at the junction of the two baileys with slightly greater projection into the outer bailey. On the edge of the motte ditch to the L (W) is the C12 Coleman Tower, which flanks the gateway into the inner bailey. A blocked doorway in the W face once communicated with a room over the gateway from which the drawbridge and portcullis were controlled. The three wall towers all contain lodgings on the upper storeys with fireplaces and latrines; the lowest level of the Rosamund Tower incorporates a postern accessed from the inner ditch separating the two baileys.

Opposite the gateway, against the NW curtain, are the remains of the principal residential complex. First the foundations of the New Hall, a 1314 rebuilding of a late C12/early C13 structure. The main entrance was at the S end of the front (E) wall, the surviving shaft bases indicating an elaborate surround of three orders. Two doorways

Pickering: Rosamund Tower from the SW.

in the S wall led to the service rooms of which vestigial traces remain. At the N end a doorway leads to a passage which gave access to the Old Hall (N) and chapel (E). The Old Hall, originally a freestanding building, predates the C12 curtain; the construction of the curtain allowed the rear (NW) wall to be demolished and the hall to be widened. Within the curtain is a C12 recess, probably for a seat. The chapel probably dates from 1220s but was substantially restored in the C19 and reroofed in the C20; very plain with lancet windows. At the E end of the bailey more foundations of another residential complex known as the Constable's Lodgings, with a hall in the NE corner. Finally, the motte and shell-keep, the top now accessed from a staircase next to the Coleman Tower. The keep is in ruins, the best surviving fragment being on the N side. It was roughly circular but facetted on the exterior. Two long loops survive, the splayed embrasures covered with tiers of corbelling. Page 1923, 463–7; Brown *et al.* 1963, 779–81; Butler 2015; Higham 2015, 96–102.

PIEL, Piel Island, Lancashire (Open – EH). In 1327 the Abbot and Convent of Furness Abbey were granted a licence to crenellate their dwelling place of Fotheray in Fourneys (Furness). This came to be known as the Peel of Foudray, or Piel Castle. In 1403 it is said to have been abandoned owing to the costs of maintenance; it was certainly decayed by 1537 and does not seem to have been refurbished subsequently.

The castle is on the S shore of Piel Island, close to the S tip of the Furness peninsula. It consisted of a quadrilateral inner ward containing a rectangular free-standing keep. An outer ward extended around the N, E and W sides of the inner ward. Both inner and outer wards were defended by a ditch and supplied with square corner towers. Unfortunately, coastal erosion has carried away the S side of the outer ward, the E and S sides of the inner ward, and the E side of the keep, so that the remains are somewhat depleted and the original extent of the castle uncertain.

The position of the outer gateway is unknown, but access to the inner ward was from the W via a centrally placed rectangular gatehouse, protected by a drawbridge and a portcullis. The keep has an unusually large footprint (some 80ft × 75ft [24.3m × 22.8m]) and is provided with a large N porch; stepped buttresses at the corners, placed diagonally and capped by canted bartizans; there are two principal storeys over a low basement, both the main floors have large, pointed windows, the upper ones once containing tracery.

The porch, which is portcullis-protected at each end, gives access to a mural lobby, with a spiral staircase on the E side leading to the portcullis room over the porch, and then the main body of the tower at a raised ground-floor level. Unusually, the interior is divided by N–S walls into three long compartments, of which only the upper floor of the W compartment has any sign of domestic convenience in the form of fireplace, latrine and window seats, though the incomplete E room may have been similarly equipped. Curwen 1910; Emery 1996, 240; Newman 1987; Perriam and Robinson 1998, 390–1.

PLESHEY, Essex (Open by appointment only). Impressive motte and bailey, possibly C11 in origin, but certainly in existence by 1142 when Geoffrey de Mandeville surrendered his castles to King Stephen. In the later C12 William de Mandeville was granted a licence to refortify the castle. In the later Middle Ages Pleshey came into the possession of the Crown, the castle being maintained into the late C15. The oval motte is some 65ft (20m) high with a large flat top. A large kidney-shaped bailey defined by a moat and high inner bank lies to the S of the motte. A gap on the SW side of the defences now provides an entrance, but the original gateway is believed to be at the NE angle adjacent to the motte, where there is an isolated mound within an enlargement of the ditch. The only building now visible is a late medieval brick bridge spanning the ditch between the bailey and the motte, but excavations have revealed the foundations of a large rectangular masonry structure, probably a hall, on top the motte, and further buildings within the bailey including a chapel. Truncated earthworks to the NE of the motte may indicate a second bailey. There are also remains of a roughly circular arrangement of defences around the village to the N comprising a ditch, and in some places an inner bank. RCHME 1921, 201–2; Christy 1923; Round 1923; Williams 1977.

PLYMPTON, Devon (Open). Early C12 motte with rectangular baily to the W, probably built by Richard de Redvers (d. 1107). It was destroyed by King Stephen's men in 1136 but rebuilt probably by Richard's son Baldwin (d. 1155), who was created Earl of Devon in 1141. In 1216 the heir of the Fifth Earl died, and his widow was forced into a marriage with Falkes de Bréauté, who, after the Fifth Earl's death the following year, became lord of Plympton. In 1224 the castle was besieged and captured on behalf of the King by Sir Robert Courtenay of Okehampton (qv) son-in-law of the Fifth Earl. His descendants became earls of Devon in 1335. The motte was moated and carries the remains of a C12 or C13 shell-keep, within which survey has provided evidence for a cylindrical keep of unknown date. The bailey is surrounded by an inner bank, but the former moat has been encroached upon. Higham *et al.* 1985.

PONTEFRACT, Yorkshire West Riding (Open). Sited on rocky spur at the NE end of the town, in a commanding position within sight of the Great North Road, Pontefract Castle was built by Ilbert de Lacy before 1086. In 1311, the estates of the last de Lacy lord, Henry, Earl of Lincoln, were inherited by his daughter, the wife of Thomas of Lancaster, and thereafter became part of the Lancaster holdings, which, as the Duchy of Lancaster, came under royal control in 1399. Richard II died here in captivity *c*.1400. During the Civil War Pontefract was a Royalist stronghold, undergoing three sieges before its surrender in 1649 when it was systematically destroyed. The site was cleared in 1881–3 to create a park and excavated in 1982–6.

The inner bailey, which crowns the spur, has a sub oval plan orientated NE–SW; there were middle and outer baileys to the SE, the former entered from a barbican to the SW, but next to nothing of these outer works survives. Access to the castle from the town is along Micklegate and Castle Garth, through the sites of the barbican and middle bailey. Immediately within the present entrance to the grounds is the outer face of the C13 keep (which occupied the S angle of the inner bailey), and, extending from it, a short length of the middle bailey curtain. The remains of the keep comprise a cluster of three (S, E and W) drum towers, the E and W towers of equal size, the S tower bigger. This cluster cases the outer face of the C11 motte; what happened on the N side of the motte is unknown, but there may have been a fourth tower to create a quatrefoil plan. Two storeys originally, an additional floor was added by John of Gaunt in 1374 and the parapet ornamented by bartizans corbelled out from the walls Northumbrian style.

Pass into the inner bailey through the largely vanished inner gatehouse, which had twin flanking towers. Around the curtain are the remains of six rectangular wall towers, named (in clockwise sequence) Gascoigne, Treasurer's, Pre-kitchen, Queen's, King's and Constable Towers; the first two have C12 origins; the three at the NE end (Queen's, King's and Constable Towers) each had an attached latrine turret and probably date from the C14 or C15. On the N side, outside the curtain and linked to the castle by a bridge, the Swillington Tower was raised 1399–1405 by the master mason Philip de Gamston. Its remains can be seen from North Baileygate by which it is truncated.

Ranged around the interior of the curtain are the remnants of some of the domestic buildings: brewhouse, bakehouse and great kitchen to the NW and great hall to the

NE linking the Queen's and King's Towers. Next to the great hall is the C12 apsidal-ended chapel, and nearby, ranged along the SW curtain, the late C16 'Elizabethan Chapel'. A little further to the S is the Constable Tower, taking its name from the Constable's lodgings which lay to the rear, and which were rebuilt in the first decade of the C15 by Robert de Gamelston (or Gamston). Roberts 2002.

PONTESBURY, Shropshire (Private). Now comprising a flat-topped mound, surrounded by later buildings, archaeological trenching in the 1960s showed that Pontesbury Castle began life as a circular ringwork defined by a ditch and inner bank. In the later C12 or C13 a great square tower was built on the E side of the ringwork. There was some evidence to suggest that this was destroyed by fire *c.*1300, an event that probably marked the end of occupation on the site. Barker 1961–4; Duckers 2006, 129–30.

PORTCHESTER, Hampshire (Open – EH). A late C11 foundation within the walls of a C3 Roman fort that formed part of the 'Saxon Shore' chain of coastal defences. In the C10 the fort became one of the Anglo-Saxon *burhs*, the system of defended settlements established by the royal house of Wessex in response to the Danish invasions. In 1086 Portchester was held by the Norman, William Maudit, who is the presumed builder of the castle. This was created by enclosing the NW angle of the fort to act as an inner bailey, whilst the greater part of the fort formed an extensive outer bailey. William's son and successor, Robert, who may have been responsible for raising the keep and providing the inner bailey with stone defences, died in 1120 in the White Ship disaster. In 1130, the Sheriff of Hampshire, William de Pontdelarche, married Robert's daughter, acquiring the Maudit estates in the process. William de Pontdelarche founded an Augustinian priory in the SE corner of outer bailey; although the priory was short-lived, the church survived. William died in 1148, and not long after Henry II (reigned 1154–87) acceded to the throne, Portchester became a royal castle, and so it remained until 1926 when it was placed in Guardianship. It was probably Henry who was responsible for converting the keep from a two-storey building to a four-storey tower. Over 200 years later, in 1396–9 Richard II vaulted over the ground storey and rebuilt the domestic buildings of the inner bailey.

Sited on a low, flat promontory at the N end of Portsmouth Harbour, the land approach is from the W via the Land Gate, a C12 rebuilding of the Roman entrance, largely reconstructed in the C14. The gatehouse is in the form of a square tower, its mostly ashlared outer face flush with that of the Roman walls. Segmental-arched gateway, and above, three large blocked openings, which probably gave access to a barbican wall walk. A staircase in the N wall led to the first-floor room. Directly opposite, in the E side of the fort, is the water gate, also a rebuilding of a Roman gate, but probably dating from before rather than after the Conquest, its inner face having a semi-circular gate arch with polychrome voussoirs. The upper storey and front (E) face with diagonal corner buttresses date from the C14.

The inner ward is enclosed to the N and W by the Roman walls, and to the S and E by a moat and C12 curtain, defining a small rectangular courtyard castle with the rectangular keep at the NW angle projecting beyond the Roman defences, a diagonally orientated rectangular tower at the SE angle, and a gatehouse to the S. The inner gatehouse is the result of an extended building history beginning with a C12 rectangular tower. An outwork with semi-circular turrets was built in front of it and

Portchester: Roofline of the early keep (first quarter of the C12).

converted into a tower in the early C14. Further extensions took place in the late C14 and C17, to give an elongated passage protected by two portcullises and drawbridges.

The courtyard is lined by domestic buildings of various periods; most important is Richard II's creation of a new set of royal apartments on the W side around a small inner courtyard, the most significant component being the hall range on the S side, with a central two-storey porch. To the L (E), demarcated by two buttresses, is the kitchen, which rose through the full height of the building. Then came a larder with service rooms above. The porch gave onto a stair rising to a first-floor screens passage running between the service rooms on the L (E), and great hall on the R (W) (which extended as far as the W range). Beneath the hall were storerooms (E) and two residential chambers (W). The W range was also given over to lodgings at ground-floor level, with the King's great chamber and inner chamber above. At the NE corner of the courtyard is the three-storey square Ashton's Tower (attributed to Robert of Ashton, constable 1376–81), an adjunct to the constable's lodgings ranged along the N side of the courtyard (largely rebuilt in the C17).

The square-plan, five-storey, keep was protected by the forebuilding ranged all across its E side. A staircase led to the first-floor entrance, immediately L (S) of which was a chapel, now represented by a large blind arch in the wall of the keep, and above it traces of its pitched roof. The tower was divided by an E–W cross-wall and served by a spiral staircase in its SW angle. On the second floor, on each side of the cross-wall, the former roof lines are to be found, showing V-shaped profiles with central valleys, a type that was also used in the keep of Bridgnorth Castle (qv). Cunliffe 1977; Cunliffe and Munby 1985.

POWERSTOCK, Dorset (Open access). Motte and bailey of unknown origin on a promontory between two streams to the SE of the village. In 1205 it was acquired from the Newburgh family by King John, who raised new domestic buildings at a cost of £373. A ditch cuts across the neck of the promontory to the E to isolate a triangular site which fans out towards the W and SW. The motte is on the N side surrounded by a ditch and crescentic bailey to the S, E and W. The bailey is protected by a bank to the E and by a rock cutting to the W; its interior is bisected by a bank. To the W and SW of the motte and bailey is a large outer enclosure defended by a bank and, to the W, also by a ditch and outer bank. Brown *et al.* 1963, 987–8; RCHME 1952, 183–4.

PRUDHOE, Northumberland (Open – EH). Stone castle with a keep, first mentioned in 1138, when, held by Odinel de Umfraville, it was besieged by William the Lion, King of Scotland. That siege was raised, but William returned to attack the castle the following year. However, the defenders were well prepared, the assault failed, and the Scots had to be content with damaging the castle and laying waste to the crops; the siege had lasted no more than five days. In 1326, when in royal custody, a peel was built outside the castle walls. Gilbert Umfraville, Earl of Angus, was the last of the line. He died in 1381, and his widow, Maud Lucy, married Henry Percy, Earl of Northumberland, thereby bringing Prudhoe into the Percy family with whom it remained except for periodic confiscation.

Sitting on a hillock to the S of the river Tyne, Prudhoe Castle is protected to the SE and E by a narrow valley in which a number of streams converge, and to the W and SW by a great L-shaped ditch. Between this outer ditch and the castle, a flat open area represents the peel of 1326. To the E of the peel a mill pond extends up to a dam carrying the track leading to the castle gate. Within these outer features is an inner ditch and above the scarp the largely C13 curtain wall, a rectangular tower projecting from the E end and a round tower from each of the two W corners.

The inner ditch is traversed by a C14 outer barbican, its very slightly pointed gateway deeply recessed between two lengths of walling, the LH (W) one truncated, but retaining a jamb of an opening into the peel. Passing through the rib-vaulted entrance into the barbican, there are staircases to L and R which led to the battlements. Nearing the gatehouse the walls terminate, denoting the position of the drawbridge, which crossed to a C13 inner barbican directly in front of the gatehouse.

The gatehouse is of three main building periods. The early C12 ground storey is pierced by a gateway of two square orders with a semi-circular arch on flat responds; above, lit by lancet windows, is the chapel, a product of a C13 rebuilding of the first floor, including the construction of the stone-roofed oriel window at the E end of the building. Inside, a large pointed chancel arch gives onto the sanctuary within the oriel, with a piscina in its S jamb. Subsequently, the tower was raised, and a second floor inserted; elements of the earlier battlements are preserved in the walling below the present parapet.

A simple barrel-vaulted passage, with a single transverse rib on corbels each carved with a pair of heads, leads to the outer ward. Here is an external staircase ascending to the upper storeys of the gatehouse. Against the N wall of the outer ward was the great hall with service rooms to the E including kitchen and brewhouse. In the S wall is a finely-preserved shouldered lintel giving access to a C14 latrine turret. Extending right across the W end of the outer ward is an early C19 house on the site of the medieval private apartments. A path around the N end of the house leads into the inner bailey the main interest of which lies in the C12 keep, a building of rectangular plan entered via a two-storey forebuilding to the E. The ground-floor entrance to the forebuilding led into a lobby with access to the basement of the keep and to a spiral stair ascending to the first floor. The second floor was reached by a staircase within the W wall. Bates 1891, 199–222; Dodds, 1926, 79–135; Keen 1982.

PULFORD, Cheshire (Visible from the churchyard). First mentioned in the early C13, the remains consist of a motte encircled by a ditch on all sides except the S where Pulford Brook provided a degree of protection, a large crescent-shaped bank to the W, and a small bailey between it and the motte. Reynolds and White 1997–8.

PULVERBATCH, Shropshire (Open access). Motte with two baileys on a ridge SW of Pulverbatch (formerly Castle Pulverbatch) village within the parish of Church Pulverbatch. Attributed to Roger Venator, a tenant of Roger of Montgomery in 1086, but not mentioned as a castle until 1153. Possibly abandoned as a residence by 1292. The earthworks comprise a motte separated by a ditch from a rectangular bailey to the NE and a larger semi-circular bailey to the W. The former is protected by a bank to the N and W and by scarping of the hillside to the E, the latter by a ditch and counterscarp bank. Brown 1989, 188–9.

QUATFORD, Shropshire (Private, but partially visible from the road). Motte and bailey on a spur overlooking a crossing of the river Severn. Raised by Roger de Montgomery, Earl of Shrewsbury, in the late C11 and abandoned by his son Robert de Bellême *c.*1101 in favour of Bridgnorth a couple of miles upstream. Oval motte at the cliff edge separated by a rock-cut ditch from a kidney-shaped bailey to the E. In the C19 a road was cut through the spur immediately to the E of the bailey, isolating it from the church of St Mary Magdalene, which lies to the west. Excavation at the E edge of the bailey in 1960, in advance of road widening, revealed numerous postholes in an indeterminate pattern, but no trace of a ditch or bank. Mason and Barker 1961–4; Duckers 2006, 130–1.

QUEENBOROUGH, Isle of Sheppey, Kent (D). Site of a stone courtyard castle built by Edward III on a new site in 1361–75. The principal mason was John Box (d. 1375). Queenborough Castle was built to a circular plan with concentric inner and outer wards, surrounded by a moat. The outer curtain had a twin-towered gatehouse to the W, and a postern gate to the E, both with barbicans. Access to the inner ward was from the E via a gateway with twin flanking towers, in addition to which there were four wall towers; all the towers in the castle were round with hexagonal interiors. The inner curtain was lined with apartments around a circular courtyard. Brown *et al.* 1963, 793–804. Time Team 2006.

RABY, County Durham (Open). In 1378, Bishop Hatfield (of Durham) granted John Lord Neville permission to make a castle at his manor of Raby and to embattle and crenellate all its towers, houses and walls. In fact, the fortification of Raby had probably begun under Neville's father, Ralph (d. 1367), and the works associated with the licence amounted to an expansion and strengthening of a castle that was already in existence. The Durham mason John Lewyn may have been involved. During the C18 the complex was drastically improved by a succession of architects, namely Daniel Garret (*c.*1740–51/2), James Paine (*c.*1752–60) and John Carr (1767–85), and again in the C19 by William Burn (1843–8). Although these schemes occasioned the destruction of much of the medieval detail, a large proportion of the C14 fabric survives.

Raby: Ground plan.

Raby today comprises an accretive collection of irregularly-placed towers, varying in shape and size, together with connecting ranges of buildings grouped around two main courtyards, all within an outer ward contained by a moated curtain wall. At the core of the medieval castle are the remains of a hall house of *c*.1300 (the Entrance Hall, the shell of which survives within the present complex). This first phase of construction, initiated by Ralph, and perhaps completed by his son John, involved the raising of a first-floor hall (the Baron's Hall) on top of the existing hall to form the E range of a tightly planned, quadrangular castle, whose nevertheless idiosyncratic

Raby: Neville Gateway of 1381–8, attributed to John Lewyn.

layout suggests an accretive development rather than a coherent design. Although the exact sequence of construction is still to be determined, at least two details distinguish the buildings of this phase from later C14 work at the castle. One is the occurrence of tunnel-vaulted basements carried on hefty stone ribs. The other is the semi-circular arched doorway.

A number of towers are associated with the hall range. The N end is enclosed by a linked group of three (the Kitchen Tower, Keep and Mount Raskelf) which, with the hall, contain a small courtyard. At the S end of the range, linked by a narrow arm, was another tower (destroyed in the C18). This arrangement of hall and towers recalls some Northumbrian defended houses of the mid C14. The W range contained a roughly central gate passage, and rectangular towers projected from its NW (the Watch Tower) and SW (Joan's Tower) angles. Originally, both towers projected beyond the outer face of the entrance range by approximately 18ft (5.49m), and by a similar distance to the N and S respectively. This front was to be dramatically altered under the licence of 1378.

Between 1381 and 1388 a monumental gatehouse (the Neville Gateway) was built in front of the existing entrance, the curtain wall between the Watch Tower and the gateway was brought forward, flush with the face of the Watch Tower, and Joan's Tower was extended to the W in order that it might project beyond the new entrance as it had projected beyond the old and continue to command the S approach to the gateway. Part of the same scheme is a group of buildings enclosing a courtyard immediately N of the main quadrangle. One of these buildings, the three-storey NW range, adjoins the N side of the Watch Tower, and is terminated to the N by Clifford's Tower, a large rectangular building of comparable magnitude, which provides an effective counterbalance to the extended Joan's Tower. A section of curtain wall (the N curtain), with a parapet on corbelled machicolations, links Clifford's Tower to the Kitchen Tower. In the new scheme, Clifford's Tower effectively assumed the former defensive function of the Watch Tower, which was to dominate the northern approach to the entrance, while also guarding access to the castle from the outer gatehouse.

One of the interests of the castle is the C14 great kitchen, which is housed in a tower to the N of the hall range. There is an architectural relationship with the kitchen of Durham Priory, and it is probable either that the overall form of the Raby kitchen provided a model for the aesthetically superior design for Durham Priory, or that Durham acted as an influence on the character of Raby.

At the SE corner of the complex a large residential tower of pentagonal plan known as the Bulmer Tower (after an ancestor of the Neville family) comprised a series of large apartments entered independently from a staircase at its SW angle. The few details that remain suggest a late C14 or C15 date. On the outside wall of the tower, within a panel, is a large heraldic device consisting of the letter 'b'. This appears on John Lord Neville's seal and that of his son Ralph, First Earl of Westmorland, and lord of Raby between 1388 and 1425. Hodgson 1880–5 and 1890–5; Hislop 1992 and 2007.

RAMPTON (Giant's Hill), Cambridgeshire and the Isle of Ely (Open access). One of several siege castles (including Burwell qv) built around the edge of the fens by King Stephen *c.*1144 to contain the notorious Geoffrey de Mandeville, Earl of Essex, then quartered in the Isle of Ramsey. When in August 1144 de Mandeville was killed attacking Burwell Castle, his rebellion disintegrated and the need for the siege castles vanished, and so Rampton was abandoned. Like its counterpart at Burwell, Rampton Castle appears to have been unfinished. The castle lies to the E of the village of Rampton, next to the main road. It consists of a sub-rectangular platform enclosed by a ditch or moat; a bank of earth on the N side represents dumping of spoil from the excavation of the ditch. Brown and Taylor 1977; Wright *et al.* 2016.

RAVENSWORTH, Yorkshire North Riding (Private). Heavily ruined stone courtyard castle of the FitzHughs SE of the village of Ravensworth. A castle was in existence by 1201, but upstanding remains appear to date from the C14. In 1391 Sir Henry FitzHugh, lord of Ravensworth from 1386–1425, received a licence to empark 200 acres of land around the castle. The last FitzHugh lord died in 1513, and by the early C17 the castle (by then a Crown property) was being used as a quarry.

Built on a low spur, largely surrounded by marshy land, and isolated from the adjacent higher ground by a ditch which curves around the N corner of the platform. Earthworks and remnants of buildings suggest that the castle was divided into a sequence of three courtyards. The best-preserved of the castle buildings is the ashlar-built gatehouse, which occupies the N angle of the platform. It comprises a single square, three-storey tower, with a latrine turret on the NE side. The front elevation is pierced by three cruciform arrow loops, one on each storey. To the R (SW) is the segmental-pointed gate arch, which pierces the curtain; it was protected by a portcullis. Access to the tower's interior was from the rear where there are ground- and first-floor doorways (the latter approached by a vanished stone staircase), both with shouldered lintels. The treatment of the doorways with a continuous convex quarter-round moulding is highly reminiscent of the doorways to the rear of the Llanfaes Gate, Beaumaris, of *c.*1296. Each floor was occupied by a single room with a fireplace and latrine and trefoil-headed windows with monolithic lintels; the fireplaces have shouldered lintels, like the doorways. Ryder 1979.

RAYLEIGH (Rayleigh Mount), Essex. Motte with two baileys built by Sweyn, son of Robert FitzWimarc who was Sheriff of Essex under Edward the Confessor and William the Conqueror. The castle was lost by Sweyn's grandson, Henry of Essex, who, in 1163, was accused by Robert de Montfort of fleeing the Battle of Coleshill during the Welsh campaign of 1157, a claim Henry denied. Trial by battle ensued, in which de Montfort prevailed. Henry's possessions were seized by the King, and he ended his days as a monk of Reading Abbey. In 1227 the Honour of Rayleigh was granted to Hugh de Burgh who moved the caput to his new castle of Hadleigh (qv). By the C14 Rayleigh Castle was no longer in use, other than as a quarry.

Now hemmed in by buildings, the castle forms a green enclave within an urban landscape. A considerable amount of tree cover, especially on the motte and around the periphery of the bailey, reduces visibility. The castle is sited on a spur, with the motte at its NW end, and the inner bailey to the E of it. An outer bailey further to the E was recorded by the RCHME in the 1920s but has since been covered with buildings. RCHME 1923,123–4; Helliwell and MacLeod 1981; Milton and Walker 1987.

REDCASTLE, Hawkstone Park, Weston-under-Redcastle, Shropshire. Stone castle built under a licence of 1227 by Henry de Audley of Heighley (qv), Sheriff of Shropshire and Staffordshire. It remained an Audley property throughout the medieval period but was probably abandoned in the C15; it was in ruins when John Leland visited *c.*1540. The castle is of sub-rectangular form, aligned N–S, but the site is an unusual one, comprising two precipitous parallel ridges and the vale between them. Rock-cut ditches formed part of the defences at the N and S ends of the vale, and a transverse ditch divided the enclosure into two, continuing into the ridges, where posterns were contrived. A curtain wall punctuated by drum towers extended all around the site, the long sides on the crests of the ridges, but survival of the stonework is fragmentary, centuries of attrition and the presence of copious undergrowth having combined to remove or obscure it. At the S end of each ridge is the stump of a round tower, but the most substantial monument is the Giant's Well Tower on the W side of the N bailey, a three-storey (once four-storey) round tower rising to a small inner (NE) bailey, sited on the E ridge. It contains a well and is pierced by cruciform arrow loops. Philips 1896; Salter 2001; Duckers 2006, 131–5.

REIGATE, Surrey (Open access). An oval enclosure castle, probably raised by William de Warenne, Earl of Surrey, from 1088. A natural hill was scarped and surrounded by a substantial ditch to form the inner bailey. There was an outer bailey to the NE of uncertain extent but defined to the N along London Road by a C13 bank, now sealed by the current bank on the N side of an artificial lake. The inner bailey was formerly enclosed by a curtain wall, but no stone remains are now visible. Underneath the inner bailey is a complex of caves. Malden 1911, 230–1.

RESTORMEL, Cornwall (Open – EH). Ringwork and bailey on a steep-sided spur to the N of Lostwithiel, possibly built by Baldwin FitzTurstin *c*.1100. Around 1270 the castle was acquired by the King's brother, Richard Earl of Cornwall. It was probably his son, Edmund, who, between 1272 and 1299, rebuilt Restormel in stone. The bailey, which lay towards the W, has been largely obliterated, and the former ringwork is now represented by the transformative creation of Earl Edmund's builders, a stone curtained inner ward of circular form some 130ft (39m) across, within which stone apartments back onto the curtain wall and surround a central courtyard. This inner ward resembles a shell-keep, a similitude that was played upon by the builders who piled up an earthen revetment around the walls in imitation of a motte, the effect accentuated by the surrounding ditch.

The rubble-built curtain wall survives relatively well, some of the battlements retaining their stone copings. From the gatehouse on the W side, a perambulation around the exterior in an anticlockwise direction brings us in turn to three large windows (SE) which indicate the position of the hall, a rectangular projection which housed the chapel (NE), and another large window to a private chamber (N). Back to the entrance, which consists of a rectangular two-storey tower predating the curtain wall; in front of it a later tower, formerly of three storeys, from which the drawbridge was controlled (the recess into which the drawbridge fitted can be seen either side of the entrance). At the innermost end of the extended gate passage is a well-preserved segmental-pointed arch, inserted in the C13, and now giving onto the circular courtyard.

Stairs led up to the parapet from either side of the gate. The two-storey domestic buildings housed service rooms and storage space at ground-floor level and residential apartments above. From the gatehouse, facing the courtyard and working anticlockwise round the building, first is the kitchen, the full height of the range, with a large fireplace, then a narrow division containing servery (ground floor) and service rooms (first floor), and beyond that, on the upper level, the hall (reached from the floor below via a stair, and containing a stair to the battlements). Next come chamber, ante chapel, chapel (in the NE projection), and another large chamber; the living rooms all have fireplaces and the whole sequence is linked by doorways. Finally, another hall or chamber isolated from the rest with its own entrance. A good example of C13 integrated castle planning. Higham 2015, 175–85; Ashbee 2020.

RICHARD'S CASTLE, Herefordshire (Open access). Motte and bailey rebuilt in stone, lying on the tip of a spur to the W of the church. Probably established before 1052 by Richard Scrob, a French follower of Edward the Confessor; at Domesday it was held by his son Osbern FitzRichard. Motte with kidney-shaped bailey to the E, the whole site surrounded by a ditch, and there was a ditch (now infilled) between the motte and bailey. Fragments of the rubble stone curtain around the bailey survive; there were also several semi-circular wall towers and a much larger rectangular tower to the E with canted corners. More than one period is represented. Excavation on the motte in the 1960s revealed the foundations of an octagonal keep with an apsidal-ended annexe to the E, probably a forebuilding containing a chapel. Curnow and Thompson (1969).

RICHMOND, Yorkshire North Riding (Open – EH). Large courtyard castle dating from *c.*1071 built for Count Alan Rufus. It comprises a triangular enclosure, its base to the S on a steep bank above the river Swale, and the apex (and gateway) to the N, towards the town. There was also an outer courtyard, or barbican, in front of the gateway, and another enclosure (the Cockpit) was added to the SE corner in the C12. Access is still from the N, first into the barbican, now dominated by a three-storey tower keep built *c.*1160 directly in front of the original gateway by Alan's great nephew, Conan IV, Duke of Brittany. The position of the present entrance is contemporary with the keep, but the original curtain containing the gateway became part of the rear wall of the keep and was thus preserved. Indeed, a great deal of C11 stonework survives generally, including the greater part of the curtain, the three eastern

Richmond: Scolland's Hall (late C11) from the NW.

towers, and the core of the main residential block, which incorporates a gateway now leading into the Cockpit, where there was a garden.

The residential block comprises a multi-period complex, but the C11 component consists of a single range extending along the S curtain; the E end was partitioned from the rest of the building, the ground floor providing access to and from the Cockpit, and the first floor acting as a chamber block to the hall with latrines in the Gold Hole Tower. The rest of the building contained Scolland's Hall over an undercroft. In front (N), two ground-floor entrances, and to the R (W) the remains of an external staircase to the conspicuously large first-floor doorway to Scolland's Hall. Also at the upper level, three windows with twin round-arch lights, and beyond (L or E), a large opening representing the later medieval conversion of a window into a doorway associated with the extended chamber block ranged along the E wall. To the R (W) of the staircase base are C12 kitchen and services. Inside, below Scolland's Hall, sockets along the side walls are for the first-floor joists, the inner ends of which were supported on a central beam supported by a row of columns. Above, the single semi-circular rear arches of the twin-light windows.

Back to the keep, the original gateway (two square orders on cushion [R] and primitive foliate [L] capitals) is now the ground-floor entrance leading to a room covered by (restored) C13 vaulting. From here, there is staircase access to the first floor, but the principal entrance was a first-floor level doorway at the SE corner formerly approached by a now-vanished external staircase. This opened to a lobby communicating both with the first- and second-floor rooms. The first floor has a central column for supporting the timber floor above, and three openings with raised sills to the N; these may be viewing windows from which the lord showed himself to his people when occasion required. The principal room at second-floor level, which is open to the roof and with clearstorey lighting at each end, was possibly an audience chamber. Goodall 2016.

ROCHESTER, Kent (Open – EH). Established by William I soon after the Conquest to control the crossing of Watling Street over the river Medway, Rochester Castle was rebuilt in stone for William II by Gundulf, Bishop of Rochester, in the 1080s. William de Corbeil, Archbishop of Canterbury, became custodian of the castle in 1127 and proceeded to erect a great tower keep, the tallest of its kind in the kingdom, the tops of the turrets rising to 125ft (138m). Rochester came under the control of the baronial opposition to King John in 1215. A siege ensued, the King's men undermined the curtain and broke into the castle, whereupon the defenders retreated to the keep; the King's miners brought down the SE corner of the building, bringing about the end of the business, although the rebels continued to hold out for a time behind the cross wall. Repairs ensued in the 1220s, including the rebuilding of the SE corner of the keep and the parts of the curtain wall. In 1264 the castle was successfully held for the King against Simon de Montfort, although much damage resulted. It was belatedly restored in the 1370s and early 1380s.

To circumnavigate the castle's enceinte by foot starting at the castle entrance (at the junction of Castle Hill and Epaul Lane), go down Epaul Lane to Boley Hill. On the L is the cathedral, and on the R, the E curtain, largely rebuilt in the 1360s with two rectilinear towers, of which the mason William Sharnhale and his men built one and completed the other. Between the towers a row of arches supports the curtain (cf. Southampton). At the SE angle is the three-quarter round Drum Tower, built

Rochester: The great tower (c.1130) from the NE.

for Henry III in the 1220s. Turning R (W) here into Baker's Walk, the keep looms up behind the curtain. Down to the Esplanade with the Medway on the L and the W curtain to the R, the best surviving section of Gundulf's C11 wall with its characteristic herringbone masonry. At the junction with Castle Hill is the NW Bastion, a diagonally projecting angle tower dating from c.1378–83, now pierced by a C19 gateway of C12 character. So, up Castle Hill back to the entrance, close to the site of the vanished medieval gateway.

The interior of the castle is now a public park (Castle Gardens) overshadowed by the keep, which exudes a raw but commanding presence. The foundations of this immense tower extend at least 14ft (4.3m) below ground level. Square plan with pilaster buttresses, and projecting corner turrets rising above the battlements, the rebuilt SE turret round in contrast to its C12 counterparts. The main block has four storeys, but five levels (the second-floor hall contains a gallery), the less vulnerable upper levels having large round-arched windows. Projecting from the N front is a three-storey forebuilding with a first-floor entrance reached via a stone staircase wrapping itself around the NW corner of the main block. A gap between the steps and the entrance was spanned by a drawbridge. Then into a vestibule within the forebuilding, and from there into the keep proper, through a doorway flanked by shafts with cushion capitals carrying a chevron-moulded arch. This entrance was protected by a portcullis and barred two-leaf door. Recesses within the entrance passage housed the servants who would have pulled open the doors to visitors.

As noted, the keep is divided (E–W) by a central cross-wall, separating the interior into interconnecting outer (N) and inner (S) section or rooms. Interestingly, the cross-wall contains at its centre a well shaft, accessible on all four storeys. Spiral staircases at the NE and SW corners allowed separate access to the two halves of the keep. The basement was for storage or service purposes, but the upper floors all had fireplaces in the N and S walls, and the first and second floors were served by latrines within the walls. The architectural high point of the keep is the second floor, which housed the hall. Here, the cross-wall contained an arcade, now open, but formerly closed by partitions, and the rooms rose higher than the other storeys to incorporate a mural gallery. Above this was a pair of private chambers.

Interesting structural details within the keep include the imprints of the formwork planks on the mortar vaults of the staircases and wall passages. Some of the passages have narrow ledges at the junction of the walls and vaults where the formwork rested. In the side walls of the third storey are angled rafter sockets implying a high-pitched roof. Brown *et al.* 1963, 806–14; Goodall 2006; Ashbee 2012.

ROCKINGHAM, Northamptonshire (Open) (Plate XII). A royal castle built for William the Conqueror on a spur on the S bank of the river Welland, now largely a Tudor mansion, although elements of the medieval castle survive. King John executed works in 1209–11, and Edward I carried out a major refurbishment in the 1270s and 1280s.

Rockingham Castle now consists of an irregularly polygonal bailey. There was formerly a motte at the SE angle and a second bailey to the SE of the motte. Of the medieval enceinte only the E curtain with its great gatehouse and a wall tower survives. The wall tower is rectangular, not unlike those associated with Henry II's works at Bamburgh, Dover and elsewhere, but the details are C13, and there is some doubt as to whether its current appearance is entirely authentic: cruciform arrow loops with basal oillet at ground-floor level, and a single narrow lancet light at first-floor level.

The gatehouse may perhaps incorporate earlier work but is conceivably all of Edward I's time. It comprises a rectangular block projecting outside the curtain with two semi-circular towers flanking the entrance. The front is ashlar faced, and like the wall towers is pierced by cruciform loops with basal oillets. Only two storeys high, the gatehouse has a squat appearance, and has probably been reduced in height. String courses to ground and first floors, stepped up over the segmental-pointed gateway.

Inside the entrance passage, a portcullis groove and opposed side doorways with pointed arches, moulded surrounds and hood moulds. These give access to the main gatehouse block and thence to the rooms within the drum towers. At the rear the ashlar facing gives way to rubblework; of the openings only the gate arch is certainly medieval.

The gatehouse brings us into a square outer courtyard with the house ranged across the LH (S) side. This range incorporates the much-altered medieval great hall, of which the C13 doorway is extant: two orders of shafts with stiff-leaf capitals and heavily moulded two-centred arch. Quite possibly of Edward I's time too. Behind the house is the rear of the wall tower, with a C13 first-floor recessed entrance: outer segmental-pointed arch with hood mould terminating in masks, and inner two-centred arch with door rebate on the outside. Brown *et al.* 1963, 815–18; Klingelhofer, E. 1983–4; Hulme 2014–15, especially 227–9; Guy 2019–20.

RUFUS (Bow and Arrow Castle), Isle of Portland, Dorset (Private, but visible from path). Late C15 tower on a rocky eminence above Church Hope Cove on the E coast of the Isle of Portland. Possibly built by Richard, Duke of York, between 1432 and 1460. It may occupy the site of an earlier castle, perhaps the one captured by Robert, Earl of Gloucester, in 1142, and/or a castle resulting from a licence to crenellate issued to Richard, Earl of Gloucester, in 1259. The existing (ruined) structure is a tower of pentagonal plan, the prow facing NW towards the approach from Easton. Each side is pierced by a circular gun loop, and the parapet was carried on corbelled machicolations. RCHME 1970, 252–3.

RUYTON-ELEVEN-TOWNS, Shropshire (Open access from the churchyard). In existence by 1148 when it was held by John le Strange. Destroyed by the Welsh in 1212. Sold in 1302 to the Earl of Arundel, who refortified the site. The remains of a square keep lie to the W of the church of St John the Baptist, on a low promontory overlooking the river Parry. Duckers 2006, 139–41.

SAFFRON WALDEN (Walden), Essex (Open). A castle of Geoffrey de Mandeville in existence by 1141, surrendered to King Stephen in 1143 and destroyed by Henry II in 1157–8. There is some reason to suppose that the castle was reoccupied before 1200. In 1347 Humphrey de Bohun, Earl of Essex, was granted a licence to crenellate several manor houses including Walden; it may have been at this time that a curtain wall (no longer extant) was built around the bailey.

De Mandeville's castle on Bury Hill took the form of a keep and roughly oval bailey, the confines of the bailey are broadly defined by Castle Street (N), Church Street (S), Museum Street (W) and Castle Hill (E). The badly ruined keep gives the appearance of being built on a low motte, but this is actually a revetment piled up around the base of the tower during construction. Rectangular plan with broad clasping buttresses at the angles, and a forebuilding on the W side approached by a staircase. The basement, which was entered from above has a central square stone base, probably for a pillar to support a first-floor arcade. The first-floor room was supplied with a large fireplace. RCHME 1916, 234; Ennis 2011.

ST BRIAVELS, Gloucestershire (Open access to exterior; restricted access to inner bailey). In existence by 1130 when it was a royal castle; at which stage it may have been little more than a ringwork containing residential accommodation, although by the 1220s it contained a rectangular keep. The curtain wall was probably built in the early C13. A monumental gatehouse was raised on the orders of Edward I in 1292–3. The keep collapsed in 1752 and a tower at the SE angle in 1777. St Briavels acted as a hunting lodge, but also as a distribution centre for weaponry from the Forest of Dean forges, notably crossbow bolts.

An irregularly polygonal enclosure is surrounded by a ditch and a curtain wall. The keep lay within the S side of the enclosure. The main point of interest is Edward I's three-storey great gatehouse at the NE angle, standing proud of the N curtain, Its twin drum towers sit on polygonal bases from which rise a wave-like arrangement of spurs, a motif otherwise found only at Tonbridge (qv) a castle of Edward's son-in-law Gilbert de Clare, Earl of Gloucester and Hereford. The chunky masonry detailing is of the same school as that of Goodrich (qv) nearly 10 miles to the N, largely rebuilt in the late C13 by Edward's uncle, William de Valence.

Although the gatehouse has undergone partial refenestration, several cruciform loops survive with oillets top and bottom. The gate passage was protected by a machicolation slot, three gates and two portcullises, and contained three pairs of opposed doors opening to (from N–S) front rooms, rear rooms and staircases. On entering the courtyard, the hall of *c.*1209–11 is on the R (W), and the two-storey early C14 chapel wing straight ahead, projecting from it at right angles. The E wall of the hall has been rebuilt, but the integral two-storey chamber block is largely intact, although, like the hall, it has retained little of its medieval character; a saving grace is that the W gable is surmounted by an *ex-situ* C13 polygonal chimney with crocketed gablets over the trefoil-headed side vents, and a cap stone topped by a sculptured horn. The first-floor chapel retains its E window, but the tracery has been lost, although a trefoil-headed piscina survives in the S wall. Curnow and Johnson 1985; Baggs and Jurica 1996; Ludlow 2021–2.

ST LEONARD'S TOWER, West Malling, Kent. See **WEST MALLING**.

SALTWOOD, Kent (Private). Ringwork and bailey, both of uncertain date, but the castle may have its origins in the late C11. Prior to the Conquest, Saltwood was a property of the See of Canterbury, but was held by Hugh de Montfort in 1086. In the mid C12 it was in the hands of Henry of Essex, Henry II's standard bearer, whose unfortunate history is related under Raleigh (qv). It was probably Henry (before 1163), or his successor Ranulph de Broc (before 1197), who was responsible for rebuilding the defences of the ringwork in stone. De Broc was administrator of the Canterbury estates during Archbishop Thomas Becket's exile (1164–70) and it was at Saltwood that Becket's assassins foregathered in December 1170 immediately before the deed. Richard I returned Saltwood to the See of Canterbury and it subsequently became an archiepiscopal residence. Substantial building work was carried out in the C14 particularly under Archbishop Courtenay (1381–96), including the rebuilding of the outer bailey defences in stone, the extension of the inner gatehouse and the reconstruction of the domestic buildings within the inner bailey. In 1540 the castle was appropriated by the King and subsequently lost its significance as a residence. A house was built to the rear of the inner gatehouse in the 1880s and some restoration carried by Sir Martin Conway and his architect, Philip Tilden, in the 1930s.

Sited on a promontory with a stream extending around its W and S sides, Saltwood consists of an oval ringwork, or inner bailey, defined by a ditch, which widens to the S to contain the stream, and is dammed at its E end to create a lake around the W and S sides. N of the dam is the junction of the inner and outer baileys, the latter irregularly polygonal and wrapped around the E and NE sides of the former. Late C14 outer curtain with cylindrical towers containing long cruciform arrow loops with oillet terminations, and, in the tower next the dam, a gun loop of inverted keyhole type. C12 rectangular gatehouse in the W curtain, refurbished in the late C14 with four-centred gate arches. At the W end of the inner bailey is the great gatehouse, the main interest being Archbishop Courtenay's late C14 W front added to the C12 gatehouse and attributed to Henry Yevele. The four-storey building is dominated by two great drum towers, their height giving them a rather slender look. They flank the recessed entrance bay, with its two-centred arch, portcullis, and corbelled and arched machicolations. This western block contains high-class domestic accommodation equipped with fireplaces, and latrines housed behind the towers. The tower battlements and much of the fenestration date from the 1880s.

Contemporary with the C12 curtain around the inner bailey is the inner part of the gatehouse, also two internally projecting rectangular towers (N and W) and two externally projecting turrets. Otherwise, the medieval buildings comprise the C14 main residential apartments ranged along the S side of the bailey. These are centred on a hall, entered via a porch, with three-storey service and chamber block at the lower (E) end, and probably a second chamber block at the upper (W) end. To the E of this complex is a two-storey extension containing a single chamber at each level, the upper floor having three large mid C14 windows to each side, containing cusped intersecting tracery. At the W end of the hall, the upper chamber block was replaced in the late C14 by two attached buildings set at right angles to one another containing first-floor chamber (E) and chapel (W). Emery 2006, 400–4.

SANDAL, Yorkshire West Riding (Open access). Remains of a motte and bailey rebuilt in stone in the mid to late C13 and the subject of a significant excavation in 1964–73. The first castle is probably attributable to William de Warenne, Earl of Surrey, who received the manor of Wakefield in the early C12; the rebuilding in stone is estimated to have occurred *c.*1240–*c.*1270. The last Warenne earl died in 1347, and the estate came to the Crown in 1361, where it resided until 1566. During the Wars of the Roses, the Battle of Wakefield took place outside Sandal Castle, then housing Richard, Duke of York, the head of the Yorkist faction. Richard led a sortie from the castle but was killed in the ensuing mêlée. In 1484, under Richard III, a tower was added to the keep and a new brewhouse and bakehouse built in the bailey. On the outbreak of the Civil War, Sandal was garrisoned for the King, but in 1645 it was besieged, bombarded, seriously damaged and captured by Parliamentarian troops. The following year it was rendered untenable, and the buildings are now very ruinous.

The castle is built on a ridge to the S of the river Calder. A path laid out around the perimeter allows the site to be circumperambulated. Orientated NW–SE, with the motte to the NW, both motte and bailey were surrounded by a ditch and counterscarp bank; there was an inner bank around the bailey and a ditch between the motte and bailey. To get into the castle from the car park bear to the R and follow the path anti-clockwise to the gatehouse. Here are the remains of a stone bridge and gatehouse, with a gap between them for a drawbridge. The gatehouse was rectangular, made T-shaped by the addition of two late medieval buttresses at its outer (N) end. Buildings ranged around the perimeter of the bailey are identified as (clockwise from the gatehouse) privy chamber, great chamber, great hall, lodging, larder, kitchen and bakehouse. Of these only the great hall retains any upstanding walls. On the opposite

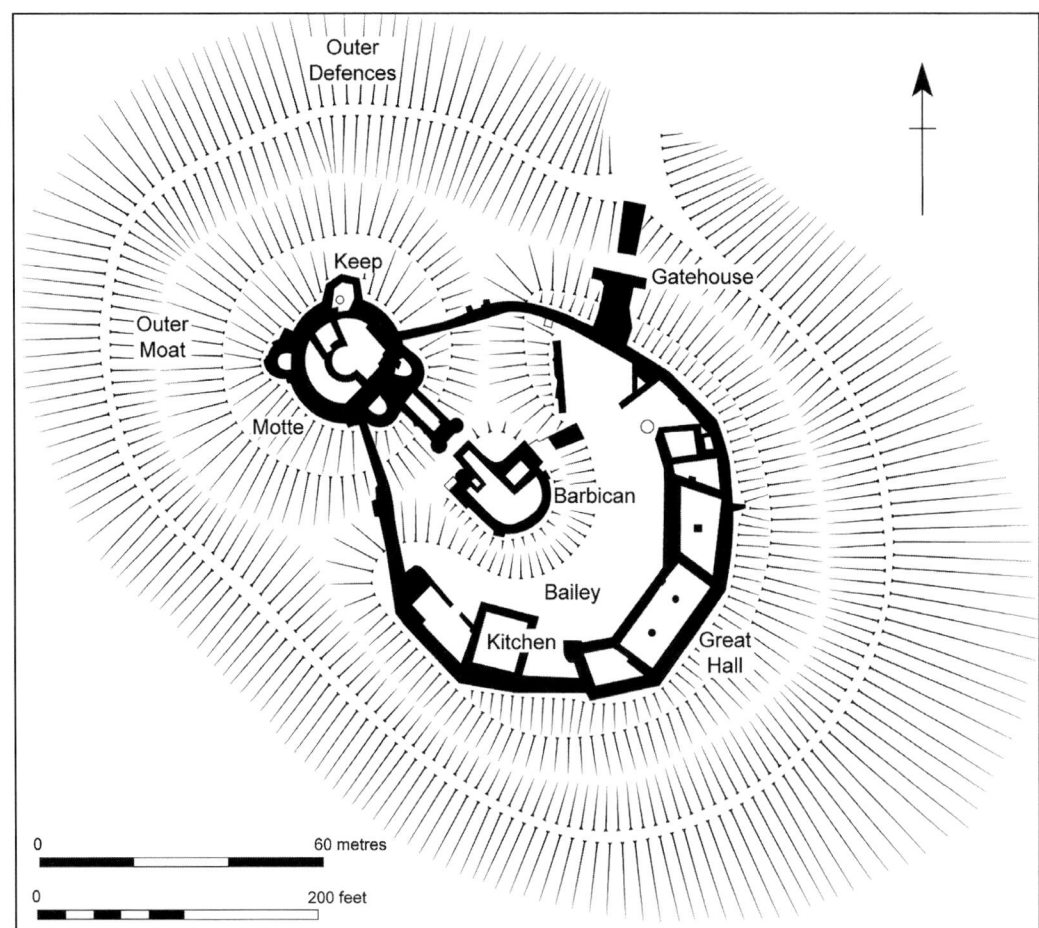

Sandal: Ground plan. After Mayes and Butler 1983.

side of the bailey, just in front of the motte, and guarding access to it, are the footings of the barbican. It was a semi-circular building with an entrance on the N side provided with a drawbridge, of which the pit for a turning bridge (now infilled) was discovered during excavation. The parallels are with the Lion Tower at the Tower of London (qv) of c.1270–80 and the barbican to Goodrich Castle (qv) of a similar date. Across the ditch at the foot of the motte is the base of the twin-towered gateway to the motte steps, the round-fronted towers with stepped batters.

The crowning glory of Sandal was the great tower, or keep, on top of the motte, a large and rather unusual building. As built, it comprised a round tower some 80ft in diameter, from which four semi-circular turrets protruded, two of which flanked the gateway on the SE side. The N turret was rebuilt in semi-polygonal form c.1484. The form of the internal plan is uncertain, but part of an inner stone ring enclosing a central area some 20ft (6m) in diameter suggests either that there was a central courtyard, or a central chamber with radiating rooms around it, a general configuration reminiscent of the great tower of Flint in north Wales begun in 1277. Mayes and Butler 1983.

SAUVEY (Castle Hill), nr Withcote, Leicestershire (Private). Two-ward enclosure castle built or rebuilt by King John c.1210–11 when nearly £450 was spent on the works of the castle and its fishpond. Situated on a low eastward-extending promontory, protected by an artificial ditch to the W and by converging streams to N and S, which were probably utilized to feed a moat (and fishpond) around the site. Rectangular ward to the W and smaller oval ward to the E, with a hollow way between them leading from the N side, possibly an entrance. An artificial bank to the SE with a gap may represent a dam and the site of a sluice gate. Page 1907, 49–50; Brown *et al.* 1963, 829; Creighton 1997, 30, 32–3.

SCALEBY, Cumberland (Private). The history of Scaleby Castle may be said to date from 1307 when Sir Robert Tilliol (whose ancestors had held the manor since *c.*1130) was granted a licence to crenellate his dwelling house of Scaleby. However, the first mention comes in 1367, in the inquisition that followed the death of Robert's belligerent grandson (another Robert), a dedicated harrier of the Scots. This younger Robert was succeeded by his son Peter who died in 1435, the last of the Tilliol male line. The greater part of the enceinte is probably owed to Robert and Peter between 1349 and 1435; from *c.*1596 a new S range was built by Sir Edward Musgrave. During the Civil War Sir Edward's grandson (also Sir Edward) held the castle for the King, and in 1648 it was burnt by Parliamentarian troops.

The castle buildings are at the centre of a circular enclosure some 500ft (152m) in diameter, defined by a moat with outer bank, and further confined within an inner moat (now infilled). Access to the outer enclosure is from the NE, and the castle gateway looks towards the NW. Outer round arch and inner pointed arch, probably late C14, with a portcullis between the two, porters' lodges to L and R of the entrance and portcullis chamber above. A curious corbelling out of the upper curtain on either side of the gate, leaving a narrow gap between them. To the R (SE) a rectangular corner tower or turret on the other side of which the curtain extends S to the S range. To the L (NW) of the gateway is a multiangular tower with narrow loops at first-floor level; opinions as to date are mixed, but the late C14/C15 cannot be discounted. It seems to be later than the rectangular four-storey solar tower at the NE corner, which it abuts, thereby protecting its W entrance, which in turn gives access to a spiral stair at the SW angle, and to a high-vaulted basement. S of this is the three-storey medieval hall range; this too has a high-vaulted basement but was refenestrated in the late C17. Further elements of the medieval castle may be incorporated into the S range. Curwen 1913, 235–7 and 1926; Emery 1996, 246–8; Perriam and Robinson 1998, 86–7.

SCARBOROUGH, Yorkshire East Riding (Open – EH). A large courtyard castle sited on an extensive headland to the E of the town jutting out into the North Sea, and in essence akin to the Northumbrian E coast castles (Bamburgh, Dunstanburgh and Tynemouth). Probably established during the reign of King Stephen (1135–54) by the Count of Aumale, William le Gros, on the site of a Roman signal station. When Henry II succeeded to the throne in 1154, Scarborough was seized and became a royal castle, remaining so until 1619. Henry II carried out substantial works between 1157 and 1169, the most notable aspect of which was the construction of the great tower. A greater sum was spent by King John (1199–1216) who rebuilt the curtain wall, in addition to domestic accommodation in the outer bailey. Henry III rebuilt the great gateway and bridge in the 1240s. In 1312 the castle was besieged by enemies of Edward II's favourite, Piers Gaveston, who had taken refuge here. It was the provisions rather than the defences that failed, and ultimately led to Gaveston's death.

Little attention was paid to the castle in the C14, until 1396 when the constable, John de Mosdale, began a programme of repairs, including the building of a new hall. In the 1420s Thomas Hyndeley, the master mason of Durham Priory, undertook the rebuilding of the inner gatehouse, or Constable Tower. During the Civil War the castle was held for the King, coming under siege in 1645 and again in 1648, actions which caused severe damage, notably to the keep, the eastern half of which was brought down by the bombardment.

The castle sits above the town, the approach being along a natural causeway which climbs up to a courtyard barbican, a roughly triangular enclosure fronted by a segmental-arched gateway with two round-fronted flanking towers, probably C13 in origin, but much altered by successive repairs, and reminiscent of the outer gatehouse of Bamburgh (qv). From the barbican, the ascent continues over a bridge and through the outer gatehouse of 1243–5 (now reduced to a pair of semicircular stumps one each side of the road), and into the inner ward which occupies the eastern angle of the headland. Here is the partially-demolished C12 keep, a square, four-storey building, the sides articulated by pilaster buttresses, the angles recessed to contain slender columns, and lit by twin-light windows. On the S side is a staircase ascending to a forebuilding containing the first-floor entrance, and, on the second floor, a chapel. The main block was divided internally by a N–S cross-wall carried on a great diaphragm arch to give a single space at entrance level, but outer (W) and inner (E) chambers on the first floor. Communication between floors was served by a spiral staircase in the centre of the W wall. Heating was by round-backed fireplaces in the centre of the E wall and there were latrines in the W wall (now only represented by the remains of the chutes). The spine wall rose only to first-floor level, and the uppermost storey was not residential; it may, in fact, have contained the roof, sunk well below parapet level.

Along the S side of the inner ward the curtain wall incorporates a series of solid round-fronted towers. This section of the curtain was probably the first phase of King John's reconstruction of the southern defences in the early C13. The continuation of the wall to the SE along the edge of the large outer ward is characterized by larger, hollow, semi-circular towers, mostly open-backed and pierced by arrow loops of the type found at Corfe Castle (qv) at a similar period. Incorporated into this wall, and utilizing one of the towers, is the so-called Mosdale Hall, King John's two-storey chamber block of which only the undercroft remains. It was divided at each level into two rooms of unequal size. Some 100ft (30m) to the N of Mosdale Hall, and evidently part of the same residential complex, is the King's Hall, now reduced to its foundations, also of John's time. It was an aisled building with an open hearth. Integral service rooms at the NW end were separated by a central passage to a detached kitchen. Page 1923, 541–9; Brown *et al.* 1963, 829–32; Goodall 2013b.

SCOTNEY, Lamberhurst, Kent (Open – NT). Moated two-courtyard castle probably built for Roger Ashburnham (d. 1392) in the late 1370s and 1380s on the NW bank of the river Bewl. This much-ruined castle occupies two islands within a substantial moat or lake. Access was from the W (to the S of the current entrance) onto the S Island/outer ward. There was a drawbridge across to the irregularly shaped E Island/inner ward, which was entered via a rectangular gatehouse with diagonally-projecting corner turrets. The inner ward was enclosed by a low curtain wall with four cylindrical corner towers, of which only the S Tower survives to any degree of completeness; it rises through two storeys and the (no longer extant) parapet was carried on arched machicolations resting on three tier corbelling. Emery 2006, 404–6; Martin *et al.* 2011 and 2012; Johnson *et al.* 2017, 95–105.

SHEFFIELD, Yorkshire West Riding (D). Vanished courtyard castle formerly situated at the confluence of the rivers Don and Sheaf, its extent now represented by the Don/Castlegate (N), Exchange Street (S) and Waingate (W). The Sheaf (now culverted), which bounded the E side of the castle, lay W of the buildings fronting the eastern section of Castlegate. First mentioned in 1183/4, when payments for repairs were mentioned. In 1270 Thomas de Furnival (d. 1291) was granted a licence to build a stone castle at his manor of Sheffield, a response perhaps to the burning of Sheffield in 1266 during the Barons' War. It seems to denote the conversion of an earlier timber castle. The castle was demolished in 1649 by the Parliamentarians, but elements of its remains have been uncovered during successive redevelopments of the site. It was surrounded by a moat connected to the Don and was entered from the S where there was a C13 monumental gatehouse with at least one (and probably two) round flanking tower(s). Moreland and Hadley 2020.

SHERBOURNE OLD CASTLE, Dorset (Open – EH). Stone enclosure castle built by Roger, Bishop of Salisbury (d. 1139), probably after 1122 on the site of an Anglo-Saxon cemetery. In 1139 Sherbourne was seized by King Stephen, and soon after held by Robert, Earl of Gloucester, returning to the Crown in 1183. Sherbourne was recovered by the Bishop of Salisbury in 1355 and remained with his successors until 1592. Bishop Langton (1485–93) was responsible for rebuilding the N gatehouse and remodelling the great tower, following a fire. In 1592 the castle was bought by Sir Walter Raleigh, who began some alterations there. During the Civil War the castle was besieged twice and in 1645 partially demolished by Parliamentary order.

Rectangular enclosure with canted corners giving an irregular, but symmetrical octagon surrounded by a ditch and counterscarp bank. Gatehouses at the NE and SW angles and in the N side, and open-backed towers at the other two angles. In the centre is an extensive residence, or palace. Access is now via the SW gatehouse, the best preserved of the three entrances. It comprises a single rectangular tower, latterly of four storeys and formerly approached by a stone bridge (the remains of which can be seen in the ditch). Pierced by a segmental-arched gateway, it retains a large C12 first-floor window with semi-circular arch, and C17 mullioned windows to the upper storeys. The NE gatehouse was similar, but the N gate quite different, comprising in its early C12 phase a narrow gateway in the curtain, with a square courtyard barbican in front approached across the ditch by a covered bridge. Three-quarter round corner turrets were added to the barbican in the C13, the courtyard barbican itself being replaced in the late C15 by a square tower and passage barbican.

The principal apartments of Bishop Roger's palace were grouped around a cloister, the ground-floor great hall to the S (demolished by Sir Walter Raleigh), lower and upper chapels in the N range, and, at the SW angle, a rectangular great tower (remodelled internally by Bishop Langton), with an attached SW turret, constituting the chamber block. Later additions include a compact accommodation block at the SW corner of the great tower (later C12), a courtyard complex to the W (*c.*1200–1355), and a courtyard and buildings to the S (late C15). The great tower was further altered by Sir Walter Raleigh, who removed the S wall and added a great oriel projection (since demolished). White and Cook 2015.

SHERIFF HUTTON, Yorkshire North Riding (Private) (Plate XIII). Shattered remnants of a quadrangular courtyard castle raised for John Lord Neville of Raby (qv) under a licence of 1382. There were formerly two wards, but the standing remains are almost entirely confined to the inner ward, and particularly to the rectangular corner towers and gatehouse. The towers rose through four or five storeys and were linked by two- or three-storey domestic ranges. The gateway is on the E side set between two towers, one being the SE corner tower. Above the entrance a line of heraldic shields, implies a date of after 1402. There was a first-floor hall, probably on the N side, with an external staircase, and an associated kitchen in the NE Tower. The W range and towers would therefore have housed the more exclusive accommodation. There were lodgings in the S range. Sheriff Hutton is best compared with the contemporary Castle Bolton (qv), which gives some reason for suspecting the involvement of John Lewyn. Emery 1996, 390–3; Dennison 2005; Hislop 2007, 24–7 and 67–8.

SHIRBURN, Oxfordshire (Private). Quadrangular castle built for Warin Lord Lisle, under a licence to crenellate of 1377. Extensively rebuilt and/or cased in brick in the early C18, probably on the original plan, and given symmetrical fenestration. The castle has cylindrical corner towers and a gate tower in the centre of the W front. Shirburn is only 12 miles away from Abingdon Abbey where the master mason William Wynford was working at about the same time that the Shirburn project was in progress; it is possible that he was involved at Shirburn also. Emery 2006, 153–7.

SHORTFLATT TOWER, Northumberland (Holiday let at the time of writing). A licence to crenellate, which also included Aydon (qv), was issued to Robert de Reymes in 1305. Now, the principal sign of fortification is a three-storey solar tower attached to the end of a much-rebuilt hall range. The origins of the latter probably lie in the C13, while the tower dates from the late C14 or early C15. Few medieval details survive, but the ground storey has a segmental-arched barrel-vault. Raimes 1954 and 1955; Emery 1996, 137–8.

SHOTWICK, Cheshire (Accessible on foot from Saughall via Dingle Wood). Motte and bailey rebuilt in stone. Possibly an C11 foundation of Hugh d'Avranches, Earl of Chester. As part of the Earldom of Chester it came to the Crown in 1237. Only the earthworks are visible now, but the stone buildings of the motte were still in evidence in the C17. They comprised an irregular hexagonal curtain with round wall towers, and a twin-towered gateway to the SW facing the old course of the river Dee, then a major channel of communication. There was also a rectangular keep, foundations of which were uncovered by excavation in the C19. The plan of this stone enclosure on the motte was very similar to that of Bolingbroke Castle (qv), a work of Ranulph, Earl of Chester, dating from the 1220s, suggesting that the two are broadly contemporary. Swallow 2016.

SHRAWARDINE, Shropshire (Open access). Royal castle near the Welsh border within the lands of the FitzAlans, lords of Clun and Oswestry. The first documentary reference to Shrawardine Castle dates from 1165, when one Philip Helgot acknowledged that he owed castle guard at Shrawardine as his predecessors had done. Repairs were carried out in the reigns of Henry II, Richard I and John. Destroyed by the Welsh probably in 1215, and in 1221 the castle guard duties owed to Shrawardine were transferred to Montgomery. It was probably at this stage, then, that the castle came to the

FitzAlans, who held it in the 1240s, and who were responsible for its reconstruction; it remained in the family until 1583. In 1645 it underwent a short siege and was slighted by the Parliamentarians. The village of Shrawardine is on the E bank of the river Severn, and the castle lies to the NE of the village, part of Montford Parish Millennium Green. The focus is a low mound, a motte or ringwork. There is an inner bailey to the E and N, outer baileys to the NE and S, and house platforms to the W. The mound retains elements of masonry; two mounds to the S may represent the former flanking towers of a gateway. Auden 1895, 120–41; Duckers 2006, 141–4.

SHREWSBURY, Shropshire (Open). A motte and bailey first mentioned in 1069, Shrewsbury Castle must have been established very soon after the Conquest. Subsequently it came to Roger of Montgomery, Earl of Shrewsbury, who created an outer bailey. In 1102, the English estates of Earl Robert de Bellême were seized by the King, and Shrewsbury became a royal castle. During the C12 a stone curtain wall was built around the inner bailey. In 1239–41 Henry III had a new chamber and tower built, generally considered to be the existing King's Hall on the N side of the inner bailey. The motte was suffering from erosion by *c.*1225, and *c.*1270 the timber great tower collapsed. Following the conquest of Gwynedd and the subjugation of Wales in the late C13, the castle's military significance was diminished, and the fabric was allowed to deteriorate. Shrewsbury was refortified by the Royalists in the 1640s at which time a barbican was built in front of the bailey gate and a postern made in the N wall. After the Restoration it was alienated from the Crown. In the late C18 Thomas Telford remodelled the King's Hall and built the summer house known as Laura's Tower on top of the motte.

The town of Shrewsbury is built within a loop of the river Severn, and the castle was built at the neck of the peninsula at the NE corner of the Saxon *burh*. The motte is directly above the W bank of the river and the inner bailey lies to the NW of it. The now-vanished outer bailey lay to the S, its E side roughly traceable from the SW corner of the inner bailey across the front of the former grammar school (now library) and along School Gardens. It then crossed Castle Street, where the gateway stood, and followed the slope above Water Lane and the river, utilizing the defences of the *burh* to the E and W. It contained the chapel of St Nicholas, demolished in 1869 and a Presbyterian church built on the site (at the time of writing, a hotel).

Now the approach to the castle is from Castle Street (just beyond the site of the chapel) where it veers off to the N, the lane to the castle continuing the NE–SW orientation of Castle Street's more southerly section; it extends through part of the outer bailey that has remained open. At the head of the lane is the C12 gateway, a simple opening through the curtain wall of two continuous roll-moulded orders preceded by the C17 barbican, which extended across the ditch. To the L (W) is a slightly smaller C12 arch, through the curtain, evidently an insertion, said to have been relocated from the demolished chapel of St Nicholas, but not recognizable from old illustrations of the building.

So, into the inner ward. There is now no ditch between the motte and bailey, but the top of the counterscarp was picked up in an excavation in 2019. A path winds up the mound, now much depleted having lost a large section towards the river. Like Laura's Tower, a ring wall around the summit dates from the C18.

The King's Hall is the main medieval survival, even though it has been much altered through refenestration. It comprises a rectangular range with drum towers at the outer (N) angles, and probably formed a chamber block with first-floor residence and undercroft. The Gothic first-floor windows date from the late C18 but are reworkings of the originals. The first-floor entrance dates from the 1920s but occupies the position of the C13 entrance. Tree-ring dating of the roof timbers has given a date of 1657–8. Radford 1957–8; Brown *et al.* 1963, 834–7.

SIZERGH, Westmorland (Open – NT). Fortified manor house of the Stricklands, comprising a much-altered hall range with crosswings, the S wing taking the form of a four-storey solar tower. Substantial alterations were undertaken in the C16 when the long wings, which now frame the entrance (W) front, were added, and the interior remodelled. In the C18 the W front of the hall was brought forward in line with the solar tower.

The tower, which dates from the C14, is the principal relic of the medieval house. At 60ft × 40ft (18.3m × 12.2m) it is abnormally large for a solar tower; also unusual is the off-centre rectangular turret that extends from the S wall; its purpose uncertain, though possibly a garderobe turret with latrines in the thickness of the wall.

On the W face, awkwardly sandwiched between the late medieval second- and third-floor windows, is an elaborate achievement of arms within an arched recess with demi-figure stops and a trio of decapitated pinnacles. Beneath a helm with holly bush crest and mantling, a shield depicts the Deincourt arms quartered with those of Strickland, a combination reflecting the marriage *c*.1239 of William Strickland and Elizabeth Deincourt, who brought the manor with her. Possibly second quarter of the C14, though whether it is in its original position is uncertain.

Inside the hall, at the S end of the original W wall, is a pointed doorway into the former cross passage. On the S side of the ex-passage a round-arched doorway gives access to the basement of the tower and the spiral stair that communicated between floors. The tower basement is barrel-vaulted and divided by an inserted late medieval cross-wall. Otherwise, the interiors are largely of C16 character. Curwen 1889; Taylor 1889; Curwen 1913, 314–16; RCHME 1936; Emery 1996, 248–50; Perriam and Robinson 1998, 366–7.

SKIPSEA, Yorkshire East Riding (Open – EH). Unusual motte and bailey to the W of Skipsea village established soon after the Conquest by Drogo de Beuvrière, lord of Holderness. In 1221 Henry III ordered the castle to be slighted following the rebellion of the then castellan William de Forz, Earl of Aumale. The earthworks comprise a motte, possibly of Iron Age origin, surrounded by a ditch and outer bank, and a crescentic bailey, some 150 yards (137m) to the W, defined on the outer (W) side by a substantial rampart and outer ditch. The motte formerly stood within Skipsea Mere and was linked to the bailey by a wooden causeway, a channel extending between the two, and acting as a harbour, being accessible to and from the North Sea. I'Anson 1917.

SKIPTON, Yorkshire West Riding (Open). The foundation of Skipton Castle is attributed to Robert de Romille who, having been granted a pre-Conquest Bolton (Abbey) estate, moved the caput of his lands to Skipton, where he had found an advantageous site for a castle. Robert de Romille's heir was his daughter Cecilia from whom Skipton descended through the female line to the de Forz earls of Aumale and, in the absence of a male heir, to Aveline de Forz, wife of Edmund Crouchback. After Edmund's death in 1296, Skipton was acquired by the Crown, and in 1310 was granted to Robert First Baron Clifford (d. 1314), who, according to his descendant Lady Anne Clifford (1590–1676), 'was the chief builder of the most strong parts of Skipton Castle'. To him have been attributed the outer gatehouse and curtain and much of the inner ward. Improvements to the domestic accommodation of the inner ward were carried out under Henry, Tenth Baron Clifford (between 1485 and 1523), whose son, Henry, First Earl of Cumberland, added a new wing in the 1530s; Henry Clifford (Fifth Earl from 1641) remodelled the outer gatehouse c.1629. Held for the King during the Civil War, Skipton was rendered untenable by Parliament, an operation that involved partial demolition. It was restored by Lady Anne Clifford in 1657–9.

Perched on the edge of a ravine, which protects its N side and allows for the ready discharge of effluent, the castle comprises an outer and inner ward, though only the full extent of the latter is now apparent. Approached from the S, the outer gatehouse is a C17 remodelling of an early C14 construction, with twin drum towers on stepped plinths, of which only the lower parts survive. Straight ahead is the inner ward, a tightly planned, irregularly pentagonal enclosure with four round angle towers, rather reminiscent of Clifford Castle (qv), Robert Lord Clifford's birthplace. Changes in the masonry testify to Lady Anne's rebuilding, showing that the upper storeys of the towers had been demolished in the slighting. Attached to the R (E) is the First Earl's 1530s wing.

The approach to the gatehouse at the W end of the inner ward is now from the S rather than the W, past the largest of the wall towers, and up a staircase to an incongruous porch of c.1500, evidently the work of the Tenth Baron, now obscuring the gateway. The gatehouse, which has a pair of flanking drum towers, probably dates from the first half of the C13, incorporating elements of its C12 predecessor. On each side of the gate passage, towards its inner (E) end is a portcullis groove and then two closely set unmoulded segmental arches, the former springing from engaged semi-polygonal responds with C13 moulded capitals. The latter was closed by a gate and secured by a drawbar.

The rooms to each side of the passage were entered independently from the courtyard (since reduced in size), and each had its own staircase to the equally separate first-floor rooms. A staircase also leads from the N room to a cellar under the gate passage, possibly a former pit for a counterbalance drawbridge, vaulted over at a later period. At ground-floor level the N arrow loop has been blocked by the construction of the later C14 NW tower. On the S side the first-floor room gives access to a chamber over the gate passage which housed the portcullis mechanism. The courtyard (Conduit Court), which has a predominantly early C16 appearance, was probably remodelled by the Tenth Baron. The medieval apartments were in the N range overlooking the ravine.

In the outer ward W of the inner ward, is the knocked-about medieval chapel: two-bay nave and chancel in one, with clasping buttresses and a sacristy projecting from the N side. Opposed N and S pointed doors of two chamfered orders, pointed N, S and E windows the latter with restored C14 Decorated tracery. Renn 1975; Leach and Pevsner 2009, 705–8.

SLEAFORD, Lincolnshire (Open access). Site of a castle built by Alexander the Magnificent, Bishop of Lincoln, between 1123 and 1139 when it was captured by King Stephen, now reduced to earthworks. When Leland saw it in the mid C16 it was still in good repair, having a moat, a gatehouse with two portcullises, and a central great tower. The site lies within a roughly rectangular field bounded by King Edward Street to the W and by drainage dykes to the N, S and E. Within this area are the earthworks representing a moated quadrangular castle. The gatehouse was on the W side protected by a barbican and there was a stone curtain wall with corner towers of which only a fragment of the NE tower remains. Mahany and Roffe 1979.

SNODHILL, Peterchurch, Herefordshire (Open access). Motte and bailey at the N end of the Golden Valley at the heart of a well-preserved medieval landscape. Probably built in the 1060s by William FitzOsbern, Earl of Hereford, and held by Hugh l'Asne. When Hugh died in 1101, Snodhill came to Robert de Chandos, and the Chandos family held it until 1428. The castle was probably slighted during the Civil War. Roughly oval bailey with a motte to the E. Fragmentary remains of a curtain wall including wing walls extending up the motte, with D-shaped N and SE towers projecting from it. The motte is crowned by the vestiges of an irregularly polygonal keep generally assigned to *c*.1200, apparently on architectural grounds. A (partly conjectural) plan drawn up by the RCHME shows an irregular twelve-sided building with a western entrance flanked by two solid round towers, but the upstanding masonry is confined to the S side of the gateway and to SE corner of the keep. The constricted size of the building suggests a tower rather than a shell-keep. An examination of the remaining section of the entrance shows a vertical building break implying transition from a simple gateway to a twin-towered gatehouse. Bowden *et al.* 2017.

SOMERFORD, Wiltshire. See **GREAT SOMERFORD**.

SOMERTON, Lincolnshire (Private). Stone quadrilateral courtyard castle built for Anthony Bek (later Bishop of Durham), being licensed in 1281. Bek gifted the manor of Somerton to the King in 1309 and it remained a royal castle until the C16. A survey of 1525 found a castle roofless and decayed and by 1601 in ruin. During the next two to three decades the castle was made habitable again by the construction of a house adjoining the SE tower on the site of S range. The stone remains stand within a large oblong moated enclosure, its southern half protected with a wider outer moat and bank around the E, W and S sides. A much smaller moated site lies to the S. The best-preserved part of the medieval fabric is the SE tower (round, like all the towers) which rises through three storeys; only the ground floors of the SW and NE towers remain; the NW tower has been largely destroyed. The ground floors of the towers are polygonal with arched recesses around the walls, being covered by plain domical vaults to the S but a by a twelve-ribbed stellar vault in the NE tower, carried on a central pillar and corbels. Cruciform arrow loops in the SE tower and an adjoining fragment of curtain. Trollope, 1857; Brown *et al.* 1963, 838–9.

SOUTHAMPTON, Hampshire (Open access). Former motte and bailey first mentioned in 1153. Rebuilding of the curtain in stone probably took place in the late C12 and early C13. A new keep was built on the motte from 1378 according to the advice of the royal masons Henry Yevele and William Wynford. It was cylindrical and encircled by a mantlet with a barbican. A major piece of architecture, its demolition was a considerable loss to the city.

The castle occupied a roughly triangular site within the NW quadrant of the walled town, the motte at the SE angle. The motte has disappeared, its former position now marked by a large block of late C20 flats (Castle House), but the W curtain and much

Somerton: NE tower. From Turner and Parker 1851.

of the NE curtain remain, as well as the base of the E gateway. This latter, on the W side of Castle Way, giving access to Castle Lane, was flanked by twin drum towers, the bases of which remain. Attached to the R (N) is the rather interesting C13 NE curtain, which curves around in a quarter circle to meet the W curtain. The rubble-built lower part, which comprises a pointed arcade, was formerly hidden within a rampart; the upper section, which rose above the rampart, has a battered base and is constructed of superior quality masonry.

The W curtain, which forms the middle section of the town wall, probably dates from the late C12. It has five chunky rectangular buttresses; between Nos 3 and 4 (counting from N to S), set between two smaller buttresses, is the late C14 water gate, with four-centred arch. To the L (N) of the gate a round-arched window to a former building inside the castle. Behind the wall to the R (S) of the gate are the remains of Castle Hall, a late C12 building with a vault. Just beyond, a modern staircase gives access to the wall walk of castle and town leading N. Brown, *et al*. 1963, 840–4; Oxley 1986.

SOUTH MIMMS, London and Middlesex (Private). Motte and bailey excavated in the 1960s, possibly the castle built by Geoffrey de Mandeville *c*.1141 and destroyed following his rebellion in 1143. Now immediately adjacent to the A1 (M) which runs through a possible outer bailey. Oval motte with kidney-shaped bailey to the E, both motte and bailey enclosed by a continuous ditch system (partly quarried away to the S) and the bailey by an inner bank; a gap on the E side of the bailey marks the site of the gateway. A hollow way formerly extended SE from the gateway to a ford over Mimmshall Brook. Excavation of the motte revealed that construction began with the raising of a low clay bank denoting the perimeter of the mound base. A timber tower was built inside, chalk rubble piled up around its lower storey and then a timber revetment constructed on top of the bank and construction of the mound around the tower completed by further dumps of earth. Kent *et al*. 2013.

SOUTH WINGFIELD, Derbyshire. See **WINGFIELD MANOR HOUSE**.

SPOFFORTH, Yorkshire West Riding (Open access – EH). An under-researched, unexcavated fortified manor house for which Henry de Percy was granted a licence to crenellate in 1308. In the mid C19 John Parker noted the remains of a courtyard house, but today, the only part of the house to survive above ground level is the W range, which formed the main residential block. The manor house occupied a rocky platform, outcropping to the W; it is against this outcrop that the split-level main block was built. The oldest part of the building is the early C13 four-bay undercroft of the great hall. In the late C13 a large two-storey chamber block was added to the N end, and during the first half of the C15, the great hall was remodelled.

Looking at the range from the E (the position of the former courtyard), the great hall is on the L (S) and the blind wall of the chamber block is to the R (N), its northern end breaking forward. The hall has tall windows of two cinquefoil-arched lights with returned hood moulds, and, in the second bay from the L (S), a large pointed doorway with moulded surround, the entrance from the courtyard to the hall. To the L of the hall doorway is a segmental-arched entrance from the service area at the S end of the hall into a now vanished S range. A third doorway at the RH (N) end of the hall led from the dais to a vanished wing of the chamber block.

Walking anticlockwise around the chamber block, a small wing incorporating a latrine turret extends from the NW angle, then a chunky pointed ground-floor window of three chamfered orders with trefoil-cusped light, two large windows to the upper chamber separated by a pilaster buttress, and at the NE corner the polygonal stair turret. Around the corner the rather imposing E front, difficult to appreciate in the restricted space, but perhaps seen to great advantage from the associated park, before the railway and the trees intervened. The chamber block to the L (N) has a good window – pointed, of two moulded orders with foliate capitals; some of the tracery is preserved – two trefoil-cusped lights with an encircled quatrefoil in the central spandrel.

Inside, the E side of the hall undercroft is the natural rock. Two staircases, one C13 (S) and one C14 (N), have been cut into it, both ascending to the courtyard. In the centre are the octagonal bases of a row of columns, inserted in the C14 to carry rib-vaulting, the corbelled responds for which survive in the walls. Odd-looking embrasures to the undercroft windows with shouldered semi-circular arches, possibly the result of a late C13 widening of the embrasures. At the N end a blocked window and a wide segmental-arched opening to the chamber block. The chamber block was accessed entirely from the hall and its undercroft and was divided into two unequal parts by a transverse wall, the most important room being to the N, so therefore, a chamber and antechamber. There was also a small inner chamber with a latrine at both levels. Emery 1996, 399–401.

STAFFORD, Staffordshire. **Castlehill** (D). Site of a castle established by William I *c.*1071 on the western edge of the town next to the river Sow. All visible traces have disappeared, but excavation of a site within the grounds of Stafford College on the S side of Broad Street in 2003 uncovered a section of C11 ditch which was identified as part of the royal castle defences. The castle appears to have been situated outside the defences of the Saxon *burh*, but subsequently incorporated within the later medieval defences. Cuttler *et al.* 2009.

Castlechurch (Open access). Motte with two baileys established on the outskirts of Stafford in the late C11 or early C12. In 1348 Ralph, First Earl Stafford, lowered the motte and built a great tower on top of it under the master mason John of Burcestre. In the 1640s Stafford Castle was slighted by the Parliamentarians, an operation that included the demolition of the keep, which was afterwards pilfered for stone. An attempt to rebuild the great tower on the C14 foundations was underway between 1811 and 1817, but only the E end of the main block and its two corner towers were ever completed. In 1962 the C19 work was partially demolished for safety reasons.

The castle is on the top of a hill to the W of the town. The earthworks are substantial: an eastern motte and a western inner bailey are supplemented by an outer bailey to the SE beyond which (SE of) are the earthworks of an attached settlement. The current approach extends along the SW side of the village site and outer bailey, but the original entrance was from the SE, through the settlement and outer bailey into the inner bailey. The only building to remain above ground level is the great tower; most of the visible stonework dates from the C19 rebuilding, although some C14 elements can be recognized. The plan is rectangular with octagonal corner turrets and a semi-octagonal turret in the centre of the SW front. There was a superficial relationship to the great tower of Dudley (qv) but the internal plan was more complex and the tower has a closer kinship with some of the compact fortified residences that were being developed from the later C13 onwards, notably along the Scottish border. Hislop 1993; Darlington 2001; Soden 2007.

STANSTED MOUNTFITCHET, Essex (Open). Ringwork and bailey of unknown date, but possibly built by Robert Gernon de Montfichet. His descendant, Richard de Montfichet, was part of the baronial opposition to King John, which resulted in the destruction of the castle. The ringwork is surrounded by a bank and ditch, with the entrance from the sub-oval bailey to the E; this latter is also banked and ditched but eroded on the S side. The RCHME recorded traces of a flint rubble wall along the top of the ringwork bank, and vestiges of a central circular feature, probably a round keep, but the earthwork has been obscured in recent years by the development of the castle as a 'Norman village', which has involved the construction of perimeter palisades and timber buildings, including a 'church' on the site of the putative keep. RCHME 1916, 276–7.

STOGURSEY, Somerset (Landmark Trust property open to guests only but the exterior can be visited on foot). Ringwork with two baileys, the ringwork subsequently converted to create a low mound with stone defences. First mentioned in 1204, but probably in existence by 1166 when William de Courcy held the Barony of Stogursey. In 1224 it was held by Falkes de Bréauté against the King and subsequently granted to Hugh de Neville, who in 1233 was ordered to refortify the castle.

The castle complex includes the moated former ringwork, a narrow bailey curving around the SE side and, further to the E, a larger and later bailey. The conversion of the ringwork into a platform involved filling the enclosure, probably with material obtained from excavating the surrounding moat; when this happened is open to question, but the C12 seems likely.

That may be the date of the earliest stonework including the base of a large rectangular tower on the W side of the enceinte that was excavated in the 1980s; however, much of the masonry is later. The great gatehouse to the E, the base of which survives incorporated into a C17 cottage, was a substantial building with a battered plinth and twin drum towers, probably C13 or C14. A similar date can be applied to the large round tower projecting from the E curtain that replaced the excavated C12 tower. Dunning 1992, 136–7, and 1995, 45–7; Guy *et al.* 2010–11, 119–25.

STOKESAY, Shropshire (Open – EH). Fortified manor house built for the wool merchant and moneylender Laurence of Ludlow between 1281, when he acquired the property, and 1294, when he died; a licence to crenellate was granted in 1291, and tree-ring dates suggest that this marks the end of building operations rather than the beginning. For the rest of the medieval period, it remained largely unaltered, but building work was in progress again in the 1640s and included the present gatehouse. Stokesay was briefly besieged during the Civil War and was slighted in 1647, although this seems to have amounted to no more than the demolition of the curtain down to courtyard level. In 1830 a fire destroyed the floors and roof in the great tower, but much has survived from the C13, making this one of the best preserved of England's medieval houses.

The current approach to the castle from the car park (on the opposite (W) side of the road) through the churchyard, provides a good opportunity to view the medieval buildings from the exterior. At the S end of the complex is the S Tower (or great tower) its unique plan based on an octagon and two dodecagons, the latter forming

Stokesay: Great hall and solar tower. From Turner and Parker 1851.

twin prows projecting beyond the curtain wall towards the SW, strategically placed to face N-bound traffic along the old road from Ludlow to Shrewsbury. The idiosyncratic form was probably an offshoot of developments at Edward I's north Walian castles, notably Caernarfon and Denbigh.

An obliquely positioned three-storey (originally two-storey) building links the tower with the main residential block ranged along the W front; it comprises a single-storey great hall of four gabled bays flanked by the solar block (R) and the N tower (L), both under hipped roofs. The N tower has a rather extraordinary timber-framed upper storey oversailing the stone walls and carried on corbelled posts and braces. This structure is substantially C13 and related to the defensive hoards (none of which survive) that once adorned many English castles.

The small sub-rectangular enclosure is entered from the E via an ornate timber-framed gatehouse tree-ring dated to 1640/41. Passing through the gateway one is confronted by the hall range, and, to the L (S), the back of the semi-independent S tower. The three large hall windows rising into the gables are all of two trefoil-arched lights with a circle over beneath a pointed arch. The fourth gable to the R (N) is blind but contains the entrance.

Inside, one is able to capture something of the atmosphere of the Middle Ages; a comparatively unaltered late C13 great hall with its original cruck-framed roof. The feet of the crucks were carried on stone corbels, raised in height as the timber has decayed. Set against each end wall is a truss of aisled form, also on corbels, which supports the ends of the purlins. Towards the upper (S) end, a polygonal arrangement of stones in the floor is the medieval open hearth, a feature that rarely survives. There is another rarity at the lower (N) end: set against the wall is a C13 timber staircase leading to the upper rooms of the N Tower.

A doorway at ground-floor level gives access to the tower basement. Lit by narrow loops it was probably a service/storage room. A pit in the N turret may have been for the evacuation of slops into the moat, but there are also traces of a painted frieze along the top of the walls suggesting a less menial use too. Wall posts and braced horizontals carry the first-floor beams. The first floor contains a two-room suite, probably a C17 conversion from a single chamber, the inner room of which is floored with reset C13 tiles, has a larger-than-normal window with an ogee arch and an inserted fireplace. The N turret has been converted into a latrine with a chute towards the W. On the second floor is a single room with a large fireplace in the S wall: fillet-moulded colonettes with moulded capitals support double corbels, which in turn carried a timber-framed hood of which only the base remains. The N turret has been turned into a bay window by insertion of C17 leaded panes.

At the upper end of the hall a doorway leads into the solar block. The ground-floor room was divided in the C17 but originally contained a single space with access to a cellar directly underneath and to a room in the link block, possibly a strongroom for valuables. In the E wall of the solar block a doorway gave onto the foot of a covered flight of steps leading to a first-floor porch and thence into the upper room of the block. This is largely Jacobean in character following a C17 refurbishment but retains its C13 E and W windows. In the N wall two windows allowed scrutiny of the great hall. A doorway in the SW corner originally led onto the wall walk but now gives access to a room resulting from a heightening of the link block in the C17.

The porch also led (across a bridge) to the three-storey South Tower, which contains more prestigious private quarters, the floors being linked by a mural staircase that led all the way up to the roof. The two upper storeys each comprise a single spacious well-lit room with a fireplace, window seats and a latrine. In fact, these seem to be the only rooms to have been provided with latrines in the C13; close stools may have been the rule. At roof level are merlons pierced by cruciform arrow loops, and two cylindrical chimney stacks. Cordingley 1963; Emery 2000, 574–6; Newman and Pevsner 2006, 609–14.

SULGRAVE, Northamptonshire (Open access). Ringwork excavated in the 1960s and 1970s, when a number of buildings were uncovered within the enclosure, including a hall and putative kitchen. The dating evidence for the site suggested continuity of occupation from the late C10 to the mid C12. The chronology of the defences is uncertain, but their origins may predate the Conquest. The ringwork is located immediately W of the Church of St James and comprises an oval enclosure some 80ft × 50ft (24.4m × 15.3m) surrounded by a ditch and inner bank; the entrance was to the NW. Davison 1977; RCHME 1982, 139–40.

SUTTON VALENCE, Kent (Open access – EH). Keep and courtyard castle of which the visible remains are the ruins of a C12 small square keep with clasping angle buttresses and a forebuilding to the N. The keep stood at the southern extremity of the castle; fragments of the W curtain and a round tower on the E side were noted in 1902. Excavation of the keep in the 1950s suggested an occupation range of c.1150–1300. Sands 1902.

SWERFORD, Oxfordshire (Open access). Motte and bailey immediately N of the village church and overlooking a crossing of the river Swere. Possibly raised by Roger d'Oilly at around the same time as Ascot d'Oilly; pottery excavated from the motte suggests a construction date in the mid C12. The motte is built of limestone lumps. The roughly kidney-shaped bailey, which lies to the S of the motte, is defined by an inner bank of earth faced with limestone and a substantial ditch. Page 1925, 326–7; Renn 1973, 318.

SWINESHEAD (The Manwar Ings), Lincolnshire (Open access). Concentric motte and bailey in existence by 1186 and probably founded by one of the de Gresley lords of the manor. It lies ½ mile NE of Swineshead village church and close to Swineshead Abbey. The large low motte is surrounded by a moat and circular bailey, and the bailey by an outer moat. A causeway across the moat to the E probably marks the position of the former entrance. Salter 2002a, 63.

TAMWORTH, Staffordshire (Open). Motte and bailey probably established by Robert le Despencer on the orders of William I soon after the Conquest. For most of the C12 and C13 Tamworth and its castle were held by the Marmion family, though a falling-out with King John resulted in an order to destroy the castle. Rebuilding included restoration of the shell-keep, the raising of the N range within it, and the construction of the gateway. The chronology is uncertain, but some rebuilding was being carried out by Philip Marmion in the 1260s, for which, as a supporter of Henry III during the Barons' War, he received royal grants. Throughout the C14 Tamworth was held by the Frevilles, and in 1423 the castle came via marriage to Thomas Ferrers; it was Thomas who was responsible for constructing the timber-framed great hall within the shell-keep. Later generations of Ferrers were responsible for a major remodelling of the shell-keep in the late C16 and C17 including the construction of the S range; in the late C18 George Marquess Townsend undertook remodelling of the N and S elevations. In 1899 the castle became a museum.

Raised on the S side of the Anglo-Saxon *burh* founded by Ethelfleda in 913 and overlooking a crossing of the river Tame to the S. Motte to the W, with bailey to the E, formerly protected to the N and E by a ditch (now largely built over) and to the S by the fall of the land towards the river. Excavation on the eastern edge of the bailey revealed evidence for timber-framed defences. However, at least parts of the fortifications were in stone. The entrance to the bailey was from the Market Place to the N, where the excavated remains of the C13 twin drum-towered gatehouse can be seen. To the R (W), on entering the bailey, is the back of the N curtain which displays a fine example of herringbone masonry, the tiers alternating with horizontal levelling courses.

This wall supports the path to the top of the motte; looming up in front of the approach, breaking forward from the shell-keep is a three-storey tower, in fact a small keep with battered plinth and pilaster buttresses, apparently C12 and contemporary with the shell-keep. A little further along, the gabled C17 Warder's Lodge and next to it the entrance, a C13 segmental-pointed arch. Then a stretch of blank curtain, two phases clearly visible, the rubble coursing of the lower part contrasting with the larger blocks of the upper section, possibly a legacy of partial demolition in 1215 and subsequent rebuilding. Next, Townsend's C18 S front, then another expanse of curtain pierced by two loops of a mural passage, and, further along, a blocked flat-lintelled postern of uncertain date, but encroached upon by a late C16 bay window base, a remnant of a scheme for the N front that was replaced by more of Townsend's Gothic windows.

The E entrance leads into a small courtyard (the shell is crowded with buildings). Directly in front is the C16 porch to the S range and great hall, brick with ashlar surround, the four-centred entrance arch flanked by pairs of engaged classical columns. Set back to the R (N) is the C15 great hall, its timber frame largely replaced by small-pane glazing from plinth to eaves. Inside, however, is one of Staffordshire's

Tamworth: Approach to the shell keep (C12 and C13).

most significant timber-framed buildings, which dendrochronology has dated to *c*.1440. It has close-studded walls, tie beam trusses, tenoned purlins and cusped wind braces.

At the R (N) end of the hall is the C16 brick porch to the N range. The range itself probably has C13 origins, but is very much altered, though a small area of stonework is visible towards the courtyard. Opposite, in the S curtain, a doorway with mutilated lintel leads to a mural staircase terminating in a latrine. Another latrine passage, in the SW curtain, is now entered from the S range. A large rounded segmental-arched doorway, evidently a C13 or C14 insertion, gives access to the basement of the keep, a high-ceilinged room devoid of facilities. On one of the merlons along the SW wall walk a lump, probably the base of a truncated sculpture or pinnacle. Meeson 1978–9 and 1983; McNeil 1987–8; Higham 2015, 103–15.

TARSET, Northumberland (Visible from the road). Fortified manor house for which John Comyn was granted a licence to crenellate in 1267. It was burnt out in 1525 by the men of Tynedale and said to be in ruins in 1538. Built on a promontory overlooking Tarset Burn, the castle consisted of a fortified hall house within a ditched enclosure. The plan of the house was rectangular with a rectangular tower at each corner, not dissimilar to that of Dally (qv), one mile to the SW. The significance of the building is that it is one of the earliest datable examples of a towered hall house, a type of fortified dwelling that gained a degree of popularity in the late C13 and C14. Dodds 1940, 242–8.

TATTERSHALL, Lincolnshire (Open – NT). A licence to crenellate was granted to Robert de Tatteshal in 1231, but Tattershall Castle is notable for having been the principal seat of Ralph Lord Cromwell (1393–1456), Lord Treasurer to Henry VI, who rebuilt the C13 castle in brick between 1434 and 1450. Remains of the earlier castle were uncovered during excavations by Lord Curzon in 1912–14, and suggest that the C15 inner ward closely follows the plan of its predecessor, which consisted of an irregularly polygonal enclosure with rounded wall towers, not unlike Bolingbroke (qv), some 10 miles to the E.

The inner ward is moated around, and in the C15 the castle was also surrounded by an outer moat with a feeder arm to the inner moat on the N side. The outer moat is now truncated to the S, but the extant arms contain two L-shaped enclosures, the outer ward (W and N) and middle ward (E and N), divided by the feeder arm. Access was from the N into the outer ward, and then across the feeder arm through a gatehouse into the middle ward. The moats, which are a major feature of the castle, together with other channels farther afield, were the work of Cromwell's water engineer, Matthew Dyker.

Admittance to the site is now from the NE into the middle ward. Here, on the LH (SE) side of the path there is a much-restored C15 brick building known as the Guardhouse, a two-storey domestic building now housing the NT shop. On the RH (NW) side of the path are some foundations of a brick range, and also of the middle gatehouse, which leads to the bridge over the feeder arm of the moat to the outer ward. On the RH (N) side of the outer ward was the outer gatehouse, and straight ahead, NW of the great tower, the C15 stable block of which the S gable and the E wall are upstanding.

Back to the middle ward and across the moat to the inner ward. The inner moat, which was scoured out by Matthew Dyker's men in 1434 is revetted in brick, a sizeable

Tattershall: Great tower from the E.

task in itself. Traces of the C13 stone wall towers remain in the centre of the S side, and to each side of the great tower, which extends into the moat on the W side of the courtyard. Next to the SW tower are the bases of the C15 brick kitchens.

The dominating spectacle is of course the great tower, a five-storey (including basement) rectangular block, plus a gallery, and a parapet carried on corbelled machicolations; projecting octagonal corner turrets rise above the battlements. The tower is built of brick laid to English bond, which makes a striking contrast with the limestone ashlar of the doorways, windows, string courses and machicolations. The great tower now appears isolated, but in the C15, in front of and parallel with it, was the stone hall of the pre-Cromwell castle, with a kitchen building at its N end. Pentices led from the hall to and across the front of the tower, where three doorways gave access (from R to L) to the ground floor, basement, and staircase in the SE turret from which the upper floors were reached.

The internal planning of the tower is comparatively simple, each floor comprising a large central room communicating with small chambers in the turrets and/or E wall. The vaulted basement was largely for storage; above this the main rooms have been interpreted as (from ground to third floor) parlour, hall, audience chamber and privy chamber. Each had a large, elaborately carved fireplace. At first- and third-floor levels the entrance is from a small rib-vaulted lobby directly next to the staircase. That to the second-floor audience chamber is more ceremonial, being via a rib-vaulted passage that extends through the length of the E wall. The stair continues to the roof, where the alure is carried on an arcaded gallery, the latter giving access to the functioning machicolation slots. False machicolations fulfilling a purely decorative function carry the parapets of the corner turrets.

There are affinities of scale and planning with the late C14 great gatehouse of Thornton Abbey, a partly brick building 50 miles distant to the N. The brick-maker was Baldwin Docheman, a Fleming or German, who has sometimes been identified as the architect, but an alternative candidate is the mason John Botiller of Toddington, who in 1435 was in charge of building works at the royal hunting lodge of Clipstone, Nottinghamshire, 40 miles to the W of Tattershall. A mason of the same name and his two servants were paid for work at Tattershall during the 1434–5 season. Curzon and Tipping 1929; Simpson 1960; Emery 2000, 308–16; Marshall 2021.

TAUNTON, Somerset (Open access to outer bailey; museum within part of the inner bailey). In origin a house of the bishops of Winchester, fortified by Bishop William Giffard (1100–29) or Bishop Henry de Blois (from 1138), one of whom was probably responsible for the great tower or keep, of which only the footings remain. In 1644 Taunton endured a siege by Royalist forces, and in 1651 Parliament ordered its slighting. Charles II gave orders for its demolition, which did not prevent Judge Jeffreys from holding his Bloody Assize in the castle hall. In 1874 half of the inner ward and its buildings were purchased by the Somerset Archaeological and Natural History Society and now house the Museum of Somerset.

The extent of the castle is broadly represented by the old mill stream next to the river Tone (N), Corporation Street (S), North Street (E) and the bus station (W). It was surrounded by a moat, a branch of which also divided the castle into an outer (S) and inner (N) bailey. The outer bailey had opposed entrances on the line of Castle Green; the W gate has disappeared, but the E gate survives at the W end of Castle Bow and is now part of the Castle Hotel: C13, rectangular with outer segmental arch of two chamfered orders, and behind it a portcullis and vaulted gate passage. The upper storeys date from the C19. This gateway leads into the inner bailey, currently a large open public space approximating to its medieval dimensions but lacking any structural remains from that period.

The buildings of the inner bailey survive to a far greater extent, mainly around the S, W and NW sides, albeit much altered by C19 refacing and refenestration. In the centre of the S front is the C13 two-storey inner gatehouse with segmental-pointed gate arch and portcullis, the upper storey refurbished in 1496 by Bishop Langton, who placed his arms on the front of the building. To the L, at the SW corner, is a C13 drum tower, and, around the corner on the W side, the boxy Bishops' *camera*, C12 in origin, retaining pilaster buttresses, with a square turret at the NE corner. Next to the *camera* on the N side, also with pilaster buttresses, is the great hall. Built as a first-floor hall, it was converted into a ground-floor hall in the C13, but later alterations have eradicated most its medieval character. Inside the courtyard there is no sign of its C12 origin, and it is no more (indeed less) than a medieval shell. To the E of the gateway is Castle House, which probably began as a late C15 two-storey lodging range. Tree-ring sampling of the arched-braced, cambered-collar roof suggest that the timber was felled *c.*1480–2, during Bishop Courtenay's arch-episcopate.

The other half of the inner bailey is part of the Castle Hotel garden. It contains the footings of the keep discovered by excavation in the 1920s, estimated to have been around 90ft (8.4m) square with a high plinth of eighteen chamfered offsets. Webster 2016.

THERFIELD, Hertfordshire (D). Motte and bailey in a field NW of the Church of St Mary, excavated in 1958 by Martin Biddle; the bailey defences were subsequently levelled. Therfield was a manor of the Abbey of Ramsey. Excavated finds and historical circumstance pointed to a date in the 1140s; Biddle suggested that the castle was built to defend the village against the ravages of Geoffrey de Mandeville (d. 1144). A small motte to the E was separated from the rectangular E–W aligned bailey by a ditch, and the bailey was defended by ditches and counterscarp banks. A continuation of the earthworks to the S denote the village defences. Biddle 1964.

THETFORD (Castle Hill), Norfolk (Open access). Motte and bailey dominating the medieval town and controlling the crossings over the rivers Thet and Little Ouse. Probably founded by Roger Bigod in the late C11, within a prehistoric fort. It was one of Hugh Bigod's castles confiscated by Henry II in 1157 and demolished in 1173. Impressively large and steep motte (the second highest in England), with bailey to the E contained by a double bank and ditch to the N. Everson and Jecock 1999.

THIRLWALL Northumberland (Open access). Tower house based on a hall and chamber block arrangement. Sited on a spur overlooking Tipalt Burn, some 100 yards N of Hadrian's Wall, the tower was constructed mainly of Roman masonry. First mentioned as a castle in 1369, when it was held by John de Thirlwall, and so described too in 1415; architectural dating evidence is sparse, but an early to mid C14 date for the tower is probable. In good repair in 1542, it was probably abandoned after the Civil War, when it was occupied by a Scottish garrison. In 1831 the greater part of the E wall collapsed, taking with it the NE turret.

Built to an L-shaped plan comprising a three-storey main block with projecting square corner turrets at the N end (of which only the NW one survives), and a four-storey solar tower projecting from the S end of the E front. The remains sit on a chamfered plinth, but the walls are otherwise unarticulated; the windows are mostly small rectangular lights with chamfered jambs. Only a fragment of the entrance (E) front remains, the gateway having been in the lost northern end. All that survives of the entrance is a remnant of the S jamb, but it was secured by an unusually substantial draw bar. To the R (N) of the entrance a staircase in the N wall extends between first- and second-floor levels. The interior was unvaulted apart from a pyramidal dome over the basement of the NW turret, and the timber floors were carried on offsets and corbels. Each floor had a large hall-like room in the main block and a chamber in the SE wing. Several openings retain shouldered lintels. Bates 1891, 323–8; Emery 1996, 140–1; Rushworth and Carlton 2004.

THORNHAM, Kent. See **THURNHAM**.

THURNHAM (Thornham, Godard's Castle), Kent (Open access). Ringwork (or motte) and bailey sited on a spur of the South Downs overlooking the Pilgrim Way. In existence by *c*.1215–19. The ringwork has a ditch and inner bank to the N and W and formerly carried a ring wall, or shell-keep. A rectangular bailey to the W was enclosed by flint rubble walls of which remains of the northern stretch survives to a height of *c*.10ft (3m); it incorporates the remains of a gatehouse at the E end. Clark 1884, 492–3.

TICKHILL, Yorkshire West Riding (Private – annual open day only). Motte and bailey rebuilt in stone. Established by Roger de Busli by 1088 as the caput of what was to become the Honour of Tickhill. In 1102 it was in the hands of Robert of Bellême from whom it was confiscated by Henry I. The construction of the keep was underway in 1178–80. From 1372 it was part of the Duchy of Lancaster. The keep was demolished in 1648.

The castle comprises a motte formed from a natural hill and a kidney-shaped bailey to the W of it, the two elements being surrounded by a continuous moat. Entry is from the W via a square two-storey gatehouse of late C11 date. Semi-circular gate arch of two square orders obscured by C15 barbican walls (cf. Tutbury [qv], another Duchy property). Above the entrance, the first-floor string acts as a base for four triangular panels resembling pediments, each containing a chequer-board pattern, of which each square bears a saltire in relief. The gatehouse is of the 'hall' type, i.e., there is no gate passage as such, simply an open space at entry level, generally an early arrangement (cf. Ludlow and Richmond [qv]).

Of great interest are the remains of a late C12 tower keep on top of the motte, even though little more than the foundations remain. These, however, show that it was a rather unusual building. The plan was hendecagonal (eleven-sided) on a circular plinth with a pilaster buttress at each angle. The geometrical basis of the plan is best compared with that of Orford keep (qv) of the 1160s, another circle-based tower. Clark 1884, 2: 494–9; Brown *et al*. 1963, 844–5.

TINTAGEL, Cornwall (Open – EH). Whatever the truth behind its renown as the birthplace of 'King' Arthur, there seems to be little doubt that Tintagel did contain an important Dark Age residence, most likely a fortress of the C5 and C6 kings of Dumnonia. Its defensive potential was obvious: a precipitous peninsular almost entirely surrounded by the sea and attached to the mainland only by a narrow peninsula. The Dumnonians improved upon this natural fortress by cutting a ditch (the 'Great Ditch') across the isthmus to control access. In the 1230s, perhaps inspired by the Arthurian associations, but no doubt also by the tactical advantages of the site, Richard, Earl of Cornwall (d. 1272), acquired the site and subsequently built a castle there, incorporating elements of the Dumnonian defences. On the death of Richard's son in 1300 the castle passed to the Crown, and in 1337 to the Black Prince, on his being created Duke of Cornwall. In the C15 it was allowed to decay.

Viewed dispassionately as architecture the castle remains may seem disappointing, and were perhaps never very imposing, but they are imbued with the romance and spectacle engendered by the legends, antiquity and wild beauty of the site. The castle was built around three wards, two on the mainland and one on the island, being connected by a bridge. A long narrow barbican was flanked on the L (W) by a cliff on which the upper ward is sited, and on the R (E) by a wall, on the other side of which is the Dark Age Great Ditch. At the end of the approach a gatehouse led into the lower ward, a quadrilateral enclosure (once extending further to the N and W) with small square towers at the NE and SE angles. Access to the upper ward was via a staircase up the side of the rock. The enclosure formerly extended further to the N, but, like the lower ward, has been truncated by collapse into the sea.

Originally, the isthmus gave direct access to the island, but erosion later necessitated the construction of a bridge, which led to an inner gatehouse, no longer extant, because, as on the landward side, landfalls have truncated the inner ward. An irregularly-shaped ward is enclosed by a curtain wall with square towers to E and NE. The main building is the hall, first built by Richard of Cornwall, possibly on the site of a Dark Age palace; its S end has disappeared down the cliff. Richard's hall was abandoned in the 1330s and rebuilt to reduced proportions *c.*1340 within the walls of the original building. A contemporary two-storey residential block lies a little further to the W. Scattered about the peninsula are further groups of ruined buildings of Dark Age date, but largely uncertain function. Thomas 1993; Batey and Holder 2019.

TITCHMARSH, Northamptonshire (Visible from the road). Quadrangular castle raised for John Lord Lovell under a licence of 1304. Described as ruinous in 1363 and now represented only by earthworks to the S of High Street. These comprise a moat surrounding a rectangular enclosure with a linked fishpond at the SE corner. Excavation in 1887 uncovered the foundations of stone buildings including a curtain wall with pentagonal corner towers. Dryden 1892; RCHME 1975, 99–100.

TIVERTON, Devon (Open). Traditionally founded in 1107, by the Redvers family, who held the castle until 1293, it was remodelled by the Courtenays from 1297 onwards, and the medieval remains are predominantly of the first half of the C14. Situated to the N of the Church of St Peter, on the edge of a cliff above the river Exe, the layout is irregularly quadrangular, with small round towers at the NW and SE angles and more substantial rectangular towers to the SW and the middle of the W curtain. Access is from the town to the E via a rectangular outer gatehouse which projects from the E curtain, being served by a polygonal stair turret at the NW corner. The Bucks' drawing of 1734 shows that it was formerly two-storied (now reduced to one) beneath a parapet carried on corbelled machicolations, and that there was a latrine turret at the SW with access from the heated first-floor room. The roof has been tree-ring dated to 1356. Like the Neville Gateway at Raby (qv) this outer gatehouse is built in front of an earlier gateway through a domestic range. It represents the completion of the medieval castle. Emery 2006, 650–5.

TONBRIDGE, Kent (Open). Motte and bailey rebuilt in stone, best known for its C13 great gatehouse. William I granted the lordship of Tonbridge to Richard FitzGilbert, patriarch of the later de Clare lords, and builder of the castle first mentioned in 1088, when it was held against William Rufus. The castle sits on a spur above the river Medway commanding a crossing, and now overlooking the bridge that carries the High Street over the river. The outer bailey lay to the N of the motte, occupying much of the area now enclosed by the road known as The Slade, but there are no visible remains. The inner bailey lies to the SW of the motte.

Entry to the inner bailey is through the great gatehouse, the exemplar of what has been dubbed the 'Tonbridge-style gatehouse', a type better known in Wales, in which a pair of large flanking drum towers is coupled with a substantial rectangular residential block, containing the gate passage and equipped with a pair of staircases usually within separate turrets. The form is largely confined to the last quarter of the C13 and the first quarter of the C14. Estimates of the date of Tonbridge itself range from *c.*1250 to *c.*1320, but, recently, a thorough and convincing argument has been made for the 1290s. The gatehouse is a consummate piece of architecture: bold drum towers, with wavy spurred bases paralleled only at St Briavels (qv) in Gloucestershire. Above the recessed gateway a tall blind arch with multiple chamfered orders dying into the flanking towers, and exquisitely detailed loops with little trefoil heads, the style and quality of the workmanship reminiscent of the King's Gate at Caernarfon begun in 1295.

In the soffit of the outer arch is a line of murder holes, then came a portcullis between the gateway and outer arch, then, within the gate passage, a pair of loops, in the vault three more lines of murder holes, then another gate and portcullis, and more murder holes. Entrance to the residential block behind the towers was from the centre of the gate passage, where opposing doorways each open to a guard room, both of which provide access to a staircase contained within a corner turret. There are two upper floors, the first floor having been divided into three rooms by upward continuations of the gate passage walls; the two outer rooms are equipped with fireplace and latrine. The upper floor contains a single chamber with a large fireplace in the S wall flanked by large, splayed window embrasures with window seats and internal hood moulds. The hood-mould stops and fireplace corbels bear sculptured heads.

Other stone elements include the lower courses of a shell-keep that crowns the motte, and sections of the curtain wall around the inner bailey, notably along the S side above the river, visible from the river promenade. Here a number of latrine turrets (which formerly discharged directly into the river) are evident; they indicate the former presence of residential buildings on the S side of the bailey. Renn 1981; Simmons 1996 and 1998; Goodall 2011, 190–3; Martin and Martin 2013; Ludlow 2021–2.

TOPCLIFFE (Maiden's Bower), Yorkshire North Riding (Private). A motte and bailey, possibly C11 in origin, but refortified in 1174 by Geoffrey, Bishop Elect of Lincoln, in support of his father Henry II. Sited on a ridge close to the confluence of the river Swale and Cod Beck. The motte is at the eastern extremity of the spur, separated from the D-shaped bailey to the W by a ditch, which extends around the bailey. NW of the castle is the site of Cock Lodge, the manor house of the Percy family that succeeded the castle. Page 1923, 71.

TOTNES, Devon (Open – EH). Motte and bailey founded by Judhael of Totnes before 1088 on the edge of the Anglo-Saxon town. Around 1273, when the castle was said to have a ruined chamber and chapel, it was acquired through marriage by the Zouche family. In 1326 William de la Zouche received permission to refortify his castle at Totnes.

A high motte, crowned by a shell-keep of sub-circular plan, faces the town, and a ditched, embanked and walled bailey extends towards the NW. Two wing walls linked the bailey defences with the shell-keep. Access to the top of the motte is via a secondary stone staircase cut into the mound but may have been along the line of the E wing wall formerly. Immediately W of this wall, the entrance to the shell-keep has a semicircular arch of two chamfered orders, narrowed by partial blocking. Unusually, the crenellations of the ring wall survive, the merlons pierced by arrow loops. On the inside face of the wall the entrance is flanked by a pair of doorways, each giving onto an intra-mural stair ascending to the parapet walk. On the W side is a doorway to a mural latrine. A line of corbels between the latrine and the nearer staircase suggests the former presence of a lean-to building. The date of the shell-keep is uncertain, but the late C12 or early C13 is likely with refurbishment in the C14. Within the enclosure excavation has revealed the stone footings of what was probably a timber keep of rectangular plan. Brown 1998.

TOTTERNHOE, Bedfordshire (Open access). Motte with three baileys, possibly on the site of a prehistoric enclosure, first mentioned as a castle in a document of 1170–6. Occupying the western tip of a spur is a ditched motte and banked western bailey. An L-shaped middle bailey, with ditch and inner and outer banks, is wrapped around the eastern and northern sides of the motte and partially encloses the western bailey. To the E of this is a large sub-rectangular outer bailey enclosed by an outer bank and ditch which straddle the spur. Petre 2012, 81–5.

TREAGO, Herefordshire (Private). Quadrangular castle considered to have been built for Sir Richard Mynors from *c.*1470 onwards, though Treago has been the seat of the family since the early C14. Substantial post-medieval alterations, most notably in the 1840s, have greatly obscured the earlier arrangements. Square plan with central courtyard (roofed over in the C19) and round corner towers, of which those to the W are no more than stair turrets; the largest (which has had its upper storey rebuilt to oversail the base) is at the SE corner. The hall (later converted to a kitchen), which was in the N range, is recorded as having a hammer beam roof. No details earlier than the C15 are visible but notes on the appearance of the castle prior to the 1840s work record that the courtyard formerly contained doorways with triangular-arched heads in the manner of Goodrich (qv), which may denote that earlier fabric was incorporated into the late C15 castle. RCHME 1931, 230–3; Emery 2000, 544–6.

TREMATON, Cornwall (Open). Motte and bailey in existence by 1086, described in the Domesday Book as a castle of Robert, Count of Mortain. Then, the manor of Trematon was held of Robert by Reginald de Valletort, whose family remained in possession until 1270, when the castle and estate were sold to Richard, Earl of Cornwall. In 1337 it became part of the Duchy of Cornwall, which was created for the Black Prince. A survey of that time records 'a well-walled castle' with a timber hall, kitchen and two-storied chamber built by Earl Edmund (i.e., between 1272 and 1300), an old chapel, and a gatehouse. In 1385–6 its defences were upgraded as a precaution against a French landing. The construction of a C19 house in the bailey was accompanied by the demolition of part of the E curtain.

The castle consists of a roughly oval motte carrying a shell-keep, and a walled bailey to the SW (the southern half of the E curtain was demolished in the C19), the two components joined by wing walls climbing the motte to the shell-keep. Access to the bailey is from the E via a C13 gatehouse – a three-storey rectangular tower pierced by the gate passage. There is a postern in the W curtain. The shell-keep has a battered base and retains its crenellated parapet, which appears to have been reconstructed, probably in the late C13. Below the parapet is a line of beam sockets for a hoarding. Wide round-arched entrance; a line of double corbels all around the interior just below parapet level indicates the position of the roof for internal structures. Toy 1933, 217–9; Brown *et al*. 1963, 846–7; Higham 2015, 133–45.

TUTBURY, Staffordshire (Open). Motte with three baileys partially rebuilt in stone, Possibly the site of an Anglo-Saxon *burh*. The castle, which became the partially caput of the Honour of Tutbury, was established *c*.1068–9 by Hugh d' Avranches probably in the aftermath of the rebellion led by Edwin and Morcar. About 1071 the castle and its lands were transferred to Henry de Ferrers and remained with the Ferrers earls of Derby until being confiscated by Henry III in 1265. Henry granted Tutbury to his son Edmund Crouchback, Earl of Lancaster. When Thomas, Earl of Lancaster, rebelled in 1322, he made his stand some four miles from Tutbury at Burton Bridge, the castle being taken by the King shortly after his defeat; it was during this period that £1,500 went missing from Tutbury, at least some of which ended up in the River Dove near Tutbury Bridge, to be rediscovered in the C19 as the Tutbury Hoard. Thomas' kinsmen managed to hold onto Tutbury, his great nephew Henry of Grosmont being created Duke of Lancaster in 1351. Henry's heir was his daughter Blanche, who married Edward III's son, John of Gaunt, and in 1361 he became Duke of Lancaster in his turn. The Duchy of Lancaster became Crown property in 1399, when Gaunt's son ascended to the throne as Henry IV.

Magnificently sited on a bluff overlooking the river Dove. A roughly triangular site with the motte at the SW apex. Immediately to the NE of the motte is the inner

Tutbury: South Tower (1440s) from the N.

bailey, also broadly triangular, protected by a ditch to the S and E, an inner bank to the E, and by the steep slope of the hill to the NW. E and NE of the inner bailey are the outer and middle baileys respectively, separated by a deep hollow-way that probably contained the early approach road to the castle. Now, entry is from the S, through the outer and middle baileys to the so-called John of Gaunt's Gateway, leading into the inner bailey. This is probably the 'new tower above the gate' on which £100 was spent by Thomas of Lancaster in 1313–14; its front is now dominated by a C15 barbican. The gatehouse itself is rectangular with large traceried first-floor windows; bold quadrant-mouldings to the loop on the SE side and the entrance arch. There was formerly a third storey, probably an addition, of which only fragments remain.

So, into the inner bailey, which was rebuilt in stone between 1400 and *c*.1460 in the following sequence: NW curtain 1400–20; S curtain 1420–42; S Tower *c*.1441–50; SE curtain *c*.1441–50; N Tower *c*.1450–60; NE curtain *c*.1450–60. The NW curtain has largely disappeared, but substantial stretches survive on the other two sides broken by the N and S towers. The S curtain was provided with three rectangular turrets, and its E half formed the S wall of the C15 great hall and great chamber, its high plinth stepping up and down battlement fashion, apparently so designed to accommodate and accentuate the window bays. These are now occupied by the windows and doorway of the King's Lodging of 1634–6, a two-storey building raised for Charles I to replace the medieval apartments. Bolsover Castle (Derbyshire) has been suggested as a possible source of inspiration. Heavily rusticated lintels and jambs; doorway with Doric pilasters and a triangular pediment with pendant keystone; unusual features are the cranked voussoirs around the round–arched doorway. The King's Lodging was swept away in 1751, but a few details survive (including a fireplace and doorway) inside the red brick house to the W that had succeeded it by 1798.

The two-storey S Tower, which was erected according to the advice of the royal mason Robert Westerley, stood at the E end of the great hall. It consists of a rectangular main block with a subsidiary wing attached to its W side and a stair turret at its NE corner. Three doorways give access from the bailey to the basements of the main block and wing, and to the stair turret. Single-light basement windows and large pointed and traceried first-floor windows, and, also at first-floor level to the R (W) of the stair turret, a monolithic window of three trefoil-headed lights beneath a square label. The basements are rather interesting in that both were intended to have stone vaults (wing plain, main block with *faux* ribs), though neither seems to have been completed beyond the springers. Above these are rows of corbels for the wall posts supporting the first floor. Presumably, both vaults were completed in timber or not at all. The stair turret gave access to a first-floor lobby in the main block which contained a single room with access to another in the wing; thus, it was a high-quality two-chamber lodging. Both rooms have a large lintelled fireplace in the E wall, the surrounds decorated with sculptures. The privy chamber in the wing formerly had access to a (now destroyed) latrine turret in the angle with the S curtain.

Of the N Tower (aka Queen Margaret's Tower, High Tower) only the W half survives and of this only the N half to full height. It was a four-storey rectangular block with separate doorways from the bailey to the basement and to a stair turret at the NW corner, the latter giving access to a series of single-chamber lodgings on the three upper floors, each with a large square-headed window and entered via a passage lit by a small monolithic window.

The motte is crowned by a round tower, a folly raised by George Venables-Vernon of Sudbury Hall between 1780 and 1791, but it stands on the site of a cylindrical keep, probably built by the Earl of Derby, between 1190 and 1247, the foundations of which were still visible in the C18, and which excavation has revealed. The keep was surrounded by a polygonal mantlet, remains of which have also been recorded in excavation. Hislop *et al.* 2011.

TYNEMOUTH, Northumberland (Open – EH). Tynemouth Priory had, since its foundation *c.*1090, been as much fortress as monastery, and in the C14 was one of the four key strongholds of the Northumbrian coast (with Bamburgh, Berwick and Dunstanburgh). In 1390, probably as a response to a Scottish incursion in the previous year in which Tynemouthshire had been harried and burnt, a major building programme was set in motion. Thus, in 1390, King Richard II contributed £500, a grant of £100 was received from the Duke of Lancaster, and the Earl of Northumberland, then Warden of the Eastern March, donated 100 marks and 1,000 trees.

The priory is sited on a North Sea promontory on the N side of the Tyne estuary. The only recognizably late C14 defence work at Tynemouth is the great gatehouse, which is recorded as having been built by Prior John Wheathamstede (1390–1419), and which is ambitious enough to account for the major share of the grants. The gatehouse comprises an imposing three-storey rectangular tower, aligned N–S, facing W, with a rectangular kitchen wing at the SE corner, a long outer barbican to the W traversing the ditch that cuts off the promontory from the mainland, and a much shorter inner barbican to the E. Craster 1907, 131–204; Emery 1996, 141–3; Hislop 2007, 38–9; McCombie 2013.

Tynemouth: Great gatehouse of 1390.

WALDEN, Essex. See **Saffron Walden**.

WALLINGFORD, Berkshire (Open). Founded soon after 1066 in the NE corner of the Anglo-Saxon *burh*, next to the Thames, on a largely undeveloped site, possibly the location of an Anglo-Saxon royal residence. Caput of the Honour of Wallingford, the castle was held by Brian FitzCount in support of the Empress Matilda during the civil war of Stephen's reign, and was besieged thrice by the King (1139, 1146 and 1152) but without success. After the accession of Henry II, the castle was acquired by the Crown, and in 1215 King John gave orders for strengthening it. Between 1231 and 1272 Wallingford was held by Henry III's brother, Richard Earl of Cornwall who spent substantial amounts on the castle in creating three concentric lines of defence. Fortified for the King during the Civil War but surrendered to a Parliamentarian army in 1646 after a 16-week siege. In 1652 it was demolished.

The early castle was of motte and bailey design with the main gatehouse towards the W. Two concentric lines of fortification being added to the N, S and W sides in the C13. The visible remains, with one or two exceptions, are the earthworks, a series of ditches and banks, and, at the S end of the inner bailey, the motte, once crowned by a stone tower. On the E bank of the inner bailey is a short length of walling of uncertain date, much patched, with a window jamb at first-floor level. Another fragment exists to the NW. To the SE of the inner bailey are some more extensive remains said to belong to the College of St Nicholas. A W-facing wall is pierced by a pointed doorway with quatrefoil-decorated spandrels and a square hoodmould, ogee-moulded with suspended returns reaching half-way down the opening. To the R (S) of this two C16 twin-light windows. Also, a S-facing wall with C16 three-light window at first-floor level to the L (W) and a turreted E end. Christie *et al.* 2013; Keats-Rohan *et al.* 2015.

WARDOUR, Wiltshire. See **OLD WARDOUR**.

WAREHAM, Dorset (Open access). Motte and bailey situated within the SW corner of the Anglo-Saxon *burh* defences overlooking the river Frome. Possibly founded soon after the Conquest, but the history of the castle is complicated by the fact that Corfe Castle (qv) was referred to as Wareham in the C11 and C12. Only the motte and part of its ditch are still visible, the mound carrying an early C20 house on the site of the C12 stone keep, the plan of which was recovered in the 1950s when a series of test pits were excavated. It was about 70ft (6.5m) square with 13ft (3.9m) thick walls and pilaster buttresses. RCHME 1970, 324–6.

WARK ON TWEED, Northumberland (Open access). A strategically important border fortress controlling a crossing of the river Tweed, Wark Castle was built by Walter Espec of Helmsley (qv) in the reign of Henry I (1100–35). Destroyed by David I of Scotland in 1138. Rebuilt by Henry II between 1158 and 1161, it held out against a siege by William the Lion in 1174. In 1329 Edward III granted Wark to Sir William Montagu (Earl of Salisbury from 1337), and in 1341 relieved a Scottish siege of the castle, then held by the Countess of Salisbury. Captured and damaged by the Scots in 1389, and again in 1399. Fortifications dismantled by the Scots in 1460. Restored by Henry VIII from 1516. Demolished by King James I. The castle remains consist of a motte and, towards the E, in linear sequence, inner and outer baileys, the latter partly occupied by village buildings. A survey carried out in 1519 recorded a three-storey gatehouse giving access to the outer bailey, and a four-storey donjon.

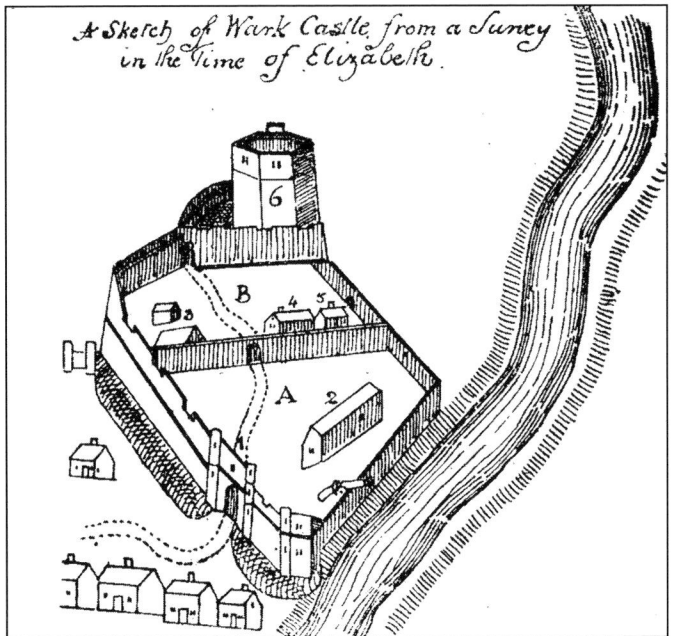

Wark: Copy of a Tudor sketch. From Bates 1891.

Both were depicted in a later C16 drawing of the castle and may have been rebuilds of medieval predecessors. Bates 1891, 331–69; Hunter Blair 1944, especially 155–60; Brown *et al.* 1963, 852–3.

WARKWORTH, Northumberland (Open – EH) (Plate XIV). In existence by the mid C12, when it was granted to Roger son of Richard FitzEustace. In 1173 it was considered too weak to be defended against the forces of the King of Scotland. Roger's son, Robert (d. 1214), who became Sheriff of Northumberland in 1203, probably began a major reconstruction of the castle in stone in the early C13, a project that may have been continued by his son, John (d. 1240). On the death of John's grandson, John de Clavering (d. 1332), Warkworth came to Henry, Lord Percy of Alnwick (qv), whose grandson, also Henry, First Earl of Northumberland from 1377, built the keep on top of the C12 motte. During the Wars of the Roses both the second and third earls were killed supporting the Lancastrian cause, and in 1464 the Yorkist King Edward IV made his supporter John Neville, Lord Montagu, Earl of Northumberland. In 1470 the title was returned to the Percys, and shortly afterwards the Fourth Earl began remodelling the bailey. His plans included a collegiate church to be built right across the bailey, but this part of the project was never completed. Over the next three centuries Warkworth suffered from neglect and decay, but the keep was partially restored in the 1850s under the direction of the architect Anthony Salvin.

The village of Warkworth lies within a loop of the river Coquet; the land rises steeply from the river to the neck of the loop where the castle is situated, on a spur, commanding the entrance to the settlement from the S, and overlooking the river crossing to the N. The castle site comprises a roughly rectangular bailey with a motte

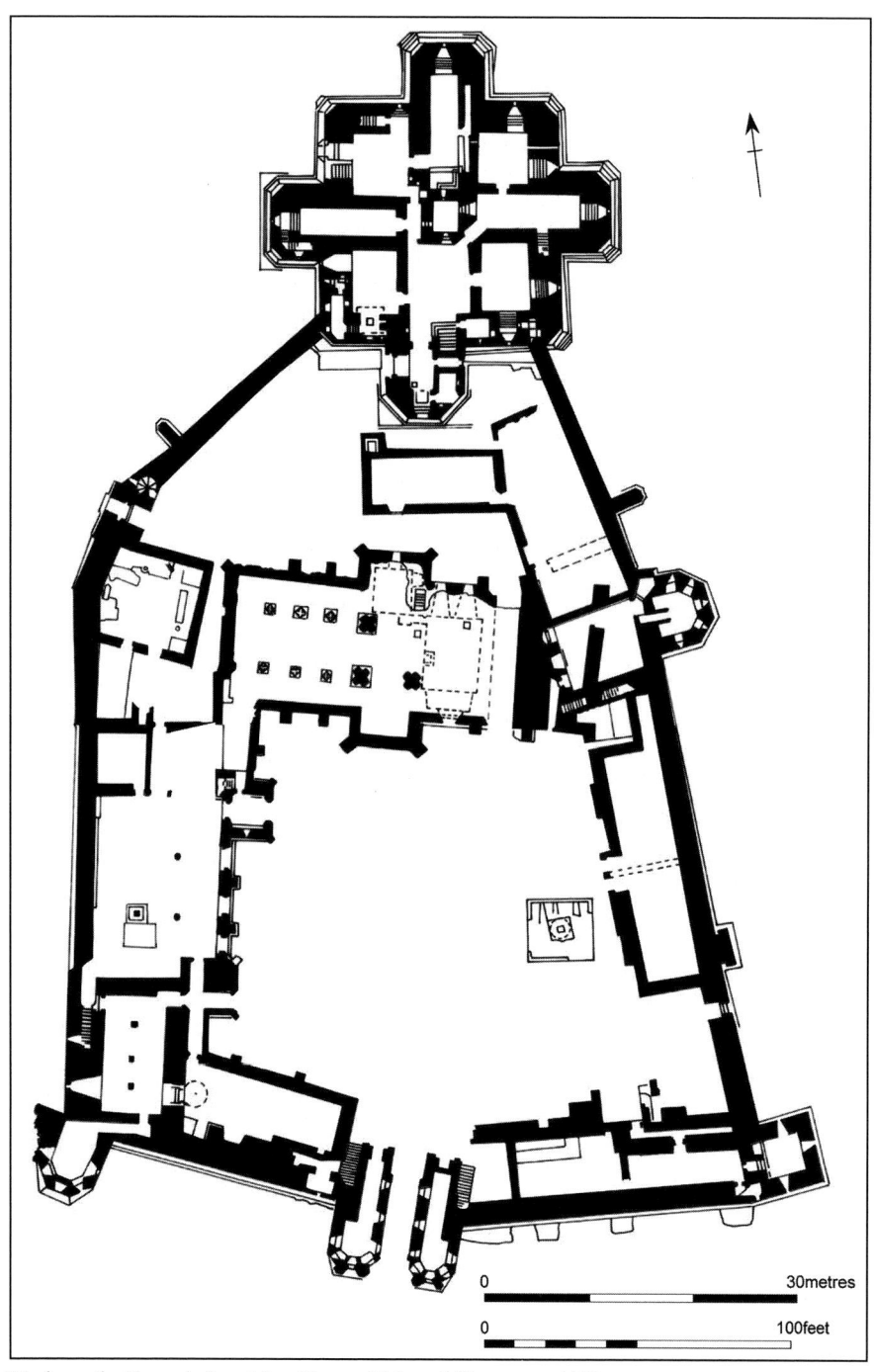

Warkworth: Ground plan. After Hunter Blair and Honeyman 1954.

at its N end. A wide berm outside the E curtain suggests that the bailey may have been larger prior to reconstruction in stone. The S front is dominated by the early C13 gatehouse with twin polygonal flanking towers and polygonal buttresses. The building was later (late C13–C14) raised in height and given a machicolated parapet over the entrance. To the L (at the SW corner) is the contemporary Carrickfergus Tower, also polygonal, and to the R the square Montagu Tower, said to have been built during the tenure of Lord Montagu *c.*1464–9. The only other wall tower is the C13 Grey Mare's Tail Tower on the E side of the castle. This too is polygonal and is distinguished by a remarkable set of arrow loops rising through two storeys with cross slits and big splayed bases. On the W side, close to the motte, an early C13 postern is set within a rectangular tower of very slight projection. To the L (N) of it is a capped polygonal buttress matching those of the main gatehouse.

The main gatehouse gives access to a quadrangular courtyard. The principal domestic apartments are to the L (W) comprising (from S to N) great chamber, great hall, service rooms (pantry and buttery) and kitchen. The most prominent aspects now are the remnants of the Fourth Earl's late C15 reconstruction of the frontage, namely the Lion Tower at the lower end of the great hall, which formed the porch, and the SE angle of the hall which includes the Little Stair Tower. A doorway to the L of the tower gave access to the hall, great chamber and chapel. Directly opposite the main gate are the remains of the collegiate church begun by the Fourth Earl; they extend across the castle from E to W, effectively creating a small inner ward in front of the keep. The church was never completed and only the lower courses of stonework survive, but the layout is clear enough. It has a four-bay nave, crossing and transepts, and a three-bay choir longer than the nave.

Moving on to the keep, it is worth pausing to appreciate the sheer power of the design. A square main block with a turret protruding from the centre of each side, the bevelled angles of the components streamlining and accentuating the perspective, the keep has a highly three-dimensional aspect. Ascending through three storeys, its height is exaggerated by its elevated site, high base, and by the Watch Tower, which rises from the centre of the block like a periscope as though keeping a watchful eye on the castle and its surroundings. The whole composition is remarkably effective and obviously the work of a talented master builder. Extending around the keep at the level of the second-floor windows is a line of (now blank) heraldic shields held by alternating angels and knights, and, on the N turret, a giant panel containing the Percy emblem, a lion rampant.

There were three entrances to the keep: a postern in the W face opening onto the top of the motte, and one on each side of the S turret, the main one on the W approached by a flight of steps, and an E doorway leading to the curtain wall walk. The compact and unusual footprint of the keep must have presented a challenge to the designer of the interior. Comparison of planning details with contemporary buildings, notably Castle Bolton (qv), which, like the Warkworth keep contains an intricate maze of rooms, suites, and staircases, suggest the involvement of John Lewyn of Durham, a notable exponent of this type of scheme.

A vestibule within the S turret, attended by a porter's lodge, gives access to a large entrance hall. The basement was largely for storage, and, except for a lantern, or light well, in the centre, was entirely barrel-vaulted. Building breaks in the stonework give clues to the sequence of construction at this level. First came the outer walls, then the vaults over the turrets, then the dividing walls of the central block and their vaults.

Warkworth: The Lion Tower from the E.

On the L (W) a room with a pit, possibly a safe for valuables, and in the W wall a small private room with latrine and fireplace. The other main room of interest is in the N turret, where rainwater was conveyed from the light well to a cistern and used to flush a drain in the N wall serving the upper-floor latrines.

Three service staircases ascend from the food store, beer cellar and wine cellar to the kitchen and upper and lower ends of the hall respectively. The main staircase, a wide straight flight, rises from the entrance hall to a lobby in the S turret, equipped with a stone bench. At the entrance to the hall is a stone seat for the attendant who controlled admission. The hall was lit by two large S windows and the two windows of the E gallery. All four have flues in their heads as vents for the smoke from the open hearth (a feature associated with Lewyn). In the C16 the open hearth was removed and one of the windows blocked to make a fireplace. Between the hall and more private apartments to the N is the chapel, the chancel within the E turret, with sedilia, piscina and candle sconces carved with angels bearing shields. A sacristy/vestry on the S side (within the E wall of the main block) has squints looking towards the altar. The chancel was open to the roof; the nave had an upper storey accessed from the private apartments. There were two residential suites, possibly male and female quarters, each comprising a great chamber and, in the N turret, a bedroom or private parlour, the two latter linked by a staircase. Access to the gallery over the nave was from the upper great chamber.

The kitchens in the NE corner of the keep are another area of particular interest. They consist of servery, outer kitchen and great kitchen, the latter, like the hall, rising through two storeys. Above the outer kitchen and servery one of the rooms dedicated to administrative staff has a series of mural storage spaces. Bates 1891, 81–166; Hodgson 1899, 18–112; Simpson 1941; Hislop 1991 and 2007, 40–5, 68–71; Goodall 2006.

WARWICK, Warwickshire (Open). A motte and bailey founded in 1068 by William I, who granted custody to Henry de Beaumont, created First Earl of Warwick in 1088. The last of the Beaumont earls died in 1242, and their estates descended through the female line to, in 1268, William Beauchamp, who became Ninth Earl of Warwick. The next five earls were Beauchamps, and it is their transformative building work, carried out during the C14, that still dominates the character of the castle. The exact chronology is uncertain, but the greater part of the rebuilding work is owed to Thomas Beauchamp, the Eleventh Earl, between *c.*1331, when he attained his majority, and 1369 when he died. A notable soldier in both the Scottish and French wars, Warwick was, from 1344, Marshal of England and a Knight of the Garter, serving as a divisional commander at both Crécy and Poitiers. Profits accrued in France may have financed his building projects.

The male line of the Beauchamps ended in 1446 with the death of Henry, the Fourteenth Earl, and in 1449, Richard Neville became Earl of Warwick by right of his wife. Warwick 'the Kingmaker' died in battle in 1471, without a male heir, and the Warwick estates were divided between his two daughters Isabel, Duchess of Clarence, and Anne, Duchess of Gloucester. Warwick Castle and the earldom fell to the Clarences, and after the Duke's death, in 1478, was appropriated by the Crown. Richard III began the construction of a great residential tower here, the last of the medieval works, but it was never completed. By 1604, when Warwick was granted to Fulke Greville, the castle was much decayed. Substantial works were carried out in the C17 by Greville, and after the Civil War by his grandson Lord Brooke, including the refurbishment of the main domestic buildings. In the latter half of the C18 further work was carried out on the main apartments including the rebuilding of the hall porch, the addition of a new dining-room block N of the hall between the porch and chapel, some refenestration and various internal changes. Much damage was done by a fire in 1871 which gutted the eastern half of the residential range including the great hall, necessitating a complete refurbishment.

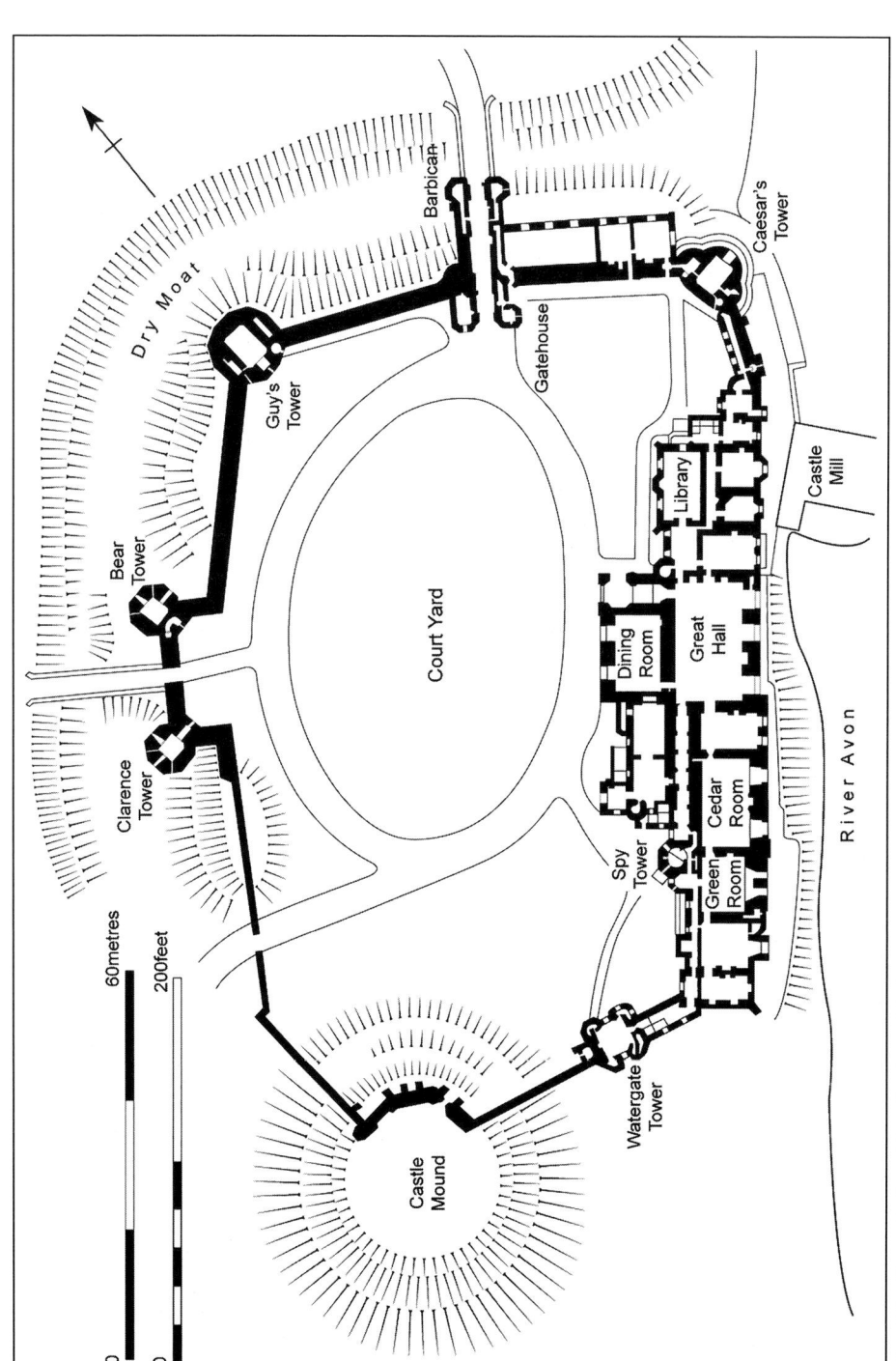

Warwick: Ground plan. After Stephens 1969.

Sited on a bluff above the river Avon, Warwick Castle lies on a NE–SW axis (treated here as though E–W) with a motte at the W end of a sub-rectangular bailey. The entrance lies to the E, whereas the main apartments are to the S ranged along the top of the river cliff, creating an inspiring spectacle from Castle Bridge. Just as notable is the E side of the bailey, which is one of the great castle frontages of England. In the centre is the admirable C14 great gatehouse, comprising a four-storey gate tower and a passage barbican with a three-storey entrance block. The segmental-pointed barbican gate arch is flanked by a pair of octagonal turrets, and the gate passage defences include a portcullis, a row of machicolations in the vault, and a gate. Then, into an open space or passage connecting the entrance block to the gatehouse, a tower in two parts, the outer with round turrets at the corners rising above the parapet and linked by battlemented open arches at a higher level to N, S and E. The inner part, which projects into the courtyard, has octagonal corner turrets.

At each end of the frontage, linked to the gatehouse by the curtain wall is a tall lodging tower, its height accentuated by being built on top of the rampart. To the R (N) is Guy's Tower, after the legendary hero, Guy of Warwick, built to a polygonal plan (based on a dodecagon) and rising through five storeys, all rib-vaulted, and all except the uppermost room provided with a fireplace and latrine. These rooms are rectangular apart from the hexagonal fifth-storey belvedere, which has a window in each of the six sides.

Caesar's Tower, to the L (S), is a six-storey building, polygonal within the curtain, but tri-lobed externally, a most unusual plan. Just as unusual is the two-tiered form of the tower, the main body terminating at fifth-floor level in a parapet on corbelled machicolations, fronting an alure, so that the upper two storeys are contained, wedding cake fashion, within a narrower second tier. As in Guy's Tower the rooms are rectangular and rib-vaulted (except for the fifth floor which has no vault). The lowest storey appears to have been a prison; the other chambers within the main body were lodgings with fireplaces and latrines.

Projecting from the N curtain are the remains of the great N tower initiated by Richard III (reigned 1483–5), planned as a massive residential block. All that remains is the ground story of the outer half with octagonal corner turrets known as the Bear Tower (N) and Clarence Tower (S), pierced by circular gun ports. A gateway was broken through in the late C18.

At the core of the main domestic block on the S side of the bailey are the medieval apartments focused on the great hall, now heavily disguised by C17, C18 and later additions and alterations. The extent of the medieval residence can to a large degree be understood by an examination of the C14 rib-vaulted undercrofts which range along the greater part of the existing block. When viewed from the S, the medieval work extends broadly from the canted bay near the RH (E) end as far as the square bay towards the LH (W) end. They now support at first-floor level (from E to W) the former pantry and buttery, great hall, Red Drawing Room, Cedar Room and Green Drawing Room, all presumably part of the C14 apartments, though now greatly altered. NW of the great hall is the chapel, again medieval in origin but changed beyond recognition. Also medieval is the Spy Tower to the W of the chapel, probably added by the Duke of Clarence in the 1470s.

In the W curtain, another C14 building is the Watergate Tower: a square gatehouse with odd polygonal corner turrets. Then comes the motte, with part of a polygonal shell wall, around the E side only. Most of the stonework belongs to the C18,

Warwick: The Clarence Tower (right) and Bear tower (left) with Guy's Tower in the background.

though the wall incorporates a segmental-arched gateway, apparently a survival from the C13. Stephens 1969, 452–75; Morris 1986; Emery 2000, 438–45; Parkyn and McNeill 2012.

WATTLESBOROUGH HALL, Shropshire (Private). A small keep, or solar tower, attributable to Richard Corbet who held Wattlesborough of Robert Corbet of Caus (qv) from *c*.1180 to *c*.1220. It occupied a roughly central position within a ditched enclosure, indications of the ditch surviving to the SW. A late C15/C16 wing has been attached to the NE and a C17 farmhouse to the SE. The 42ft (13m) square tower is built of large stone blocks of near-ashlar quality with a battered plinth, chamfered mid-height offset and pilaster buttresses at the angles. It survives to full height minus the battlements.

The basement was lit by little rectangular loops, of which one survives to the W; the first floor was illuminated by twin rectangular lights beneath monolithic lintels incorporating semi-circular tympana, the northern one replaced by a C14 window with twin ogee lights. Also in the C14, an extra floor was inserted, windows of that date surviving to the NE and SE (the latter obscured by the farmhouse). At the junction with the NE wall of the farmhouse, an arch springer extends from the angle buttress, apparently a gateway within an attached wall (a division of the courtyard?).

The C12 entrance to the tower is on the S side at first-floor level; it is similar in style to the windows, the tympanum (actually a round-arched recess within the lintel) giving the impression of defying gravity (was it the mason's intention to create an illusion?). This doorway is mostly of two chamfered orders (the LH side of the outer arch dies into the SW corner buttress), the RH outer arch ends in an unusual beakhead derivative stop. The door was secured by a draw bar and led straight through the wall into the first-floor chamber.

In the basement are various inserted doorways into the later wings including, directly below the blocked segmental-arched first-floor entrance, a wide C14 pointed arch, probably relocated. The first-floor chamber was served by the latrine to the NE and a barrel-vaulted spiral staircase to the SW leading to the roof; there are large semi-circular (E and W) and segmental (N and S) window embrasures, the former taking advantage of the greater headroom afforded by the clearly visible gable ends of the sunken roof. Squeezed in next to the W window a C15 fireplace with flat lintel and moulded surround; above it at inserted second-floor level a similar but plainer fireplace, and above that, a relocated sculptured head. Davis 2021–2.

WAYTEMORE (Bishop's Stortford), Hertfordshire (Open access). Late C11 motte and bailey, probably raised by William the Conqueror to control a crossing of the river Stort and granted by him to the Bishop of London. Dismantled by King John in 1208; rebuilt from 1213; licence to crenellate of 1346. Large oval motte with irregularly-shaped bailey to the S. On top of the motte are remains of a stone enclosure or tower of unknown date. RCHME 1910, 63–4; Page 1912b, 292–306.

WEETING, Norfolk (Open access – EH). Fortified manor house on a site occupied since the C10 or C11. The manor house itself was built by Hugh de Plais, a tenant of the Earl of Surrey; it is believed that the design of the Weeting house was based on that of a building at the earl's Castle Acre. The remains consist of a rectangular moated site containing the ruins of a late C12 manor house comprising an aisled hall aligned N–S, a three-storey chamber block at the S end with attached latrine turret (now the most prominent element of the ruins), and a two-storey service block at the N end. Heslop 2000.

WELBOURN (Castle Hill), Lincolnshire (Open access). Ringwork in existence by 1158, when it was being rebuilt in stone for Hugh of Bayeux. The manor of Welbourn had been divided in the early C12, and the castle served as the focus of the northern half. In 1288 the castle buildings included a hall with two chambers, kitchen, brewhouse, oxhouse, cowshed and sheep fold. In the C14 the two manors were reunited and by 1374 the site had been abandoned in favour of the manor house further S. Situated on Castle Hill towards the N end of the village, the castle enclosure is roughly D-shaped, the flat side to the S. A ditch, partly encroached upon by modern roads and housing, extends around the N, E and W sides, whereas to the S there are three parallel E–W ditches and banks, the southernmost encroached upon by an adjoining property. There are also remnants of an inner bank to the NW and E. Roffe 1997.

WEOBLEY, Herefordshire (Open access). In existence by 1138, when it was captured by King Stephen, but probably built by the de Lacys in the C11. A C17 schematic plan of the castle shows a quadrilateral enclosure tapering from S to N and surrounded by a ditch, with round corner and semi-circular mid-wall towers, and, at the S end, a rectangular keep with round corner towers. Nothing of this is now evident, but a date in the C13/C14 for buildings of this nature would seem probable. Presently, only a confusing collection of earthworks is now visible, suggesting a rather less regular arrangement than that shown in the plan. However, it is apparent that a ditch, or moat, did extend around the site, accompanied on the S and E sides by an inner bank. The entrance was at the N end, from the town, and gave access to a bailey occupying about half the site. To the S of this are the remains of a so-called ringwork defined around its E side by a bank, but otherwise not particularly instructive. This, presumably, is the site of the keep. Nash and Redwood 2006.

WEOLEY, Worcestershire (Visible from a viewing platform but rarely open). Fortified manor house of the lords of Dudley (qv). Excavation has suggested that the site was occupied by *c.*1100, and that the early structures were surrounded by a ditch and inner bank carrying a palisade. In addition, the remains of early C13 buildings have been recorded, including a stone hall destroyed by fire between 1248 and *c.*1260, and a timber kitchen. In 1264 Roger de Somery obtained a licence to crenellate his manor houses at both Weoley and Dudley, and it was probably after this that stone defences were erected.

Now firmly embedded within the Birmingham conurbation, and fenced off from the surrounding C20 housing, the site of Weoley Castle forms a beleaguered island of the former medieval landscape. The castle enclosure consists of an irregular quadrangle with three roughly straight sides, with the W side forming an angular curve. Stone defences of well-executed ashlar masonry, with a series of projecting rectangular towers, but surviving little above courtyard level, so that it is largely the battered plinth that remains. The base of each sloping stone is chamfered to give a vertical face so that the courses rise in a series of little steps. At intervals vertical buttresses rise from the slope; possibly they supported little turrets. The gatehouse is at the N end of the W front, its high threshold obviously reached by a bridge across the moat; two large flanking buttresses/turrets which project into the moat may have housed a raised drawbridge, but the greater part of the gatehouse was inside the curtain. Inside, the main apartments (including hall, chamber block, kitchen and service rooms), were ranged along the E side of the courtyard. The chapel and another residential block were on the N side. Oswald 1962 and 1962–3; Smith 1965; Emery 2000, 445–7.

WEST BITCHFIELD, Northumberland. See **BITCHFIELD**.

WEST MALLING (St Leonard's Tower), Kent (Open access to exterior only – EH). Small tower built by Gundulf, Bishop of Rochester *c.*1100, the main surviving component of a larger residential complex. The tower, which is built of coursed ragstone rubble with tufa dressings, measures *c.*33ft (10m) square at the base, has 6ft (2m) thick walls, and rose through three storeys, though only two survive in full. Clasping buttresses at the angles, those of the NW corner enlarged to accommodate a spiral stair. The E side contains the original ground-floor entrance (now blocked); above, stretching across this elevation and to the S (i.e., the two faces exposed to public view) is a display of arcading with central windows lighting the basement, but otherwise blind. At first-floor level a series of large windows with plain semi-circular arches, like those of the arcading, single lights to N, S and W, but two to the entrance (E) front. The present (C19) entrance is through the W wall into the basement, whence there was access to the upper rooms via the NW stair. There seems to have been a lack of amenities (eg, fireplaces and latrines) and the tower may have served a ceremonial rather than residential purpose, the upper room perhaps as an audience chamber. Elements of medieval walling and earthworks in the vicinity testify to the former existence of associated buildings. North 2001.

WEST TANFIELD (Marmion Tower), Yorkshire North Riding (Open access – EH). When John Leland visited West Tanfield he saw 'no notable building but a fair toured Gateway and a Haule of squarid stone'. The hall has since disappeared, but a gatehouse tower remains, now the only remnant of the castle to have survived above ground level.

A licence was obtained in 1348 by Maud, the widow of Sir John Marmion, to crenellate the manor of 'Westtanfeld'. After a later John Marmion died without issue in 1387, whilst taking part in John of Gaunt's Spanish campaign, the property came to his niece, Elizabeth, the wife of Henry FitzHugh of Ravensworth (qv). Elizabeth and her husband may have been the builders of the gatehouse, which appears to date from *c*.1400.

The three-storey gatehouse lies immediately SW of the church, facing E along Church Street, which it terminates. Rectangular in plan with a NW stair turret, the tower is pierced by a four-centred gateway and vaulted passageway, giving access to the grounds of the Old Rectory which occupies the manor house site. To the L (S) of the gate is a rectangular window lighting a porter's lodge. Placed centrally, and corbelled out from the first floor, is a polygonal oriel window with a stone roof, and above that, at second-floor level, a C16 mullioned and transomed window inserted into an earlier opening.

The porter's lodge, which is entered from the gate passage, occupies the entire S side of the ground storey; it is equipped with a fireplace and latrine. On the opposite side of the passage is the door to the staircase. This leads to the two upper floors. At first-floor level is a fireplace with partially surviving segmental-pointed arch. The uppermost floor retains twin-light windows with trefoil-headed lights and stone benches in the embrasures; it is also furnished with a latrine corbelled out from the S wall. Page 1914, 384–9; Emery 1996, 412.

WESTON TURVILLE, Buckinghamshire (Private). Motte with two baileys, first mentioned *c*.1145, when Geoffrey de Turville held it of the Earl of Leicester. In 1173/74 the castle was slighted on the orders of Henry II, an action probably prompted by the rebellion of the Earl of Leicester, Robert de Beaumont. The Turvilles continued to occupy the manor of Weston Turville throughout the C13. In 1333 a licence to crenellate the site of the manor of Weston Turville granted to John de Molyns and his wife Egidia probably refers to the castle site. Situated NW of St Mary's Church, the castle comprises a motte with baileys to the SW (containing the current manor house) and SE. Excavation of a trench across the motte ditch in 1985 recovered blocks of C12 dressed masonry and roof tile, interpreted by the excavator as evidence for the late C12 slighting. Hagerty 1986; Yeoman 1986.

WHITCHURCH (Bolebec Castle), Buckinghamshire (Ringwork accessible from Castle Lane). Ringwork and bailey, caput of the Barony of Bolebec, possibly the castle works erected by Hugh de Bolebec and complained about by Pope Eugenius in 1147. In the C13 the barony came to the de Vere earls of Oxford through marriage. The castle was dismantled at the end of the Civil War. The ringwork and its triangular bailey are now separated, lying to the S and N respectively of Castle Lane. The ringwork was surrounded by a large ditch with counterscarp bank, and there are also traces of an inner bank and an entrance to the W towards Weir Lane, where a drawbridge is said to have been visible until the end of the C18; the bailey was enclosed by a bank and outer ditch. Page 1925, 443–4.

WHITCHURCH, Shropshire. A castle was founded at or near Whitchurch soon after the Conquest by William de Warenne. There are two sites to which this could refer: **Castle Hill**, Traditional site of a castle near the town centre, but the location is uncertain, and no remains can be confirmed. Duckers 2006, 176–8. **Pan Castle**, motte and bailey 1 mile to the SW of Whitchurch. Sited on the edge of a former marsh, which lay to the N and E, the castle consists of an irregularly-shaped motte surrounded by a moat and counterscarp bank, with a sub-rectangular bailey to the S, bounded by a moat and inner bank on the S and W sides, and by a scarp on the E, where the castle was protected by the marsh. Duckers 206, 125–6.

WHITTINGTON, Shropshire (Open). Fronting the main road through the village and exuding an air of rural tranquillity by virtue of its limpid moat, Whittington is a former motte and bailey castle established within a prehistoric fortification and rebuilt in stone in the C13. The castle is first mentioned in 1138 when William Peverel held it for the Empress Matilda. Henry II confiscated Whittington, but in 1204 it was granted to Fulk FitzWarren III of Alberbury (qv) whose claim was based on kinship with the Peverels. In 1221 Fulk was given permission to strengthen the castle against the Welsh, who, under Llywelyn ab Iorwerth, laid the castle to siege two years later, perhaps before the rebuilding work had been completed. In the C14 a garden was created inside the castle.

Established in a flat marshy site, the castle's W and S sides are enclosed by three banks and ditches, prehistoric in origin, once part of a large enclosure, while the N and E sides were protected by a pool of water fed by natural springs, a feature which probably extended all around the castle. The outer (E) gatehouse, facing onto the road, and reached by a bridge across the moat, is C13 in origin, possibly part of Fulk FitzWarren's works of the 1220s, but substantially rebuilt in 1809, as much picturesque folly as medieval fortification. This leads into the NE bailey, an area now devoid of medieval buildings, and separated from a W bailey by a C14 ditch, into which the water defences intruded. This W bailey seems to have been the site of the garden; a mound to the SE, formerly moated, has been interpreted as a viewing mount.

To the E of the mound, in the SE corner of the castle, is the irregularly polygonal inner bailey, a C13 stone-walled enclosure with projecting round towers. This, in fact, was the motte of the early castle, remodelled and probably extended by Fulk FitzWarren to create a strongly defended citadel raised above the level of the baileys and surrounded by water. The twin-towered gatehouse is at the NW angle; the mound in front of it represents the bridge abutment. The LH (E) tower (the best preserved of all the towers) has a cruciform arrow loop with fishtail base. Inside the enclosure are the foundations of a rectangular keep, probably C12, with the base of a staircase on the E side. Brown 2003; Duckers 2006, 178–82.

WHORLTON, Yorkshire North Riding (Clearly visible from the road). Motte and bailey probably built by the Meynells who were in possession by the beginning of the C12. In 1348, after the male line of the Meynells failed, the manor came through marriage to the Darcy family. A squarish motte defined by a ditch lies to the W of a roughly crescentic bailey, now divided by the modern road which runs along the SE flank of the motte. The castle was refurbished under the Darcys, their efforts concentrating on the motte, which was lowered and given a stone great tower and three-storey gatehouse, though only the latter remains standing. This faces E, is built of ashlar, and has a rectangular plan with a projecting stair turret at its NW angle. Heraldic shields above the central segmental-arched gateway suggest that Philip Darcy was the builder between *c.*1370 and 1398 when he died. The principal windows are rectangular with recessed frames and central mullions and transoms. Inside traces of the gate passage vaulting ribs are still visible; rooms to either side at ground- and first-floor levels, the latter with fireplaces in the end walls, all rooms with latrines. Page 1923, 309–13; Emery 1996, 413–14.

WIGMORE, Herefordshire (Open access – EH). The chief castle of the powerful Mortimer family, founded by William FitzOsbern soon after the Conquest and granted to Ralph Mortimer in 1075. Roger Mortimer, who, with Queen Isabella, forced the abdication of Edward II, was created First Earl of March in 1328. The last of the Mortimer lords, Edmund Mortimer, Fifth Earl of March, was heir presumptive to Richard II until Henry Bolingbroke, who had a weaker claim, usurped the throne in 1399. Edmund died in 1425 without issue, and the Mortimer estates, as well as his claim to the throne, were inherited by his nephew, Richard, Duke of York, and subsequently by York's son, who ascended the throne as Edward IV, at which point Wigmore became a royal castle. From that time onwards its significance declined, and in 1601 it was sold to Thomas Hartley of Brampton Bryan (qv). In 1643 it was slighted to prevent the Royalists from using it as a fortress and is now very much a ruin.

Built on a spur NW of the village of Wigmore, and cut off by ditches from the high ground to the N. The footpath from the village passes through the middle of the outer bailey, heralded by some earthworks on the R (E) and then through the bank that constitutes the S side of the enceinte. Looming up beyond is the stone-curtained inner bailey, and above it, the high point of the spur which forms a natural motte crowned by the walls of a shell-keep. The towering castle on its sloping site must have provided a stirring vista before the ruination of the buildings and the encroachment of vegetation combined to enfeeble the potency of its impact.

There is a climb up to the inner ward, which was protected by a ditch. Of the C14 rectangular gatehouse, a single segmental-pointed gate arch survives, rebated for gates to the rear (N). Two storeys are evident, and there is a roof crease above the gate arch. In the side wall to the R (E) of the arch at first-floor level is a doorway giving access to a largely vanished latrine turret. Along the curtain, some 25 yards to the L (W) of the gatehouse, is the broad face of the C14 S tower, a two-storey rectangular lodging tower with trefoil-headed windows. Further along to the W, the smaller but similar SE tower before the curtain ascends the motte to join the shell-keep. On the other (E) side of the gatehouse are the semi-circular E tower, possibly C13, and the semi-polygonal NE tower, possibly C14. Adjacent to this tower within the inner ward, a platform with traces of walling may have been the site of a residential complex.

Finally, another climb to the top of the motte, the (SE) approach dominated by a rectangular tower-like projection, the two-horned profile of its upper section exaggerated by a headless central window. The broadly oval enclosure is largely devoid of stone around its S and W sides, an exception being a tall finger of masonry to the SW which contained a staircase. In contrast, there is a well-preserved section of curtain to the N with a shallow rectangular projection, probably a turret, about mid-way along its length, and, at the E end, the stub of the wing wall that once descended the motte to the NE tower. Remfry 1995; Rátkai 2015.

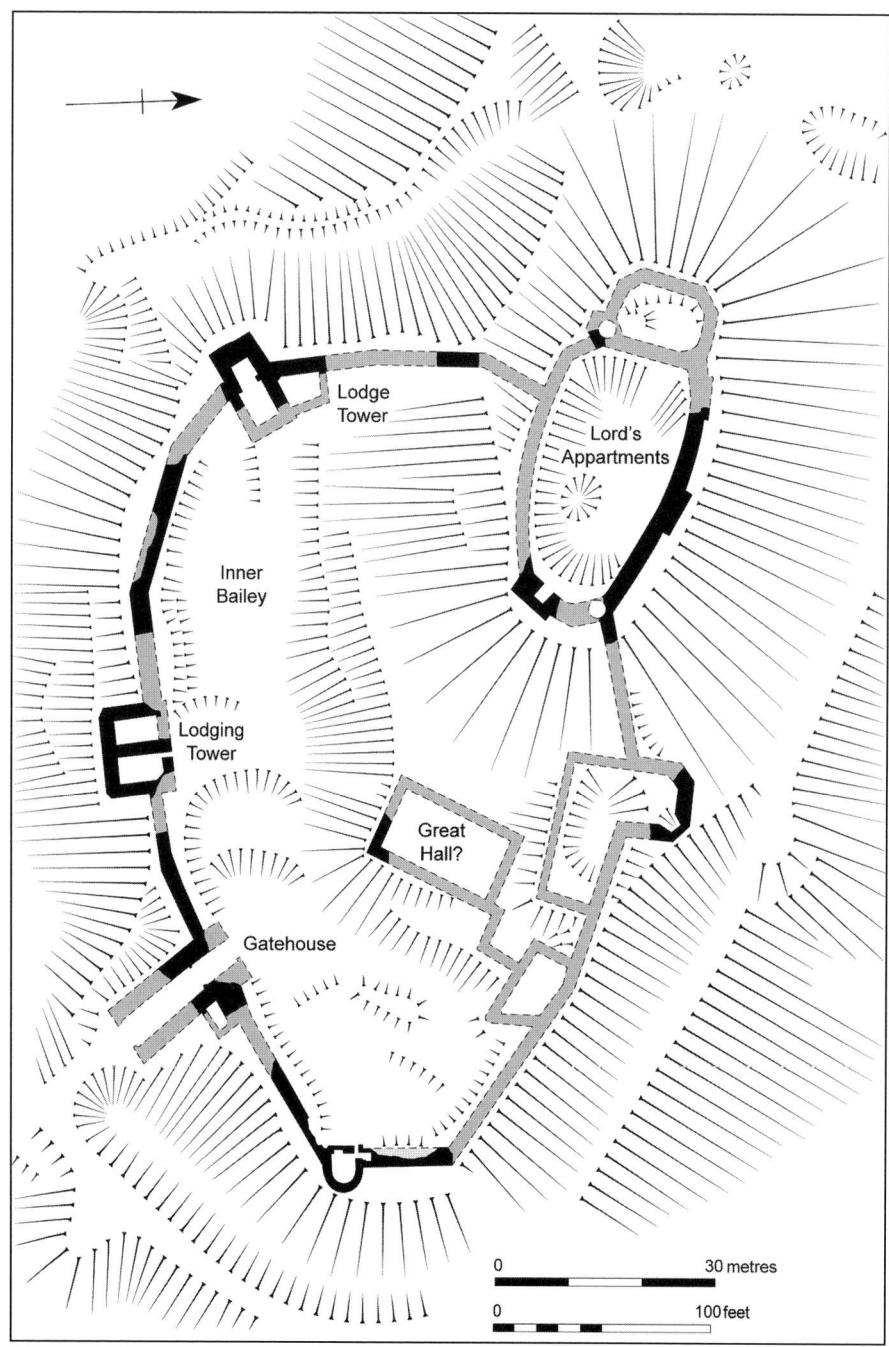

Wigmore: Ground plan of the inner bailey. After English Heritage 2015.

Wigmore: The inner gatehouse from the SE.

WILTON, Herefordshire (Private). Stone castle in existence by 1188, when it was held by Longchamp family, but rebuilt during the C13 and C14. Around 1250 Wilton came into the hands of the de Grey family and remained with them until the late C16 when it was sold, and a house built across the S front. The castle was burnt out during the Civil War, but a new house was built within the ruins during the C18.

    Sub-rectangular enclosure overlooking a crossing of the river Wye, the disparate nature of the towers suggesting that the construction of the stone castle was carried out over a long period rather than in one fell swoop. The entrance, of which there is now no trace, must have been in the S front, but here, one is now confronted by the ruined C16 house, though its rounded SE corner has been cited as a possible reflection of one of the flanking towers.

At the SW angle is a great tower some 75ft (22m) long with an apsidal W end projecting beyond the curtain; such a plan is a curiosity in an English castle but would be at home in C13 north Wales (e.g., Castell-y-Bere, Carndochan, both in Merioneth). However, the details, which include steep segmental-pointed arches with wide chamfers, are consistent with other English castles along the border, notably Goodrich (qv). Immediately E of the apse on the S side, the remains of a turret probably housed a latrine (cf. Castell-y-Bere S tower).

At the NW corner is an octagonal tower with integral latrine turret, probably a derivation of the late C13 royal works in north Wales (Caernarfon for the polygonal form; Rhuddlan, Conwy, Harlech for the latrine turret). The NE tower has largely disappeared but a roundish mid-wall tower on the E side has survived, complete with arrow loops and a restored trefoil-arched window. RCHME 1931, 29–31; Remfry 1998.

WINCHESTER, Hampshire (Open). An important royal castle established *c*.1067, of which the great hall is now the only significant element to survive above ground level. Winchester Castle occupied a sub-rectangular site aligned NNE–SSW (for the sake of simplicity described here as N–S). There was a motte at the N end, and later a second motte, or raised platform, at the S end, forming an upper ward and containing a great tower. The great hall was towards the N end.

In 1216 the castle was besieged and captured by Prince Louis, who caused considerable damage with his assault engines. Substantial reconstruction works were undertaken by Henry III, beginning in 1222, when the great hall was taken down and the current hall begun under the supervision of the royal mason Master Stephen. The great gatehouse at the E end of the castle was rebuilt and a large new round tower erected at the NE angle. The great tower on the motte was rebuilt in 1259–60 under the direction of John of Gloucester. Held for the King during the Civil War, it was besieged and captured by Parliament in 1645 and the fortifications subsequently demolished. An army barrack was established in the castle in the 1790s and rebuilt after a fire of 1894 around what is now known as Peninsular Square, which occupies that greater part of the former castle.

The approach to the castle is from the N, down Castle Avenue to a terrace in front of the great hall of 1222–36. N of the terrace the remains of the NE round tower are exposed to view, its circular plan marked out in concrete. Steps descend to two sally ports which extended beyond the castle walls N and E. The great hall is a single-storey, five-bay building of aisled construction, possibly on the site of the Norman Hall that it replaced. As built in the C13 there were service and main doorways in the first and second bay from the L (E) respectively with windows above; the present central entrance dates from the end of the C19, and replaces a window. Originally, the eaves level was lower, and the upper halves of the windows rose above it under gables containing circular oculi (cf. Stokesay [qv] of *c*.1280); the eaves were raised in the 1390s and the gables disappeared. The spacious interior, its giant arcades carried on shafted piers in Purbeck marble, evokes something of the splendour of a medieval great hall of royal status. On the wall at the S end is the famous round table probably made for Edward I in 1289. Biddle *et al.* 2000; Guy 2020–1.

WINDSOR, Berkshire (Open). The greatest castle in the kingdom, Windsor was founded by William I *c.*1070 to control the Thames valley, later becoming an important royal residence. Built on a ridge above the river, it comprises a very substantial motte set between large upper (E) and lower (W) wards. There is also a small middle ward between the motte and the lower ward. The original extent of the castle is uncertain, but the current parameters had probably been obtained by the C12, when Windsor became a significant royal residence.

Henry II was responsible for transforming the upper ward by the construction of a courtyard house which became the nucleus of the royal apartments, and by rebuilding the defences in stone, characterized by rectangular wall towers; he may also have crowned the motte with a shell-keep. In 1216 Windsor was besieged by the forces of Prince Louis of France, Louis himself then directing the siege of Dover (qv). The siege was unsuccessful but some damage to the castle was sustained, and Henry III was to carry out major works there in the 1220s, including the reconstruction of the western and southern defences of the lower ward and the raising of a new wall around the S side of the motte, typified by round-fronted towers. In the 1240s Henry created a new suite of royal apartments in the NE corner of the lower ward, set around a cloister with the royal chambers to the N and the Chapel of St George to the S.

Between 1350 and 1377 Edward III effected a transformation of the interior by the creation of a college associated with the newly-created Order of the Garter in the lower ward (1350–6), by remodelling the Round Tower (1353–7), rebuilding the royal apartments in the upper ward (1357–65), and constructing the lodging ranges on the E and W sides of the upper ward (1364–77). The work was under the direction of the master mason John Sponlee assisted by William Wynford. The master carpenters included William Herland, William Hurley and William Wintringham. The last great work of the Middle Ages was the Edward IV's construction of a new collegiate chapel of St George 1477–83 and accommodation for the associated priests; the master mason was Henry Janyns and the master carpenter John Squyer. Under Henry VII, Henry III's chapel was largely reconstructed as the lady chapel to the new church.

Access to much of the exterior is restricted, but a consoling thought is that this does not include the W front facing High Street which can be viewed by all, and which despite the C19 refenestration, refacing of the towers and partial reconstruction, is still recognizable as the work of Henry III of the 1220s. Decorative banded masonry, the curtain punctuated by the three round-fronted towers with battered bases, named (from L to R) Curfew, Garter and Salisbury. Around the corner in Castle Hill is the early C16 Henry VIII Gate, on the site of the medieval gateway to the lower ward, and further along, flanking the motte, the Henry III and Edward III Towers, the termini of Henry III's (now replaced) enclosing wall on this side of the motte, and the only parts of the scheme to survive, albeit much altered.

Lower Ward. Entering the castle via the C19 St George's Gate next to the Edward III Tower, a perambulation around the motte leads to the lower ward, the natural starting point for the visitor, albeit reached via a circuitous route. The lower ward is home to the collegiate complex founded by Edward III in the C14 but radically transformed by Edward IV and completed by Henry VII. It centres around the late C15 St George's Chapel, the dominating focus of the outer ward, built on the scale of a medium-sized cathedral. Aisled nave and choir of equal length with an additional ambulatory bay at the E end, a central crossing with short semi-octagonal transepts, and an aisleless Lady Chapel with semi-polygonal E end, this latter a reconstruction of the chapel first raised by Henry III and endowed by Edward III for the Order of the Garter scheme. Polygonal chapels project from all except the NE corner, where the church connects with the C14 college buildings.

Panel-traceried windows with four-centred arches, those to the clearstorey slightly less depressed, the bays articulated by flying buttresses with panelled pinnacles capped by statues of heraldic beasts; figure sculptures are to be found in buttress niches at aisle level. An openwork parapet extends between the upper buttress finials. The nave W end is framed by a pair of polygonal turrets, the elevated threshold of the W door now approached by a late C19 grand staircase. Blind panels to either side of the door, and above, the great W window with five tiers of fifteen lights beneath traceried intersecting arches.

The richly-decorated interior features blind panelling and heavily-moulded arches and piers, the latter dispensing with capitals to segue into rib clusters bordering and fanning out to blend into the lierne vault. The nave vault was in place by 1506 when John Aylmer and William Vertue contracted to build the choir vault to the same pattern as that over the nave, with a stipulation to complete it by 1508. Fan-vaults over the aisles and crossing, the latter of 1527–8, probably to a design by Vertue (d. 1527).

In the ambulatory E of the altar screen is an exciting survival from the C13, nothing less than the *in situ* western entrance to Henry III's chapel which was incorporated into the new church. A tripartite arrangement of pointed openings (the outer two blocked) with Purbeck marble shafts, the glory of the scheme being the original paired doors in the centre which are covered with a display of decorative ironwork: a vertical line of three large vesicas on each door augmented with multiple scrolls with foliate terminations. a hugely important relic of the medieval smith's art, in this case stamped several times with the maker's name: 'GILEBERTVS', probably Gilbert de Bonnington of Canterbury, a moneyer and probable goldsmith.

More delicate examples of medieval ironwork can be seen on the door to Edward IV's first-floor chantry chapel in the choir N aisle, which occupies the two easternmost bays (see the oriels overlooking the choir). The door and its furniture date from *c.*1480, the metalwork including a lock plate, handle plate and squint. Of the same period are the *ex situ* gates from the chantry on the N side of the High Altar, a highly significant piece of ironwork of *c.*1480 by John Tresilian, framed by twin polygonal towers, and very architectural in character with buttresses, traceried windows and an upper tier of little oriels or lanterns.

The main fixtures in the choir, however, are the stalls of 1477–84 made under the direction of the master carver, William Berkeley. There were originally twenty-one along the N and S sides and eight along the W side, all with highly elaborate canopies (originally capped with spires) and seats carved with misericords. Two additional stalls were added at the E end of both long sides in the late C18.

Exiting the chapel via the W end brings us face to face with the C15 Horseshoe Cloister, around which are ranged the timber-framed lodgings of the vicars choral. At the opposite (E) end is the former Lady Chapel, now the Albert Memorial Chapel, which incorporates elements of Henry III's chapel. To the N of this is the Dean's Cloister, representing the first phase (1350–2) of Edward III's college, which was based around the courtyard house built by Henry III. Edward kept the courtyard and elements of the buildings surrounding it including the chapel, which became the collegiate chapel of St George, and created a cloister. The N, S and W walls all seem to pre-date the C14 work, the most conspicuously C13 part being the N wall of the chapel, which retains a blind arcade with engaged columns bearing stiff leaf capitals. The E range (now part of the Deanery) was rebuilt entirely to accommodate (from S to N) vestry, chapter house and warden's lodge; flanking the chapter house door was a pair of Perpendicular windows (one now converted to a doorway) with cusped outer arch fringe, the tripartite arrangement linked by a continuous hood mould springing from slender castellated corbels. New cloister alleys were constructed around the quadrangle, with openings of four cinquefoil-headed lights under sub-arches containing split- or double-cusped quatrefoils within twin supermullions.

North of the Dean's Cloister is the Canons' Cloister of 1353–6, around which the priests were lodged in two-storey timber-framed ranges. The final stage of construction was the Aerary, or treasury, of 1353–4 at the NW corner of the Dean's Cloister, the principal interest of which is the ground storey, an elaborately decorated porch giving access to the cloister from the W. Perpendicular traceried wall panelling and masterly lierne vault.

Back towards the motte, we come to the middle ward. Looking N, rising above the C19 building (Lord Chamberlain's Upper Stores) lining the RH (W) side of the court, is the Winchester Tower of 1356, a rectangular wall tower at the junction of the middle and upper wards with a stair turret at the SE corner, rising above the parapet, and a latrine turret at the NW angle, outside the curtain wall. The rectangular form is characteristic of the towers raised during Edward III's reconstruction of the upper ward, which were once a prominent feature of the castle.

Middle Ward. The middle ward is dominated by the motte and its crowning C12 Round Tower, sub-circular in plan and articulated by pilaster buttresses. The two upper storeys and machicolated battlements are a C19 fabrication, transforming what was a rather squat building into something more tower like. The medieval shell represents a reconstruction of an earlier shell-keep, seemingly occasioned by subsidence on the S side of the motte, perhaps a result of undermining during the 1216 siege. Edward III's remodelling of 1353–7 involved the construction of timber-framed two-storey apartments backing onto the walls of the keep and ranged around the four sides of a central courtyard (now covered). Remarkably, the hefty timber framing largely survives, and appears to have contained an exclusive, if compact, residence with hall, chambers, kitchen and service rooms. It may represent temporary accommodation for the King and Queen during the reconstruction of the upper ward.

The entrance is via a C15 covered staircase on the NW side, entered from the Engine Court at the NW angle of the upper ward; before that one has to pass through the inner gatehouse of 1359/60 (the misleadingly named Norman Gate), much altered but retaining the basic character of central entrance recessed between two tall drum towers rising to approximately the same height as today. It forms, as it did in the C14, a powerful introduction to the upper ward, and heralds a series of later C14 gatehouses of this general form. Beneath the pseudo-medieval machicolations, the C14 pointed gateway survives; it was protected by a portcullis and opens to a rib-vaulted gate passage of two octopartite bays with ringed sculptured bosses at the three main intersections.

Upper Ward. Passing into the upper ward the trefoil-headed entrance to the Round Tower staircase is on the R (S); it probably dates from the late C14. The upper part of the stairway was probably built by the master mason John Cantelow in

1439–40. There is no public access to the upper ward itself, nor indeed is there much of interest generally accessible to the visitor whose prime interest is the medieval castle, but the present buildings almost entirely occupy the footprint of their C14 predecessors, and although much has been altered, the skeletal pattern remains, along with a good deal of medieval fabric.

As completed by Edward III in the C14, the main block along the N side of the ward, now containing the state apartments, was grouped around three courtyards, E (Kitchen Court), W (Little Cloister) and central (Great Cloister), separated by the main and privy staircases to E and W respectively, and lined around the perimeter by domestic ranges. Facing the upper ward, the 350ft (106m) S front was articulated by two gatehouses each flanked by a pair of octagonal towers, and at the SW corner by the polygonal Rose Tower, which survives. The Spicerie (W) Gate (replaced by the State Entrance) gave access to the central and W courts and the privy stair, while the Kitchen (E) Gate (replaced by the Guests' Entrance but surviving in part at ground-floor level) led to the Kitchen (E) Court.

The main apartments were at first-floor level, the S range between the two gatehouses containing the great hall (E) and chapel (W), the royal apartments being ranged around the Little Cloister and the N side of the Great Cloister. To give some idea of how the present layout relates to the C14 plan the following should be noted along the route of the public tour. The Grand Staircase is on the site of the Little Cloister, the Grand Vestibule on the site of the privy staircase, the Waterloo Chamber occupies the Great Cloister, the Grand Reception Room the site of the main stair, and St George's Hall replaces both the great hall and chapel.

The main visible remains from the medieval period are at ground level. Within the S range (from E–W) are the Armoury Undercroft, Great Undercroft and Steward's Hall, the first two indubitably C14, each with quadripartite vaulting carried on a central line of octagonal columns and half-column responds, the Steward's Hall possibly a C13 building incorporated into the later scheme. Immediately N of the Steward's Hall, is the Larderie Passage, a C14 arcaded and vaulted construct, looking into the Kitchen Court, and built to carry the N wall of the Great Hall above, which oversails the rear (N) wall of the Steward's Hall. On the opposite (N) side of the Kitchen Court is the remarkably preserved C14 kitchen, a rectangular building retaining its roof and lantern, predominantly a rebuild of 1489 incorporating C14 material. St John Hope 1913; Wilson 2002; Emery 2006, 192–208; Brindle 2018.

WINGFIELD, Suffolk (Private). Moated quadrilateral castle built for Richard II's chancellor, Michael de la Pole, under a licence to crenellate of 1385. It was probably raised to celebrate Pole's elevation to the peerage as Earl of Suffolk in the same year. The outstanding aspect of Wingfield is the entrance (S) front, which survives to full height, in contrast to the rest of the enceinte which has largely disappeared. The two corner towers and the twin towers of the not quite central gatehouse are all semi-octagonal, an unusual choice for a castle at this date, and perhaps harking back to earlier in the century when polygonal towers had been in vogue (cf. Alnwick, Maxstoke, Newark, Stafford [qv]). The fenestration pattern shows there were two storeys of apartments set against the curtain wall; the towers rise through three storeys and there is a single storey above the gateway. At the two N angles was a pair of quadrilateral towers and on the E side a rectangular postern tower. Aldwell 1925, 7–34; Emery 2000, 160–4; Liddiard 2015.

WINGFIELD MANOR HOUSE, South Wingfield, Derbyshire. Situated at the N end of a spur above the village of South Wingfield, the eye-catching properties of Wingfield Manor House make a stirring sight, the verticality of its high gables, turrets, buttresses, chimneys and great tower (the 'High Tower') contributing to a spikey skyline of theatrical quality, presenting itself unequivocally as the house of a man of consequence. This castellated great house was built between 1439/1440 and *c*.1450 by Ralph, Lord Cromwell (d. 1456), treasurer (1433–43) to Henry VI, on a castle site occupied since the C12. The initial site work was carried out by John Entrepas, and probably included the razing of the earlier castle, of which no part remains upstanding, although traces of the castle ditch have been discovered during excavation and survey.

Cromwell died in 1456, and Wingfield was purchased by the Earl of Shrewsbury. The Sixth Earl was charged with keeping Mary Queen of Scots in custody; she was at Wingfield in 1569 and 1584. In 1644 the manor house was besieged by the Parliamentarians, bombarded, captured, and in 1646 slighted. Subsequently it was bought by the Haltons who patched up the shell of the great hall and lived there until the 1770s. Since then, the site has continued to be occupied as a farm, the house to which occupies part of the range dividing the two courtyards. At the time of writing Wingfield was closed to the public for safety reasons.

The house comprises outer (S) and inner (N) courtyards; there was a garden and orchard to the N of the inner courtyard. Approached from the Amber valley to the E, the track led to the outer gatehouse at the SE angle of the complex, a rectangular block divided into pedestrian and carriage entrances, recessed between two rectangular turrets. On entering the inner courtyard to the L (S) of the gateway, is an aisled building, formerly with an upper floor, and still roofed owing to its latter-day use as a barn. Its C15 purpose is uncertain, but storage and administrative purposes are

Wingfield Manor House: Great hall and chamber block.

possible. The rest of the S range has largely disappeared owing to the intrusion of farm buildings, and the E and W ranges are also incomplete, though they probably contained staff lodgings.

The better-preserved N range divides the inner and outer courtyards. The RH (E) side is occupied by the farmhouse, the LH (W) side is a ruin, and at the W end is the truncated High Tower, extending beyond the curtain wall. A notable aspect of the frontage is a splendid array of hefty chimney stacks, breaking forward into the courtyard, their tapering tops carrying lofty chimneys. In the centre is the inner gatehouse, also with carriage and pedestrian entrances, and flanked by a pair of rectangular turrets. Above the gateway an armorial panel bearing the arms of Cromwell and his associates and Cromwell's personal device of crossed purses.

Moving through the gateway into the inner courtyard, directly ahead is the two-storey porch giving access to the principal accommodation complex on the N side of the inner courtyard. Doorway with continuous moulded surround, the pointed arch decorated with square fleurons. Parapet frieze of large fleurons, and crenellations with continuous coping around merlons and embrasures; the merlons are carved with heraldic shields. To the L (W) the gable of a crosswing containing a first-floor chamber with large traceried window. To the R (E) a gap where the front of the great hall should be; only its eastern end survives in the form of a canted bay, or oriel, containing tall traceried windows under four-centred heads.

Inside the porch are stone benches L and R and then the doorway into the former cross-passage of the great hall with a door opposite leading to the N porch and garden. To the L (W) is a laver under a four-centred arch. The ground-floor hall was open to the roof and lit by highly placed windows with four-centred arches; the C17 cross windows beneath them were introduced by the Haltons who also inserted a first floor. A doorway at the upper (E) end of the hall led to a now-vanished suite of apartments, probably Lord Cromwell's private rooms, and to a staircase which descends to the hall undercroft. The undercroft is covered by an elaborate rib vault carried on a row of central columns and half-column responds with large carved bosses at the intersections. It is evidently an insertion resulting from an early change of plan, to judge from its rather awkward layout.

At the lower (W) end of the hall is a tri-partite arrangement of pointed doorways, the larger central opening giving onto a passage leading to the kitchen and the two flanking doors to the pantry (L) and buttery (R). A heated room N of the buttery was evidently residential. These spaces are beneath the first-floor guest suite, which was reached from a stair in the N porch. The central passage descends towards the kitchen; food and drink could be collected from serving hatches to the L (S) and at the very end of the passage (this latter now a doorway). The great kitchen has three large fireplaces. The area to the N of the kitchen represents incremental infilling, providing further residential accommodation at the upper level.

In addition to the accommodation in the N range there were lodgings in the S range and a W range (only the W wall of which survives) each with a fireplace and latrine. There may also have been an E range, but of this there is now no trace. Also accessed from the inner courtyard was the five-storey High Tower, a rectangular keep-like structure with an attached latrine turret, containing individual lodgings reached via a stair at the NE angle. These were set above a ground-storey communal latrine probably flushed from a roof-top cistern. Despite its function, this tower, similar in concept to the slightly later High Tower at Tutbury (qv), which also contained a series of lodgings, and which likewise projected from the curtain, was no doubt inspired by the keeps of yesteryear, and intended to proclaim Lord Cromwell's noble status. Thompson, 1976 and 1981; Emery 1985, and 2000, 449–59; Dixon 2019.

WITTON-LE-WEAR, County Durham (Centre of a holiday and caravan park and open to guests). A licence to crenellate granted to Ralph de Eure in 1410 included a pardon for having begun, without permission, to fortify his manor house by enclosing it with a wall of stone and lime. This licence marks the final stage in the construction of a fortified manor house begun here in the C14. Additions were made in 1796, 1846 and 1881, but the present building is still largely contained by the medieval curtain wall.

The remains of the castle completed by Ralph de Eure *c.*1410 comprised a roughly square courtyard surrounded by a curtain wall, interrupted on the N side by a late C14 great tower. Opposed gateways in the centres of the E and W sides, are each protected by a machicolated projection of the parapet. Formerly, there was a bartizan at each corner of the curtain: three round and one square, of which only three survive.

The rectangular tower measures *c.*80ft × 35ft (24.3m × 10.6m); a turret projects from each corner: those to the E are placed diagonally and have side-machicolated battlements (cf. Raby and Brancepeth [qv]) carried on two tiers of corbels. The W turrets are square and of uneven projection; on the battlements are two stone figures of warriors (cf. Raby and Hylton, [qv]).

The basement is barrel-vaulted and has small chambers in the corner turrets. A newel stair in the E wall of the tower ascends to the first floor, probably a hall or great chamber. At this level the southern turrets housed small chambers accessible from the main room. The staircase coming up from the basement terminates here and in order to continue the ascent to the second-floor chamber and roof, there is a second newel stair situated in the NW turret. At second-floor level there was a garderobe in the NE turret, and a mural passage in the W wall. Emery 1996, 155–7.

WOLVESEY, Winchester, Hampshire (Open – EH). Remains of a C12 fortified bishop's palace on the site of the Anglo-Saxon episcopal residence, in the SE corner of the Roman town, the greater part being the work of King Stephen's brother, Bishop Henry de Blois (1129–71). Substantial works had been completed by 1138, and when, in 1141, the Empress Matilda and her army occupied Winchester and besieged Wolvesey, they would have seen a defendable walled and moated enclosure with at least one tower projecting from its perimeter. The bishop's men reacted to the siege by raining fire down on the enemy, so causing a conflagration in the town. Wolvesey held out until reinforcements arrived and the besiegers were themselves besieged.

The remains lie to the N and E of the C17 former bishop's palace, which occupies part of the medieval site and which is inaccessible to visitors. The buildings of the castle were arranged around an irregular quadrangle, and several phases have been recorded. The earliest of the buildings is the West Hall, which is assigned to Bishop William Giffard (1107–29); it occupied the entire W side of the courtyard, but only its north end survives, and the greater part of its site lies within the grounds of the later palace. Despite its name, the West Hall was actually a chamber block housing the private apartments of the bishop and his household.

There was also a great hall, but this was replaced by Bishop Henry, who built the East Hall on the opposite side of the courtyard and added a porch to the West Hall. He subsequently appended a chapel and latrine block to the West Hall, raised a great tower on the E side of the complex together with a smaller tower (Wymonds Tower) further S. Most of these components date from c.1135–41. During the first few years of Henry I's reign, when Bishop Henry's castles were slighted by the King, the bishop himself was in exile in Cluny, but returned in 1158 and built a substantial new N front, the centrepiece of which was a large gatehouse (Woodman's Gate).

Access to the ruins is now via a footpath from College Road, which leads to the SE corner of the complex. Straight ahead, just beyond some foundations, is the S gable end of Bishop Henry's East Hall of c.1135–8, a three-tier elevation framed by pilaster buttresses, with round-arched openings including a central door flanked by small rectangular loops, two large windows above which lit the first-floor hall, and then, above a bold string course, two smaller windows, this upper section above the string course belonging to Bishop Henry's heightening of the building probably between c.1141 and 1154. Beyond the LH (W) buttress is the end of an aisle that ran the full length of the W front. To the R is the entrance to an aisle-like building which extends only part of the way along the side of the hall. At the SE angle of this structure, rising above and projecting beyond the adjacent curtain wall, is Wymond's tower, initially a latrine turret, later converted into a tower by encasing with buttressed walling.

Through the central doorway into the hall range; its S end formed a two-storey chamber block. The longitudinal walls are reduced to their footings, but the N gable end is as well preserved as the S; it retains elements of pointed blind arcading, added by Bishop Henry to support the greater thickness of the superimposed upper storey; below the arcading are the scars of the former supporting buttresses, which rose from ground level. Next, at the N end of the courtyard, is Woodman's Gate, of 1158–71, placed in front of the earlier C12 enclosing wall: rectangular, with a central passage and flanking guard rooms. Then the West Hall of c.1100, or at least its northern end, nicely faced with Quarr-stone ashlar. In front are the vestiges of Bishop Henry's Caen-stone porch of c.1135–8. At the N end of the building is the commodious latrine block of c.1138–41, which was flushed by a stream. Biddle 1986; Wareham 2000.

WRESSLE, Yorkshire East Riding (Periodic open days). Quadrangular castle built of excellent quality ashlar masonry for Sir Thomas Percy, younger brother of the Earl of Northumberland, probably in the 1390s. Percy was executed in 1402 for his part in the rebellion of that year and his property confiscated. It returned to the Percy family c.1471 and was refurbished in the first quarter of the C16 by the Fifth Earl of Northumberland. The greater part of the castle was demolished in 1650, but the S range and towers continued in occupation until the 1790s, when fire broke out and gutted the remaining buildings.

What survives is the S range and the two attached corner towers, as well as a later bakehouse which incorporates the NW junction of the C14 courtyard ranges. However, floor plans and a perspective drawing of c.1600 by T.F. Hampe allow a faithful reconstruction of its plan and elevations. Comparison with the plans of Castle Bolton (qv) and Lumley (qv) suggest the involvement of John Lewyn of Durham. The gatehouse was in the centre of the E front opposite the first-floor great hall in the W range. The entrance to the hall was at the N end of the courtyard frontage, approached by an external staircase. It was heated by an open hearth, and the dais at the S end by a large fireplace which survives in the wall of the SW tower; like other fireplaces in the castle, it has a three-centred arch. Above is the scar of the nearly flat roof.

The S front comprises a range with two-storey centre and three-storey end blocks recessed between the three-storey Lord's Tower (SW) and the four-storey Chapel Tower (SE). In each of the re-entrant angles is a latrine turret, structurally later than the other components and perhaps an afterthought. The ground floor was lit by small trefoil-headed loops (now blocked), the upper floors by large twin-light transomed windows; those of the great chamber in the centre of the range are cinquefoil-headed with quatrefoils above in the manner of plate tracery; a similar technique was used in the first-floor chapel S and E windows, in imitation of panel tracery, the chunky proportions presenting an original, but curious appearance. Later phases of fenestration include the remains of a C15 first-floor oriel window in the Lord's Tower and a number of C16 windows with three-centred heads, mostly at ground-floor level. Octagonal stair turrets rise above the two towers at the courtyard angles, and an octagonal chimney with crenellated top survives at the E end of the range.

The S range, which is entered from the former courtyard, contained two storeys of residential apartments, both apparently centred on a hall with end rooms formerly divided by timber partitions (also a characteristic of Lumley). Large central ground- and first-floor fireplaces in the N and S walls respectively. In the E wall a large brick blocking rising from first-floor level represents the chapel chancel arch. The chapel nave, then, was in the S range. Above was a gallery including the Lord's own pew. In the chapel a piscina survives; the other rooms were residential, as in the Lord's Tower, with fireplaces and latrines. Emery 1996; Hislop 2007; Brears 2011.

YANWATH HALL, Westmorland (Private). A fortified manor house of the Threlkeld family built on a bluff above a crossing of the river Eamont looking N. Begun in the C14 with the construction of a residential tower, to which two domestic ranges were added in the C15 to enclose the N and E sides of a courtyard; remodelled in the C16 by the Dudley family. The three-storey tower displays two structural phases, the ground storey being built from coursed rubble, with better-quality dressed stone blocks of near-ashlar quality above. This suggests a hiatus in construction, but not necessarily a long one. Crenellated parapet with four square corner turrets. The principal windows are all C16 insertions, but a C14 window with trefoiled ogee head survives to the W. Attached to the E side of the tower is the hall range, which retains a number of C15 windows with trefoil-headed lights including (on the S side) a bay window for lighting the dais. The C16 witnessed the insertion of several windows, an upper floor over the eastern half of the hall, a chimney stack backing onto the cross passage, and a doorway at the N end of the passage. Also, the kitchen at the E end of the range was reconstructed, though this retains its medieval great fireplace. Over the hall is a C15 arched-braced collar roof with three tiers of purlins, cusped wind braces and king posts. At the N end of the E wall a doorway provides access to the tower. A mural lobby opens to the barrel-vaulted basement and to a spiral stair in the NE angle. The first floor is largely C16 in appearance but retains a latrine in the NW corner with a wash basin. At second-floor level are two twin-light windows with stone benches in the embrasures. Curwen 1913, 319–22; RCHME 1936, 250–2; Emery 1996, 259–61; Perriam and Robinson 1998, 320–1.

YELDEN, Bedfordshire. See **YIELDON**.

YIELDON (Yelden), Bedfordshire (Private). Motte with two baileys. A castle of the Traylly family dating from the C11 or C12. Mentioned in 1173–4 and said to be decayed in 1360. Motte and SW bailey of one build surrounded by a moat, the bailey also enclosed by an inner bank. Excavation in 1881–2 found debris from robbed stone buildings on the motte and in the bailey, in addition to foundations of a stone curtain behind the bank, and, within the moat at the SW angle, foundations of a circular tower, possibly an element of a bridged entrance complex. A roughly triangular bailey to the N of the earthworks is thought to be a later addition. Petre 2012, 86–8.

YORK. In 1068 William the Conqueror established a castle in York as part of his policy to deal with the northern rebellion of Edgar the Aetheling, Anglo-Saxon claimant to the English throne. The following year a resurgent rebel army attacked the city and killed the constable, Robert FitzRichard. William returned, put the rebels to flight and built a second castle to supplement the first. Later that year a Danish army joined forces with the Northumbrians and marched on York; the two Norman castles were captured and destroyed. William marched N again, chased off the rebels, set in motion the devastating Harrying of the North, and rebuilt the two castles. It is not entirely certain which of the two strongholds came first, but opinion generally favours the better known and preserved of these, on the N side of the Ouse, which incorporates Clifford's Tower; the other, which came to be known as the 'Old Baile', is directly opposite, on the S side of the river.

York Castle (Open). York Castle comprised a motte with a bailey to the SE; there may have been a second bailey to the W, but of this all trace has been lost. Prior to the C13 the castle superstructure was mainly of timber. The keep on top of the motte was burnt down during the anti-Semitic riots of 1190, thereby killing the Jews who had sought safety there. A new keep was erected but, along with other parts of the castle, it probably blew down in 1228 during a gale. When Henry III visited York in 1244, he decided to rebuild the castle in stone, a project carried out over the next 20 years.

The pride of York Castle and the principal surviving element from Henry III's reconstruction is Clifford's Tower, an unusual structure built to a quatrefoil plan according to the advice of the King's master mason Henry de Reyns. Its footprint has often been compared to that of the early C12 great tower of Etampes, and indeed, the correspondence of the dimensions is too great to be coincidental. However, despite its comparative lack of height, it is arguably a more arresting building, an effect partly occasioned by the high quality of its limestone ashlar. The two-storey tower has a battered base, and survives up to parapet level, but the crenellations themselves have been swept away. Very unusual openings pierce the walls at both levels; their upper parts are windows, their lower parts arrow loops with basal oillets. The first-floor windows mostly have shouldered lintels, an early use of this form in the royal works, but two pointed windows flank the entrance. To the N, E and W, at the junctions of the lobes, round turrets rising from first-floor level house staircases (E and W) and latrines (N). In the centre of the S front is the forebuilding containing the entrance, now reached by a flight of fifty-five steps, but formerly approached from the bailey across a bridge. Now largely of C17 date, the forebuilding incorporates the remains of its C13 predecessor (essentially the E wall) including one jamb of the gateway and part of its arch.

Through the forebuilding a pointed arch gives access to a portcullis-protected passage to the great tower, now one large space; how it was divided originally is uncertain; there are no signs of wall divisions, so any partitions must have been of timber. The two northern lobes each have a fireplace and a latrine, suggesting a division into two rooms at this end, but otherwise the original plan is a matter of conjecture. In the centre was a central octagonal pillar which must have formed a support for the upper floor and probably the roof, both of which must have presented particular technical challenges. A pair of spiral staircases flanking the entrance ascend to first-floor level, and then to the wall walk, with direct access from the W stair to the chapel where the N and E wall arcades partially survive, their pointed arches decorated with dogtooth ornament. At first-floor level is a single latrine and no fireplace.

Apart from Clifford's Tower, parts of the bailey defences survive, including two towers. The main stretch is from Tower Street at the N end of Skeldergate Bridge. It includes the S corner tower, its ashlar facing and smoothly-battered base emulating the excellent masonry work of Clifford's Tower. Only a little further along to the N is a blocking denoting the former position of the S gatehouse, and beyond that the SE tower, half round with cruciform arrow loops. Cooper 1911; RCHME 1972.

The Old Baile and Baile Hill (Visible from the city walls). Now represented only by its motte (Baile Hill), the Old Baile lay within the SW corner of the city defences. The city wall is later than the castle but may follow the line of the Anglo-Saxon defences. The bailey is now covered by housing but occupied a rectangular area, its NE and NW sides broadly following the lines of Cromwell Street and Falkland Street. The now isolated motte was therefore at the E angle. Excavations of Baile Hill in the 1960s showed that it was built on top of C11 occupation deposits and was raised in a series of horizontal layers. On the summit evidence was found for a timber perimeter wall with an entrance on the W side and, inside the enclosure, a central rectangular timber building with a turret at the E angle opposite the entrance to the motte top. Addyman and Priestly 1977.

CASTLES BY COUNTY

Bedfordshire
  Bedford
  Biggleswade
  Cainhoe
  Eaton Socon
  Meppershall
  Totternhoe
  Yielden
Berkshire
  Brightwell
  Donnington
  Hinton Waldrist
  Wallingford
  Windsor
Buckinghamshire
  Boarstall
  Castlethorpe
  Lavendon
  Weston Turville
  Whitchurch
Cambridgeshire and the Isle of Ely
  Bourn Hall
  Burwell
  Cambridge
  Ely
  Rampton
Cheshire
  Aldford
  Beeston
  Chester
  Halton
  Pulford
  Shotwick
Cornwall
  Launceston
  Restormel
  Tintagel
  Trematon

County Durham
  Barnard Castle
  Brancepeth
  Durham
  Hollinside
  Hylton
  Lumley
  Raby
  Witton-le-Wear
Cumberland
  Bewcastle
  Carlisle
  Cockermouth
  Dacre
  Egremont
  Greystoke
  Kirkoswald
  Muncaster
  Naworth
  Penrith
  Scaleby
Derbyshire
  Bakewell
  Bolsover
  Duffield
  Haddon
  Peveril
  Wingfield
Devon
  Bampton
  Barnstaple
  Berry Pomeroy
  Bickleigh
  Compton
  Exeter
  Gidleigh
  Lydford
  Okehampton
  Plympton

  Tiverton
  Totnes
Dorset
  Corfe Castle
  Marshwood
  Powerstock
  Rufus
  Sherbourne
  Wareham
Essex
  Castle Hedingham
  Clavering
  Colchester
  Great Canfield
  Hadleigh
  Ongar
  Pleshey
  Rayleigh
  Saffron Walden
  Stansted Mountfichet
Gloucestershire
  Berkeley
  Brimpsfield
  Bristol
  Dymock
  Miserden
  St Briavels
Hampshire and the Isle of Wight
  Ashley
  Bishop's Waltham
  Carisbrooke
  Christchurch
  Merdon
  Odiham
  Portchester
  Southampton
  Winchester
  Wolvesey

Herefordshire
Brampton Bryan
Bredwardine
Bronsil
Clifford
Croft
Dorstone
Eardisley
Ewyas Harold
Goodrich
Hereford
Huntington
Kilpeck
Llancillo
Longtown
Lyonshall
Pembridge Castle
Richard's Castle
Snodhill
Treago
Wigmore
Wilton

Hertfordshire
Anstey
Benington
Berkhamsted
Hertford
Therfield
Waytemore
Weoley

Huntingdonshire
Buckden
Huntingdon

Kent
Allington
Canterbury
Chilham
Cooling
Dover
Eynsford
Folkestone
Hever
Leeds
Leybourne
Lympne
Newnham
Queenborough
Rochester
Saltwood
Scotney
Sutton Valence
Thurnham
Tonbridge
West Malling

Lancashire
Aldingham
Castlestede
Clitheroe
Gleaston
Lancaster
Penwortham
Piel

Leicestershire
Ashby de la Zouche
Groby
Hallaton
Kirby Muxloe
Leicester
Mountsorrel
Sauvey

Lincolnshire
Bolingbroke
Bourne
Castle Bytham
Castle Carlton
Kingerby
Lincoln
Owston Ferry
Sleaford
Somerton
Swineshead
Tattershall
Welbourn

London and Middlesex
London, Tower of
Montfichet's Tower
South Mimms

Norfolk
Baconsthorpe
Caister
Castle Acre
Castle Rising
Mileham
North Elmham
Norwich
Thetford
Weeting

Northamptonshire and the Soke of Peterborough
Barnwell
Fotheringhay
Longthorpe
Peterborough
Rockingham
Sulgrave
Titchmarsh

Northumberland
Alnwick
Aydon
Bamburgh
Belsay
Berwick-upon-Tweed
Bitchfield
Blenkinsop
Bothal
Bywell
Cartington
Chillingham
Chipchase
Cocklaw
Cocklepark
Corbridge
Crawley
Cresswell
Dally
Dunstanburgh
Edlingham
Elsdon
Embleton
Etal
Featherstone
Ford
Halton
Harbottle
Haughton
Langley
Mitford
Morpeth
Nafferton
Newcastle upon Tyne
Norham
Prudhoe
Shortflatt

Tarset
Thirlwall
Tynemouth
Wark
Warkworth
Nottinghamshire
Cuckney
Newark
Nottingham
Oxfordshire
Ascot d'Oilly
Bampton
Banbury
Broughton
Deddington
Middleton Stoney
Oxford
Shirburn
Swerford
Rutland
Oakham
Shropshire
Acton Burnell
Adderley
Alberbury
Bridgnorth
Brockhurst
Castell Bryn Amlwg
Caus
Cheney Longville
Clun
Ellesmere
Holdgate
Hopton Castle
Knockin
Ludlow
Morton Corbet
Myddle
Oswestry
Pontesbury
Pulverbatch
Quatford
Redcastle
Ruyton-Eleven-Town
Shrawardine
Shrewsbury
Stokesay
Wattlesborough
Whitchurch
Whittington
Somerset
Bridgwater
Castle Cary
Castle Neroche
Crewkerne
Dunster
Farleigh Hungerford
Montacute
Nether Stowey
Nunney
Over Stowey
Taunton
Staffordshire
Alton
Chartley
Dudley
Eccleshall
Heighley
Newcastle under Lyme
Stafford
Tamworth
Tutbury
Suffolk
Burgh
Clare
Framlingham
Haughley
Lidgate
Little Wenham
Mettingham
New Buckenham
Old Buckenham
Orford
Surrey
Abinger
Bletchingley
Farnham
Guildford
Reigate
Sussex
Amberley
Arundel
Bodiam
Bramber
Hastings
Herstmonceux
Knepp
Lewes
Pevensey
Warwickshire
Beaudesert
Brandon
Brinklow
Castle Bromwich
Fillongley
Hartshill
Kenilworth
Maxstoke
Warwick
Westmorland
Appleby
Brough
Brougham
Kendal
Pendragon
Sizergh
Yanwath
Wiltshire
Castle Combe
Devizes
Great Somerford
Ludgershall
Old Wardour
Worcestershire
Elmley
Hanley Castle
Inkberrow
Yorkshire East Riding
Great Driffield
Scarborough
Skipsea
Wressle
York
Yorkshire North Riding
Ayton
Bowes
Castle Bolton
Crayke
Danby
Gilling
Helmsley
Hutton Colswain
Middleham
Mortham Tower

Mulgrave
Nappa Hall
Pickering
Ravensworth
Richmond
Sheriff Hutton
Topcliffe
West Tanfield

Whorlton
Yorkshire West Riding
Almondbury
Barwick-in-Elmet
Burton-in-Lonsdale
Cawood
Conisbrough
Harewood

Knaresborough
Pontefract
Sandal
Sheffield
Skipton
Spofforth
Tickhill

BIBLIOGRAPHY

Adams, P. (2005–6), 'Clitheroe Castle', *Castle Studies Group Journal* 19: 79–92.
Addyman, P.V. and Priestly, J. (1977), 'Baile Hill, York', *Archaeological Journal* 134: 115–56.
Alcock, L., King, D.J.C., Putnam, W.G. and Spurgeon, C.J. (1967–8), 'Excavations at Castell Bryn Amlwg', *Montgomeryshire Collections* 60: 8–27.
Alcock, N.W. and Buckley, J. (1987), 'Leicester Castle: The Great Hall', *Medieval Archaeology* 31: 73–9.
Alcock, N.W., Faulkner, P.A. and Jones, S.R. (1978), 'Maxstoke Castle, Warwickshire', *Archaeological Journal* 135: 195–233.
Aldwell, S.W.H. (1925), *Wingfield: Its Church, Castle and College*. Ipswich: W.E. Harrison.
Alexander, M. (2006), *"With ramparts crown'd". The Early History of Guildford Castle*. Guildford Museum.
Alexander, M. and Westlake, S. (2009), 'Hadleigh Castle, Essex', *English Heritage Historical Review* 4: 4–21.
Allen, D. and Stoodley, N. (2010), 'Odiham Castle, Hampshire: Excavations 1981–1985', *Hampshire Studies* 65: 23–101.
Ashbee, J. (2004), '"The Chamber called Gloriette": Living at Leisure in Thirteenth- and Fourteenth-century Castles', *Journal of the British Archaeological Association* 157: 17–40.
Ashbee, J. (2005), *Goodrich Castle*. London: English Heritage.
Ashbee, J. (2006), 'Thomas Earl of Lancaster and the Great Gate of Dunstanburgh Castle', *English Heritage Review* 1: 28–35.
Ashbee, J. (2012), *Rochester Castle*. London: English Heritage.
Ashbee, J. (2020), *Restormel Castle*. London: English Heritage.
Ashbee, J. and Oswald, A. (2007), *Dunstanburgh Castle*. London: English Heritage.
Auden, J.E. (1895), 'Notes on the Church, Castle, and Parish of Shrawardine', *Transactions of the Shropshire Archaeological and Natural History Society* (2nd series), 7 (Pt 1): 120–202.
Austin, D. (2007), *Acts of Perception: A Study of Barnard Castle in Teesdale*. 2 volumes. Architectural and Archaeological Society of Durham and Northumberland Research Report No. 6.
Baggs, A.P., Crowley, D.A., Pugh, R.B., Stevenson, J.H. and Tomlinson, M. (1975), 'The Borough of Devizes: Town, Castle and Estates', in E. Crittall (ed.), *A History of the County of Wiltshire. Volume 10*. London: Victoria County History.
Baggs, A.P. and Jurica, A.R. (1996), 'St Briavels', in C.R. Currie and N.M. Herbert (eds), *A History of the County of Gloucester. Volume 5: Bledisloe Hundred, St Briavels Hundred, the Forest of Dean*. London: Victoria County History, 247–71.
Baggs, A.P. and Siraut, M.C. (1992), 'Bridgewater Castle', in R.W. Dunning (ed.), *A History of the County of Somerset. Volume 6: Andersfield, Cannington and North Petherton Hundreds*. London: Victoria County History, 206–7.
Barker, P.A. (1957–60), 'Medieval Pottery from Sites in Shropshire: II A Group from the Motte at Adderley', *Transactions of the Shropshire Archaeological Society*. 56 (3): 258–62.
Barker, P.A. (1961–4), 'Pontesbury Castle Mound Emergency Excavations 1961', *Transactions of the Shropshire Archaeological and Historical Society* 57: 206–23.
Barker, P.A. and Barton, K.J. (1978), 'Excavations at Hastings Castle, 1968', *Archaeological Journal* 134: 80–100.
Barley, M.W. (1951), 'Cuckney Church and Castle', *Transactions of the Thoroton Society of Nottinghamshire* 51: 26–9.
Barnes, H.D. and Simpson, W.D. (1951), 'The Building Accounts of Caister Castle (AD 1432–1435)', *Norfolk and Norwich Archaeological Society* 30 (3): 178–88.

Barton, K.J. and Holden, E.W. (1977), 'Excavations at Bramber Castle, Sussex, 1966–67', *Archaeological Journal* 134: 11–79.

Bates, C.J. (1885), 'The Barony and Castle of Langley', *Archaeologia Aeliana* (2nd series), 10: 38–56.

Bates, C.J. (1891), *Border Holds of Northumberland*. London and Newcastle: Andrew Reid. Also published as Volume 14 of *Archaeologia Aeliana* (2nd series).

Bateson, E. (ed.) (1893), *A History of Northumberland. Volume 1*. Newcastle and London: Northumberland County History Committee.

Bateson, E. (ed.) (1895), *A History of the County of Northumberland. Volume 2*. Newcastle and London: Northumberland County History Committee.

Batey, C.E. and Holder, N. (2019), *Tintagel Castle*. London: English Heritage.

Bennett, P., Frere, S.S. and Stow, S. (1982), *Excavations at Canterbury Castle*. Maidstone: Kent Archaeological Society.

Biddle, M. (1964), 'The Excavation of a Motte and Bailey Castle at Therfield, Herts', *Journal of the British Archaeological Association* 27: 53–91.

Biddle, M. (1986), *Wolvesey: The Old Bishop's Palace, Winchester, Hampshire*. London: English Heritage.

Biddle, M., Clayre, B. and Morris, M. (2000), 'The Setting of the Round Table: Winchester Castle and the Great Hall', in M. Biddle, *King Arthur's Round Table: An Archaeological Investigation*. Woodbridge: Boydell Press, 349–74.

Bilson, J. (1906–7), 'Gilling Castle', *Yorkshire Archaeological Journal* 19: 105–93.

Blaylock S. and Higham, R. (2021), *Rougemont, Exeter: A Medieval Castle in its Urban Context. Excavation and Building Recording at Exeter Castle 1985–2016*. Devon Archaeological Society Monograph 2.

Blood, N.K. and Taylor, C.C. (1992), 'Cawood: An Archiepiscopal Landscape', *Yorkshire Archaeological Journal* 64: 83–102.

Bond, J. (2001), 'Earthen Castles, Outer enclosures and the Earthworks at Ascot D'Oilly, Oxfordshire', *Oxoniensia* 46: 43–69.

Bowden, M., Lane, R., and Small, F. (2017), *Snodhill Castle, Herefordshire: Archaeological, Architectural and Aerial Survey and Investigation*. English Heritage Research Report Series No. 76-2017.

Brakspear, H. (1914), 'Dudley Castle, Staffordshire', *Archaeological Journal* 71: 1–24.

Braun, H. (1934), 'Some Notes on Bungay Castle', *Suffolk Institute of Archaeology and Natural History* 22 (1): 109–19.

Braun, H. (1935), 'Bungay Castle: Report on the Excavation', *Suffolk Institute of Archaeology and Natural History* 22 (2): 201–23.

Brears, P. (2011), 'Wressle Castle: Functions, Fixtures and Furnishings for Henry Percy "The Magnificent" Fifth Earl of Northumberland, 1498–1527', *Archaeological Journal* 167: 55–114.

Brindle, S. (2012), 'The Keep at Conisbrough Castle, Yorkshire', *Château Gaillard* 25: 61–73.

Brindle, S. (2013), 'Henry II, Anglo-Scots Relations, and the Building of the Castle Keep, Newcastle upon Tyne', in J. Ashbee and J. Luxford (eds), *Newcastle and Northumberland: Roman and Medieval Architecture and Art*. British Archaeological Association Conference Transactions 36, 90–114.

Brindle, S. (2018), *Orford Castle*. London: English Heritage.

Brindle, S. (ed.) (2018), *Windsor Castle: A Thousand Years of a Royal Palace*. Royal Collection Trust.

Brindle, S. and Sadrei, A. (2015), *Conisbrough Castle*. London: English Heritage.

Brown, A.E., and Taylor, C.C. (1977), 'Cambridgeshire Earthwork Surveys II: Rampton: Giant's Hill', *Proceedings of the Cambridge Antiquarian Society* 67: 97–9.

Brown, P. (2003), *Whittington Castle, Shropshire*. Whittington Castle Preservation Trust.

Brown, R.A. (1964), *Orford Castle, Suffolk*. London: HMSO.

Brown, R.A. (1978), *Castle Rising*. London: HMSO.

Brown, R.A. (1989), *Castles from the Air*. Cambridge University Press.

Brown, R.A., Colvin H.M., and Taylor, A.J. (1963), *The History of the King's Works. Volumes 1–2: The Middle Ages*. London: HMSO.

Brown, R.A. and Curnow, P.E. (1984), *Tower of London, Greater London*. London: HMSO.

Brown, S. (1998), *Totnes Castle*. London: English Heritage.

Butler, L. (2015), *Pickering Castle*. London: English Heritage.

Cantor, L. (1966), 'The Medieval Castles of Staffordshire', *North Staffordshire Journal of Field Studies* 6: 38–46.

Bibliography

Chatwin, P.B. (1955), 'Brandon Castle, Warwickshire', *Transactions and Proceedings of the Birmingham Archaeological Society* 73: 61–83.
Cherry, B. and Pevsner, N. (1991), *Devon*. The Buildings of England. Yale University Press.
Christie, N., Creighton, O., Edgeworth, M. and Hamerow. H. (2013), *Transforming Townscapes. From Burh to Borough: The Archaeology of Wallingford, AD 800–1400*. The Society for Medieval Archaeology Monograph 35.
Christy, M. (1923), 'The Excavations of Foundations on the Castle Keep at Pleshey', *Transactions of the Essex Archaeological Society* (new series), 16: 190–204.
Clapham, A.W. (1928), 'An Early Hall at Chilham Castle', *Antiquaries Journal* 8: 350–3.
Clark, G.T. (1884), *Mediaeval Military Architecture in England*. 2 volumes. London: Wyman and Sons.
Clough, T.H. McK. (1981), *Oakham Castle. A Guide and History*. Leicestershire Museums, Art Galleries and Record Services.
Coad, J.G. (1971), 'Recent Excavations within Framlingham Castle', *Proceedings of the Suffolk Institute of Archaeology and History* 32: 152–63.
Coad, J.G. (1995), *Dover Castle*. London: Batsford.
Coad, J.G. and Streeten A.D.F. (1982), 'Excavations at Castle Acre, Norfolk, 1972–77: Country House, and Castle of the Norman Earls of Surrey', *Archaeological Journal* 139: 138–301.
Cole, M. (1994), *Report on Geophysical Survey 1994, Merdon Castle, Hursley, Hampshire*. Ancient Monuments Laboratory Report 26/94 (available online).
Conway, M. (1909), 'Allington Castle', *Archaeologia Cantiana* 28: 337–62.
Cook, M. and Kidd, N. (2020), *The March of Ewyas. The Story of Longtown Castle and the de Lacy Dynasty*. Eardisley: Logaston Press.
Cooper, T.P. (1911), *The History of the Castle of York*. London: Elliot Stock.
Cordingley, R.A. (1963), 'Stokesay Castle: The Chronology of its Buildings', *Art Bulletin* 45: 91–107.
Coulson, C. (1992), 'Some Analysis of the Castle of Bodiam, East Sussex', in C. Harper-Bill and R. Harvey (eds), *Medieval Knighthood. Volume 4*. Woodbridge: Boydell Press, 51–107.
Craster, H.H.E. (ed.) (1907), *A History of Northumberland. Volume 8*. Newcastle: Northumberland County History Committee.
Craster, H.H.E. (ed.) (1914), *A History of Northumberland. Volume 10*. Newcastle: Northumberland County History Committee.
Creighton, O. (1997), 'Early Leicestershire Castles: Archaeology and Landscape History', *Transactions of the Leicestershire Archaeological and Historical Society* 71: 31–2, 34.
Creighton, O. (1999), 'Early Castles in the Medieval landscape of Rutland', *Rutland Record* 73: 19–33.
Creighton, O. (2000), 'Early Castles in the Medieval Landscape of Wiltshire', *Wiltshire Archaeological and Natural History Magazine* 93: 114.
Croft, O.G.S. (1949), *The House of Croft of Croft Castle*. Hereford: E.J. Thurston.
Crow, J. (2004), 'Harbottle Castle: Excavation and Survey', in P. Frodsham, *Archaeology in the Northumberland National Park*. CBA Research Report 136, 264–61.
Crowley, D.A. (ed.) (1991), *A History of the County of Wiltshire. Volume 14: Malmesbury Hundred*. London: Victoria County History.
Cunliffe, B. (1977), *Excavations at Portchester Castle. Volume 3: Medieval, the Outer Bailey and its Defences*. London: Society of Antiquaries.
Cunliffe, B. and Munby, J. (1985), *Excavations at Portchester Castle. Volume 4: Medieval, the Inner Bailey*. London: Society of Antiquaries.
Curnow, P.E. (1989), 'The Tower House at Hopton Castle and its Affinities', in C. Harper-Bill, C.J. Holdsworth and J.L. Nelson (eds), *Studies in Medieval History presented to R. Allen Brown*. Woodbridge: Boydell Press, 81–102.
Curnow, P.E. and Johnson, E.A. (1985), 'St Briavel's Castle', *Château Gaillard* 12: 91–114.
Curnow, P.E. and Thompson, M.W. (1969), 'Excavations at Richard's Castle, Herefordshire 1962–1964', *Journal of the British Archaeological Association* 32: 105–28.
Curwen, J.F. (1889), 'Sizergh No. 2', *Transactions of the Cumberland and Westmorland Antiquarian and Archaeological Society* 10: 66–74.
Curwen J.F. (1908), 'Kendal Castle', *Transactions of the Cumberland and Westmorland Antiquarian and Archaeological Society* 8: 84–102.

Curwen, J.F. (1910), 'Piel Castle, Lancashire', *Transactions of the Cumberland and Westmorland Antiquarian and Archaeological Society* 10: 271–87.

Curwen, J.F. (1911), 'Cockermouth Castle', *Transactions of the Cumberland and Westmorland Antiquarian and Archaeological Society* 11: 129–58.

Curwen, J.F. (1912), 'Castlestede, near, Hornby, Lancashire', *Transactions of the Cumberland and Westmorland Antiquarian and Archaeological Society* 12: 412–14.

Curwen, J.F. (1913), *Castles and Fortified Towers of Cumberland, Westmorland and Lancashire North of the Sands*. Cumberland and Westmorland Antiquarian and Archaeological Society Extra Series 13.

Curwen, J.F. (1922), 'Bewcastle', *Transactions of the Cumberland and Westmorland Antiquarian and Archaeological Society* 22: 186–97.

Curwen, J.F. (1926), 'Scaleby Castle', *Transactions of the Cumberland and Westmorland Antiquarian and Archaeological Society* 26: 398–414.

Curzon, G.N. (1926), *Bodiam Castle. A Historical and Descriptive Survey*. London: Jonathan Cape.

Curzon, G.N. and Tipping, H.A. (1929), *Tattershall Castle, Lincolnshire: A Historical and Descriptive Survey*. London: Jonathan Cape.

Cushion, B. and Davison, A. (2003), *East Anglian Archaeology: Earthworks of Norfolk* 104, 173–5.

Cuttler, R., Hunt, J. and Rátkai, S. (2009), 'Saxon Burh and Royal Castle: Re-thinking Early Urban Space in Safford', *Staffordshire Archaeological and Historical Society Transactions* 43: 39–85.

Dallas, C. and Sherlock, D. (2002), *Baconsthorpe Castle. Excavation and Finds, 1951–1972*. East Anglian Archaeology 102.

Darlington, J. (ed.) (2001), *Stafford Castle: Survey, Excavation and Research 1978–1998. Volume 1. The Surveys*. Stafford Borough Council.

Davis, P. (2015–16), 'Interpretations of the Roof and Upper Works of the Great Tower of Conisbrough Castle', *Castle Studies Group Journal* 29: 250–62.

Davis, P. (2021–2), 'Wattlesborough Tower, Shrewsbury', *Castle Studies Group Journal* 35: 82–104.

Davison, B.K. (1972), 'Castle Neroche: An Abandoned Norman Fortress in South Somerset', *Somerset Archaeology and Natural History* 116: 16–58.

Davison, B.K. (1977), 'Excavations at Sulgrave, Northamptonshire, 1969–76: An Interim Report', *Archaeological Journal* 134: 105–114.

Dennison, E. (ed.) (2005), *Within the Pale: The Story of Sheriff Hutton Park*. By the Sheriff Hutton Women's Institute Community Pale Project. York: William Sessions.

Dennison, E. and Richardson, S. (2012), *Harewood Castle, West Yorkshire: Archaeological and Architectural Survey and Recording*. Ed Dennison Archaeological Services: EDAS Report 2003/212. R01. Available online: archaeologydataservice.ac.uk.

Detsicas, A. (ed.) (1981), *Collectanea Historica: Essays in Memory of Stuart Rigold*. Kent Archaeological Society.

Dixon, P.W. (1979), 'Towerhouses, Pelehouses and Border Society', *Archaeological Journal* 136: 240–52.

Dixon, P.W. (1988), *Aydon Castle*. London: English Heritage.

Dixon, P.W. (1990), 'The Donjon of Knaresborough: The Castle as Theatre', *Château Gaillard* 14: 121–139.

Dixon, P.W. (1992), 'From Hall to Tower: The change in Seigneurial Houses on the Anglo-Scottish Border after c.1250', in P.R. Coss and S.D. Lloyd (eds), *Thirteenth Century England 4*. Proceedings of the Newcastle upon Tyne Conference 1991. Woodbridge: The Boydell Press, 85–107.

Dixon, P.W. (1993), '*Mota Aula et Turris*: The manor-houses of the Anglo-Scottish Border', in G. Meirion-Jones and M. Jones (eds), *Manorial Domestic Buildings in England and Northern France*. London: Society of Antiquaries, 22–48.

Dixon, P.W. (2019), *Wingfield Manor*. London: English Heritage.

Dixon, P.W. and Bourne, P. (1978a), 'Halton Castle Reconsidered', *Archaeologia Aeliana* (5th series), 6: 131–9.

Dixon, P.W. and Bourne, P. (1978b), 'Coparcenary and Aydon Castle', *Archaeological Journal* 135: 234–8.

Dixon, P.W. and Marshall, P. (1993a), 'The Great Tower at Hedingham Castle: A Reassessment', *Fortress* 18: 16–23.

Bibliography

Dixon, P.W. and Marshall, P. (1993b), 'The Great Tower in the Twelfth Century: The Case of Norham Castle', *Archaeological Journal* 150: 410–32.

Dixon, P.W. and Marshall, P. (2002), 'Norwich Castle and its Analogues', in Meirion-Jones *et al.*, 235–43.

Dodd, A. and Moss, P. (1991), 'The History of Brimpsfield Castle and the Giffard Family', *Glevensis* 25: 34–7.

Dodds, M.H. (ed.) (1926), *A History of Northumberland. Volume 12*. Newcastle: Northumberland County History Committee.

Dodds, M.H. (ed.) (1935), *A History of Northumberland. Volume 14*. Newcastle: Northumberland County History Committee.

Dodds, M.H. (ed.) (1940), *A History of Northumberland. Volume 15*. Newcastle: Northumberland County History Committee.

Donaldson-Hudson, R. (1956–8), 'Naworth Castle', *History of the Berwickshire Naturalist Club* 34: 221–31.

Drage, C. (1989), *Nottingham Castle. A Place Full Royal*. Thoroton Society.

Drewett, P.L. (1975), 'Excavations at Hadleigh Castle, Essex, 1971–72', *Journal of the British Archaeological Association* 38: 90–154.

Drury, P.J. (1982), 'Aspects of the Origins and Development of Colchester Castle', *Archaeological Journal* 139: 302–419.

Drury, P.J. (2002), 'Norwich Castle keep', in Meirion-Jones *et al.*, 211–34.

Drury, P.J. (2014), *Bolsover Castle*. London: English Heritage.

Dryden, H. (1892), *Associated Architectural Societies Reports and Papers* 21: 247–8.

Duckers, P. and Duckers, A. (2006), *Castles of Shropshire*. Stroud: Tempus.

Dunning, R.W. (1981), 'The Origins of Nether Stowey', *Proceedings of the Somerset Archaeological and Natural History Society* 125: 124–6.

Dunning, R.W. (ed.) (1992), *A History of the County of Somerset. Volume 6*. London: Victoria County History.

Dunning, R.W. (1995), *Somerset Castles*. Somerset Books.

Eales, R. (2018), *Peveril Castle*. London: English Heritage.

Ellis, P. (ed.) (1993), *Beeston Castle, Cheshire: Excavations by Laurence Keen and Peter Hough, 1968–85*. London: Historic Monuments Commission for England (English Heritage).

Ellis, P. (ed.) (2000), *Ludgershall Castle, Wiltshire: A Report on the Excavations by Peter Addyman, 1964–72*. Wiltshire Archaeological and Historical Society Monograph 2.

Elrington, C.R. (ed.) (1973), *A History of the County of Cambridge and the Isle of Ely. Volume 5*. London: Victoria County History.

Elsworth, D.W. and Mace, T. (2015), *Aldingham Motte, Cumbria and its Environs in the Medieval Period*. Cumberland and Westmorland Antiquarian and Archaeological Society: Cumbria Archaeological Research Reports 5.

Emery, A. (1985), 'Ralph, Lord Cromwell's Manor at Wingfield (1439–*c*.1450): Its Construction, Design and Influence', *Archaeological Journal* 142: 276–339.

Emery, A. (1996–2006), *Greater Medieval Houses of England and Wales*. Volume 1: Northern England (1996), Volume 2: East Anglia, Central England and Wales (2000), Volume 3: Southern England (2006). Cambridge University Press.

Ennis, T. (2011), 'Investigations on the Medieval defences of Walden Castle, Saffron Walden, 2005–2009', *Transactions of the Essex Society of Archaeology and History* 2: 98–106.

Everson, P. (1996), 'Bodiam Castle, East Sussex: Castle and its Designated Landscape', *Château Gaillard* 17: 70–84.

Everson, P. and Jeacock, M. (1999), 'Castle Hill and the Early Medieval Development of Thetford', in P. Pattison, D. Field and S. Ainsworth, *Patterns of the Past: Essays in Landscape and Archaeology for Christopher Taylor*. Oxford: Oxbow Books.

Fairclough, G. (1982), 'Edlingham Castle. The Military and Domestic Development of a Northumbrian Manor, Excavations 1978–80: Interim Report', *Château Gaillard* 9–10: 373–87.

Fairclough, G. (1984), 'Edlingham Castle, Northumberland: An Interim Account of Excavations, 1978–83', *Transactions of the Ancient Monuments Society* (new series), 28: 40–60.

Fairclough, G. (1992), 'Meaningful Constructions: Spatial and Functional Analysis of Medieval Buildings', *Antiquity* 66: 348–66.

Farrar, W. and Brownbill, J. (1911), *A History of the County of Lancaster. Volume 6*. London: Victoria County History.

Faulkner, P.A. (1961), 'Haddon Hall and Bolsover Castle', *Archaeological Journal* 118: 188–98.

Faulkner, P.A. (1963), 'Castle Planning in the Fourteenth Century', *Archaeological Journal* 120: 215–35.

Ferguson, C.J. (1878–9), 'Naworth Castle', *Transactions of the Cumberland and Westmorland Antiquarian and Archaeological Society* 4: 486–95.

Fosbrooke, T.H. (1911), *Ashby-de-la-Zouche Castle: Historic and Descriptive*. W.K. Morton & Sons.

Fox, L. (1944–5), 'Leicester Castle', *Transactions of the Leicestershire Architectural and Archaeological Society* 22: 125–70.

Gardener, H. and Jope, M. (1940), 'The Earthwork at Hinton Waldrist', *Berkshire Archaeological Journal* 44: 49–60.

Gardener, W. (1904), 'Ancient Defensive Earthworks', in H.A. Doubleday and W. Page (eds), *A History of the County of Warwick. Volume 1*, 360–2.

Gaydon, A.T. (ed.) (1968), *A History of the County of Shropshire. Volume 8*. Oxford University Press for the Institute of Historical Research, University of London.

Gibson, J. (1926), 'Featherstone Castle, Northumberland', *Archaeologia Aeliana* (4th Series) 2: 125–31.

Giggins, B. (2005), 'Northampton's Forgotten Castle', *Castle Studies Group Bulletin* 18: 185–7.

Giggins, B. (2018–19), 'Barnwell Castle, Northamptonshire Part 1', *Castle Studies Group Journal* 32: 294–315.

Giggins, B. (2020–21), 'Barnwell Castle, Northamptonshire Part 2', *Castle Studies Group Journal* 33: 285–306.

Girouard, M. (2012), *Old Wardour Castle*. London: English Heritage.

Godard, E. (1930), 'The Mount at Great Somerford', *Wiltshire Archaeological and Natural History Magazine* 45: 88–9.

Godrey, W.H. (1929), 'The Barbican, Lewes Castle', *Sussex Archaeological Collections* 70: 9–18.

Goodall, J. (2004), 'The Great Tower of Carlisle Castle', in M. McCarthy and D. Weston (eds), *Carlisle and Cumbria. Roman and Medieval Architecture, Art and Archaeology*. British Archaeological Association Conference Transactions 27: 39–62.

Goodall, J. (2006), 'The Great Tower of Rochester Castle', in T. Ayers and T. Tatton-Brown (eds), *Medieval Art, Architecture and Archaeology at Rochester*. British Archaeological Association Conference Transactions 28: 265–99.

Goodall, J. (2006a), *Warkworth Castle and Hermitage*. London: English Heritage.

Goodall, J. (2011), *The English Castle*. Yale University Press.

Goodall, J. (2013a), 'The Early Development of Alnwick Castle', in J. Ashbee and J. Luxford (eds), *Newcastle and Northumberland Roman and Medieval Architecture and Art*. British Archaeological Association Conference Transactions 36, 232–47.

Goodall, J. (2013b), *Scarborough Castle*. London: English Heritage.

Goodall, J. (2015), *Ashby de la Zouche Castle and Kirby Muxloe Castle*. London: English Heritage.

Goodall, J. (2016), *Richmond Castle and St Agatha's Abbey, Easby*. London: English Heritage.

Gough, R. (1875), *Antiquities and Memoirs of Myddle*. Shrewsbury.

Gould, I.C. (1900), 'The Castle of Ongar', *Transactions of the Essex Archaeological Society* (new series), 7: 136–41.

Grundy, J., McCombie, G., Ryder, P., Welfare, H. and Pevsner, N. (1992), *Northumberland*. The Buildings of England. Harmondsworth: Penguin.

Guy, N. (2014–15a), 'The Berkeley Castle Shell Keep', *Castle Studies Group Journal* 28: 18–21.

Guy, N. (2014–15b), 'Lancaster Castle Revealed – Part 1 – The Keep', *Castle Studies Group Journal* 28: 140–89.

Guy, N. (2016–17a), 'CSG Annual Conference "Castles of the Welsh Marches" – Hereford April 2016', *Castle Studies Group Journal* 30: 4–150.

Guy, N. (2016–17b), 'Lancaster Castle – The Gatehouse Revealed', *Castle Studies Group Journal* 30: 168–217.

Bibliography

Guy, N. (2018–19), 'A Few Notes on Bampton Castle, Oxfordshire', *Castle Studies Group Journal* 32: 175–208.
Guy, N. (2019–20), 'CSG Northampton Conference – Rockingham Castle', *Castle Studies Group Journal* 33: 65–85.
Guy, N. (2020–21), 'The Art and Architecture of Henry III with a Focus on Winchester – Part 1', *Castle Studies Group Journal* 34: 238–80.
Guy, N., Coe, B., Bartlett, D., White, P. (2010–11), 'The Castle Studies Group Annual Conference "Castles of Wessex" – Taunton April 2010', *Castle Studies Group Journal* 24: 4–146.
Guy, N., Marshall, P., Davis, P. and Hislop, M. (2012–13), 'CSG Annual Conference "Castles of Co. Durham" – Durham April 2012', *Castle Studies Group Journal* 26: 4–150.
Guy, N., Mercer, D. and Burton, P. (2021–2), 'Bridgnorth Castle, Shropshire: Description and Possible Layout of the Baileys', *Castle Studies Group Journal* 35: 65–81.
Hagerty, R.P. (1986), 'The Turvilles and the Castle of Weston Turville', *Records of Buckinghamshire* 28: 179–81.
Harbottle, B. and Ellison, M. (1981), 'An Excavation in the Castle Ditch, Newcastle-upon-Tyne', *Archaeologia Aeliana* (5th series), 9: 75–250.
Harbottle, B. and Salway, P. (1960), 'Nafferton Castle, Northumberland. Interim Report', *Archaeologia Aeliana* (4th series), 38: 129–44.
Harbottle, B., Salway, P. and Edwards, B.J.N. (1961), 'Nafferton Castle, Northumberland. Second Report', *Archaeologia Aeliana* (4th series), 39: 165–78.
Hare, J. (1988), 'Bishop's Waltham Palace, Hampshire: William of Wykeham, Henry Beaufort and the Transformation of a Medieval Episcopal Palace', *Archaeological Journal* 145: 222–54.
Hartwell, C., Pevsner, N. and Williamson, E. (2016), *Derbyshire*. The Buildings of England. Newhaven and London: Yale University Press.
Helliwell, L. and MacLeod, D.G. (1981), *Documentary Evidence and Report on Excavations 1969–1970*. Rayleigh Mount Local Committee.
Herbert, N.M. (ed.) (1976), *A History of the County of Gloucester. Volume 11: Bisley and Longtree Hundreds*. London: Victoria County History.
Heslop, T.A. (1991), 'Orford Castle Nostalgia and Sophisticated Living', *Architectural History* 34: 36–58.
Heslop, T.A. (1994), *Norwich Castle Keep: Romanesque Architecture and Social Context*. Centre of East Anglian Studies.
Heslop, T.A. (2000), '"Weeting Castle": A Twelfth-Century Hall House in Norfolk', *Architectural History* 43: 42–57.
Higham, R.A. (1977), 'Excavations at Okehampton Castle, Devon. Part 1: The Motte and Keep', *Proceedings of the Devon Archaeological Society* 35: 3–42.
Higham, R.A. (2015), *Shell-keeps Revisited: The Bailey on the Motte?* Castle Studies Group online publication (www.castlestudiesgroup.org.uk).
Higham, R.A. and Allan J.P. (1980), 'Excavations at Okehampton Castle, Devon. Part 2: The Bailey. A Preliminary Report', *Proceedings of the Devon Archaeological Society* 38, 19–151.
Higham, R.A., Allan, J.P. and Blaycock, S.R. (1982), 'Excavations at Okehampton Castle. Part 2: The Bailey', *Proceedings of the Devon Archaeological Society* 40: 19–151.
Higham, R.A., Goddard, S. and Rouillard, M. (1985), 'Plympton Castle, Devon', *Proceedings of the Devon Archaeological Society* 43: 59–73.
Higham, R.A., and Hamlin, A. (1990), 'Bampton Castle, Devon: History and Archaeology', *Proceedings of the Devon Archaeological Society* 48: 101–10.
Hill, N. (2013), 'Hall and Chambers: Oakham Castle Reconsidered', *Antiquaries Journal* 93: 163–216.
Hislop, M. (1991), 'The Date of the Warkworth Donjon', *Archaeologia Aeliana* (5th series) 19: 79–92.
Hislop, M. (1991–2), 'Master John of Burcestre and the Castles of Stafford and Maxstoke', *Transactions of the South Staffordshire Archaeological and Historical Society* 33: 14–20.
Hislop, M. (1992), 'The Castle of Ralph Fourth Baron Neville at Raby', *Archaeologia Aeliana* (5th series), 20: 91–7.
Hislop, M. (1996a), 'Bolton Castle and the Practice of Architecture in the Middle Ages', *Journal of the British Archaeological Association* 149, 10–22.

Hislop, M. (1996b), 'Lumley Castle, its Antecedents and its Architect', *Archaeologia Aeliana* (5th series), 24: 83–98.
Hislop, M. (2007), *John Lewyn of Durham: A Medieval Mason in Practice*, BAR British Series 438, Oxford: Hedges.
Hislop, M. (2010), 'A Missing Link: A Reappraisal of the Date, Architectural Context and Significance of the Great Tower of Dudley Castle', *Antiquaries Journal* 90: 211–33.
Hislop, M. (2018), 'The Round Tower of Barnard Castle', in N. Guy (ed.), *Castles: History, Archaeology, Landscape, Architecture and Symbolism: essays in honour of Derek Renn*. Castle Studies Group: 81–104.
Hislop, M. (2019), *Barnard Castle, Bowes Castle and Egglestone Abbey*. London: English Heritage.
Hislop, M. (2020), *James of St George and the Castles of the Welsh Wars*. Barnsley: Pen and Sword.
Hislop, M., Kincey, M. and Williams, G. (2011), *Tutbury: 'A Castle Firmly Built': Archaeological and Historical Investigations at Tutbury Castle, Staffordshire*. BAR British Series 546. Oxford: Archaeopress.
Hodder, M. (Forthcoming), 'Castle Bromwich Motte and Bailey Castle: Excavations by W.J. Ford, 1969–70'.
Hodgson, J. (1820–39), *A History of Northumberland*. Part 2, Vol. 1 (1827); Part 2, Vol. 2 (1832); Part 2, Vol. 3 (1840); Part 3, Vol. 1 (1820); Part 3, Vol. 2 (1828); Part 3, Vol. 3 (1835).
Hodgson, J.C. (ed.) (1897), *A History of Northumberland. Volume 4*. Newcastle: Northumberland County History Committee.
Hodgson, J.C. (ed.) (1899), *A History of Northumberland. Volume 5*. Newcastle: Northumberland County History Committee.
Hodgson, J.C. (ed.) (1902), *A History of Northumberland. Volume 6*. Newcastle: Northumberland County History Committee.
Hodgson, J.C. and Parker Brewis, J.O.W. (1921), 'The Manor and Tower of Bitchfield', *Archaeologia Aeliana* (3rd series), 18: 101–16.
Hodgson, J.F. (1880–1885 and 1890–1895), 'Raby', *Transactions of the Architectural and Archaeological Society of Durham and Northumberland* 3: 113–27, and 4: 49–122.
Hope, W.H. St John (1908), 'The Castle of Ludlow', *Archaeologia* 61: 257–328.
Hope-Taylor (1950), 'The Excavation of a Motte at Abinger in Surrey', *Archaeological Journal* 107: 15–43.
Horsman, V. (1988), 'Eynsford Castle: A Reinterpretation of its Early History in the Light of Recent Excavations', *Archaeologia Cantiana* 105: 39–58.
Hudson, T.P. (ed.) (1986), *A History of the County of Sussex. Volume 6*. London: Victoria County History.
Hudson, T.P. (ed.) (1997), *A History of the County of Sussex. Volume 5*. London: Victoria County History.
Hugill, R. (1979), *Castles of Durham*. Newcastle upon Tyne: Frank Graham.
Hulme, R. (2014–15), '"Well-placed for Waging War": Strategic aspects of William the Conqueror's Rural Castles', *Castle Studies Group Journal* 28: 225–8.
Hunter Blair, C.H. (1932–4), 'Norham Castle', *History of the Berwickshire Naturalist Club* 28: 27–75, 257–8.
Hunter Blair, C.H. (1937), 'Mitford Castle', *Archaeologia Aeliana* (4th series), 14: 74–94.
Hunter Blair, C.H. (1944), 'The Early Castles of Northumberland', *Archaeologia Aeliana* (4th series), 22: 116–70.
Hunter Blair, C.H. (1947–9), 'Elsden', *History of the Berwickshire Naturalists Club* 31: 40–7.
Hunter Blair, C.H. (1955), 'Mitford Castle', *Archaeologia Aeliana* (4th series), 33: 27–34.
Hunter Blair, C.H. and Honeyman, H.L. (1954), *Warkworth Castle, Northumberland*. London: HMSO.
I'Anson, W.M. (1913), 'The Castles of the North Riding', *Yorkshire Archaeological Journal* 22: 303–99.
I'Anson, W.M. (1917), 'Skipsea Castle', *Yorkshire Archaeological Journal* 24: 258–62.
Impey, E. (2008a), *Castle Acre Priory and Castle*. London: English Heritage.
Impey, E. (ed.) (2008b), *The White Tower*. New Haven and London: Yale.
Impey, E. (2014), *Longthorpe Tower*. London: English Heritage.
Impey, E. and Parnell, G. (2006), *The Tower of London. The Official Illustrated History*. Revised edition. London: Merrell Publishers.

Bibliography

Ivens, R.J. (1984), 'Deddington Castle, Oxfordshire, and the English Honour of Bayeux', *Oxoniensia* 49: 101–19.

Jardine-Rose, P. (2012–13), 'Newnham Castle Excavations, Kent. Interim Report', *Castle Studies Group Journal* 26: 196–200.

Jenkins, J.G. (ed.) (1963), *A History of the County of Stafford. Volume 8*. London: Victoria County History.

Johnson, M. (ed.) (2017), *Lived Experience in the Later Middle Ages: Studies of Bodiam and Other Elite Landscapes in South-eastern England*. Southampton: The Highfield Press.

Johnson, S. (1983), *Burgh Castle: Excavations by Charles Green 1958–61*. East Anglian Archaeology 20.

Jope, E.M. and Threlfall, R.I. (1959), 'The Twelfth-century Castle at Ascot Doilly, Oxfordshire: Its History and Excavation', *Antiquaries Journal* 39: 219–73.

Keats-Rohan, K.S.B., Christie, N. and Roffe, D. (eds) (2015), *Wallingford: The Castle and Town in Context*. BAR British Series 621. Oxford: Archaeopress.

Keen, L.J. (1982), 'The Umfravilles, the Castle and Barony of Prudhoe, Northumberland', in R.A. Brown (ed.), *Anglo-Norman Studies: Proceedings of the Battle Conference* 5: 165–84.

Kent, J., Renn, D. and Streeten, A. (2013), *Excavations at South Mimms Castle, Hertfordshire 1960–91*. London and Middlesex Archaeological Society Special Paper 16.

Kenyon, J. (2015), *Middleham Castle*. London: English Heritage.

Kenyon, J. (2017), *Helmsley Castle*. London: English Heritage.

Kerr-Peterson, M. (2013), 'The End of Bridgwater Castle', *Proceedings of the Somerset Archaeology and Natural History Society* 156: 127–34.

Kightly, C. (2011), *Berry Pomeroy Castle*. London: English Heritage.

Klingelhofer, E. (1983–4), 'Rockingham Castle in 1250: Form and Function of a Royal Castle Under Henry III', *Northamptonshire Past and Present* 7.1: 11–25.

Knocker, G.M. and Sabben Clave, E.E. (1958–60), 'Hall's Close, Ashton Keynes', *Wiltshire Archaeological and Natural History Magazine* 57: 241–2.

Knoop, D., Jones, G.P. and Lewis, G.B. (1934), 'Some New Documents concerning the Building of Cowling Castle and Cobham College', *Archaeologia Cantiana* 46: 52–6.

Knowles, W.H. (1895), 'Cocklaw Tower', *Transactions of the Architectural and Archaeological Society of Durham and Northumberland* 4: 309–15.

Knowles, W.H. (1898), 'The Vicar's Pele, Corbridge', *Archaeologia Aeliana* 19: 171–8.

Knowles, W.H. (1926), 'The Castle, Newcastle upon Tyne', *Archaeologia Aeliana* (4th series), 2: 1–51.

Leach, P. and Ellis, P. (2004), 'Roman and Medieval Remains at Manor Farm, Castle Cary', *Somerset Archaeology and Natural History* 147: 80–128.

Leach, P. and Pevsner, N. (2009), *Yorkshire West Riding: Leeds, Bradford and the North*. The Buildings of England. Yale University Press.

Liddiard, R. (2015), 'Reconstructing Wingfield Castle', in P. Blore and E. Martin (eds), *Wingfield College and its Patrons: Piety and Prestige in Medieval Suffolk*. Woodbridge: Boydell and Brewer, 77–96.

Liddiard, R. and McGuicken, R. (2007), *Beeston Castle*. London: English Heritage.

Lindley, P. (ed.) (2004), *The Early History of Lincoln Castle*. Society for Lincolnshire History and Archaeology Occasional Papers 12.

Longstaffe, W.H.D. (1860), 'The New Castle upon Tyne', *Archaeologia Aeliana* (2nd series), 4: 45–139.

Ludlow, N. (2021–2), 'London or Wales? The Gatehouses at Tonbridge and Leybourne in Context', *Castle Studies Group Journal* 35: 178–246.

McCarthy, M.R., Summerson, H.R.T. and Annis, R.G. (1990), *Carlisle Castle: A Survey and Documentary History*. London: Historic Buildings and Monuments Commission.

McCombie, G. (2013), *Tynemouth Priory and Castle*. London: English Heritage.

McGuicken, R. (2006), 'Castle in Context? Redefining the Significance of Beeston Castle, Cheshire', *Chester Archaeological Society Journal* 81: 65–82.

McNeil, R. and Jamieson, A.J. (eds) (1987), *Halton Castle: A Visual Treasure*. North West Archaeological Report 1. McNeill, J. (2006), *Old Sarum*. London: English Heritage.

McNeill, T.E. (1987–8), 'Excavations at Tamworth Castle, 1972 and 1974', *Transactions of the South Staffordshire Archaeological and Historical Society* 29: 1–54.

McNeill, T. and Scott, G., 'Langley Castle', in Guy (2018), 314–49.
Maddison, J. (1993), 'Building at Lichfield Cathedral during the Episcopate of Walter Langton (1296–1321)', in J. Maddison (ed.), *Medieval Archaeology and Architecture at Lichfield*. British Archaeological Association Conference Transactions 13 for 1987, 65–84.
Mahany, C. and Roffe, D. (1979), 'Sleaford', *South Lincolnshire Archaeology* 3: 1–33.
Malden, H.E. (ed.) (1911), *A History of the County of Surrey. Volume 3.* London: Victoria County History.
Malden, H.E. (ed.) (1912), *A History of the County of Surrey. Volume 4.* London: Victoria County History.
Manby, T.G. (1959), 'Duffield Castle Excavations 1957', *Derbyshire Archaeological Journal* 79: 1–21.
Marshall, P. (1998), 'The Twelfth-Century Castle at Newark', in A. Alexander, *Southwell and Nottinghamshire: Medieval Art, Architecture and Industry*. British Archaeological Association Conference Transactions, 110–25.
Marshall, P. (2009–10), 'The Internal Arrangement of the Donjon at Colchester in Essex: A Reconsideration', *Castle Studies Group Journal* 23: 178–90.
Marshall, P. (2021), 'The 15th-Century Great Tower at Tattershall Castle: Aspiration, Display and the Practicalities of Social Distinction', *Château Gaillard* 29: 263–72.
Marshall, P. and Samuels, J. (1997), *Guardian of the Trent. The Story of Newark Castle*. Newark Castle Trust.
Martin, D. and Martin, B. (2013), 'A Reinterpretation of the Gatehouse at Tonbridge Castle', *Archaeologia Cantiana* 133: 235–76.
Martin, D., Martin, B. and Clubb, J. (2011), 'An Archaeological Survey of the Old Castle, Scotney, Lamberhurst. Part 1', *Archaeologia Cantiana* 131: 321–43.
Martin, D., Martin, B. and Clubb, J. (2012), 'An Archaeological Survey of the Old Castle, Scotney. Part 2', *Archaeologia Cantiana* 132: 111–51.
Martin, E. (1998), 'Little Wenham Hall: A Reinterpretation', *Proceedings of the Suffolk Institute of Archaeology and History* 39.2: 151–64.
Mason, J.F.A. and Barker, P.A. (1961–4), 'The Norman Castle at Quatford', *Transactions of the Shropshire Archaeological and Historical Society* 57: 37–62.
Mayes, P. and Butler, L. (1983), *Sandal Castle Excavations 1964–1973*. Wakefield: Wakefield Historical Publications.
Meeson, R.A. (1978–9), 'Tenth Tamworth Excavation Report, 1977: The Norman Bailey Defences of the Castle', *Transactions of the South Staffordshire Archaeological and Historical Society* 29: 15–28.
Meeson, R.A. (1983), 'The Timber Frame of the Hall at Tamworth Castle, Staffordshire and its Context', *Archaeological Journal* 140: 329–40.
Meirion-Jones, G., Impey, E. and Jones, M. (2002), *The Seigneurial Residence in Western Europe AD c.800–1600*. BAR International Series 1088.
Middleton, A. (1910), *An Account of Belsay Castle in the County of Northumberland*. Privately printed.
Miles, T.J. (1986), 'Excavations of a Saxon Cemetery and Norman Castle at North Walk, Barnstaple', *Proceedings of the Devonshire Archaeological Society* 46: 59–84.
Milton, B. and Walker, H. (1987), 'Excavations at Bellingham Lane, Rayleigh, Essex', *Essex Archaeology and History* 18: 39–44.
Moreland, J. and Hadley, D. (2020), *Sheffield Castle: Archaeology, Archives, Regeneration, 1927–2018*. White Rose University Press.
Morley, B. (1976), 'Hylton Castle', *Archaeological Journal* 133: 118–34.
Morley, B. (1979), *Hylton Castle*. London: HMSO.
Morley, B. and Gurney, D. (1997), *Castle Rising, Norfolk*. East Anglian Archaeology 81.
Morris, R.K. (1986), 'The Architecture of the Earls of Warwick in the Fourteenth Century', in W.M. Ormrod (ed.), *England in the Fourteenth Century*. Proceedings of the 1985 Harlaxton Symposium. Woodbridge: Boydell Press, 161–74.
Morris, R.K. (2011), 'Sidelights on the 14th Century Architecture at Kenilworth Castle', in L. Monckton and R.K. Morris (eds), *Coventry: Medieval Art, Architecture and Archaeology in the City and its Vicinity*. British Archaeological Association Conference Transactions 33, 349–62.
Morris, R.K. (2015), *Kenilworth Castle*. 3rd edition. London: English Heritage.

Bibliography

Munby, J., Norton, A., Poore, D. and Dodd. A. (eds) (2019), *Excavations at Oxford Castle 1999–2009*. Thames Valley Landscape Monograph 44. Oxford: Oxford Archaeology.

Nash, G.H. and Redwood, B. (eds) (2006), *Looking Beyond the Castle Walls: The Weobley Castle Project, Herefordshire*. BAR British Series 415. Oxford: Archaeopress.

Nelson, I.S. (2013), *Etal Castle*. London: English Heritage.

Newman, J. and Pevsner, N. (2006), *Shropshire*. The Buildings of England. Yale University Press.

Newman, R. (1987), 'Excavations and Survey at Piel Castle, near Barrow-in-Furness, Cumbria', *Transactions of the Cumberland and Westmorland Antiquarian and Archaeological Society* 87: 101–16.

North, M. (2001), 'St Leonard's Tower: Some Aspects of Anglo-Norman Building Design and construction', *Archaeologia Cantiana* 121: 269–86.

Oliver, B. (1928), 'The Castle of Barnstable', *Transactions of the Devonshire Association* 60: 215–23.

Oswald, A. (1962), 'Excavation of a 13th Wooden Building at Weoley Castle, Birmingham, 1960–61', *Medieval Archaeology* 6–7: 109–34.

Oswald (1962–3), 'Interim Report on the Excavations at Weoley Castle, 1955–60', *Transactions and Proceedings of the Birmingham Archaeological Society* 78: 61–85.

Oswald, A. and Ashbee, J. (2006), 'Dunstanburgh Castle – Northumberland's own Camelot?', *Research News* 4: 40–3.

Oxley, J. (ed.) (1986), *Excavations at Southampton Castle*. Southampton Museums.

Page, W. (ed.) (1907a), *A History of the County of Leicester. Volume 1*. London: Victoria County History.

Page, W. (ed.) (1907b), *A History of the County of Oxford. Volume 2*. London: Victoria County History.

Page, W. (ed.) (1908a), *A History of the County of Hereford. Volume 1*. London: Victoria County History.

Page, W. (ed.) (1908b), *A History of the County of Kent. Volume 1*. London: Victoria County History.

Page, W. (ed.) (1911), *A History of the County of Suffolk. Volume 1*. London: Victoria County History.

Page, W. (ed.) (1912a), *A History of the County of Hampshire. Volume 5*. London: Victoria County History.

Page, W. (ed.) (1912b), *A History of the County of Hertford. Volume 3*. London: Victoria County History.

Page, W. (ed.) (1914a), *A History of the County of Hertford. Volume 4*. London: Victoria County History.

Page, W. (ed.) (1914b), *A History of the County of York North Riding. Volume 1*. London: Victoria County History.

Page, W. (ed.) (1923), *A History of the County of York North Riding. Volume 2*. London: Victoria County History.

Page, W. (ed.) (1925), *A History of the County of Buckingham. Volume 3*. London: Victoria County History.

Page, W. (ed.) (1927), *A History of the County of Buckingham. Volume 4*. London: Victoria County History.

Page, W. (ed.) (1928), *A History of the County of Durham. Volume 3: The City of Durham*. London: Victoria County History.

Page, W. (ed.) (1930), *A History of the County of Northampton. Volume 3*. London: Victoria County History.

Page, W. and Ditchfield, P.H. (eds) (1924), *A History of the County of Berkshire. Volume 4*. London: Victoria County History.

Page, W., Proby, G. and Ladds, S.I. (eds) (1932), *A History of the County of Huntingdon. Volume 2*. London: Victoria County History.

Page, W. and Willis-Bund, J.W. (eds) (1913), *A History of the County of Worcester. Volume 3*. London: Victoria County History.

Page, W. and Willis-Bund, J.W. (eds) (1924), *A History of the County of Worcester.Volume 4*. London: Victoria County History.

Parkyn, A. and McNeill, T. (2012), 'Regional Power and the Profits of War: The East Range of Warwick Castle', *Archaeological Journal* 169: 480–518.

Pattison, P., Brindle, S. and Robinson, D.M. (2020), *The Great Tower of Dover Castle. History, Architecture and Context*. Swindon: Historic England.

Perriam, D.R. (2008), 'William Strickland's Tower in Penrith: Penrith Castle or Hutton Hall?', *English Heritage Review* 3: 36–45.

Perriam, D. and Robinson, J. (1998), *The Medieval Fortified Buildings of Cumbria*. CWAAS Extra Series 29.

Petre, J.S. (ed.) (2012), *The Castles of Bedfordshire*. Donington: Shaun Tyas.
Philips, W. (1896), 'Red Castle, Shropshire', *Journal of the British Archaeological Association* 2: 126–9.
Plowman, D. (2005), 'Framlingham Castle: A Political Statement?', *Proceedings of the Suffolk Institute of Archaeology and History* 41.1: 43–9.
Popescu, E. (2009), *Norwich Castle: Excavations and Historical Survey 1987–98. Part 1: Anglo-Saxon to c.1345* (East Anglian Archaeology 132.1). *Part 2, c.1345 to Modern* (East Anglian Archaeology 132.2).
Porter, R. (2020), *Pevensey Castle*. London: English Heritage.
Powell, W.R. (1956), *A History of the County of Essex. Volume 4: Ongar Hundred*. London: Victoria County History.
Pugh, R.B. (ed.) (2002), *A History of the County of Cambridge and the Isle of Ely. Volume 4*. London: Victoria County History.
Radford, C.A.R. (1957–8), 'The Medieval Defences of Shrewsbury', *Transactions of the Shropshire Archaeological Society* 56: 15–20.
Rahtz, S. and Rowley, T. (1984), *Middleton Stoney. Excavation and Survey in a North Oxfordshire Parish 1970–1982*. Oxford University Department for External Studies.
Raimes, A.L. (1954), 'Shortflat Tower and its Owners, 1200–1600, with a Description of Building and its History by H.L. Honeyman', *Archaeologia Aeliana* (4th series) 32: 126–59.
Raimes, A.L. (1955), 'Shortflat Tower and its Owners. Part 2', *Archaeologia Aeliana* (4th series) 33: 134–41.
Rátkai, S. (2015), *Wigmore Castle, North Herefordshire: Excavations 1996 and 1997*. Society for Medieval Archaeology Series 34.
Reeve, M.M. and Thurlby, M. (2005), 'King John's "Gloriette" at Corfe Castle: Masons, Patrons and the Question of Style in Early Gothic Castles', *Architectural History* 64: 168–85.
Remfry, P.M. (1994a), *Clifford Castle 1066 to 1299*. SCS Publishing.
Remfry, P.M. (1994b), *Clun Castle 1066 to 1282*. SCS Publishing.
Remfry, P.M. (1995), *The Mortimers of Wigmore, Part 1: Wigmore Castle 1066–1181*. SCS Publishing.
Remfry, P.M. (1997a), *Buckenham Castles 1066–1649*. SCS Publishing.
Remfry, P.M. (1997b), *Brampton Bryan Castle 1066 to 1309, and the Civil War 1642 to 1646*. SCS Publishing.
Remfry, P.M. (1997c), *Kington and Huntington Castles 1066 to 1298*. SCS Publishing.
Remfry, P.M. (1998), *Wilton Castle, 1066–1646*. SCS Publishing.
Remfry, P.M. (1999), *Moreton Corbet Castle, 1066–1700*. SCS Publishing.
Remfry, P. (2009), *Berkhamstead Castle and the Families of the Counts of Mortain, the Earls of Cornwall and the Crown*. SCS Publishing.
Renn, D. (1961), 'The Keep of New Buckenham', *Norfolk Archaeology* 32: 232–5.
Renn, D. (1973a), *Norman Castles in Britain*. 2nd edition. London: John Baker.
Renn, D. (1973b), 'Defending Framlingham Castle', *Proceedings of the Suffolk Institute of Archaeology and History* 33.1: 58–67.
Renn, D. (1975), 'An Angevin Gatehouse at Skipton Castle', *Château Gaillard* 7: 172–82.
Renn, D. (1981), 'Tonbridge and some other Gatehouses', in Detsicas, 93–103.
Reynolds, S. and White, G. (1997–8), 'A Survey of Pulford Castle', *Cheshire History* 37: 23–5.
Riall, N. (2003), 'The New Chapels of Henry of Blois as Bishop of Winchester: The Case Against Farnham, Surrey', *Medieval Archaeology* 47: 115–29.
Rigold, S.E. (1956), *Nunney Castle, Somerset*. London: HMSO.
Rigold, S.E. (1962–3), 'The Anglian Cathedral of North Elmham, Norfolk', *Medieval Archaeology* 6–7: 67–108.
Rigold, S. (1971), 'Eynsford Castle and its Excavation', *Archaeologia Cantiana* 86: 109–71.
Rigold, S. (1980), 'New Buckenham Castle', *Archaeological Journal* 137: 353–5.
Rigold, S. and Fleming, A.J. (1973), 'Eynsford Castle: The Moat and Bridge', *Archaeologia Cantiana* 88: 87–116.
Rimmington, F.C. and Rutter, J.G. (1967), *Ayton Castle: Its History and Excavation*. Scarborough and District Archaeological Society Research Report No. 5.
Roberts, I. (2002), *Pontefract Castle. Archaeological Excavations 1982–86*. Yorkshire Archaeology 8. West Yorkshire Archaeology Service.

Bibliography

Rodwell, W. (1976), 'Excavations on the Site of Banbury Castle, 1973–4', *Oxoniensia* 41: 90–147.
Roffe, D. (1997), 'Welbourn Castle, Lincolnshire', *Nottingham Medieval Studies* 41: 54–6.
Round, J.H. (1900), 'The Honour of Ongar', *Transactions of the Essex Archaeological Society* (new series), 7: 142–52.
Round, J.H. (1923), 'Pleshy (Pleshey)', *Transactions of the Essex Archaeological Society* (new series), 16: 268–72.
Royal Commission on the Historical Monuments of England (RCHME) (1910), *An Inventory of the Historical Monuments in Hertfordshire*. London: HMSO.
RCHME (1912), *An Inventory of the Historical Monuments in Buckinghamshire. Volume 1: South*. London: HMSO.
RCHME (1913), *An Inventory of the Historical Monuments in Buckinghamshire. Volume 2: North*. London: HMSO.
RCHME (1916), *An Inventory of the Historical Monuments of Essex. Volume 1: North West*. London: HMSO.
RCHME (1921), *An Inventory of the Historical Monuments in Essex. Volume 2: Central and South West*. London: HMSO.
RCHME (1923), *An Inventory of the Historical Monuments in Essex. Volume 4: South East*. London: HMSO.
RCHME (1926), *An Inventory of the Historical Monuments in Huntingdonshire*. London: HMSO.
RCHME (1931), *An Inventory of Historical Monuments in Herefordshire. Volume 1: South West*. London: HMSO.
RCHME (1932), *An Inventory of the Historical Monuments in Herefordshire. Volume 2: East*. London: HMSO.
RCHME (1934), *An Inventory of the Historical Monuments in Herefordshire. Volume 3: North West*. London: HMSO.
RCHME (1936), *An Inventory of the Historical Monuments in Westmorland*. London: HMSO.
RCHME (1952), *An Inventory of the Historical Monuments in Dorset. Volume 1: West*. London: HMSO.
RHME (1959), *An Inventory of the Historical Monuments in the City of Cambridge*. London: HMSO.
RCHME (1968), *An Inventory of the Historical Monuments in the County of Cambridgeshire. Volume 1: West Cambridgeshire*. London: HMSO.
RCHME (1970), *An Inventory of the Historical Monuments in Dorset. Volume 2*. London: HMSO.
RCHME (1972), *An Inventory of the Historical Monuments in the City of York. Volume 2: The Defences*. London: HMSO.
RCHME (1975), *An Inventory of the Historical Monuments in the County of Northampton. Volume 1: North-east Northamptonshire*. London: HMSO.
RCHME (1982), *An Inventory of the Historical Monuments in the County of Northampton. Volume 4: South-West Northamptonshire*. London: HMSO.
Rushworth, A. and Carlton, R. (2004), 'Thirlwall Castle: A Gentry Residence in Medieval Tynedale', in P. Frodsham (ed.), *Archaeology in the Northumberland National Park* CBA Research Report 136, 272–94.
Ryder, P. (1979), 'Ravensworth Castle, North Yorkshire', *Yorkshire Archaeological Journal* 51: 89–100.
Ryder, P.F. (1992), 'The Gatehouse of Morpeth Castle', *Archaeologia Aeliana* (5th series), 20: 63–77.
Ryder, P.F. (2003), 'Cresswell Tower', *Archaeologia Aeliana* (5th series), 32: 73–90.
St John Hope, W.H. (1913), *Windsor: An Architectural History*. 2 volumes and plans. London: Country Life.
Salter, M. (1997a), *The Castles and Tower Houses of Northumberland*. Malvern: Folly Publications.
Salter, M. (1997b), *The Castles and Moated Mansions of Staffordshire*. Malvern: Folly Publications.
Salter, M. (2001a), *The Castles and Moated Mansions of Shropshire*. Malvern: Folly Publications.
Salter, M. (2001b), *The Castles and Tower Houses of Yorkshire*. Malvern: Folly Publications.
Salter, M. (2002a), *The Castles of the East Midlands*. Malvern: Folly Publications.
Salter, M. (2002b), *The Castles of Gloucestershire and Bristol*. Malvern: Folly Publications.
Salzman, L.F. (1940), *A History of the County of Sussex. Volume 7*. London: Victoria County History.
Salzman, L.F. (1945), *A History of the County of Warwick. Volume 3*. London: Victoria County History.
Salzman, L.F. (1947), *A History of the County of Warwick. Volume 4*. London: Victoria County History.

Salzman, L.F. (ed.) (1951), *A History of the County of Warwick. Volume 6*. London: Victoria County History, 143–8.
Sands, H. (1902), 'Sutton Valence Castle', *Archaeologia Cantiana* 25: 198–206.
Sands, H. and Braun, H. (1934), 'Conisbrough and Mortemer', *Yorkshire Archaeological Journal* 32: 147–59.
Saunders, A. (1964), *Lydford Saxon Town and Castle*. London: HMSO.
Saunders, A. (1980), 'Lydford Castle, Devon', *Medieval Archaeology* 24: 123–64.
Saunders, A. (2006), *Excavations at Launceston Castle, Cornwall*. Society for Medieval Archaeology Monograph 24.
Scott Robertson, W.A. (1877), 'Coulyng Castle', *Archaeologia Cantiana* 11: 128–44.
Sheppard, R. (2003), 'Excavation of a Medieval Building and a Civil War Refortification at Bolsover Castle, Derbyshire', *Derbyshire Archaeological Journal* 123: 111–45.
Serjeantson, R.M., Ryland, W. and Adkins, D. (eds) (1906), *A History of the County of Northampton. Volume 2*. London: Victoria County History.
Shoesmith, R. (1980), *Hereford City Excavations Volume 1: Excavations at Castle Green*. CBA Research Report 36.
Shoesmith, R. (2009), *Castles and Moated Sites of Herefordshire*. Monuments in the Landscape Volume 2. Logaston Press.
Shoesmith, R. (ed.) (2014), *Goodrich Castle: Its History and its Buildings*. Logaston Press.
Shoesmith, R. and Johnson, A. (eds) (2000), *Ludlow Castle: Its History and its Buildings*. Logaston Press.
Simmons, S. (1996), 'Tonbridge Castle: Further Observations on an Ancient Castle', *Archaeologia Cantiana* 116: 101–47.
Simmons, S. (1998), 'The Lords and Ladies of Tonbridge Castle', *Archaeologia Cantiana* 118: 465–62.
Simpson, W.D. (1939), 'The Castles of Dudley and Ashby de la Zouche', *Archaeological Journal* 96: 141–54.
Simpson, W.D. (1940), 'Belsay and the Scottish Tower Houses', *Archaeologia Aeliana* (4th series), 17: 75–84.
Simpson, W.D. (1944), 'Dudley Castle: The Renaissance Buildings', *Archaeological Journal* 101: 119–25.
Simpson, W.D. (1949), 'The Town and Castle of Appleby: A Morphological Study', *Transactions of the Cumberland and Westmorland Antiquarian and Archaeological Society* 49: 118–33.
Simpson, W.D. (1951), 'Haughton Castle', *Archaeologia Aeliana* (4th series), 29: 118–34.
Simpson, W.D. (1960), *The Building Accounts of Tattershall Castle 1434–72*. Lincoln Record Society No. 55.
Smith, J.T. (1965), 'The Structure of the Timber Kitchen at Weoley Castle, Birmingham', *Medieval Archaeology* 9: 82–93.
Soden, I. (ed.) (2007), *Stafford Castle: Survey, Excavation and Research 1978–1998. Volume 2 – The Excavations*. Stafford Borough Castle.
Spurrell, M. (1995), 'Containing Wallingford Castle, 1146–1153', *Oxoniensia* 60: 257–70.
Stacey, N. (2009), *Framlingham Castle*. London: English Heritage.
Stephens, W.B. (ed.) (1969), *A History of the County of Warwick. Volume 8*. London: Victoria County History.
Summerson, H., Trueman, M. and Harrison, S. (1998), *Brougham Castle, Cumbria. A Survey and Documentary History*. Cumberland and Westmorland Antiquarian and Archaeological Society Research Series No. 8.
Swallow, R. (2012), 'Landscape of Power: Aldford Castle, Cheshire', *Cheshire History Journal* 52: 5–28.
Swallow, R. (2016), 'Cheshire Castles of the Irish Sea Cultural Zone', *Archaeological Journal* 173: 288–341.
Swanton, M.J. (1972), 'Castle Hill, Bakewell', *Derbyshire Archaeological Journal* 92: 16–107.
Taylor, M.W. (1889), 'Sizergh No. 1', *Transactions of the Cumberland and Westmorland Antiquarian and Archaeological Society* 10: 48–65.
Thacker, A.T. and Lewis, C.P. (eds) (2005), *A History of the County of Chester. Volume 5, Part 2: The City of Chester: Culture, Buildings, Institutions*. London: Victoria County History.
Thomas, C. (1993), *The English Heritage Book of Tintagel: Arthur and Archaeology*. London: Batsford.

Bibliography

Thompson, A.H. (ed.) (1913–20), 'The Building Accounts of Kirby Muxloe Castle, 1480–1484', *Transactions of the Leicestershire Archaeological Society* 11: 193–345.
Thompson, M.W. (1957), 'Excavation of the Fortified Medieval Hall of Hutton Colswain at Huttons Ambo, near Malton, Yorkshire', *Archaeological Journal* 114: 69–81.
Thompson, M.W. (1960), 'Recent Excavations in the Keep of Farnham Castle, Surrey', *Medieval Archaeology* 4: 81–94.
Thompson, M.W. (1966), 'The Origins of Bolingbroke Castle, Lincolnshire', *Medieval Archaeology* 10: 152–8.
Thompson, M.W. (1967), 'Excavations in Farnham Castle Keep, Surrey, England 1958–60', *Château Gaillard* 2: 100–05.
Thompson, M.W. (1969), 'Further Work at Bolingbroke Castle', *Medieval Archaeology* 13: 216–17.
Thompson, M.W. (1976), 'The Construction of the Manor at South Wingfield, Derbyshire', in G. de G. Sieveking, I.H. Longworth and K.E. Wilson (eds), *Problems in Economic and Social Archaeology*. London: Duckworth, 417–38.
Thompson, M.W. (1977a), 'Three Stages in the Construction of the Hall at Kenilworth Castle, Warwickshire', in M.R. Apted, R. Gilyard-Beer and A.D. Saunders, *Ancient Monuments and their Interpretation: Essays Presented to A.J. Taylor*. London and Chichester: Phillimore.
Thompson, M.W. (1977b), *Kenilworth Castle, Warwickshire*. London: HMSO.
Thompson, M.W. (1981), 'The Architectural Significance of the Building Works of Ralph Lord Cromwell (1394–1456)', in Detsicas, 155–62.
Thornber, W. (1856–7), 'The Castle Hill of Penwortham', *Transactions of the Historic Society of Lancashire and Cheshire* 9: 61–76.
Time Team 1995 'Medieval Dining Hall' (Hylton).
Time Team 2001 'The Leaning Tower of Bridgnorth' (Bridgnorth).
Time Team 2002 'Every Castle Needs a Lord' (Beaudesert).
Time Team 2006 'Castle in the Round' (Queenborough).
Time Team 2010 'Massacre in the Cellar' (Hopton Castle).
Time Team 2011a 'House of the White Queen' (Groby).
Time Team 2011b 'Castle of the Saxon Kings' (Bamburgh).
Time Team 2012 'How to Lose a Castle' (Crewkerne).
Time Team 2013 'Horseshoe Hall' (Oakham).
Tipping, H.A. (1921), *English Homes Period 1, Volume 1: Norman and Plantagenet 1066–1485*. London: Country Life.
Toomey, J.P. (2001), *Records of Hanley Castle, Worcestershire c.1147–1547*. Worcestershire Historical Society.
Toy, S. (1933), 'The Round Castles of Cornwall', *Archaeologia* 83: 203–26.
Trollope, E. (1857), 'Somerton Castle and its Builder', *Associated Architectural Societies Reports and Papers* 4: 83–91.
Turnbull, P. and Walsh, D. (1994), 'Recent Work at Egremont Castle', *Transactions of the Cumberland and Westmorland Antiquarian and Archaeological Society* 94: 77–89.
Turner, T.H. and Parker, J. (1851–9), *Some Account of Domestic Architecture in England*. Volume 1: From the Conquest to the End of the Thirteenth Century (1851). Volume 2: From Edward I. to Richard II (1853). Volume 3, Parts 1 and 2: From Richard II to Henry VIII (1859).
Uhlman, D. (1993), *Croft Castle*. London: National Trust.
Vallance, A. (1927), 'The Engraved Plate at Cooling Castle', *Archaeologia Cantiana* 39: 176–80.
Varley, W.J. (1973), *Castle Hill, Almondbury: A Brief Guide to the Excavations 1939–1972*. Huddersfield: Tolson Memorial Museum.
Vickers, K.H. (ed.) (1922), *A History of Northumberland. Volume 11*. Newcastle: Northumberland County History Committee.
Wareham, J. (2000), *Three Palaces of the Bishops of Winchester: Wolvesey (Old Bishop's Palace), Hampshire; Bishop's Waltham Palace, Hampshire; Farnham Castle Keep, Surrey*. London: English Heritage.
Watson, B. (1992a), 'The Norman fortress on Ludgate Hill in the City of London, England: Recent Excavations 1986–90', *Chateau Gaillard* 15: 335–45.
Watson, B. (1992b), 'The Excavation of a Norman castle on Ludgate Hill', *London Archaeologist* 16.4: 371–7.

Watson, G.P.H. and Bradley, G. (1937), *Carlisle Castle, Cumberland*. London: HMSO.
Webster, C.J. (2016), *Taunton Castle*. Somerset Archaeological and Natural History Society.
West, J.J. (1981), 'Acton Burnell Castle in Shropshire', in Detsicas, 85–92.
White, H.M. (1905), 'Excavations in Castle Hill, Burton-in-Lonsdale', *The Antiquary* 41: 411–17.
White, P. and Cook, A. (2015), *Sherborne Old Castle, Dorset: Archaeological Investigation 1930–90*. London: Society of Antiquaries.
White, R. (2012), *Belsay Hall, Castle and Garden*. London: English Heritage.
Whitehead, D. (2007), *The Castle Green at Hereford: A Landscape of Ritual, Royalty and Recreation*. Hertfordshire: Logaston Press.
Wilcox, R. (1980), 'Excavations at Farleigh Hungerford Castle, Somerset', *Somerset Archaeology and Natural History* 124: 87–109.
Williams, F. (1977), *Pleshey Castle, Essex (XII–XVI Century): Excavations in the Bailey, 1959–1963*. BAR British Series 42. Oxford: British Archaeological Reports.
Wilson, C. (2002), 'The Royal Lodgings of Edward III at Windsor Castle: Form, Function, Representation', in Keen, L. and Scarff, E. (eds), *Windsor: Medieval Archaeology, Art and Architecture of the Thames Valley*. British Archaeological Association Conference Transactions 25: 15–94.
Wilson, M.D. (2016), 'The Castle Builders. Part 1. The "embattled walls" of Hartshill', *Coventry and District Archaeological Society Bulletin* 494.
Wilson, M.D. (2017a), 'The Castle Builders. Part 2. The Celebration of Divine Worship', *Coventry and District Archaeological Society Bulletin* 494.
Wilson, M.D. (2017b), 'The Castle Builders. Part 3. Ludford's Hartshill Castle', *Coventry and District Archaeological Society Bulletin* 498.
Wilson-North, R. (1991), 'Bampton Castle: An Earthwork Survey by the Royal Commission on the Historical Monuments of England', *Proceedings of the Devon Archaeological Society* 49: 115–19.
Wright, D.W. and Creighton O.H. (2016), *Castles, Siegeworks and Settlement: Surveying the Archaeology of the Twelfth Century*. Oxford: Archaeopress, 118–23.
Wright, D., Trick, S. and Creighton, O. (2016), 'Rampton "Giants Hill", Cambridgeshire', in Wright and Creighton, 118–23.
Yeoman, P.A. (1986), 'Excavations at the Motte, Weston Turville Manor, 1985', *Records of Buckinghamshire* 28: 169–78.
Young, C.J. (2000), *Excavations at Carisbrooke Castle, Isle of Wight, 1921–1996*. Wessex Archaeology Report No. 18.
Young, C.J. (2010), *Carisbrooke Castle*. London: English Heritage.
Zeepvat, R.J. and Cooper-Reade, H. (1994–6), 'Excavations within the Outer Bailey of Hertford Castle', *Hertfordshire Archaeology* 12: 15–40.

INDEX OF PEOPLE

Abberbury, Richard de   79
Abinger, Robert of   1
Adeliza of Louvain, Queen of England   57, 157, 168
Alan Rufus   191
Alan Niger, Earl of Richmond   35
Albini, Nigel d'   46
Albini, William d', Earl of Sussex   ix, 9, 11, 57, 58, 157, 168
Aldeburgh, William de   107, 108
Alexander (the Magnificent), Bishop of Lincoln   19, 156, 157, 205
Alfred, son of Judhael   22
Allington, Avelina   3
Allington, William of   3
Alverton, John of, carpenter   90
Amundeville, Peter d'   121
Angus, Gilbert Umfraville, Earl   184
Anstey, Nicholas de   8
Armstrong, William, 1st Baron   18, 51
Arnold, William, architect   89
Arundel, Richard FitzAlan, 1st Earl   65
Ashburnham, Roger   200
Asne, Hugh l'   206
Astor, William Waldorf   114
Audley family   156
Audley, Henry de   109, 189
Aumale, William de Forz, Earl   55, 66, 204
Avranches, Hugh d', 1st Earl of Chester   202, 223
Aylmer, John, mason   244
Ayton, William   15

Badlesmere, Bartholomew de, 1st Baron   128
Badlesmere, Margaret, Baroness   128
Bailleul, Reginald de   172
Baldwin, Abbot of Bury St Edmunds   132
Balliol, Edward   108
Balliol, Guy de   19
Baliol, John de, *see* John, King of Scotland   19
Bayeux, Hugh of   235
Bampton, Robert of   18
Barton, Roger de, mason   67
Beauchamp family   21, 24, 91, 93, 231
Beauchamp, Guy de, 10th Earl of Warwick   19

Beauchamp, Henry, 14th Earl of Warwick   231
Beauchamp, Thomas, 11th Earl of Warwick   231
Beauchamp, William, 9th Earl of Warwick   60, 231
Beauchamp, Richard, 2nd Baron of Powick   42
Beaufort, Henry, Bishop of Winchester   30, 31
Beaumont, Henry de, 1st Earl of Warwick   231
Beaumont, Robert de, 1st Earl of Leicester   103, 129
Beaumont, Robert de (le Bossu), 2nd Earl of Leicester   129, 154
Beaumont, Robert de (Blanchmains), 3rd Earl of Leicester   129, 237
Beuvrière, Drogo de   204
Becket, Thomas, Archbishop of Canterbury   28, 84, 174, 196
Bek, Anthony, Bishop of Durham   4, 89, 206
Berkeley, Thomas, Third Baron   27
Berkeley, William, carver   244
Bertram, Sir Robert, Sheriff of Northumberland   35
Bertram, William   151
Beverley, Robert of, mason   132, 135
Biddle, Martin, archaeologist   218
Bigod, Hugh, 1st Earl of Norfolk   45, 98, 218
Bigod, Roger   218
Bigod, Roger, 2nd Earl of Norfolk   x, 99
Bigod, Roger, 4th Earl of Norfolk   45
Blenkinsopp, Robert de   31
Blois, Henry de, Bishop of Winchester   30, 96, 148, 217, 249
Blundeville, Ranulph de, 6th Earl of Chester   xi, 24–5, 34, 61, 109
Bohun family   115
Bohun, Humphrey de, Earl of Essex   195
Bolebec, Hugh de   237
Boleyn, Anne   138
Bolingbroke, Henry de, *see* Henry IV
Bonnington, Gilbert de, metalworker   244
Botiller, John   217
Boulogne, Eustace, Count of   8, 80
Box, John, mason   185
Brampton, Brian de   37

Braose, Reginald de   115
Braose, William I de   36
Braose, William II de   90, 123
Bréauté, Falkes de   24, 60, 181, 210
Brewer, William   41
Brittany, Brian of   127
Brittany, Conan IV, Duke, and Earl of Richmond   191
Brittany, Geoffrey, Duke, and Earl of Richmond   35
Broc, Ranulph de   196
Brooke, Francis Greville, 1st Baron   231
Broughton family   44
Burcestre, John of, mason   147, 209
Burn, William, architect   185
Burnell, Robert, Bishop of Bath and Wells   1–2, 114
Busli, Roger de   219

Camville, Richard de   151
Cantelow, John, mason   245–6
Carew family   30
Caröe, W.B., architect   3
Carr, John, architect   185
Cartington, John de   50
Chandos, Robert de   156, 206
Charles I, King of England and Scotland   48, 224
Charles II, King of England and Scotland   217
Chesney, William de   79
Chester, Hugh d'Avranches, 1st Earl   202, 223
Chester, Ranulph de Gernon, 4th Earl   161
Chester, Ranulph de Blundeville, 6th Earl   xi, 24–5, 34, 61, 109, 132
Chester, John the Scot, 7th Earl   25
Cheyne, Sir Hugh   61
Clare, Gilbert de, 4th Earl of Gloucester   107
Clare, Gilbert de, 7th Earl of Gloucester   xi, 196
Clare, Gilbert de, Earl of Pembroke   101
Clare, Richard (Strongbow) de, 2nd Earl of Pembroke   101
Clare Richard de, 6th Earl of Gloucester   195
Clare, Robert de, 1st Earl of Gloucester   41, 195, 201
Clavering, John de   227
Clifford, Henry, 10th Baron   205
Clifford, Henry, 1st Earl of Cumberland   205
Clifford, Henry, 5th Earl of Cumberland   205
Clifford, John, 9th Baron   9
Clifford, Robert, 1st Baron   xii, 9, 42, 43, 44, 174, 205
Clifford, Roger de   43
Clifford, Roger, 5th Baron   9, 43, 44
Clifford, Lady Anne   9, 42, 174, 205

Clinton, Geoffrey de   39, 117
Clinton, William, Earl of Huntingdon   147
Clinton, Lescelina   39
Cobham, John, Lord   72, 74, 113, 114
Coleville, William de   55
Columbers family   156
Comyn, John   215
Conan IV, Duke of Brittany   191
Constance, Countess of Richmond   35
Conway, Sir Martin   3, 196
Corbeil, William de, Archbishop of Canterbury   192
Corbet, Sir Andrew   152
Corbet, Richard   152, 234
Corbet, Robert   60, 234
Cornwall, Edmund, 2nd Earl   190, 222
Cornwall, Reginald, de Dunstanville, Earl   127
Cornwall, Richard, 1st Earl   114, 127, 146, 190, 219, 220, 222, 226
Courcy, William de   210
Courtenay family   30, 167, 220
Courtenay, Hugh, Earl of Devon   167
Courtenay, John, Marquis of Devon   167
Courtenay, Sir Robert   181
Courtenay, William, Archbishop of Canterbury   196, 197, 218
Cousin, John, Bishop of Durham   90
Cowper, John, mason   121
Crewe, Nathaniel, 3rd Baron, Bishop of Durham   17
Criol family   95
Cromwell, Ralph, Lord   xiii, 215, 247, 248, 249
Crumbwelle, Idonea de   42
Crump, Thomas, mason   73
Cuckney, Thomas de   78
Cumberland, Henry Clifford, 1st Earl   205
Cumberland, Henry Clifford, 5th Earl   205

Dacre family   78, 153
Dacre, Humphrey, Lord   122
Dacre, Ralph, Lord   155
Dacre, Thomas, Lord   122
Dalyngrygge, Sir Edward   32, 34
Darcy family   238
Darcy, Philip   239
David I, King of Scotland   226
Deincourt, Elizabeth   204
Derby, William Ferrers, 3rd Earl   87
Derby, William Ferrers, 4th Earl   7, 61, 225
Despencer, Hugh   107
Despencer, Robert le   213
Despenser, Henry, Bishop of Norwich   162
Devereux family   146
Devereux, John, Lord   146–7
Devon, Baldwin de Redvers, 1st Earl   78, 181

Index of People

Docheman, Baldwin, brick maker   217
Dudley family   251
Dudley, John, Duke of Northumberland   86
Dudley, Robert, Earl of Leicester   118
Dunstanville, Alan de   2
Dunstanville, Petronilla   2
Dunstanville, Reginald, Earl of Cornwall   127
Dunstanville, Walter de   2
Dyker, Matthew, water engineer   215

Edgar the Aetheling   252
Edmund Crouchback, Earl of Lancaster   123, 129, 161, 178, 204, 223
Edward I, King of England   xi, xii, 19, 25, 29, 65, 74, 122, 128, 129, 135, 137, 138, 164, 167, 194, 195, 196, 211, 242
Edward II, King of England   27, 28, 41, 47, 48, 61, 107, 122, 128, 178, 199, 239
Edward III, King of England   xii, 105, 147, 185, 223, 226, 243, 244, 245, 246
Edward IV, King of England   xiv, 11, 141, 164, 227, 239, 243, 244
Edward, Prince of Wales (the Black Prince)   219, 222
Edward the Confessor, King of England   viii, 64, 112, 189, 191
Edward the Martyr, King of England   74
Eleanor of Castile, Queen of England   128, 165, 175
Elias, mason   87
Entrepas, John   247
Epaignes, Alfred d'   156, 172
Errington family   67
Espec, Walter   110, 226
Essex, Geoffrey de Mandeville, 1st Earl   46, 91, 180, 188, 195, 208, 218
Essex, Henry de   189, 196
Essex, Humphrey de Bohun, 5th Earl   195
Etton, Thomas de   100
Eure, Ralph de   15, 249
Eynsford, William de   95

Fastolf, Sir John   xiii, 46
Felsted, Richard de   107
Felton, William   91
Ferrers family   103, 165, 213
Ferrers, Henry de   87, 223
Ferrers, Thomas   213
Ferrers, Walkelin de   165
Ferrers, William, 4th Earl of Derby   7, 61, 225
Fiennes family   44
Fiennes, Sir Roger   xiii
Fiennes, William   44
FitzAlan family   11, 65, 151, 202–3
FitzAlan, Richard, 1st Earl   65

FitzAnsculf, William   1, 84
FitzCount, Brian   226
FitzEustace, Richard   227
FitzEustace, Roger (*see also* Roger de Lacy)   106
FitzHarding, Robert   27
FitzHugh, Lady Elizabeth   237
FitzHugh, Sir Henry   189, 237
FitzGilbert, John   139
FitzGilbert, Richard   220
FitzOsbern, William, 1st Earl of Hereford   27, 47, 64, 95, 206, 239
FitzRalph, Harold   95
FitzRanulph, Robert   148
FitzRichard, Osbern   191
FitzRichard, Robert   252
FitzRobert, Sweyn   189
FitzRoger, Robert, Sheriff of Northumberland   227
FitzTurstin, Baldwin   190
FitzWarren, Fulk III   3, 238
FitzWymarc, Robert   64
Flanders, Walter of, water engineer   135
Flambard, Ranulph, Bishop of Durham   89, 162
Fleming, Michael le   3
Fleming, Winemar   60
Forz, Aveline de, Countess of Lancaster   204
Forz, Isabella de   48
Forz, William de, Earl of Aumale   55, 66, 204
Fossard, Nigel   154
Fox, Richard, Bishop of Durham   89, 90
Furnivall family   7
Furnival, Thomas de, 1st Baron   201

Gamelston, Robert de, mason   182
Gamston, Philip de, mason   181
Garret, Daniel, architect   185
Gaveston, Piers, Earl of Cornwall   122, 199
Geneville, Geoffrey de   141
Geoffrey, Bishop of Lincoln (illegitimate son of Henry II)   221
Geoffrey, Bishop of Coutances   41
Geoffrey, Prince, Duke of Brittany   35
Gianibelli, Federigo   48
Giffard family   41
Giffard, John   41
Giffard, William, Bishop of Winchester   217, 249
Gilbert family   69
Glasham, Robert de, carpenter   107
Gloucester, John of   242
Gloucester, Gilbert de Clare, 4th Earl   107
Gloucester, Gilbert de Clare, 7th Earl   xi, 196
Gloucester, Richard de Clare, 6th Earl   195

Gloucester, Robert, 1st Earl   41, 195, 201
Gloucester, Richard, Duke of, *see* Richard III, King of England
Grentmesnil, Hugh de   129
Grentmesnil, Ivo de   129
Greville, Fulke, 1st Baron Brooke   231
Greville, Francis, 3rd Baron Brooke   231
Grey, Lady Jane   138
Greystoke family   153
Greystoke, Ralph, Lord   154
Greystoke, William, Lord   103, 154
Gros, William le, Earl of York and Count of Aumale   55, 199
Grosmont, Henry of, Duke of Lancaster   223
Gundulf, Bishop of Rochester   192, 193, 236

Halton family   247, 248
Handlo, John   31
Harley family   37
Harold Godwinson, King of England   138, 146
Harrington, Sir John de   100
Harrington, Sir Robert de   100
Hartley, Thomas   239
Haschenperg, Stephan von   49
Hastings, John, 1st Baron   97
Hastings, William, 1st Baron   xiii, xiv, 11, 13
Hatfield, Thomas, Bishop of Durham   89, 90, 185
Heley, John, mason   106
Helgot   114
Helgot, Philip   202
Henry I, King of England   ix, 2, 9, 18, 28, 39, 57, 58, 63, 74, 117, 123, 127, 132, 157, 168, 175, 176, 226, 250
Henry II, King of England   x, 9, 11, 17, 18, 27, 28, 35, 41, 42, 45, 49, 63, 70, 76, 79, 80, 83, 84, 96, 98, 103, 107, 109, 115, 129, 138, 158, 170, 173, 176, 178, 182, 194, 195, 196, 199, 202, 218, 219, 221, 226, 237, 238, 243
Henry III, King of England   xi, 17, 24, 25, 41, 55, 74, 83, 101, 121, 123, 130, 135, 137, 138, 139, 146, 154, 158, 159, 161, 164, 167, 175, 178, 193, 203, 204, 213, 223, 226, 242, 243, 244, 252
Henry IV, King of England   34, 123, 124, 149, 176, 178, 223, 239
Henry VI, King of England   xiii, 113, 215, 247
Henry VII, King of England   19, 243
Henry VIII, King of England   39, 138, 169, 226
Henry (son of David I of Scotland), 3rd Earl of Northumberland and 3rd Earl of Huntingdon   15–16
Henry of Essex   189, 196

Henry of Grosmont, Duke of Lancaster   223
Herland, William, carpenter   243
Hereford, Henry FitzRalph, Earl   95
Hereford, Ralph, Earl   112
Hereford, Roger, 2nd Earl   90
Hereford, William FitzOsbern, 1st Earl   27, 64, 95, 206
Hereford, Walter of   2
Heron, Alexander   63
Heron, Sir John   77
Heron, Sir William   98
Heton, Thomas de   63
Heydon, Henry   15
Heydon, John   15
Holebrok, Roger de   134
Holme, Henry, mason   87, 88
Hopton family   115
Howard family   11
Howard, Katherine   138
Hubert de Burgh   80, 105
Hull, William, mason   113
Hungerford, Sir Edward   96
Hungerford, Sir Thomas   96
Hungerford, Sir Walter, 1st Baron   96
Huntingdon, Simon de Senlis, Earl   98
Huntingdon, William Clinton, Earl   147
Hurley, William, carpenter   243
Hylton, William Lord   116–17
Hyndeley, Thomas, mason   200

Inge, William   95
Isabella of France, Queen of England   128, 164, 167, 239

Janyns, Henry   243
Jeffreys, George, Judge   217
John, King of England   x, xi, 24, 74, 75, 76, 80, 82, 83, 91, 107, 119, 121, 122, 123, 124, 139, 151, 153, 164, 167, 184, 192, 194, 198, 199, 200, 202, 210, 213, 226, 235
John Balliol, King of Scotland   19
John the Scot, Earl of Chester   25
Joy, William, mason   28
Judhael   22

Kemp, John, Archbishop of York   60
Kirkeby family   95
Knollys, Sir Robert   32

Lacy family   65, 235
Lacy, Gilbert de (the elder)   139, 140, 142
Lacy, Gilbert de (the younger)   140
Lacy, Henry de   8, 24
Lacy, Henry de, Earl of Lincoln   8, 106, 132, 181

Index of People

Lacy, Ilbert de   181
Lacy, Robert de   65
Lacy, Roger de   91, 146
Lacy, Roger de (formerly Roger FitzEustace)   106
Lacy, Walter de   138–9, 139
Lancaster, Edmund Crouchback, 1st Earl   123, 129, 161, 178, 223
Lancaster, Henry of Grosmont, Duke   223
Lancaster, John of Gaunt, Duke   xiii, 34, 87, 113, 117, 123, 223, 224, 225
Lancaster, Thomas, 2nd Earl   7, 8, 65, 87, 106, 120, 132, 178, 181, 223, 224
Langley, Edmund of, Duke of York   98
Latimer, William Lord   79
Langton, Thomas, Bishop of Salisbury   31, 201, 217
Langton, Walter, Bishop of Coventry and Lichfield   91
Leicester, Robert de Beaumont, 1st Earl   103, 129
Leicester, Robert (le Bossu) de Beaumont, 2nd Earl   129, 154
Leicester, Robert (Blanchmains) de Beaumont, 3rd Earl   129, 237
Leicester, Robert Dudley, Earl   118, 119, 120, 121
Lese family   95
Lewyn, John, mason   xiii, 9, 17, 18, 38, 46, 49, 52, 54, 87, 88, 90, 108, 117, 143, 145, 175, 185, 202, 229, 231, 250
Leybourne, Roger de   132
Lincoln, Henry de Lacy, Earl   8, 106, 132, 181
Lindsey, Sir David de   78
Lionel, Duke of Clarence and Earl of Ulster   147
Lisle, Warin, 2nd Baron   202
Longchamp family   241
Longchamp, Osbert de   3
Lorimer, Sir Robert, architect   146
Louis, Prince, French Dauphin   xi, 28, 80, 82, 113, 167, 242, 243
Lovel, John, 5th Baron   169, 220
Lucy, Countess of Chester   132
Lucy, Maud   66, 127, 184
Lucy, Richard de   170
Lucy, Thomas de   125
Ludlow, Laurence of   210
Lumley, John, Lord   143
Lumley, Ralph, 1st Baron   xiii, 143
Luttrell, Lady Elizabeth   89
Luttrell, Sir Hugh   89

Mandeville, Geoffrey de, 1st Earl of Essex   46, 91, 180, 188, 195, 208, 218

Mandeville, William de, 3rd Earl of Essex   180
Manners family   104, 111
Manners, Sir Robert   94
March, Edmund Mortimer, 5th Earl   239
March, Roger Mortimer, 1st Earl   141, 164, 239
Mare, John de la   2, 165
Marlborough, Alfred de   95
Marmion family   97, 213
Marmion, John, 4th Baron (of Winteringham)   237
Marmion, Maud   237
Marmion, Philip, 5th Baron (of Tamworth)   213
Mary Stuart, Queen of Scots   52, 98, 247
Matilda, Dowager Holy Roman Empress   ix, x, 79, 127, 139, 173, 226, 238, 249
Maudit, Robert   182
Maudit, William   182
Maudit, William, 8th Earl of Warwick   60
Maurice, engineer, mason   80, 84, 158, 161
Merlay family   153
Meschines, William de   92
Metcalfe, Thomas   155
Meynell family   238
Middleton, Christiana   125
Middleton, Henry   25
Middleton, John de   25
Mohun, Lady Joan   89
Mohun, William de   89
Molyns, Egidia   237
Molyns, John de   237
Montagu, John Neville, Lord   227, 229
Montagu, Sir Edward   22
Montagu, Sir William, Earl of Salisbury   164, 226
Montalt family   57
Montfichet family   152
Montfichet, Richard de   210
Montfichet, Robert Gernon de   210
Montfort, Hugh de   109, 196
Montfort, Peter de   24
Montfort, Robert de   189
Montfort, Simon de   7, 39, 117, 129, 130, 167, 175, 192
Montford, Thurstan de   24
Mortain, Robert de, Count of   28, 57, 110, 127, 151, 175, 222
Mortain, William de   28, 151
Mortimer, Edmund, 5th Earl of March   239
Mortimer, Ralph   239
Mortimer, Roger, 1st Earl of March   141, 164, 239
Morville, Hugh de   42, 174

Mowbray, Robert, Earl of Northumberland 15, 158
Mowbray, Roger de 173
Moyne, Berenger le xi, 22, 23
Musard, Robert 151
Muschamp, Geoffrey de, Bishop of Coventry 91
Mynors, Sir Richard 222

Neville, Anne, Duchess of Gloucester 19
Neville family xiii, 46, 150
Neville, Hugh de 210
Neville, Isabel, Duchess of Clarence 231
Neville, John, 5th Baron xiii, 79, 185, 188, 202
Neville, John, Lord Montagu 227, 229
Neville, Ralph, 4th Baron 149, 185
Neville, Ralph, 6th Baron and 1st Earl of Westmorland 38, 147, 174, 188
Neville, Richard, Earl of Warwick 19, 231
Neville, Robert, 2nd Baron 148
Neville, Robert, Bishop of Durham 77
Newburgh family 184
Newcastle, William Cavendish, 1st Duke 164, 165
Nigel the Physician 2
Norfolk, Hugh Bigod, 1st Earl 45, 98, 99, 218
Norfolk, Roger Bigod, 2nd Earl x, 99, 100
Norfolk, Roger Bigod, 4th Earl 45
Norman, Thomas, carpenter 113
Northumberland, John Dudley, Duke 86, 87
Northumberland, Robert Mowbray, Earl 15, 158
Northumberland, Henry Percy, 1st Earl xiii, 66, 127, 184, 225, 227, 250
Northumberland, Henry Percy, 4th Earl 227, 229
Northumberland, Waltheof, Earl 89
Norwich, Sir John 148

Odo, Bishop of Bayeux 79, 80
Ogle family 35
Oilly, Robert d' 173
Oilly, Roger d' 11, 212
Osbert, mason 18
Oxford, Aubrey de Vere, 1st Earl ix, 55

Paine, James, architect 185
Paterson, John, architect 38
Paynel family 1, 84
Paynel, Gervaise 84
Pembroke, William de Valence, 1st Earl 101, 196
Pembroke, Aymer de Valence, 2nd Earl 19, 101
Pembroke, Gilbert de Clare, 1st Earl 101

Pembroke, Richard (Strongbow) de Clare, 2nd Earl 101
Pembroke, William Marshal, 1st Earl 101, 117, 139
Penchester, Lady Margaret 3
Penchester, Sir Stephen 3, 113
Pennington family 154
Pentecost, Osbern 95
Percy family xii, 4, 149, 184, 221, 227, 250
Percy, Henry de, the elder 4, 7, 208
Percy, Henry de, the younger 4, 6, 227
Percy, Henry, 1st Earl of Northumberland 66, 127, 184, 225, 227, 250
Percy, Henry, 4th Earl of Northumberland 227, 229
Percy, Sir Thomas xiii, 250
Peverel, William 176, 238
Picot, Sheriff of Cambridgeshire 35
Pitt-Rivers, Augustus 97
Plais, Hugh de 235
Plantagenet, Hamelin (half-brother of Henry II) x, 70
Plukenet, Alan de 75
Poitou, Roger de 123
Pole, Michael de la, Earl of Suffolk 246
Pontdelarche, William de 182
Pomeroy, Henry 28–9
Pomeroy, Sir Richard 29
Prouz, Sir William 100
Pugin, A.W.N., architect 7
Puiset, Hugh du, Bishop of Durham 89, 90, 162

Raleigh, Sir Walter 201
Ralph, mason 63
Ralph, Earl of Hereford 112
Rede, William, Bishop of Chichester 8
Redvers, Baldwin de, Earl of Devon 78
Redvers family 220
Redvers, Richard de 47, 63, 181
Reymes, Robert de 14, 202
Reyns, Henry, mason 252
Reymes, Hugh de 14
Richard, 1st Earl of Cornwall 114, 127, 146, 190, 219, 220, 226
Richard I, King of England 80, 135, 164, 196, 202
Richard II, King of England xii, 117, 176, 182, 183, 225, 239, 246
Richard III, King of England xiv, 19, 21, 22, 197, 231, 233
Richard of York 141, 195, 197, 239
Richmond, Alan Niger, Earl 35
Richmond, Conan, Earl 191
Richmond, Constance, Countess 35

Index of People

Richmond, Geoffrey, Earl   35
Robert Curthose, Duke of Normandy   158
Roger, Bishop of Salisbury   201
Roger the Poitevin   65
Rokeby family   152
Romille, Cecilia   204
Romille, Robert de   204
Ros, Robert de   111
Ros, William de   111
Rotherham, Thomas, Bishop of Lincoln   45
Russell, John, Bishop of Lincoln   45
Russell, Matthew   38

St Pol, Marie de, Countess of Pembroke   98
Salisbury, Edward of, Sheriff of Wiltshire   138
Salisbury, Sir William Montagu, Earl of   164, 226
Salvin, Anthony, architect   6, 7, 89, 90, 155, 227
Sanceler, Reginald   132
Savoy, Peter, Count   175
Say, Picot de   65
Scott, George Gilbert, architect   83
Scrob, Richard   191
Scrope, Richard le   xiii, 52
Senlis, Simon de, Earl of Huntingdon and of Northampton   98
Seymour, Edward, Duke of Somerset   29
Seymour, Lord Edward   29
Seymour, Sir Edward, 1st Baron   29
Sharington, Sir William, architect   86
Sharnhale, William, mason   73, 192
Sharp, Dr John   17
Shrewsbury, George Talbot, 6th Earl   247
Shrewsbury, John Talbot, 1st Earl   7
Shrewsbury, Robert de Bellême, 3rd Earl   2, 185, 203
Shrewsbury, Roger de Montgomery, 1st Earl   9, 93, 185, 203
Simon, mason   175
Siward le Gros   61
Skirlaw, Walter, Bishop of Durham   143, 145
Smythson, John, mason   164
Smythson, Robert, mason   169
Somerset, Edward Seymour, Duke   29
Somery, John de   84
Somery, Ralph de   84
Somery, Roger de   236
Spenser, Henry, mason   118
Sponlee, John, mason   243
Squyer, John, carpenter   243
Stafford, Ralph 1st Earl   xiii, 209
Stephen, King of England   ix, x, 3, 8, 11, 18, 24, 30, 45, 46, 49, 52, 55, 77, 78, 79, 95, 98, 114, 132, 139, 148, 151, 169, 173, 175, 180, 181, 188, 195, 199, 201, 205, 226, 235, 249
Strange, Guy le   123
Strange, John le   155, 195
Strickland, William   204
Stryvelyn, Cristiana   29
Stryvelyn, Sir John   25, 29
Suffolk, Michael de la Pole, Earl   246
Surrey, William de Warenne, 1st Earl   51, 130, 190, 238
Surrey, William de Warenne, 2nd Earl   197
Sussex, William, d'Albini, Earl   ix, 9, 11, 57, 58, 157, 168

Talbot, George, 6th Earl of Shrewsbury   247
Talbot, John, 1st Earl of Shrewsbury   7
Tatteshal, Robert de   215
Telford, Thomas   203
Thanet, Margaret, Countess   9
Thanet, Thomas, Earl   9
Thirlwall, John de   218
Thorpe, Robert de   138
Threlkeld family   251
Tilden, Philip, architect   3, 196
Tilliol, Sir Peter   199
Tilliol, Sir Robert   199
Titchmarsh, Hugh of, mason   122
Toret, Bartholomew   152
Tosny, Ralph de   64
Tracey, Henry de   22
Trailly family   251
Tresilian, John, blacksmith   244
Tunstall, Cuthbert, Bishop of Durham   89, 90
Turville, Geoffrey de   237

Ulecotes, Philip de   155
Umfraville, Gilbert, Earl of Angus   184
Umfraville, Odinell de   107, 184
Umfraville, Richard de   155
Umfraville, Robert de   93

Valence, Aymer de, 2nd Earl of Pembroke   19, 101
Valence, William de, 1st Earl of Pembroke   101, 196
Valletort, Reginald de   222
Valoines, Theobald de   42
Valonges, Peter de   26
Valonges, Roger de   26
Vanburgh, Sir John, architect   145
Vane, Sir Henry   19
Venables-Vernon, George   225
Venator, Roger   185
Verdun, Bertran de   7
Verdun, Norman de   39

Vere, Aubrey de, 1st Earl of Oxford   ix, 55
Vernon family   104
Vernon, Sir George   104
Vernon, Richard   104
Vertue, William, mason   244
Vescy, Ivo de   4
Vescy, William de   4
Vieuxpont, Isabella   9
Vieuxpont, Robert de   9, 42, 43, 44

Walcher, Bishop of Durham   89
Waltheof, Earl of Northumberland   89
Warenne, William de, 1st Earl of Surrey   51, 130, 190, 238
Warenne, William de, 2nd Earl of Surrey   197
Warwick, Guy de Beauchamp, 10th Earl   19
Warwick, Henry Beauchamp, 14th Earl   231
Warwick, Henry Beaumont, 1st Earl   231
Warwick, Thomas, 11th Earl   231
Warwick, Richard Neville, Earl   19, 231
Warwick, William Beauchamp, 9th Earl   60, 231
Westerley, Robert, mason   112, 224
Westmorland, Ralph de Neville, 1st Earl   38, 149, 174, 188
Wheathamstede, John, Prior of Tynemouth   225
William I, King of England   ix, 24, 47, 61, 67, 74, 80, 89, 93, 95, 109, 113, 115, 130, 132, 158, 163, 164, 168, 173, 175, 176, 178, 189, 192, 194, 209, 213, 220, 231, 235, 243, 252
William (Rufus) II, King of England   ix, 49, 158, 163, 175, 192, 220
William the Lion King of Scotland   115, 184, 226
Winemar the Fleming   60
Wintringham, William, carpenter   113, 118, 243
Wode, Henry, mason   46
Wolveston, Richard, mason   35, 36, 162
Wright, William, carpenter   49
Wyatt, Sir Henry   3
Wyatt, James, architect   90
Wykeham, Thomas   44
Wykeham, William of, Bishop of Winchester   30, 31, 44
Wynford, William, mason   169, 202, 206

Yevele, Henry, mason   73, 197, 206
Yevele, Robert, mason, 137
York, Edmund of Langley, Duke   98
York, Richard, Duke   141, 195, 197, 239, 243
York, William le Gros, Earl, and Count of Aumale   55, 199

Zouche family   11, 221
Zouche, William de la   221